KING, Robert R. Minorities under Communism; nationalities as a source of tension among Balkan Communist states. Harvard, 1973. 326p map tab bibl 72-95184. 14.00. SBN 674-57632-2
For the third time in as many years, King has published on the problems of Balkan nationalities, but this time his scholarly net is cast wider and the catch is bigger and better. With tables, maps, and impressive documentation, he ranges through the complex history and contemporary prospects of relations between the Communist states of Europe with respect to national minorities. His post at Munich's Radio Free Europe is well suited to keeping abreast of such an exotic specialty, and he has. In authoritative detail, he reminds his readers that the proximity of Soviet power has reduced the "disruptive" effect of Balkan nationalisms on international relations; that much of the aggressive energy of East European irredentism has been sublimated into subtle debates over historical interpretations, administrative adjustments, and selected fine-points of Communist ideology; but that despite a century of atrocities perpetuated on national minorities and a quarter-century of Communist rule, nationalism still exerts a stronger "influence on men than do class interests." For graduates and upper-division undergraduates.

Minorities under Communism

Nationalities as a Source of Tension
among Balkan Communist States

Robert R. King received his Ph.D. from the
Fletcher School of Law and Diplomacy and is
currently senior analyst for Rumania and
Bulgaria in Radio Free Europe, Munich,
West Germany.

Minorities under Communism

Nationalities as a Source of Tension among Balkan Communist States

Robert R. King

Harvard University Press, Cambridge, Massachusetts   1973

Acknowledgments

Many people have helped in the writing of this book, though only a few can be singled out here. Professor Uri Ra'anan of the Fletcher School of Law and Diplomacy encouraged me to deal with this topic and offered critical advice during its writing. Professor William E. Griffith of the Massachusetts Institute of Technology gave me access to his files. The staffs of Harvard University's Russian Research Center and its libraries helped me to make the best use of their extensive materials. Charles Andras of Radio Free Europe gave helpful suggestions on the original draft and made his files on the Hungarian minorities available. My other colleagues at Radio Free Europe called many developments to my attention and assisted with translations of Hungarian and Slovak materials. Unity Evans gave me careful editorial assistance and helped with the proofreading; Maria Hofheinz and Susan Hoover typed the manuscript.

For the encouragement and support of my parents, I am grateful. To them, and to my wife Kay for her patience and assistance, this book is dedicated.

Munich   Robert R. King
February 1973

Contents

Maps

Minorities under Communism

Nationalities as a Source of Tension
among Balkan Communist States

Introduction

The relationship between nationalism and communism is the subject of much of the literature dealing with the political elements of communism. Certain questions of nationalism and communism have been treated extensively, but others have been largely ignored. The "national question" has two aspects with which communist parties have been forced to deal. First, there is the question of the relationship of the *Staatsvolk** to party and government. Communist ideology places the party above nationality as the nonnational vanguard of workers of all nationalities. It thus derives its right to rule as the representative of the interests of the working class on a specific territory, but not for a specific nationality. Noncommunist governments, on the other hand, generally derive their legitimacy from the fact that they represent the interests of the nation, and in the case of a state with more than one nationality, of the leading nationality. The relationship between the *Staatsvolk*

---

* *Staatsvolk,* a German expression coined in the nineteenth century, refers to the major nationality, the dominant nationality of a state, as opposed to the national minorities or subject nationalities of the state.

1

and the communist party which rules over it is complex and varies from state to state. The Russian nationality's role as *Staatsvolk* of the Soviet Union has produced an interesting mixture of Russian nationalism and Russian messianism with communist internationalism and Soviet domination of the communist commonwealth.[1] However, in those states in which communist rule has been imposed by the Soviet Union, *Staatsvolk* nationalism has frequently assumed an anti-Soviet and anticommunist flavor. This triangular relationship between Soviet imperialism, local nationalism, and communist ideology has been the subject of numerous studies.[2]

The second aspect of the national question deals with the relationship between the *Staatsvolk* and national minorities under communism. In this case, the national question is concerned with linguistic, educational, and cultural rights, as well as some form or combination of territorial or administrative autonomy for minorities. Many of the studies on this aspect of the national question have dealt with the non-Russian nationalities of the Soviet Union. Since their proportion now approaches 50 percent of the Soviet population and is continually increasing, the question of the national minorities is a highly significant element in the Soviet internal situation.[3] The People's Republic of China and Yugoslavia are also multinational states whose internal nationality relations are an important factor in the politics of the country.[4] The question of national minorities cannot, however, be dealt with in isolation from the question of *Staatsvolk* nationalism and its relationship to the ruling communist party. Rising nationalism among the *Staatsvolk* invariably brings greater pressure for assimilation of the minorities. Those communist parties which have attempted to identify themselves with *Staatsvolk* nationalism have found that pursuit of the interests of the leading nationality frequently demands policies which limit minority rights.

This study considers both elements of the national question, but focuses specifically on a neglected aspect of the relationship between communism and nationalism—the impact which national minorities have on relations among communist states. Although national minorities have not been the principal factor in relations among the countries of Eastern Europe since 1945, they do play a significant role. Most of the previous literature has examined East European nationalism principally from the viewpoint of the relations between the Soviet Union and the other states in the communist area. While the present study does deal with this problem, its primary focus is on the effect national minorities have had upon relations among these states.

Because it deals with the effect of minorities upon interstate relations, the study is limited to those minorities that are ethnically linked to a neighboring communist state. The Jewish minority is one of the most interesting and one of the most discussed of the minority groups in Eastern Europe, but in this case its situation is not relevant. The same is true of the Gypsy, Tartar, and similar nationalities without links to another state. The Turks in Bulgaria and Yugoslavia and the Italians in Yugoslavia have also been omitted because they are linked with the *Staatsvolk* of states not ruled by communist parties. The internal national problems of communist states with two or more major nationalities (Czechs and Slovaks in Czechoslovakia; Serbs, Croats, Slovenes, Macedonians, and Montenegrins in Yugoslavia) become an issue only to the extent that they affect the relations of that state with its communist neighbors over the question of minorities. The question of the German minorities is complicated by the existence of two German states and by the expulsion of most of the ethnic German population from Eastern Europe after World War II, and so this aspect is also considered only peripherally. Since the focus of the study is on the effect of national minorities on international relations among communist states, discussion of a communist party's policies toward its own minorities is relevant only as it relates to the effect those minorities have on relations among states. More detailed consideration of the communist party-states' internal nationality policies is a question too broad in scope to be encompassed in a reasonably complete single-volume work, and this aspect of the national question is one that has frequently been considered by students of the subject.

Geographically, the states included in the study were all at one time or another a part of the Turkish Empire in Europe, and are today included in communist Eastern Europe—Slovakia, Hungary, Rumania, Bessarabia (or Soviet Moldavia), Bulgaria, Yugoslavia, and Albania. The specific minority groups discussed are the Hungarian minorities in Czechoslovakia, Rumania, and Yugoslavia; the Macedonians, who are ethnically Bulgarian according

3

to Sofia, but are a separate nationality according to Belgrade; the Rumanians of Soviet Moldavia, who are called "Moldavians" by Moscow; the Albanian minority in Yugoslavia; and, to a lesser extent, the Ukrainian, Bulgarian, Slovak, and other less numerous national minorities.

Chapter 1

Nationalism and Communism

"A nation," according to a derisive European saying, "is a group of people united by a common error about their ancestry and a common dislike of their neighbors."[1] Although there is more than enough truth in this statement to make it humorous, "nationalism" and "nation" are not easily reduced to a single-sentence definition. The abundance of works that have appeared attempting to define or determine the foundations of nationality gives some indication of the problem.[2] Despite the complexity and scope of the study of nationalism, however, there are certain fundamentals upon which most students of nationalism agree.

Because men are communal beings, they can only be fully understood within the context of their social relations. Men function as members of various groups in society—religious, class, vocational, family, state, and national, among others. An individual is usually a member of many groups. Furthermore, the membership of some groups may be identical with the membership of others, as in the Balkans where religious and national groups are almost always identical. However, groups are more often composed of people with conflicting group consciousness.

A number of factors distinguish national groups from other groups into which men are organized. First, the national group is generally "the group consciousness to which the individual, in case of conflict of group loyalties, owes supreme loyalty."[3] Allegiance to nation can and has in the past pitted men of the same religious conviction, of the same class, even of the same state, against each other. It was this supreme loyalty to nation which led the British journalist and economist, Sir Norman Angell, to observe during the ultranationalist era of the 1930's: "Political nationalism has become for the European of our age the most important thing in the world, more important than civilization, humanity, decency, kindness, pity; more important than life itself."[4] This highest allegiance to nation, which Angell and others have condemned, is sometimes mitigated by conflicting allegiances to other groups. For the most part, however, national loyalty is the supreme group loyalty.

A second feature of nationalism which distinguishes it from other group consciousness is its connection with a state or a territory. Although nationality is by no means synonymous with state citizenship, the national group almost always strives for state-political recognition. Walter Sulzbach emphasizes this aspect of nationality by defining a nation as "a group of people which wishes to be sovereign among other peoples and therefore desires a state of its own."[5] A nation can exist without possessing its own sovereign state, as was the case with the Czechs before 1918 or the Poles between 1795 and 1918. National identity may even exist without striving for separate statehood as, for example, the Jews between the Diaspora and the advent of Zionism. However, nationalism is closely connected with the possession of, or the striving for, political sovereignty within a state.

Another feature of the national group distinguishing it from other social groups is the possession of a distinct culture, the most obvious elements of which are language and literature. Language has long been the prime means of differentiating nations, but language does not by itself determine nationality. The American, British, British-Canadian, Australian, and New Zealand nationalities all speak English, but each has a separate national consciousness. This culture-communication aspect of nationality has been expressed in terms of communications theory and cybernetics by Karl Deutsch, whose work gives a modern, social science analysis of and quantitative support to this cultural aspect of nationalism.

Although these are not the only characteristics which distinguish national from other group consciousness, they are the major elements. Nationalism, however, is not a uniform phenomenon. It developed in different geographic areas during different periods of time at different rates and under different conditions. Therefore, the dominant elements of nationalism vary greatly from one area to another. In Western Europe, where nationalism first developed, the growth and centralization of the power of the state occurred concurrently with the evolution of national consciousness. Hence, "nation" and "state" became synonymous. As the nation came to be identified with the state, it was accepted that the nation was entitled to its own state. Therefore, in Western Europe nationality became an essentially territorial concept, with citizenship determining nationality. Thus, the ethnic German of the Alsace declares: "Ich bin ein Franzose!" This territorial concept of nationality developed primarily in France and England, but it also became the principal basis for nationality in the British colonies. Although territory is the prime element in West European nationalism, it is by no means exclusive, as the recent resurgence of national minorities in Western Europe indicates.

Although elements of national consciousness were evident in both Britain and France long before Bastille Day 1789, the French Revolution ushered in the era when nationalism became a dominant element in world politics. The French Revolution and the European conflicts which followed in the years from 1792 to 1815 also hastened the spread of nationalism from Western to Central Europe. In contrast to Western Europe, where a common state territory, a strong central government, and a unified economic system preceded or developed concomitantly with nationalism, the area east of the Rhine was governed by political systems which were not conducive to the rise of nationalism. The Russian, Prussian (later German), Austrian, and Turkish Empires encompassed numerous peoples separated by culture, religion, language, and tradition. German-, Polish-, and Italian-language areas were ruled by separate governments, and, since economic and political unification along national lines came after the development of national consciousness, elements of language and culture were stressed. German nationalism affected the ethnic Germans of Prussia and the small German principalities of northewestern and southern Germany, as well as the German population of the Austrian Empire. Italian nationalism embraced Italian-speaking citizens of the Papal States, Austria's Italian provinces, and the various independent Italian states. It was this emphasis on language and culture that gave Central European nationalism its ethnic emphasis. Nationality was something determined by birth, by race, and by culture—not by citizenship.

In the Balkan Peninsula, nationalism developed even later because social conditions contributing to the rise of nationalism were even less advanced in areas which had been part of the Turkish Empire than in Central Europe. Ottoman administrative structure had a profound impact on the type of nationalism that emerged in its former territories. The Turks virtually eliminated the local nobility as they conquered the Balkans, preferring to control their subjects indirectly through religious leaders. Since religious leaders were the most conscious segment of Balkan society, nationalism in the Balkans was strongly influenced by religious identification.[6] The Serbian struggle for independence was closely linked with the struggle for a Serbian Patriarchate. Greek national identity was maintained primarily through the Greek Orthodox Church. Montenegrins, who never officially surrendered to the Turks, were led by priest-princes who ruled in both secular and religious affairs. The real beginning of Bulgarian nationalism was the Sultan's recognition of the Bulgarian Exarchate in 1870. Serbs and Croats speak essentially the same language, but Serbs are distinguished by their Orthodox faith and Croats by their Roman Catholic conviction. Serbo-Croatian-speaking Moslems of Bosnia-Herzegovina have preferred to call themselves Yugoslav Moslems rather than Serbs or Croats in postwar Yugoslav censuses. Hence, nationalism in the former Turkish territories is not determined by territory or ethnicity, but by religion.*

Nationalism did not have much impact on the peoples of Africa and Asia until the twentieth century, and in these areas it was strongly influenced by colonial domination, which all of these de-

* Albanians are the exception. About 70 percent of the Albanians are Moslem, 20 percent are Orthodox, and 10 percent are Roman Catholic.

veloping countries experienced. Hence, nationalism in the Third World is linked with the drive for modernity. The native races, and especially their Western-educated intelligentsia, desired equality with the white Europeans, and this has become a definite characteristic of Third-World nationalism. In many cases the anti-colonial impetus has become the chief cornerstone of national unity.[7]

Following World War II and the excesses of negative nationalism which led to this conflict, many social scientists concluded that nationalism as a force in world politics was declining.[8] Although there are some signs that Western Europe is moving in the direction of a more mature supranationalism, nationalism as a force in world politics appears to be gaining, not losing, strength. The mass mobilization which is occurring at a rapid rate and the greater penetration of governments into the everyday lives of their citizens have led to an increasing consciousness of national identity. This growth of nationalism has had a far-reaching impact on world politics: The number of states to receive independence has multiplied, colonial powers have been unable to maintain dominance over other peoples, and intervention by great powers in the affairs of small states has been greatly limited. American involvement in Vietnam is the classic example of this, but the Soviet Union also found Hungary in 1956 and Czechoslovakia in 1968 difficult to control despite overwhelming Soviet military superiority. Rumania has been permitted considerable autonomy within the Soviet sphere because the cost of intervention has increased owing to the mobilization of Rumanian nationalism. Another effect of increased nationalism has been the reassertion of national sovereignty in the Eastern and Western blocs which emerged from the cold war. France reduced its participation in NATO and limited its integration within the Common Market system in order to reassert French sovereignty. Even the communist block has split into national communisms. Cuba, Yugoslavia, China, and the Soviet Union all consider themselves models of orthodox communism.

One of the most pervasive effects of increasing nationalism can be observed in relations among nationalities within multinational states. Mass mobilization has not only heightened the nationalism of the *Staatsvolk,* it has also increased the consciousness of the national minorities. This is particularly true in the newly independent coun-

9

tries of the Third World, where national unity has heretofore been tenuous. Moslem Pakistan was separated from Hindu India when independence was granted in 1947. India has since been divided into federal states along linguistic-ethnic lines and continues to show increasing centrifugal tendencies. The civil war between East and West Pakistan and the establishment of Bangladesh are perhaps the most dramatic evidence of this trend on the subcontinent. The Nigerian civil war ended the secession of Biafra from the Nigerian state, but at the cost of hundreds of thousands of lives, and the hostilities have further alienated the Ibo nation from the other Nigerian nationalities. Even in the developed West, national minorities are showing increased consciousness. The Irish Catholic minority's assertion of its rights vis-à-vis the Protestant majority of British Northern Ireland has clear national implications. In recent years Britain has also witnessed a revival of Welsh and Scottish nationalism. The question of special treatment or separation for Canada's French population has become one of the major internal questions facing the Canadian federation. Belgium, which has two separate cultural and linguistic groups (Walloon and Fleming), faces similar internal problems. Even Switzerland, which for centuries has been the epitome of the harmonious union of diverse ethnic, linguistic, and religious groups, has been affected. The French-speaking Catholics of the Jura district in German-speaking Protestant Bern canton are seeking greater autonomy from Bern, though not separation from Switzerland.[9]

The states of southwestern Europe provide a fascinating subject for the study of minority nationalism. The establishment of communism after World War II has in some cases dampened and in some cases amplified the sense of nationalism of minorities and *Staatsvolk*. The intricate ethnic map of Eastern and Central Europe has also complicated the impact of nationalism. The area has been the focal point of conflicting forces for centuries: Migrations of peoples from Asia were halted there by the Germans and Greeks in the centuries after the fall of Rome. Conflict between Slavs, Germans, Greeks, Hungarians, and Turks left the area an incredible maze of ethnic confusion. Later Austrian, Russian, and Turkish competition led rulers to transplant and mix peoples in order to secure borders, and the lack of natural boundaries and the continual threat of external invasion led Central European principalities into feudal federal relationships. It became tradition for a state to embrace several principalities which included various linguistic and religious groups for protection, but, at the same time, these groups retained some semblance of autonomous existence.

This ethnic patchwork within multinational empires led to intense and bitter national conflict. In 1848–1849 the revolt of the Hungarians against Vienna was opposed by Slovaks and Croats. The Slavs justly feared that Hungarian autonomy would intensify the attempt of the rising Hungarian nationalists to assimilate the non-Magyars of the Hungarian realm. Thus nationalism drove Hungarians and Slavs to opposite sides of the barricades. From the Revolution of 1848 until the end of World War I, the most serious problem facing the Austrian Empire was the internal nationality question. In the Russian Empire, Polish, Finnish, Baltic, and Ukrainian peoples were held in check only by severe repression. The Turkish Empire, internally corrupt and inefficient, gradually gave up its territories to the indigenous Balkan peoples during the nineteenth century. Montenegro, Serbia, Greece, Rumania, and Bulgaria were successively established as autonomous states before 1914.

The defeat of Germany, Austria-Hungary, and Turkey in World War I and the internal revolution that convulsed Russia eliminated the external forces that had dominated Eastern Europe for centuries. A series of new, independent states were established, and national minorities were reduced, but not eliminated, by the new national boundaries. Certain areas, such as Transylvania and the Vojvodina, were of such confused ethnographic makeup that no amount of gerrymandering could eliminate some minorities. More often, however, ethnic principles were disregarded in drawing the new boundaries, and states which enjoyed the sponsorship of one of the victorious great powers received territory inhabited by another nationality for economic, strategic, or historic reasons. Thus, what is now southern Slovakia became part of Czechoslovakia, although a large, compact, ethnic Hungarian population inhabited the territory contiguous to the border of Hungary. Rumania received the eastern edge of the Hungarian Plain, where, had the boundary been shifted slightly in some places, compact Hungarian populations would also have remained in Hungary rather than in Rumania. Although the new political boundaries reduced the number of national minorities, after the Paris Peace Conference between one-fifth and one-fourth of the population of Eastern Europe were still national minorities. Each of the states of Eastern Europe had a core nationality or *Staatsvolk,* but in some cases this *Staatsvolk* constituted less than half the population. Every East European state had a sizable national minority population.*

Because national discontent had been a serious source of international unrest in Eastern Europe before World War I, the peacemakers at the Paris Peace Conference were anxious to reduce ethnic tension as much as possible. Besides attempting to redraw boundaries along roughly ethnic lines, the peace treaties included provisions for minority treatment. The defeated powers, which included Austria, Hungary, Bulgaria, and Turkey, were bound by such provisions in their treaties. Newly created states or states receiving new territories—Poland, Czechoslovakia, Rumania, Yugoslavia, and Greece—concluded special treaties with the victorious powers which also contained such provisions. The Charter of the League of Nations also ensured these rights. Although the League system was based on good intentions, it failed because of the weaknesses of the procedure, the opposition of those states which had signed treaties for minority protection, and the ultimate demise of the League.[10]

National minorities were poorly treated by East European governments between the wars because the minorities were an alien element within a national state. The East European governments claimed that a nation is entitled to its state independence and that it has a right to pursue its own national interests. Since the governments primarily represented the dominant nationality, the creation of a *Staatsvolk* required some statistical manipulation. In Czechoslovakia, Czechs and Slovaks were considered to be two branches of the same nationality, thus giving the state a *Stattsvolk* which totaled 65 percent of the population. In Yugoslavia, Serbs, Croats, Macedonians, Bosnian Moslems, and some Albanians were all considered to be the Serbo-Croatian-speaking *Staatsvolk* of Yugoslavia, despite considerable cultural, historical, and religious differences among them.

The interwar East European governments were strongly cen-

* See Appendix for figures on the minorities in Eastern Europe between the two world wars.

tralized regimes. Though there was widespread sympathy in Croatia and Transylvania for a loose federal structure in their respective states, Belgrade and Bucharest allowed their provinces less autonomy than they had enjoyed under Austria. The national minorities were discontented because of the rigid central control and the discrimination against them. At the same time the East European governments were uneasy about national minorities which could not accept the legitimacy of a regime ruling as the representative of the *Staatsvolk,* and these mutual distrusts reinforced each other.

Compounding the problem was the desire of the former defeated powers for revision of their borders. They regarded the fact that their ethnic kinfolk inhabited territories which they had formerly held as the strongest basis for their claim to the old lands. These states encouraged linguistic and cultural links with the minorities, and carried out overt and covert propaganda. (From 1923 to 1934, the Bulgarian government permitted and encouraged Macedonian revolutionary groups to conduct terrorist raids on Yugoslavia territory from sanctuaries in southwest Bulgaria.)

This, of course, had a significant impact on foreign relations in interwar Europe. The vehemence of Hungarian opposition to its territorial losses under the Treaty of Trianon led Czechoslovakia and Yugoslavia to form an alliance against Hungary. Later, Rumania joined these two states in the anti-Hungarian coalition which came to be known as the Little Entente. The purpose of this alliance was to ensure that the three states retain those territories which Hungary had been forced to cede to them after World War I. Although the members of the alliance later established a more pemanent organizational structure, what cemented the Little Entente was the common fear of Hungarian revisionism. Bulgaria was the other principal revisionist power, and the Balkan Entente, created in 1934, was clearly aimed at that country. In the protocol to the agreement creating the Entente, the signatories—Rumania, Yugoslavia, Greece, and Turkey, all powers which held territory claimed by Bulgaria—pledged themselves to maintain the territorial status quo in the Balkans and to guarantee existing frontiers against aggression by any Balkan state. The Bulgarian government was invited to join the Entente, but Sofia openly declared that these territorial provisions made the agreement unacceptable.

The question of Bessarabia was the prime source of friction in the relations between the Soviet Union and Rumania. Moscow signed nonaggression pacts with the states on its western borders, implying Soviet recognition of the existing frontiers. However, no such agreement was signed with Rumania. Both states refused to exchange ambassadors during most of the interwar period.

The overt desire of the revisionist states for territorial changes and the opposition of the status quo powers to boundary adjustments produced a wave of nationalism that swept through Eastern Europe during the 1930's. In every state except Czechoslovakia, national demands took precedence over the requirements of democracy. Nationalist governments were elected because they promised to protect the national interest, and they continued to promote nationalist fervor in order to justify their retention of power. Each East European state had one or more of the ultranationalist groups —the Arrow Cross Party in Hungary, the Iron Guard in Rumania, the Ustaši in Croatia, and the Chetniks in Serbia. Although these parties did not necessarily represent the views of the majority of the population, they do indicate the nationalist tenor of the 1930's. Extreme nationalism became a religion; it dominated the political life of almost every East European state.

These unresolved territorial and national minority questions made it impossible for the East European states to unite in opposition to German and Italian imperialism. The Fascist states were able to play off one Central European state against another, to the detriment of all states. Germany secured Polish and Hungarian support for the rape of Czechoslovakia by giving each a piece of Czechoslovak territory. Bulgaria was given parts of Rumania, Yugoslavia, and Greece. Transylvania was divided between Hungary and Rumania; hence, each of these states sought to demonstrate greater loyalty to Hitler in order to secure all of that contested territory. Nationality, national aspirations, and national minorities constituted a crucial element in determining the sympathies and the fate of the East European states during World War II.[11]

Another major influence on the nations of Eastern Europe after the war was communist ideology. It is important, therefore, to consider communist theory and practice with regard to the national question. Communist treatment of the national question is fraught with contradictions. Although "Marxist" ideology has come to be identified with specific policies on the subject, Karl Marx, the founder of the ideology, was little concerned with questions of nationality and nationalism. His thought was dominated by economics, which he considered to be the determining factor in history and society, and his active interest was in social and political revolution, not national revolution. In his extensive writings he touched on nationality only peripherally, and he offered no definition of nation. In fact, he used the terms "nation" and "national" with unscholarly ambiguity to refer to the state, the ruling class of a country, or even a society. He most frequently used "nation" in the West European sense to refer to the people living on the territory of a state, and he specifically denied that language, culture, and history were important in determining nationality.[12]

When Marx did consider a national movement, it was solely from its revolutionary and economic aspects. Some national movements were to be supported, others were not. For example, the Poles were numerous enough to establish an economically viable state and were noted as revolutionaries, so Marx favored Polish independence. But he opposed independence for Czechs, Croatians, and other Slavic nationalities of the Habsburg Empire because these peoples had helped defeat the Viennese and Hungarian revolutions of 1848–49 by siding with monarchy, and they were too few in number to establish viable economic units.[13] Marx opposed pan-Slavism because it was a tool of tsarism, which he regarded as the bastion of reaction. Thus, revolutionary strategy and emphasis on his own materialist concept of history led him to overlook the significance of national revolutions and of nationalism as a force in history.

In the *Communist Manifesto,* which reflects Marx's ideas on nationalism, the distinguishing feature of the communist movement is proclaimed to be its nonnational character: "In the national struggles of the proletarians of the different countries, [communists] point out and bring to the front the common interests of the entire proletariat, independently of all nationality."[14] Later, in the *Manifesto,* Marx declared, "The workers have no country." However, in order to gain power the proletariat "must rise to be the leading class of the nation, must constitute itself as *the* nation, though not in the bourgeois sense of the word."[15] This last state-

15

ment has led some critics to conclude that Marx did not deny the nation but that he expected the revolution to occur within a national framework.[16] Although he may have expected the revolution to occur separately within each state, Marx did not see nations continuing to exist after the revolution. In the *Manifesto* he observed, "National differences and antagonisms between peoples are vanishing gradually from day to day," and "the supremacy of the proletariat will cause them to vanish still faster."[17] Although Marx treated the national question as a peripheral concern and denied that nationalism had any permanent significance, he is the source of the most important slogan in communist theory on the national question—the national "right of self-determination." Hence, modern communists ascribe the genesis of communist nationality policy to Marx even though the founding prophet ignored the national question.

Marx and his followers in Western Europe could regard the national question as being of peripheral concern. Socialists in Eastern and Central Europe were confronted head on by the issue, however. Awakening national consciousness began to affect the peoples of Eastern Europe just as the ideology of socialism spread into the multinational empires of Austria and Russia and into the Balkans. Many intellectuals in Eastern Europe accepted Marxism for its international appeal. Ethnic minorities, particularly Jewish intellectuals, did so because they found themselves excluded from the national states envisioned by East European nationalism. Many socialist members of the *Staatsvolk,* in contrast, saw Marxism as supporting the continued rule of their nationality: the aristocracy could be replaced by a social-democratic regime, but the leading role of the ruling *Staatsvolk* would remain unaltered. For these Marxists "internationalism" became a justification for national interests. National minorities in Eastern Europe during the interwar period supported communist candidates largely because the communist parties were the most antigovernment (and therefore the most anti-*Staatsvolk*). Thus, although communism disavowed nationalism, it received support specifically because it championed the national interests of the oppressed minority populations.[18]

This complex national-international contradiction within Marxism became a major issue within the social democratic movements in the Austrian and Russian Empires. In these two multinational

16

states the rising national aspirations of the subject peoples assumed such importance that socialists could not ignore the problem. In Austria, the socialist movement was reorganized by Victor Adler in 1889 after decades of internal dissension. Although it was intended that the party be a unified nonnational organization, in 1891 a sizable faction of Czech socialists broke away from Adler's Austrian Socialist Party to pursue national socialist goals. By the beginning of the twentieth century Ukrainians, Poles, Italians, Slovenes, and Rumanians, as well as the Czechs, had formed separate national socialist parties,[19] which forced Austrian socialists to take a vital interest in the national question and to develop a socialist approach toward it.

The first Austrian social democratic proposal for solving the national problem was adopted at Brünn (Brno) in 1899 at a congress of the federated social democratic parties. The *Brünner Programm* called for reorganization of the Habsburg Monarchy into a democratic federation of nationally homogeneous territories in which national minorities would be protected by special guarantees. The German socialists proposed that the administrative competence of these national units be limited to cultural affairs and that German be retained as the leading language. The Czechs led Slav opposition to these proposals and forced the Germans to yield on both points. The nationality provisions in the final text of the *Brünner Programm* were very moderate and represented a compromise between the positions of the German Austrians and the Slavs. The program favored the continued existence of the Austrian state in a somewhat altered form, and it remained the party's official position on the national question until the end of World War I.[20]

Although their views received little attention at Brünn, Otto Bauer and Karl Renner became the leading Austrian socialist theoreticians to deal with the nationality question from the socialist point of view. Renner had joined the socialist movement after having published a number of important writings on the national question, and he continued to advocate his earlier beliefs. However, his later arguments stressed social democratic premises. Otto Bauer, who was a socialist all his life, was perhaps more consistently Marxian in his analysis of the nationality problem.

Bauer and Renner were in general agreement on the socialist

position regarding the national question. Both felt that the political and economic unity of Austria should be maintained in order to permit the evolution of capitalism as a precondition to the establishment of socialism. The national question was, in effect, a smoke screen used by the bourgeoisie to cover their class interests and weaken the solidarity of the proletariat of all nationalities. In order to prevent the national question from obscuring the true economic interests of the workers, Renner proposed a system of state reorganization that would permit satisfaction of the national aspirations of the nationalities but at the same time would guarantee the unity of the state. He proposed the creation of nonnational provinces based on purely economic and administrative considerations. In addition, each nationality would be organized into local, regional, and state-wide national associations, independent of the territorial divisions for state administration, that would have jurisdiction in matters of culture and education. Religious affiliation could not be put on a territorial basis; nor could the question of nationality be solved in that way. Therefore, every man should be entitled to choose his own nationality and to exercise his national rights anywhere within the Austrian state. Bauer urged the resolution of nationality conflict so that the proletariat could unite in fighting for its common interests. He supported Renner's system of administrative reorganization under the principle of personal autonomy and his ideas were, if anything, more centralistic than Renner's.[21]

The *Brünner Programm* and the proposals of the Russian social democrats were quite conventional compared with the revolutionary proposals of Bauer and Renner. Their unique contribution was the principle of personal autonomy—disconnecting nationality from territory. All other attempts to deal with the national question had been based on granting national *and* territorial rights in some form or another. Because the proposed nationality organizations would be given authority to deal with "national affairs" but not political or economic matters, the Renner-Bauer program was unacceptable in practice.

Personal autonomy implied that, once nationality became a matter of personal choice unconnected with territory, national discrimination would cease and socialists would be able to concentrate on economic problems. However, just as granting freedom of religion did not eliminate special privileges for national churches, granting personal autonomy with regard to nationality did not eliminate the *Staatsvolk*. The nonnational territorial government would still employ people who were aware of their nationality, and these people would continue, consciously or unconsciously, to pursue the interests of their nationality. Renner did not propose a nationality quota system for the nonnational state administration, and he even suggested that German be used as the language of communication on the highest levels, as well as among organizations using different national languages. Although he did not propose that special privileges be granted to the German nationality, he clearly saw the Germans as continuing to play the leading role.

The arguments advanced by Renner and Bauer were based upon socialist premises and emphasized economic and class interests over national interests; they did, however, support the German national position for the continuation of an Austrian Empire. The social democratic theoriticians and the *Brünner Programm* were pro-Austrian to the extent that some historians considered socialism to be one of the pillars of the empire.[22] Neither Bauer nor Renner was a German nationalist in the usual sense, but, after the disintegration of Austria in 1918, both advocated *Anschluss* with Germany. Although they were consistent in their devotion to socialism, their ideological views supported the German national cause in Austria.

In Russia the national question also became a major issue with socialists, and later with communists. Before World War I Russia was a multinational empire in which ethnic Russians made up less than half the total population. As in Austria, the movement for liberation from tsarist absolutism became entangled with the question of national liberation; hence, the national question became a concern of the revolutionaries. The revolutionary movement also attracted many non-Russians. As in Austria, Russian social democrats were forced to deal with the national question because nationality divisions developed within the movement. The Jewish *Bund,* which represented a large proportion of the Jewish workers, first joined the Social Democratic Party and then withdrew when its demand for federation of the party along national lines was rejected. A short time later, however, the *Bund* rejoined the party, though the national question had not been clarified. Social democrats in Poland, Latvia, and Lithuania separated for some time from the central party organization. The questions of cultural-national autonomy and federalization of the party were recurrent national issues that divided the social democrats prior to World War I. The Russian socialists were never as divided as the Austrian socialists, however, because the Austrian social democratic movement was federated along national lines almost as soon as Adler reorganized the party and it remained federated until it separated into national units with the dissolution of Austria-Hungary in 1918. The Russian social democrats were also divided on the national question, but national factions were short-lived and the party did not become a federation.

Differing circumstances, leaders, and ideology explain this situation. In the Austrian half of the Dual Monarchy, universal franchise and the secret ballot had been achieved by 1907. The Austrian socialists were a legal party seeking to participate in the Austrian parliament. This forced them to seek popular support and required alliances with socialists of various nationalities in order to gain influence over the government. Since the Austrian socialists were a mass party, they were forced to make concessions to the demands of the nationalities concerning party organization and party program in order to gain popular support. Russian revolutionaries operated under more repressive conditions. The tsarist government was much slower to extend the franchise and to permit parliamentary influence on government. The Russian social democrats, particularly the Bolshevik faction under Lenin, adopted the strategy of forming a small conspiratorial party to lead the masses. Because of this different concept of party organization and because it was driven underground, the party did not have to make concessions to national sentiment. Since the goal was revolution, propaganda slogans could appeal to national sentiment without actually making concessions to nationalism.

The rising wave of national discontent in Russia on the eve of World War I made nationalism a potential ally of the Bolshevik cause. Lenin, who had previously ignored the issue, became concerned to enunciate a Bolshevik policy on the national question as a tactical expedient to further the cause of proletarian revolution. He frequently denounced "Great-Russian chauvinism" both before and after coming to power, but his intolerance of non-Russian peoples and cultures prevented him from developing a truly internationalist attitude. His opposition to federalization of the party or state and his insistence upon rigid centralization in effect supported the continued rule of the Russian *Staatsvolk*. Many Russian socialists published their views on the national question, but the writings of Lenin and Stalin are of more permanent concern because it is from them that current Soviet national policy has evolved. For Lenin, nationalism was a product of capitalistic development, destined to die with capitalism:

Capitalism's world-historical tendency to break down national barriers, obliterate national distinctions, and assimilate nations . . . is one of the greatest driving forces transforming capitalism into socialism.

Marxism cannot be reconciled with nationalism, be it even of the "most just," "purest," most refined and civilized brand. In place of all forms of nationalism Marxism advances internationalism, the amalgamation of all nations in the higher unity. . . .[23]

Because he apparently saw nationalism as an element of the capitalist superstructure, Lenin attempted only indirectly to define it or to analyze its nature in his own works.[24] Stalin, who formulated the Bolshevik position in his *Marxism and the National Question*, developed his ideas under the supervision of Lenin, and Stalin's early writings can be said to reflect Lenin's thinking.[25]

Lenin saw the principal value of nationalism to be its usefulness in furthering the cause of the revolution. Hence, Bolshevik support for national causes was to be "strictly limited to what is progressive in such movements."[26] Therefore, "the working class supports the bourgeoisie only in order to secure national peace . . . and to create optimum conditions for the class struggle." The proletariat "values above all and places foremost the alliance of the proletarians of all nations, and assesses any national demand, any national separation, from the angle of the working-class struggle."[27]

For Lenin, the key to the national question was the right of a nation to "self-determination," which for him meant simply "the political separation of these nations from alien national bodies, and the formation of an independent national state."[28] However, he specified that there were certain conditions under which separation of a nation from the state was progressive and certain situations in which it was not. The party would, of course, be the agency to determine whether separation was appropriate under the circumstances.[29]

Lenin's opportunism on the national question provoked criticism from other Marxists who foresaw serious consequences resulting from his slogan of "self-determination" for the non-Russian nationalities. Rosa Luxemburg was one of the most articulate of Lenin's critics in this connection. She pointed out that in the Polish areas of Russia, Lenin's policy of supporting national self-determination would mean turning Poland over to the landlords and the bourgeoisie, while in Central Asia self-determination would bring feudal chiefs and Moslem religious leaders to power. Despite the validity of Rosa Luxemburg's reasoning, Lenin realized the powerful appeal of nationalism and sought to harness it to bring about the collapse of the tsarist system. Once the Bolsheviks had come to power there would be an opportunity to adjust demands for self-determination to the needs of the proletariat.

During the few short years following the November 1917 coup d'état that Lenin remained in control of the Russian state, the problems of the civil war and foreign intervention pushed the national question into the background. With the gradual establishment of communist control over most of the former Russian Empire, the right of self-determination remained a propaganda phrase, but the communist party determined that secession under present conditions was counterrevolutionary. At the seventh party congress in May 1917 Stalin, who had become the party spokesman on national questions, explained that "a people has the right to secede, but it may or may not exercise that right, according to circumstances."[30] He was even more adamant in 1920 when he stated the policy of the Soviet government toward the national question, insisting that the victory of the revolution made it necessary for Russia and the border nations to support each other against the forces of imperialism.[31] The successful conclusion of the civil war and the end of foreign intervention permitted the consolidation of communist power. A federal state structure was established with national units theoretically entering the union as equal republics.[32] Lenin, who had originally opposed a federal state or party structure, now recognized the strength of non-Russian nationalism and supported the establishment of constituent federal republics. In addition, the communist government sought to appeal to the former peoples of the Russian Empire now separated from the Soviet state by at least giving the appearance of accepting the idea of national autonomy. However, the federal form was merely a facade covering a politically monolithic, centralized Soviet state. Those of Russian nationality remained the *Staatsvolk* of the Soviet Union, and Stalin, the Georgian who succeeded Lenin as party and state leader, became a nationalist Russian ruler.

The Soviet government grants more on paper than in practice. In theory the communist nationality policy admits the right of a nation to self-determination (separation); encourages the development of a national culture; permits administration and education to be conducted in the native language; and grants some form of territorial autonomy or recognition. In actuality, however, Soviet policy has been much more antinational. The right of secession cannot be exercised in practice. National culture is permitted only to the extent that is supports Soviet, not national, purposes. When the theory of the amalgamation of nations is being emphasized, a policy of Russification is followed; at other times distinctive national features are tolerated. Territorial and administrative autonomy is severely limited. Though in many cases administrative positions are held by local nationals, Moscow exercises absolute control over the constituent republics of the USSR.[33]

The establishment of communist governments in Eastern Europe following World War II thus confronted the states of that area with two conflicting traditions. One was the tradition of nationalism which had been awakened during the struggles of the nationalities for liberation from multinational empires. National consciousness had been heightened during the interwar period and World War II by ultranationalist governments, economic crisis, conflict over ethnic minorities, and demands for territorial revision. The other tradition was the communist national policy, which was introduced into the nationalist atmosphere of Eastern Europe by the Red Army and Moscow-installed communist parties. The Soviet treatment of nationalism emphasized ideological slogans and international (that is, Soviet) rather than national goals. Proletarian internationalism and the unity of nationalities in the class struggle were almost the antithesis of the nationalism that had pervaded Eastern Europe before 1945. However, communist nationality policy can hardly be said to have triumphed in present-day Eastern

Europe. National conflict has been banned by the Soviet Union and its client communist parties, but, behind a facade of unity and "internationalism," nationalism and national conflict continue to exist. Although communist policy has affected the form and intensity of the conflict, the basic national problems that have disturbed Eastern Europe for generations continue to pierce the communist veneer.

Chapter 2

Aftermath of World War II: Redrawing National Boundaries

As the victorious Red Army pushed the invading Nazi *Wehrmacht* back into Central Europe, new governments were established in which local communists controlled key ministries and exercised an influence much greater than their popular support would warrant. The first national question to face the Soviet Union and these client regimes in Eastern Europe was the readjustment of frontiers. Soviet policy proclaimed the right of self-determination and implied that the will of the people should be the principal factor in establishing boundaries. However, it was Soviet national interest and not ideology that determined the action of communist leaders. As the most powerful force in the area, the Soviet Union took what it wanted.

Soviet policy toward the Ukrainian irredenta in Czechoslovakia, Poland, and Rumania fluctuated in the period between the two world wars. At the fifth Comintern congress in 1924, the Communist International instructed the communist parties of the three countries to launch a general slogan urging "separation of the Ukrainian lands from Poland, Czechoslovakia, and Rumania and their union with the Soviet Ukraine, and through this, with the Union of Soviet Socialist Republics."[1] At the same time, however, the leaders of the Soviet Union were reluctant to risk encouraging nationalism in the Soviet Ukraine by conducting a campaign advancing ethnic claims to the Ukrainian irredenta outside the Soviet frontiers. Under Stalin, the Soviet government had undertaken a vicious campaign to eradicate Ukrainian nationalism, and until this process was completed Soviet leaders were reluctant to undertake the annexation of Ukrainians living beyond its borders. These western Ukrainians (those living in Czechoslovakia, Poland, and Rumania) were the most anticommunist, anti-Russian, and nationalist, and would certainly prove difficult to control. On the other hand, these territories were the major source of nationalist propaganda aimed at Soviet Ukranians and the base of a Ukrainian liberation movement. Control of these territories would permit the Soviet Union to crush the nationalist movement and eliminate it as a source of unrest in the Soviet Ukraine. There was also historical incentive to regain territory which had been part of tsarist Russia, and, briefly, of the Soviet Union. (After the defeat of Germany in World War I, the Soviet Union temporarily regained the northern Ukrainian territories which Germany had occupied during the war. However, the defeat of the Red Army by the Polish army forced the Soviet government to cede these territories to Poland under terms of the Treaty of Riga, March 18, 1921.)

By the late 1930's the deportation of kulaks, the great purge, and police terror had effectively suppressed Ukrainian nationalism in the Soviet Union, and Stalin began actively to pursue a policy of uniting Ukrainian lands under Soviet hegemony. By the terms of the Secret Protocol to the Soviet-German nonaggression pact of August 23, 1939, the Soviet "sphere of influence" in Poland was extended westward to the line of the Narew, the Vistula, and the San Rivers. This gave the Soviet Union most of the Polish territory inhabited by Ukrainians and Byelorussians. Ten months later the Soviet government demanded that Rumania cede northern Bukovina, with its Ukrainian ethnic majority, and Bessarabia, with a Ukrainian minority, to the Soviet Union. Though these Ukrainian territories were occupied by Germany and Rumania for almost three years during the war, when the Soviet armies reconquered them in 1944 they were reincorporated into the Soviet Union.

After they decided to claim these Ukrainian lands, it was entirely consistent for the Soviet leaders to annex the Carpatho-Ukraine.* The population of the Carpatho-Ukraine is primarily Ukrainian, although there is a sizable Magyar minority along the Hungarian border. The Czechoslovak census of 1921 recorded a "Russian (Great Russian, Ukrainian, Carpatho-Russian)" population of 375,117 (61.8 percent). Hungarians numbered 104,177 (17.2 percent); Jews, 81,529 (13.4 percent); and Czechs and Slovaks, only 19,945 (3.3 percent).[2] The 1959 Soviet nationality census recorded a population of 686,464 (74.6 percent) Ukrainians; 146,247 (15.9 percent) Hungarians; 29,599 (3.2 percent) Russians; and smaller numbers of Rumanians, Slovaks, and Jews.[3] Technically the territory was taken from Hungary since part of it had been awarded to Hungary by an Italian-German decision in 1938 and the remainder was occupied by Hungarian troops at the time German troops occupied all of Czechoslovakia in 1939. Since the Carpatho-Ukraine had been part of pre-Munich Czechoslovakia, however, it became an issue in Czechoslovak-Soviet relations. Although there is substantial evidence to suggest that Czechoslovak President Edvard Beneš did not strongly oppose ceding the Carpatho-Ukraine to the Soviet Union, there has been considerable controversy about whether he actually offered to cede the territory to the Soviet Union before the Red Army occupied it and began to integrate it into the Soviet Union. An official of the Czechoslovak government-in-exile claimed that, when Beneš was in Moscow for the signing of the Soviet-Czechoslovak alliance in December 1943, he suggested to Stalin that "Carpathian Ruthenia might find its new destiny within the Soviet Ukraine," but according to this account Stalin "emphatically refused Beneš's suggestion."[4] In a letter written to Beneš in January 1945, Stalin reminded him: "You yourself told me in Moscow that you were prepared to cede the Transcarpathian Ukraine to the Soviet Union, to which, as you will remember, I did not at that time give my approval."[5] Two Slovaks—one communist and one noncommunist—claimed that Beneš had told them in London that he had made such an offer to

---

* This territory is called "Podkarpatska Rus" (Subcarpathian Rus or Subcarpathian Ruthenia) in the Czechoslovak constitution of 1920. In Hungarian it is referred to as "Ruthenia," and in Soviet terminology it is "Zakarpatskaia Ukraina" (Transcarpathian Ukraine).

27

Stalin and that the latter had accepted it,[6] but there is evidence to the contrary from other sources. The brother of the Czechoslovak president reported that on January 6, 1944, when Beneš returned to London after negotiating the treaty with the USSR, a Soviet envoy handed him a letter from Stalin demanding that he cede the Carpatho-Ukraine to the Soviet Union. He called this "the heaviest blow suffered by Dr. Beneš since Munich."[7] According to Beneš's political secretary, when Stalin's letter arrived reminding him of the offer to cede the Carpatho-Ukraine to the Soviet Union, Beneš emphatically denied that he had made such an offer.[8]

Unfortunately the Czechoslovak president did not clarify this question before his death. After the Soviet Union and Czechoslovakia signed the treaty transferring Ruthenia to the USSR, Beneš stated that as early as 1919 he and President Masaryk had envisioned the annexation of the Carpatho-Ukraine to the Soviet Union "as soon as the Ukrainian people were nationally united." He added, "This occurred when eastern Galicia became a part of the Ukraine, and thereby of the Soviet Union."[9] However, these statements were published *after* the Carpatho-Ukraine had been lost to Czechoslovakia, when it would not benefit Czechoslovakia to antagonize the Soviet Union by revealing details unfavorable to Moscow. Statements made by Beneš before Soviet troops entered the Carpatho-Ukraine are not clear on this point. He did make a number of references to the Carpatho-Ukraine remaining a part of Czechoslovakia.[10] In his February 3, 1944, report to the Czechoslovak State Council in London on his return from Moscow, after signing the Czechoslovak-Soviet alliance, Beneš clearly included the Carpatho-Ukraine in postwar Czechoslovakia.[11] Nevertheless, his references to that area were almost always ambiguous. Though he stated that the Carpatho-Ukraine should be restored to Czechoslovakia, he implied that this might not be permanent: "The pre-Munich constitution of the Republic remains in force until such time as it may be changed by us," and "this applies also to Carpathian Ruthenia." But he added that "if there are to be any changes in the constitution of Carpathian Ruthenia" they must be made with the consent of the population.[12] In the same speech Beneš told the State Council that he was not telling all that had been decided in Moscow: "This is, however, not the moment to examine concretely the matters we negotiated, and on which we reached mutual understanding." But, he assured them, "There were no secret agreements and conventions between us."[13] In Beneš's mind the status of Ruthenia was not explicitly clarified during his first visit to Moscow in 1943. He does not seem to imply that he gave away the territory at that time.

From many of his statements as well as from what actually took place, it is possible to piece together Beneš's real position. With Germany, Poland, and Hungary all claiming parts of Czechoslovakia, Beneš insisted that the territorial integrity of Czechoslovakia must be restored. If Ruthenia were kept by the Soviet Union, instead of being freely ceded to the USSR by Czechoslovakia after the latter's pre-Munich boundaries had been re-established, it would set a dangerous precedent which might be followed by other neighboring states having claims on Czechoslovak territory, and this would be a serious blow to the international prestige of Czechoslovakia.[14] Beyond this legal argument Beneš, remembering the Little Entente, would like to have retained a geographical link with Rumania. Before 1944, however, it had become clear to Beneš that the Soviet Union would play a dominant role in Central European affairs; hence, he was not willing to antagonize the Soviet leaders. The Carpatho-Ukraine was the least developed area of Czechoslovakia, and the force of Ukrainian nationalism, which had become evident in Ruthenia during 1938 and 1939, did not bode well for the future of Ruthenia within Czechoslovakia. After the westward expansion of the Soviet frontiers in 1939–1940, Ruthenia was the only area with a substantial Ukrainian population not included in the Soviet Union. Since the Red Army would liberate all of Czechoslovakia and the USSR would play a major role in postwar Eastern Europe, Beneš strongly desired Soviet friendship. Therefore, he could do little more than he did, which was to accept the loss of the Carpatho-Ukraine with good grace.

The position of the Czech, Slovak, and Carpatho-Ukrainian communists during the time the fate of the Carpatho-Ukraine was being decided indicates either that the Soviet leaders were undecided until very late about annexing the territory, or that they did not clearly communicate their decisions to the local communists. By late October 1944 the Red Army was in control of most of the Carpatho-Ukraine. Under the terms of a Czechoslovak-Soviet agreement, a representative of the London government-in-exile arrived to restore Czechoslovak administrative authority. On October 29, 1944, at a mass meeting in Hust, in the presence of the Czechoslovak government delegation, Ivan Turyanitsa, the leading communist of the Carpatho-Ukraine, proclaimed that liberated Ruthenia must remain a part of Czechoslovakia. Ten days earlier he had said substantially the same thing in an article for a communist newspaper.[15] It was only after November 4, when Soviet Army and NKVD personnel began advocating union of Ruthenia with the Soviet Ukraine, that Turyanitsa changed his position. Czech and Slovak communist émigrés in Moscow, concerned about the separatist movement in Ruthenia, sent a representative from Moscow to speak with Turyanitsa and put a stop to his agitation for Soviet annexation of Ruthenia.[16]

The fact that the local communist leaders in the Carpatho-Ukraine did not support annexation until after November 4 and the Czech and Slovak communists in Moscow did not support it until after November 26 may indicate that it was grass roots Ukrainian nationalism or the overzealousness of local army and NVKD personnel that started the movement.[17] It seems much more likely, however, that Moscow made the decision and failed to communicate it to the Czech and Slovak communists. Soviet military and police personnel would not take such initiative without instructions from above. Also, there was ample reason for Moscow to annex the area. The Carpatho-Ukraine had a Ukrainian ethnic majority even though it was never part of tsarist Russia (the Soviet Union had used such a claim to annex northern Bukovina); possession of Ruthenia would give the Soviet Union control of the passes through the Carpathian Mountains into the valley of the Danube; and, without the Carpatho-Ukraine, the Soviet Union would have no common border with Hungary.

The actual take-over was accomplished quickly. Soviet military authorities gave the Czechoslovak government representative authority only in the eastern section of the province. Military control was retained in the more heavily populated and larger western section because it was near the front and, hence, still a "war zone." Under Soviet military pressure, communist slates were chosen for the local government bodies. Mobilization of the population for the Czechoslovak Army, which was to have been carried out in the eastern zone by the Czechoslovak government delegation, was

30

thwarted by the Soviets, who enlisted more "volunteers" in the Red Army than could be conscripted by the Czechoslovak representatives. The Czechoslovak delegation was prevented from entering western Ruthenia, while communist political leaders traveled throughout the area encouraging sentiment for union with the Soviet Ukraine. The Czechoslovak group's communications went through Soviet military channels to Moscow and then to London, but none of these messages could be sent in code. Turyanitsa called a conference of district government committees to be held in the western zone of the Carpatho-Ukraine, but the representatives of the Czechoslovak government-in-exile could not attend because that zone was not under their control. However, all local district representatives received permission from Soviet military authorities to attend. The conference adopted a resolution—copies of which had been posted by some overenthusiastic local communists the day before the conference began—calling for union of Ruthenia with the Soviet Ukraine. Leaders in the Kremlin at once declared that the will of the people could not be thwarted. The Mosow-based Czech and Slovak communists, now fully aware of Moscow's will, began to demand that Czechoslovakia immediately and unilaterally cede the Carpatho-Ukraine to the Soviet Union as a demonstration of Czechoslovak goodwill.[18] Because of the concern of the Czechoslovak government in London, Stalin magnanimously agreed in January 1945 to postpone the cession until such time as "the two governments thought it opportune."[19] The treaty of cession was signed in Moscow on June 19, 1945.

The Carpatho-Ukraine had never been a part of either tsarist Russia or the Soviet Union, but it did have a Ukrainian ethnic majority. The same was true of northern Bukovina, which the Soviet Union had seized from Rumania in 1940. The Soviet claim to Bukovina was based almost completely on the fact that it had a Ukrainian population. In June 1940, when the German ambassador in Moscow reminded Molotov that Bukovina had never been part of even tsarist Russia and suggested that withdrawal of the Soviet claim to this area would facilitate a peaceful solution of the Bessarabian problem, Molotov countered by saying that "Bukovina is the last missing part of a unified Ukraine and that for this reason the Soviet government must attach importance to solving this question simultaneously with the Bessarabian question."[20] Later, however, the Soviet Union reduced its demand for all of Bukovina and only required the northern part including the city of Czernowitz (Cernăuți, Chernovtsy), an area with a predominantly Ukrainian population.[21] According to the 1930 Rumanian census, the areas which became part of the Soviet Union included 90.6 percent of the population of Bukovina which claimed to be of Ukrainian nationality; those areas which remained part of Rumania included 64.3 percent of those of Rumanian nationality.[22]

Bessarabia, which on the other hand had been part of tsarist Russia for over a hundred years prior to 1919, has a Rumanian ethnic majority. This area was also seized by the Soviet Union, but for historical and strategic, not ethnic, reasons. Bessarabia was ceded to Russia by Turkey in 1812, but, in the chaos of the Russian Revolution, Rumania annexed the territory in 1918. The question of Bessarabia was the major issue that prevented an improvement in Soviet-Rumanian relations throughout the period between the two world wars. In the secret protocol to the Soviet-German non-aggression pact of August 23, 1939, the boundaries of "their respective spheres of influence" were delineated. The agreement specified: "With regard to southeastern Europe attention is called by the Soviet side to its interest in Bessarabia. The German side declares its complete [political] disinterestedness in these areas."[23] On June 26, 1940, the Soviet Union, with twenty-four divisions massed on the Rumanian border, issued an ultimatum to Rumania demanding Bessarabia. Since the German government suggested yielding to the demand, Rumania had no choice but to agree, and the territory passed into Soviet hands.

According to the Rumanian census of 1930, the population of Bessarabia included 56 percent Rumanians; Russians and Ukrainians together made up only 23 percent; the remainder were Jewish, Bulgarian, Turkish, and German.[24] The actual territory of Bessarabia includes only the area between the Prut and Dniester Rivers. While the majority of the population is Rumanian, those areas bordering on the Black Sea are Ukrainian and Bulgarian. When the USSR took Bessarabia in 1940, these non-Rumanian areas became part of the Soviet Ukraine. While most of the Rumanians living in the Soviet Union are to be found in Bessarabia, there is a small area across the Dniester River with a Rumanian population which has never been part of Rumania, and the Soviet Union has always acknowledged it to be ethnically non-Ukrainian. Prior to

1940 the area was known as the Moldavian Autonomous Republic, but on August 2, 1940, this area and the parts of Bessarabia inhabited by Rumanians were combined into the Moldavian Soviet Socialist Republic, and the territory was elevated to the status of a Union Republic.

When Germany invaded the Soviet Union a year after the annexation of Bessarabia, Rumania joined with the Nazi forces in order to regain her lost province. Rumania reannexed Bessarabia directly and also took over the administration of a much larger part of the Soviet Union, including the port of Odessa and territory east to the Bug River. This area, called Transnistria, was administered by a Rumanian-appointed governor; it was given to Rumania by Hitler as compensation for the loss of northern Transylvania, which had been awarded to Hungary on August 30, 1940. Rumania had no real interest in annexing Transnistria, though some Rumanians hoped to use it as a bargaining device to regain northern Transylvania from Hungary.[25]

As the Axis armies were forced back toward the prewar Soviet boundaries, the Soviet government made it clear that its right to Bessarabia was not to be questioned. On April 2, 1944—just after Soviet troops had occupied most of Bessarabia and just two days before they were to cross the Prut River into Rumania proper—Soviet Foreign Minister Molotov called in representatives of the Soviet and foreign press and informed them that "the Red Army [has] emerged on the Prut River, which formed the state frontier between the USSR and Rumania. This [has] laid the beginning of the full re-establishment of the Soviet state frontier established in 1940 by a treaty between the Soviet Union and Rumania." While leaving no doubt that the Soviet Union would keep Bessarabia, Molotov, in an attempt to allay Rumanian fears about Soviet intentions, further declared that the Soviet Union had no intention "of acquiring any part of Rumanian territory or of changing the existing social system in Rumania."[26] Soviet troops would enter Rumania only to pursue the retreating German armies.

Secret negotiations were already under way between the allies and representatives of Rumania's King Michael in Cairo, and, unknown to the Western allies, between the Soviet Union and the government of General Ion Antonescu in Stockholm. The negotiations were hampered by communications problems between Bucharest and Cairo, and by Soviet attempts to get the highest price.[27]

Bessarabia and Northern Bukovina

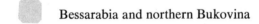 Bessarabia and northern Bukovina

‒·‒·‒· Moldavian ASSR (before 1940)

‒ ‒ ‒ ‒ Moldavian SSR (since 1944)

‒‒‒ International boundaries (since 1945)

An armistice agreement was signed September 12, 1944—twenty days after King Michael had arrested Marshal Antonescu, broken the alliance with the Axis powers, announced a cessation of hostilities with the allies, and declared war on Hungary. The armistice agreement, to which the three principal allies agreed, specified that "the state frontier between the Union of Soviet Socialist Republics and Rumania established by the Soviet-Rumanian Agreement of 28th June 1940 is restored."[28] There was no mention of the Soviet-Rumanian frontier at the peace conference.

The Soviet Union made no pretense about determining the will of the people of Bessarabia. In 1940 the Rumanian government had suggested that a plebiscite be held before Bessarabia should be ceded to the Soviet Union, but the Soviets refused. In 1944 there was no hint that the Bessarabians might have a right to self-determination. The Soviet Union wanted Bessarabia and northern Bukovina and took them. The Rumanian communists had consistently supported Soviet claims to Bessarabia. In 1943, when the leader of the Peasant Party, Iuliu Maniu, offered the Communist Party an opportunity to collaborate with him in opposing Marshal Antonescu, the communists refused because they were unwilling to pledge themselves, as had all other parties in the opposition bloc, to work for the restoration of Rumania's former territorial borders.[29]

While the Carpatho-Ukraine and Bessarabia-northern Bukovina were the only territories in southeastern Europe that the Soviet Union took for itself, it played a major role in all other boundary settlements in the area. As with territory the Soviet Union annexed, the national question was not the determining factor in the distribution. Aside from major changes in the borders of the USSR and of the defeated nations Germany and Japan, and the need to compensate Poland for its loss of territory in the east, Soviet leaders opposed major boundary adjustments. This did not, however, prevent them from using the boundary question to further their aims in southeastern Europe. The Soviet Union compensated countries for land they had lost to the USSR at the expense of a third country. This was clearly the case with Poland, and it was also a factor in the disposition of Transylvania.*

* The term Transylvania is used here to refer to the entire territory which Rumania annexed from Hungary after World War I. Historically Transylvania is only that half of the area which lies east of the Bihar Mountains and is

35

Just over half the population of Transylvania is Rumanian, but there are large Hungarian and German minorities. The Rumanian census of 1930 showed the population of Transylvania (including the Banat, Crișana, and Maramureș) to be 58.5 percent Rumanian, 24.4 percent Hungarian, 9.8 percent German, and 3.2 percent Jewish.[30] These figures, which are for the entire region, do not reflect the fact that there are areas contiguous to Hungary, in addition to the Szekler lands in eastern Transylvania, which have local Hungarian majorities. In the Second Vienna Award of August 30, 1940, Ciano and Ribbentrop gave Hungary the northern part of Transylvania, including slightly less than half the contested territorry. The Rumanian government resigned and King Carol abdicated, while the Hungarian government insisted on its historical rights to all the territory. During the war Rumania and Hungary competed for Hitler's favor in order to gain the other half of Transylvania.

As Hitler's defeat drew near, the Rumanians realized there was no hope of regaining Bessarabia, so they concentrated their efforts on regaining all of Transylvania. The Soviets were quite willing to compensate Rumania for the loss of Bessarabia and northern Bukovina at Hungary's expense. Not only would this sweeten relations between Rumania and the Soviet Union, but, if Rumania should ever advance revisionist claims to Bessarabia, it would be useful to remind Rumania that Hungary also had claims on Transylvania. King Michael issued a proclamation on August 23, 1944, which announced Rumania's renunciation of the Axis alliance and the cessation of hostilities against the allies, and accepted the allied armistice terms which, he said, had "guaranteed the independence of Rumania and . . . recognized the injustice of the Vienna *Diktat* by which Transylvania was torn from us." The King also declared war on Hungary, proclaiming: "At the side of the Allied Armies and with their help, I mobilize all forces of the nation, and we shall cross the frontiers unjustly imposed upon us at Vienna so as to liberate our Transylvania from enemy occupation."[31] Though negotiations had been going on for some time, the terms of the

enclosed on the south and east by the bend of the Carpathian Mountains. The rest of the territory that Rumania gained from Hungary is the eastern edge of the Hungarian plain and includes Maramureș, Crișana, and the eastern part of the Banat.

SOVIET UNION

HUNGARY

Mara-Mureş

Crişana

Transylvania

Banat

RUMANIA

YUGOSLAVIA

BULGARIA

HUMAPS

Hungarian-Rumanian Boundary Changes

....-.~ Hungarian-Rumanian boundary before 1918

--- -   Hungarian-Rumanian boundary, 1919–1940, 1945–

Northern Transylvania (given to Hungary in Second Vienna Award, 1940; returned to Rumania, 1945)

------ International boundaries

Rumanian armistice had not been agreed upon at the time Michael issued his proclamation. The Soviet Union issued another statement reaffirming Molotov's April disclaimer that the Soviet Union had territorial ambitions with regard to Rumania. The new Soviet statement clearly implied that Transylvania would compensate for the loss of Bessarabia and for Rumania's help against the Axis forces:

If the Rumanian troops will cease military action against the Red Army, and if they will pledge, hand in hand with the Red Army, to carry on the liberation war against the Germans for the independence of Rumania, or against the Hungarians for the liberation of Transylvania, then the Red Army . . . will help them fulfill this honorable task.[32]

The Rumanians quickly rallied and gave the Soviets considerable assistance against the German and Hungarian armies in northern Transylvania. The Hungarians, who had been balking under German domination, fought vigorously in Transylvania, while the Germans strengthened their position in central Hungary. Hungary's stubborn refusal to yield Transylvania to Rumania and her new ally from the east was one of the reasons behind the anti-Hungarian attitude of the Soviet Union during the first few years following the war.

The specific terms of the armistice agreement restored Transylvania to Rumania, but left open the possibility of revisions in favor of Hungary. The allies declared the decision of the Second Vienna Award regarding Transylvania null and void, agreeing that "Transylvania (or the greater part thereof) should be returned to Rumania, subject to confirmation at the peace settlement."[33] At Stalin's direction, the Soviet military authorities turned over the administration of all of Transylvania to the Rumanian government in March 1945, more than a full year before the peace treaties were concluded. Stalin, however, did insist that the Rumanian government "secure the rights of the nationalities" in Transylvania.[34]

Once the Soviet leaders decided to return Transylvania to Rumania, they were completely consistent. Communist leaders in both Hungary and Rumania supported the Kremlin decision. As the Hungarian government began to draw up its plans for the Paris Peace Conference, the communist Vice-Premier, Mátyás Rákosi, knowing Moscow's decision and the futility of trying to change it, admitted with acerbity that "now he would have to consider the Hungarian Peace Treaty."[35] When it was decided to present claims for part of Transylvania, Rákosi proposed that they should not exceed 4,000 to 10,000 square kilometers—the smallest area suggested by a member of the Hungarian government.

In April 1945 a Hungarian delegation visited Moscow and presented, among other things, a plan to claim 22,000 square kilometers of Transylvania. Stalin asked to see maps of the area, had Molotov read the relevant section of the Rumanian armistice agreement, and agreed that the Hungarians could legally introduce the Transylvanian question at the Paris Peace Conference. Later, at dinner in Moscow, Molotov told the Hungarian Premier that Hungary should negotiate directly with Rumania on the subject. When Ferenc Nagy, the Hungarian leader, pointed out the futility of negotiating with the Rumanians over Transylvania, Molotov only repeated his earlier suggestion. The Hungarians asked the Soviet Union to recommend to the Rumanian government that it negotiate with the Hungarian government, but Molotov declined.[36] Apparently Stalin was willing to permit frontier adjustments in Transylvania only if Rumania approved, and the Rumanian government refused to negotiate when a Hungarian representative was sent to Bucharest to discuss the question. At the session of the Council of Foreign Ministers in Paris on May 7, 1946, all of Transylvania was awarded to Rumania, with no change in its boundaries. James F. Byrnes, the American Secretary of State, proposed minor border rectifications in favor of Hungary, but Molotov insisted that all Transylvania should go to Rumania because "Stalin had already so decreed."[37]

While the Hungarian communists were thus put in the position of opposing Hungarian national goals because of Moscow's decision, the Rumanian communists were able to play on Rumanian nationalism. In an article written just after the decision of May 7 restored all of Transylvania to Rumania, Vasile Luca, secretary of the Rumanian Communist Party, claimed:

The point of view of the Rumanian Communist Party has been and still is consequent [sic—consistent?]. We have stood resolutely against the Vienna Verdict, we have stood against the alliance with

Hitlerite Germany, and we have stood and fought against the war of Hitler and Antonescu.

"The Rumanian Communist Party considers that a true and lasting peace in the Danube Basin cannot be established, that the national independence of the small countries in Central Europe cannot be secured, unless all remnants of the Hitlerite 'New Order' are completely obliterated and the Vienna Verdict thus abolished."[38]

The most consistent line followed by the Rumanian Communist Party was that of subservience to Moscow on national questions. The party remained silent with regard to Rumania's claims to Bessarabia and northern Bukovina, though these were ethnically and historically at least as valid as the claims to Transylvania. Had the tables been turned and had Stalin favored Hungary at Rumania's expense, it would have been Luca, and not Rákosi, who would have denounced the bourgeois nationalism of his government while still praising the "consistency" of communist national policy.

At the Paris Peace Conference of 1946, the Hungarians again presented their case for a part of Transylvania. Again it was the Soviet Union and other communist delegations that opposed Hungary's claims most strongly. When the Australian delegate proposed that Hungary give its views on Transylvania to the Territorial and Political Commission for Rumania, the Soviet, Ukrainian, Byelorussian, and Czechoslovak delegations opposed the action. When the time came for Hungary to present its case, the delegate from the Ukraine insisted upon inviting the Rumanian delegation to attend. At a plenary session of the Peace Conference, Molotov insisted that "the question of Transylvania be settled to the satisfaction of the Rumanian people."[39]

One major reason for the Soviet Union's consistent support of Rumania's claims in Transylvania was the desire to compensate Rumania for Bessarabia-northern Bukovina. But here, as elsewhere, the Soviet Union also used support for territorial claims to reward and to punish. When the postarmistice government was set up in Rumania, the Soviets were not satisfied. The first government, under General Santescu, failed to grant enough power to the communists, and after three months and two cabinet reorganizations he was forced to resign. Despite his pleas, the Soviet Union did not again put northern Transylvania under Rumanian administration during his term of office. General Rădescu succeeded him as Prime Minister, but because he was not pro-Soviet enough, he was forced out of office within three months by communist-inspired demonstrations and an ultimatum from Stalin via Vishinsky to King Michael. At Vishinsky's insistence, Dr. Petru Groza became Prime Minister of a government that included a substantial number of representatives of the communist and procommunist parties.

The Groza government was announced on March 6, 1945. On March 8, Groza and his new Foreign Minister, Tărtărescu, addressed a letter to Stalin pledging that Rumania would adhere to the "principles of equality, democracy, and justice in respect to the entire population" of Transylvania, and requesting that the territory be returned to Rumanian administration.[40] On March 9, Stalin directed Soviet military leaders to turn over the administration of northern Transylvania to the new Rumanian government. At a meeting of Rumanian officials celebrating the restoration of Transylvania to Rumania, Groza gave some of the details of the transaction. He left no doubt that the move was intended to help the Groza government and weaken opposition to it:

> Then I said to the gentlemen of the historical parties: if your conscience is clear you should become genuine democrats and work hard to make the Soviet Union feel confidence in us; [if you do this] we will receive northern Transylvania back in 24 hours.
>
> With great effort we have swept away the remnants of Hitlerism, and established a democratic regime in this country. The first thing we did was to ask the USSR to give us back northern Transylvania. We addressed the great Marshal Stalin in Moscow, and within one hour he gave us a favorable reply.[41]

A year later, when the Rumanian people again had reason to be thankful to Molotov and the Soviet Union for refusing, at a meeting of the Council of Foreign Ministers in Paris, to consider any revision of the Hungarian-Rumanian boundary, Vasile Luca spelled out in unmistakable terms the lesson of the return of northern Transylvania:

> The Rumanian people will never forget that only by removing Maniu-Brătianu followers from the commanding posts of the country, has it been possible to restore northern Transylvania to Ruma-

CZECHOSLOVAKIA

POLAND

SOVIET UNION

19

AUSTRIA

HUNGARY

5

4

2

3

1

9

6

18

7

11

8

RUMANIA

10

YUGOSLAVIA

17

12

BLACK

SEA

13

14

BULGARIA

ITALY

15

16

ALBANIA

GREECE

TURKEY

ADRIATIC SEA

HUMAPS

Southeastern Europe: Territorial Changes, 1938–1947

International boundaries as of January 1938

Boundaries of territories altered between 1938 and 1947

1. *Bessarabia*—ceded to the Soviet Union by Rumania, June 28, 1940; invaded by Axis forces, June 1941, and annexed by Rumania; reannexed to the Soviet Union, April 1944.

2. *Northern Bukovina*—same as No. 1.

3. *Northern Transylvania*—given to Hungary in Second Vienna Award, August 1940; returned to Rumania, March 1945.

4. *Ruthenia or the Carpatho-Ukraine*—part given Hungary in First Vienna Award, November 1938; remainder occupied by Hungary in March 1939; entire territory ceded to Soviet Union by Czechoslovakia, June 1945.

5. *Southern Slovakia*—part given Hungary in First Vienna Award, November 1938; remainder occupied in March 1939; returned to Czechoslovakia in 1945.

6. *Part of Croatia*—occupied and annexed by Hungary in April 1941; restored to Yugoslavia in 1945.

7. *Baranja and Bačka*—same as No. 6.

8. *Banat*—autonomous province with large German minority; administered by Germany, 1941–1944; returned to Yugoslavia, 1945.

9. *Part of Slovenia*—annexed to Germany (Austria), April 1941; restored to Yugoslavia in 1945.

10. *Parts of Slovenia and Croatia*—annexed by Italy or under Italian (later German) control, 1941–1945.

11. *Independent Republic of Croatia*—a German satellite, 1941–1945.

12. *Serbia*—nominally independent, but under German control, 1941–1944.

13. *Montenegro*—nominally independent but under Italian (later German) control, 1941–1944.

14. *Kosovo and part of Macedonia*—annexed by Albania with Italian assistance, 1941–1944.

15. *Yugoslav Macedonia*—occupied by Bulgaria, 1941–1944; retaken by Yugoslavia in 1944.

16. *Eastern Greek Macedonia and Western Thrace*—occupied by Bulgaria in 1941; returned to Greece, 1944.

17. *Southern Dobruja*—ceded to Bulgaria by Rumania under terms of the Second Vienna Award, August 1940; retained by Bulgaria after 1945.

18. *Venezia Giulia* (including the Istrian Peninsula)—ceded to Yugoslavia by Italy under terms of the Italian Peace Treaty, 1947.

19. *Eastern Galicia*—occupied by the Soviet Union, 1939; invaded by Germany, 1941; reoccupied and annexed by the Soviet Union, 1944–1945.

nia, even previous to the peace conference. The Rumanian people, by the very fact that it has installed in power a government of large democratic concentration, has won the confidence of the Soviet Union—that powerful state which, after vanquishing fascism, has restored to us Transylvania the second day after Dr. Petru Groza's government had come to power.[42]

After forcing King Michael to install a government unpopular with the majority of Rumanians but clearly favorable to the Soviet Union, Stalin immediately granted the new government the territory which the Rumanian people had been demanding. In this case the Soviets cynically used the national question in carrot-and-stick fashion to bring about the government they wanted in Rumania.

It was also to Rumania's advantage that the Soviet Union was not on good terms with the Hungarian government. Hungary was not only the last of the German satellites to come to terms with the Red Army, but the Hungarian army—unlike those of Rumania and Bulgaria—did not turn against the Germans. Even more important, however, the relatively free elections in November 1945 had given the Smallholder Party 57 percent of the votes cast, while the Hungarian Communist Party came in third, with only 17 percent of the vote. Even in Budapest the Smallholders gained an absolute majority of the seats on the municipal council, while the joint Social Democratic-Communist ticket received only 42 percent.[43] Also, the Hungarian government openly attempted to gain the support of the United States and Great Britain by sending government delegations, including the Prime Minister, to Washington and London. No government trying to court Moscow's support would have done more than address its appeals to the Kremlin. Thus not only was the Transylvanian issue a good way to show support for the Groza government in Bucharest, it was also an excellent way to weaken and to show disapproval of the Nagy government in Budapest.

In the case of the Yugoslav claims to southern Austrian Carinthia and Trieste, the degree of Soviet support was based on the state of Belgrade-Moscow relations. When relations were good, the Soviet Union supported Yugoslav claims on national grounds. But when Yugoslavia was expelled from the Cominform, the USSR denounced these claims. But support for Yugoslav territorial claims

44

by the Soviet Union was never wholehearted. Though the Soviet leaders were willing to push claims which would extend their sphere of influence, the Yugoslavs were too aggressive and not sufficiently subservient to Moscow to suit Stalin. Nevertheless, while relations were ostensibly friendly, the Soviets gave at least formal diplomatic support to Yugoslavia's claims as an indication of support for the Yugoslav government.

In November 1943 the partisan-dominated provisional government of Yugoslavia—the Anti-Fascist Council of National Liberation—declared that the Italian province of Venezia Giulia, with Trieste, had been annexed to Yugoslavia. As the Germans withdrew from this area, Yugoslav partisans occupied most of the Istrian Peninsula and were actually fighting inside Trieste when an allied ultimatum forced them to withdraw their troops from the city. The argument over the Italian-Yugoslav border was taken up at the London Conference of Foreign Ministers which met in September 1945 to consider the peace treaty with Italy. The Yugoslav government claimed northern Venezia Giulia where, according to Belgrade, in the entire region, except the town of Gorica [Gorizia], there was not a single village or town with an Italian majority. Even in Gorica the Austrian census of 1910 showed Slavic inhabitants outnumbering Italian inhabitants 49 percent to 41 percent, and its natural hinterland to be "100 percent Slovene." The Istrian Peninsula and the Adriatic islands, despite "forceful denationalization of Yugoslavs and . . . the systematically organized immigration of Italians," were only one-third Italian. To establish ethnic claims to Trieste was more difficult. But the Yugoslavs, undaunted, pointed out that the Trieste population "consists almost entirely of newcomers" since only two hundred years ago the four thousand inhabitants were almost all Slavic. The Yugoslav memorandum concluded by arguing against the creation of a neutral zone in Trieste or Venezia Giulia. The area is "geographically, ethnographically, economically, and by the will of its population a constituent part of Yugoslavia."[44]

The London Conference was unable to reach agreement on Yugoslavia's claims because the Soviet Union supported the Yugoslavs while the United States, Britain, and France opposed them. At Soviet direction, the Italian Communist Party urged the transfer of Trieste and Venezia Giulia to Yugoslavia as a gesture of magnanimity "to strengthen the forces of democracy."[45] Moscow also placed the disputed area under its own "Giulian" Communist Party, which operated from Ljubljana, and prohibited the Italian party from functioning there. Despite the East-West deadlock, the London Conference did agree that Trieste should become a free port, that the Italian-Yugoslav frontier should be the ethnic line as far as possible, and that a commission of experts of the four powers should recommend the line that conformed best to local geographic and economic factors. The four experts, of course, each recommended a different boundary line. The Soviet line was far to the west, and, while it left no Slavs in Italy, it would have given 500,-000 Italians to Yugoslavia. The four powers finally agreed to accept the French boundary proposal, which balanced Slavs in Italy with Italians in Yugoslavia and created the Free Territory of Trieste.

The southern part of the Free Territory was to be occupied by Yugoslavia and the northern part, including the city of Trieste, was left under allied control until the government of the Free Territory should become functional. The United Nations Security Council agreed to accept responsibility for government of the area, but in the Security Council the Soviet Union prevented appointment of a governor-general for the territory. Meanwhile the Yugoslavs administered their zone as an integral part of their own territory. While Yugoslav-Soviet relations were still friendly, the Soviet Union delayed the establishment of a government in Trieste and worked to weaken any government that might be established in order to allow Tito to retain the area under his occupation and permit the Yugoslavs to seize the whole area, if possible.

Following Yugoslavia's expulsion from the Cominform in 1948, the Soviet Union placed the Trieste party in the hands of a trusted former Comintern agent who severed all links with Ljubljana. The Trieste organization was eventually returned to the control of the Italian Communist Party. After 1948 the Soviet Union also made an about-face in the Security Council and insisted upon the appointment of a strong governor of Trieste in order to force Tito to relinquish control of the Yugoslav-administered southern half of the Free Territory and limit his influence in Trieste. To influence the Italian elections of 1948, the Western powers had promised that Trieste would be returned to Italy. Roles were now reversed: the Soviet Union demanded selection of a governor and immediate implementation of the Trieste agreements; the West prevented action for fear of alienating Italy.[46]

Yugoslavia also advanced territorial claims against Austria on the basis of nationality. At the close of the war Belgrade requested that the Yugoslav army participate in the occupation of Austria. When the British arrived in their zone of occupation, they found Yugoslav partisans in control of several areas of Carinthia. A warning note from Britain and finally a curt order from the Soviet military command were required before the Yugoslavs withdrew. Stalin apparently feared that too-vigorous prosecution of Yugoslav claims in the British zone of Austria might provoke British opposition with regard to Soviet zones of influence. The Yugoslavs nevertheless organized demonstrations and set up subversive organizations among the Slovenes to encourage "local" support for annexation.

Activities on the diplomatic front began in January 1947 at the London meeting of foreign ministers' deputies, with the Soviets supporting the Yugoslavs. Yugoslavia claimed 130 square kilometers of the Austrian province of Styria, including the city of Radkersburg (Radgona), which is primarily German, and 10,000 people, 6,000 of whom were said to be Slovene. Claims were also advanced to "Slovene Carinthia," an area of 2,470 square kilometers in the province of Carinthia with a population of 180,-000, two-thirds of whom were said to be Slovene. This area would have included the cities of Villach and Klagenfurt, which are overwhelmingly German. The Yugoslavs also demanded the enactment of a special statute to guarantee national rights to the 70,000 Croats in Austrian Burgenland, or an exchange of the German-speaking populations living in areas the new frontier would still leave in Austria.[47] The Western powers absolutely refused to consider the Yugoslav claims, citing the plebiscites of 1920 which showed that majorities in some of the contested areas favored remaining with Austria. The question of the Yugoslav claims was one of the major issues of the Austrian treaty upon which the Soviet Union and the Western allies could not agree. Two more years of negotiations failed to produce a solution acceptable to both the Soviet Union and the West.[48]

When the foreign ministers met in Paris in the spring of 1949 the Soviet Union and Yugoslavia were embroiled in the Cominform controversy. The Soviet Union withdrew its support for Tito's claims, alleging that Yugoslavia had held secret negotiations with the British in 1947. In an official communiqué dated June 20, 1949, the foreign ministers stated that the treaty should guarantee the rights of Slovene and Croat minorities in Austria.[49] Thus, the Soviet Union could justify its national ideology and at the same time drop its support for the recalcitrant Yugoslavs. Since the Soviets—to show their disapproval of the Tito government—refused to support the Yugoslav claims against Austria, but at the same time were not interested in signing the Austrian treaty, a new excuse had to be found for delaying the State Treaty. At almost the same time that Molotov announced that his government would no longer uphold Tito's claims, he said that no Austrian treaty could be signed until the provisions of the agreement creating the Free Territory of Trieste had been implemented. Moscow's support for Yugoslavia's claims against Italy and Austria clearly appear to have been based on political, not national, considerations. The Slovenes in Venezia Giulia and Austria and the Croats in Istria and Burgenland had little to do with the Soviet attitude.

The disposition of Dobruja was another example of the Soviets' using a national question to show support for a pro-Moscow government. However, there was an ethnic justification in this case, since that area is more Bulgarian than Rumanian. Southern Dobruja was part of Rumania from 1913 until the German and Italian foreign ministers returned it to Bulgaria under the terms of the Second Vienna Award of August 30, 1940. During the time this territory was part of Rumania, the government in Bucharest encouraged Rumanians to settle there. However, by the time of the 1930 census, after several years of Rumanian rule, the two southern districts of Dobruja contained only 21 percent Rumanians, as against 38 percent Bulgarians and 34 percent Turks.[50] Though the Vienna Awards were denounced by all communist leaders as unjust remnants of Hitlerism that had to be eliminated, the restoration of southern Dobruja to Rumania was never suggested. Bulgaria had the advantage of a long history of friendship with Russia. In addition, Bulgaria refused to fight the Soviet Union. When the Red Army crossed its frontiers, Bulgaria declared war on the Soviets only to permit the USSR to have a voice in her fate at the peace negotiations. After a coup on September 9, 1944, the Communist Party was firmly ensconced in power in Sofia, and Bulgaria became

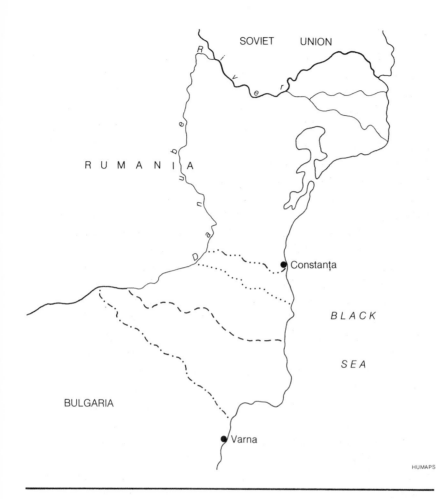

SOVIET UNION

R U M A N I A

BLACK

SEA

BULGARIA

Constanța

Varna

HUMAPS

Bulgarian-Rumanian Boundaries in Dobruja

· · . · · · · ·   Treaty of San Stefano (1878)

· · · . - · · ·   Treaty of Bucharest (May 1918)

· - · . - · - ·   Treaty of Bucharest (August 1913); confirmed by
               Treaty of Neuilly (1919)

~ - - -   Treaty of London (May 1913); re-established in 1940

⁓⁓   Other international boundaries

one of Moscow's favorites. Where Bulgaria was involved, territorial claims were not limited to former enemies. Bulgaria, a defeated German satellite, proposed to the peace conference that it be given western Thrace, territory seized with Germany's help from Greece —one of the United Nations. Stalin was quite willing to expand his empire by expanding Bulgaria at the expense of his Greek "ally." The Bulgarian claims were supported by other Slav states. The Polish delegate "made a plea for humane and generous treatment of Bulgaria," and the Ukraine delegate observed that "Bulgaria should have a peace of justice . . . and therefore should recover western Thrace."[51] It is possible that the Bulgarian claims were advanced to counter Greek demands for a strip of Bulgarian territory. Whether the claims were seriously advanced or not, there was an obvious advantage in having Moscow's support, and the key to this was a communist-dominated government under Moscow's direct control.

Though the Soviet Union claimed to have a developed ideology on the national question, postwar boundary decisions in southeastern Europe were not based upon it. Soviet historic and national interests were the first consideration in redrawing the boundaries. Next came the political considerations of the Soviet leaders—compensation of some states at the expense of others for land seized by the Soviet Union, and the use of territorial settlements to reward pliant and punish recalcitrant governments. Local communist leaders were willing tools of Moscow in supporting the Kremlin's decisions: when these edicts were favorable, they used them to gain popular support; when they were not, they remained silent or attempted to obscure the issues.

Chapter 3

From Coalition Cabinets to Stalinist Satellites: The National Question, 1945–1955

The redrawing of national boundaries involved all communist states of southeastern Europe. Almost as extensive in scope was the transfer of populations, which became a major aspect of postwar communist nationality policy. Though the concept was not originally a communist idea, the Soviet Union and the local communists were its most avid advocates in southeastern Europe. Population transfers were not aimed at removing nationals who had left their country during the war and settled outside its boundaries. Peoples who had inhabited the same lands for centuries found that boundaries drawn after both world wars left them separated from the national state in which the majority of their own ethnic nationality lived. Large-scale population transfers were used after World War I to relocate almost two million Greeks, Turks, and Bulgarians in their own national states. During World War II, Hitler negotiated a number of agreements to transfer German populations from outlying territories to Germany or to territory newly acquired by the Third Reich. There were agreements between Germany and the Soviet Union before June 1941 to exchange and resettle populations. Stalin also used population transfers as a major element in Soviet nationality policy. He uprooted whole populations from one part of the Soviet Union and resettled them in another almost at whim. In his secret speech to the Twentieth CPSU Congress Khrushchev said, half in jest and half seriously, that the Ukrainians had escaped this fate under Stalin "only because there were too many of them and there was no place to which to deport them."[1]

Though the Soviet Union was the strongest supporter and envisioned the most extensive use of population transfers after World War II, leaders of the United States and Great Britain and some of the noncommunist leaders of southeastern Europe also favored the system. President Beneš of Czechoslovakia considered the removal of at least some of the *Sudetendeutsche* before the Munich crisis of 1938,[2] and he secured British, American, and Soviet support for the removal of German and Hungarian minorities from his country in the spring of 1943.[3] At the Potsdam Conference the big three recognized that "the transfer to Germany of German populations or elements thereof remaining in Poland, Czechoslovakia, and Hungary will have to be undertaken."[4] The inclusion of Hungary as one of the countries which would expel its German population was apparently a Soviet suggestion. Hungary, fearing the expulsion of Hungarian minorities by the Czechoslovak, Rumanian, and Yugoslav governments, neither requested nor desired to expel its German minority. The anti-German moves in Hungary came primarily from the Soviet occupation authorities and the Hungarian communists, who wanted to expel the Germans from Hungary in order to make room for Hungarians expelled from Czechoslovakia.[5]

The Soviets were particularly adamant in their insistence on expelling the German minorities from southeastern Europe. Though communist nationality policy was willing to permit minorities of most nationalities to live in the same state and even grant them minority rights, the German minorities were considered "a problem apart and . . . singled out from the general complex of minority problems." Because Germany had used the *Volksdeutsche* as a fifth column against the states of central and southeastern Europe, the Soviets concluded that the nations of Europe must either "remain subject to the constant menace of pan-Germanism" or "transfer the German population from a number of countries to Germany."[6] Under communist direction, the states of southeastern Europe with

German minorities—Rumania, Yugoslavia, Hungary, and Czechoslovakia—passed sweeping laws denying citizenship to, confiscating the property of, and in many cases expelling all Germans who had collaborated with the Nazi government.[7] Since the Ministry of the Interior interpreted and enforced these laws, and since the Minister of the Interior was in all cases a communist or a willing fellow traveler, the laws were used to eliminate the Germans as a whole. In Hungary, for example, when László Rajk became Minister of the Interior he took vigorous action against the German minority— though Rajk himself was of *Volksdeutsche* origin. In July 1946 Rajk protested so vigorously when American authorities suspended the expatriation of Germans from Hungary that agreement was reached to continue the expulsion.[8] Between Germans fleeing from their homes with the retreating German army and those forcibly expelled, the German minority in Czechoslovakia was virtually eliminated by 1948. In Hungary it was reduced to less than a third, and in Yugoslavia, to less than a tenth of its prewar size. In Rumania the government did not expel its German population, but, through enlistments in the German army during the war, the flight of pro-Nazi Germans with the retreating German armies, and Soviet deportation of Germans to aid in postwar Soviet reconstruction, the German minority in Rumania was reduced to half of its former size. The Rumanian government, however, did confiscate property of Germans who could be shown to have had Nazi sympathies, thus undermining the minority's economic status.[9]

The Czechoslovak government was as interested in eliminating its Hungarian minority as it was in expelling the Germans. In his plans for postwar Czechoslovakia, President Beneš made it clear that Hungarians were to be assimilated or eliminated. "There is no room for minority problems [in Czechoslovakia]," he said. "Members of minorities who refuse to return to their national state (for example, Slovaks who stay and Hungary and Hungarians who stay in Czechoslovakia) will be definitely sacrificed and given up to national assimilation by the other state."[10] Official government documents and decrees denying citizenship, requiring forced labor, and expelling the minorities were applied to the Magyar minority with the same severity with which they were enforced upon the German minority.[11]

Despite Czechoslovak attempts to eliminate the Magyar minority, the Hungarian government consistently declined to accept them. Finally, at the insistence of the Allied Control Commission in Budapest, negotiations were undertaken by the two countries in December 1945. These talks finally produced the agreement of February 27, 1946, which provided that, in exchange for Czechs or Slovaks in Hungary who chose to remove to Czechoslovakia, the Czechoslovak government could select and transfer to Hungary an equal number of Hungarians living in Slovakia.[12] Both sides agreed that further attempts to solve the problem would be made. The very day this agreement was signed Vladimír Clementis—the Slovak communist in the Czechoslovak Foreign Ministry who had signed the agreement for Czechoslovakia—addressed a letter to the Hungarian government proposing an agreement under the terms of which 150,000 to 200,000 Hugarians in Slovakia would be transferred to Hungary. This, said Clementis, would eliminate the Hungarian population in Slovakia, because the Czechoslovak government would restore "Czechoslovak citizenship to a large number of persons of Slovak origin (ancestry) who belong to this [Hungarian minority] population." Clementis explained that "re-Slovakization" would not be difficult because the Magyar minority "includes all those who though of Slovak origin and still speaking the Slovak language today declare themselves to be Magyars under the influence of a long national oppression."[13] Although there is some truth to the claim that a part of the Hungarian minority is of Slovak ancestry, many of these people consider themselves to be Hungarian despite their parentage. However, there is also a sizable minority in Slovakia who are Hungarian by culture and parentage. The Hungarian government's reply to the Clementis letter rejected re-Slovakization and forcible transfer and requested the Czechoslovak government to grant the Hungarians full minority rights. The Hungarian government also suggested that Czechoslovakia resolve its difficulties by ceding to Hungary some 8,000 square kilometers of territory inhabited predominantly by Hungarians. Clementis, as well as the British and American representatives, opposed this proposal, and no progress was made on the issue before the Paris Peace Conference.

In late December 1945 or early January 1946, representatives of the Hungarian and Slovak Communist Parties met in Budapest. Ernö Gerö, Jozsef Révai, and Antal Apro led the Hungarian delegation, while Viliam Široký, Gustáv Husák, and Daniel Okali led the Slovak group. The Hungarians protested to their Slovak comrades against the persecution of the Hungarian minority in Slovakia, pointing out that the atrocities committed against the Hungarians were a violation of Marxist-Leninist theory. Also, they added, in supporting these actions the Slovak Communist Party was acting contrary to its own interests. The Hungarians were one of the most democratic elements in Slovakia, and many Hungarians belonged to the prewar leftist movements. Realizing the Slovak position that all Hungarians should leave Czechoslovakia, Révai raised the question of the cession to Hungary of territories inhabited by an overwhelming majority of Hungarians, or the establishment of a Hungarian autonomous region within the Czechoslovak republic. Široký and the Slovak delegation were adamantly opposed to both propositions, and the delegations separated on somewhat less than amicable terms.

About the end of February 1946 György Heltai, the communist political director of the Ministry of Foreign Affairs, went to Bratislava and Prague in an attempt to see what could be done about the treatment of the Hungarian minority. Jan Masaryk, the Czechoslovak Foreign Minister, told Heltai that he deplored the policies being carried out against the Hungarian minority, but added that he was powerless to alter the policy because of Beneš's changed attitude toward the national minorities as a result of the bitter experience of 1938. He also reminded Heltai of the new platform of the Slovak Communist Party, which favored expulsion of the Hungarians. Široký, who at the time was Deputy Prime Minister, was even more antagonistic to the Hungarian minority than he had been the previous December. On the question of the Hungarian minority, Široký told Heltai, *in perfect Hungarian,* that "Gerö and Révai tried to convince us with dogmatic, theoretical arguments; we turned to the living practice—Stalin—and he said we were right. What more do you want?"

Some Yugoslav party leaders, apparently including Tito, attempted to intercede with the Czechoslovak communists on the treatment of the Hungarian minority in Slovakia at several interparty meetings. There was no Yugoslav intervention at an official or government level, although an agreement between Yugoslavia and Hungary was signed (but never put into operation) on the voluntary exchange of populations. The agreement was intended to show the Czechoslovak communists and the Prague government that it was possible to conclude reasonable treaties with Hungary.[14]

The fact that Stalin had considered the question of the Hungarians in Slovakia and given the Czech and Slovak communists approval to transfer the population indicates something of his calculations on the use of national minority issues to further communist aims. The elimination of the Hungarian minority was a popular national issue with the Slovaks. By directing the Slovak Communist Party to support the expulsion of the Hungarians, Stalin hoped to gain Slovak national support for the Communist Party. At the time, the Czech and Slovak parties were seeking to gain power through parliamentary means. The communists had received the largest number of votes of any single Czechoslovak political party in the relatively free elections following the war. Communist support for cession to Hungary of Hungarian minority territory or for the creation of a Hungarian autonomous region would have seriously undermined communist support in Slovakia, and perhaps also in the Czech areas. There was little to be gained for the communist cause in Hungary by appealing to Hungarian sentiment. The Hungarian Communist Party had run a poor third in the first postwar elections—an indication of Hungarian national antagonism to Russia and to communism. In addition, Stalin's role in returning all of Transylvania to Rumania had so antagonized the Hungarians that concessions to the Hungarian minority in Slovakia would not, by themselves, be adequate to improve the Hungarian communists' position. Also, the Soviet Union dominated the Hungarian Allied Control Commission, and there were large numbers of Soviet troops stationed in the country; hence, there was little need to appeal to popular support to further the cause of the Hungarian communists.

When a Hungarian government delegation visited Stalin in Moscow in April 1946, they raised the question of the Hungarian minority in Slovakia. The Soviet leader told them, "I believe in an exchange of population." But he also added, "You are just in desiring equal citizenship rights for the Hungarian population on Czechoslovakian territory, and I state herewith that the Soviet Union will support such undertakings."[15] If Stalin gave instructions to support the rights of the Magyar minority in Slovakia, this was not apparent from the actions of the Soviet delegation at the Paris Peace Conference.

By the time of the Paris conference, no progress had been made by Czechoslovakia and Hungary toward solving the problem. Therefore, the Czechoslovak delegation proposed an amendment to the Hungarian Peace Treaty which would authorize Czechoslovakia to transfer no more than 200,000 inhabitants of Magyar ethnic origin from Czechoslovak territory to Hungary. The proposed amendment would also have required Hungary to accept these ethnic Hungarians and to recognize them as nationals.[16] The Czechoslovak position was presented to the Territorial and Political Commission for Hungary by Vladimír Clementis, the Slovak communist who had vigorously defended Slovak national interests.[17] The Soviet Union fully supported the Czechoslovak government position, giving the Czech and Slovak communists the opportunity to wave the banner of nationalism. They could further communist popularity by contrasting the opposition of Britain and the United States with the unequivocal support of the Soviet Union and its satellites. Though Hungary did not advance claims to Slovak territory, several times during the peace conference the Hungarian delegation expressed a willingness to accept Hungarians in Slovakia if the territory on which they lived were ceded to Hungary.[18] The conference rejected the original Czechoslovak amendment requiring Hungary to accept expelled Magyars, but adopted an article requiring Hungarian-Czechoslovak bilateral negotiations on the question.[19] The Hungarian peace treaty, however, added insult to injury by approving a Czechoslovak-proposed amendment that Hungary cede land across the Danube from Bratislava to permit expansion of that city's port facilities.[20]

Federation—a favorite communist scheme to solve national questions—was a primary issue in the postwar relations between communist regimes of southeastern Europe. A federation of Balkan communist states seemed particularly promising, with the communist governments in both Belgrade and Sofia supporting the idea. As early as the 1870's socialists in the Balkans had been suggesting federal schemes for the area. Socialist unity on federation, however, was shattered at the outbreak of the First World War, when Serbian and Bulgarian socialists each supported their own government's claim to Macedonia. Following the end of the war and the Russian Revolution, most of the Balkan socialist parties reorganized and emerged as communist parties, once again advocating Balkan federation. This time the Soviet Union officially favored the scheme. The Fifth Comintern Congress in Moscow approved "the slogan launched by the communist parties of the Balkan countries advocating a Balkan Federation of equal and independent Workers' and Peasants' Republics."[21] A Balkan Communist Federation, consisting of a secretariat and other organs, was organized to include the parties of the Balkans, but it, like the socialists, split up over Macedonia.[22]

At the end of the Second World War, the communists in Yugoslavia were firmly in control, the communist-dominated Fatherland Front governed Bulgaria, the Albanian Communist Party, under Yugoslav tutelage, was tightening its hold, and in Greece the communists, though not in control of the government, had begun guerrilla operations against Athens. The Western powers were anxious to demobilize and were involved elsewhere. A more propitious time could hardly have existed for the creation of a Balkan federation. In the past such schemes had aimed at the creation of a larger unit to strengthen the Balkans against great-power influence and to end nationality strife. Now, with the Soviet Union acting the part of protector of the communist regimes in the area, the federation became more important as a means of fostering economic development and solving the national questions between the friendly governments of the area. According to the communists, the question of Macedonia would be solved in the context of a Balkan union by making it an integral federal unit. Also, the Albanian minority in Yugoslavia's Kosovo region could have closer relations with Albania in a federal context. The later inclusion of Rumania and Hungary would bring about some solution to the problems of Hungarians in the Vojvodina and Transylvania. Although these grandiose plans appeared to be theoretically reasonable, the communist article of faith that creation of a federation eliminates national conflict is erroneous. Boundaries must also be drawn between federal units, and the contested territory can belong to only one unit. The creation of a federation would hardly solve the problems of national minorities; it would merely transform an international question between independent states into an internal question involving separate federal units. The current situation in Yugoslavia is eloquent evidence of this.

The question of Macedonia led to differences between the Yugoslav and Bulgarian communist parties both before and after the Nazi defeat of Yugoslavia in 1941. The Bulgarian party used the Bulgarian occupation of Macedonia during World War II to extend its jurisdiction over all of Macedonia, and Moscow was finally called in to settle the dispute between the Bulgarian and Yugoslav parties regarding jurisdiction over the area. It was given to Yugoslavia, probably because Stalin took an essentially conservative view of territorial changes. The usual explanation, that Yugoslavia received the area because of the Yugoslav partisans' greater war efforts, is not true. The decision was made by Moscow in mid-1941, before the partisans had begun to offer effective resistance. In November 1943 the Yugoslav communists recognized Macedonia as a separate republic within the Yugoslav federation, and the inhabitants of Macedonia were declared to be a separate nationality —the "Macedonians." When the communist-led Fatherland Front seized power in Bulgaria in September 1944, Macedonia immediately became a central issue in relations between the communist governments in Sofia and Belgrade.[23]

The reason both Bulgaria and Yugoslavia became advocates of Balkan federation after the communist seizure of power, however, was not primarily because they wished to solve the national question in the Balkans. The Yugoslav communists had recognized the existence of a Macedonian nationality during World War II, and after coming to power established a Macedonian Republic as one of the six federal units of the new Yugoslavia. One of Yugoslavia's purposes in advocating Balkan federation was to add to the Macedonian Republic those parts of Macedonia held by Bulgaria and Greece. If a Macedonian nationality in fact existed, the Slavs of Bulgarian and Greek Macedonia belonged to it; thus Macedonian unification under a Balkan federation would strengthen Yugoslav communist claims that there was such a thing as a separate Macedonian nationality. The Yugoslav communists were interested in expanding their hegemony, and the Balkan federation which they envisioned would, in effect, have added Bulgaria, Albania, and parts of Greek Macedonia to the Yugoslav federation.

The Bulgarian communists, on the other hand, saw Balkan

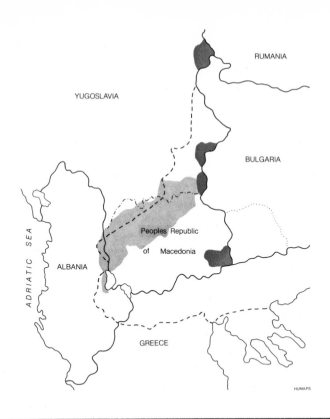

Macedonia: Territorial Changes

- - - Bulgarian boundary established by the Treaty of San Stefano (1878)

Zone to be arbitrated by the Russian Tsar under terms of the secret Bulgarian-Serbian treaty (1912)

Territory ceded by Bulgaria to Yugoslavia by the Treaty of Neuilly (1919)

- - - Boundary of the Yugoslav People's Republic of Macedonia (1945–   )

.... Blagoevgrad district (Pirin Macedonia)—Bulgaria

International boundaries (since 1920)

federation as a way of regaining Macedonia. Bulgaria, as one of the defeated Axis powers, would surely be denied those parts of Yugoslavia and Greek Macedonia which she had acquired through German generosity during the war. That the Bulgarian communists were interested in having Macedonia under their control was demonstrated by the conflict between the Bulgarian and Yugoslav parties for jurisdiction over the area throughout most of World War II. Through the creation of a Balkan federation, the Bulgarian communists expected to be able to establish a special relationship with the non-Bulgarian parts of Macedonia because of the traditional historic and ethnic links between Bulgaria and Macedonia. Thus, both Yugoslav and Bulgarian communists sought to further their own interests in Macedonia through Balkan federation. The federation was destined to fail from the beginning.

The vigorous fight of the Yugoslav partisans against the Germans won them support of Moscow and increased their prestige among the peoples of Eastern Europe. The Bulgarian communists, who had supported Bulgarian national aims and come into conflict with the Yugoslav party over Macedonia during the war, had lost their former pre-eminence among Balkan communists. The Yugoslavs, who intended to dominate any Balkan federation, took the initiative with regard to creation of the federation in September 1944, almost as soon as the communist-led Fatherland Front had seized power in Bulgaria. Two leaders who had played important roles in securing Yugoslav communist domination of Macedonia, Svetozar Vukmanović-Tempo and Lazar Koliševski, were sent to Sofia to exchange opinions on the Macedonian question. According to Yugoslav accounts, the Bulgarians agreed to give Pirin (Bulgarian) Macedonia administrative and cultural autonomy, while the Yugoslavs agreed that the unification of Pirin with Yugoslav Macedonia would not be made into an "action slogan" and would be postponed until "conditions were right for it." It was also made clear, according to Tempo and Koliševski, that the question of the unification of Macedonia should not be linked to that of the formation of "a close union between Yugoslavia and Bulgaria." The Bulgarians also agreed to a number of steps which, according to Koliševski, were to prepare Pirin Macedonia "for union with the Macedonian democratic federal state of Tito's new Yugoslavia."[24]

The Bulgarian party was far from united in granting these concessions to the Yugoslav communists. At a regional party conference in the Pirin district held in Gorna Dzumaya, the Bulgarian Macedonian communist Poptomov was reputed to have given "a serious warning concerning [Yugoslavia's] intention to incorporate Pirin Macedonia." Ljubčo Arsov, of the Yugoslav Macedonian party Central Committee, who was present, protested.[25] Poptomov also asked, "Why should the Gorna Dzumaya region [Pirin Macedonia] unite with Macedonia in Yugoslavia? Why not vice versa, and have the Tsaribrod and Bosiligrad districts [taken from Bulgaria by the Treaty of Neuilly after World War I] returned to us?" He claimed that the question of Pirin Macedonia's detachment from Bulgaria was not an "actual" one among the people there, that the Bulgarian people were not yet ready for such a move, and that the Macedonian question was closely tied to the projected Yugoslav-Bulgarian union. A further insult to the Yugoslavs was Poptomov's contention that, while Bulgaria was safely under Soviet influence, no one knew who would predominate in Yugoslavia; might it not be the British?[26]

The Yugoslavs became further concerned because the Bulgarian press and radio were giving "undue" prominence to the liberating activities of Bulgarian units in Macedonia and because the Bulgarians were treating Macedonia as an "independent" state, separate from Yugoslavia.[27] In October 1944 Tempo wrote a sharply worded letter to Kiro Miljovski, the Yugoslav Macedonian representative to the Bulgarian communists, protesting that Bulgarian propaganda claimed: "Our National Army is fighting shoulder to shoulder with the glorious Red Army, the National-liberation Army of the legendary Marshal Tito, and the Macedonian partisans and brigades." Tempo insisted that the Bulgarians be told that "the Macedonian partisans and brigades are part of the National-liberation Army of the legendary Marshal Tito" and that "our units are called the *Macedonian units of the National-liberation Army of Yugoslavia*.'"[28] The Bulgarian communists were aware of the prestige enjoyed by Marshal Tito among the Western powers and with Stalin for his partisan exploits, and thus had little hope for the unification of Macedonia under Bulgaria. However, they opposed its becoming an integral part of Yugoslavia and advocated an autonomous Macedonia which could later be united with Bulgaria.

Following Tempo's criticism, the Bulgarians sent Tito a mollifying letter, signed by Traicho Kostov, a secretary of the Bulgarian Central Committee. "Our people are conscious of their great guilt with regard to the Yugoslavs and especially the Serbian and Macedonian peoples," apologized Kostov, and went on:

Especially in connection with the creation of a free Macedonian state in the framework of a new, federative Yugoslavia, which represents the first decisive step toward realization of the Macedonian ideal of a free, united Macedonia, we give you our assurance that our party and our people acclaim the new Macedonian state most warmly. We shall work to popularize it. . . . Especially among the inhabitants of the Bulgarian part of Macedonia, we shall help to arouse a Macedonian national consciousness among the population, utilizing the heroic past and present of the Macedonian people . . . publishing Macedonian newspapers, etc. . . . We shall agitate broadly . . . for the most painless realization of the Macedonian ideal of a free, united Macedonia within the framework of the new Yugoslavia.[29]

Although the Bulgarian party officially acknowledged the existence of a Macedonian nationality and declared its support for a Macedonia united under Yugoslavia, there was still strong opposition to this policy, even from leading Bulgarian party members. Despite their approval of the Yugoslav plans to unify Macedonia, the Bulgarians retained firm control over party and government organs in Pirin Macedonia.

In December 1944 Edward Kardelj, one of Tito's close associates, went to Sofia to win Bulgarian approval for Yugoslavia's plan for a Bulgarian-Yugoslav federation. Although Tempo and Koliševski had stated in their earlier letter from Sofia that the question of Macedonian unification was not to be tied to Bulgarian-Yugoslav union, once talks on federation got under way the question of Macedonia became enmeshed in the question of federation. In discussions with Kardelj, the Bulgarians favored a defense pact between the two countries. After the pact had been concluded, a joint commission would draw up plans for union. Calling this plan inadequate, Kardelj proposed immediate movement toward federation, including a meeting between representatives of all the Yugoslav republics and the Bulgarians. Disagreement over the makeup of a commission to draw up plans for federation was the first evidence of the conflicting Bulgarian-Yugoslav views which later hampered agreement on federation. The Yugoslav proposal called for Bulgaria to become the seventh republic in the Yugoslav federation. The Bulgarians favored a federation in which the two countries would be equal. A Bulgarian proposal which was sent to the Yugoslavs in January 1945 called for a South Slav federation with common ministries and a common national assembly. The transition to full federation would be carried out by a temporary executive body composed of equal numbers of Yugoslavs and Bulgarians. This the Yugoslavs rejected, advocating instead that a commission composed of representatives of the seven federal units be formed to draw up a constitution. Yugoslav accounts maintain that Stalin favored the Yugoslav proposal to include Bulgaria as one of several republics.[30]

After the failure of Kardelj's mission to Sofia, both parties sought to revitalize the stalemated negotiations by appealing to the Kremlin. High-level delegations from both Yugoslavia and Bulgaria traveled to Moscow to present their case to the Soviet leaders. However, Britain had expressed opposition to any federal arrangement, and Stalin declared that the time was not propitious for any change in the status quo. The Yugoslav party temporarily relaxed its efforts to annex Pirin Macedonia and concentrated on consolidating its own position in Vardar Macedonia. Although the federation issue between Bulgaria and Yugoslavia remained dormant for almost two years, the Yugoslav and Albanian governments took steps to bring their two states closer together. In November 1946 a treaty was signed providing for a common currency, common economic planning—including Yugoslav assistance in the reconstruction of Albania—and the establishment of a customs union.[31] Currency reforms were carried out in Albania in preparation for the introduction of a common currency. In addition, joint Yugoslav-Albanian enterprises were established, modeled after Soviet undertakings with the satellite states.

According to a Yugoslav account, Georgi Dimitrov, the head of the Bulgarian party, continued to favor Macedonian unification though the federation question was temporarily shelved. He was quoted as having told the National Assembly in Sofia on December 6, 1945, that the solution to the Macedonian question lay "not in the division of Macedonia, not in a struggle over it, but in respect for the will of its people, the majority of whom have obtained freedom and equality in the framework of the FPRY."[32] Delegates from the Pirin Region who attended the January 1946 plenum of the Bulgarian Central Committee claimed that 70 percent of the people there had declared themselves to be Macedonian.[33] Party secretary Vulko Chervenkov, however, replied that talk about the unification of Macedonia would damage the Fatherland Front, the noncommunist elements of which were decisively against any move that would result in loss of Bulgarian territory. They were joined by a number of party leaders from Pirin Macedonia itself, notably Vladimir Poptomov and Dimitar Ganev. The latter expressed his doubts about Yugoslavia's future on the basis of the danger represented by the Yugoslav communists' "adventuristic policies on the Trieste question."[34]

In a speech on Ilinden (August 2), 1946, commemorating the Macedonian uprising against the Turks, Koliševski voiced Yugoslavia's continued interest in Bulgarian Macedonia. He told the First Congress of the People's Front of Macedonia that the Bulgarian government should "make it possible for our [Macedonian] people in Pirin Macedonia to have the same opportunities for free national development which the Bulgarian national minority enjoys in Yugoslavia." He also re-emphasized the Yugoslav claim that "to raise the question of the union of Macedonia outside the borders of Yugoslavia is simply provocation, and runs counter to the independence and the interests of the Macedonian people."[35] The Bulgarians were quick to respond to Koliševski's statement. Four days later, at its tenth plenum, the Bulgarian party resolved that efforts to unite the remaining parts of Macedonia should include cultural rapprochement between the Pirin Region and the MPR, but that unification must be achieved on the basis of a treaty of alliance which would define exactly the borders of Bulgarian Macedonia. The Bulgarian party insisted that the population of the Pirin Region should have the right to opt for Bulgarian citizenship, and that there be no customs barriers between Macedonia and Bulgaria.[36] The resolution was not released to the public.

The Bulgarian party was in an awkward position. The Yugoslavs were again insisting upon Macedonian unification. Negotiations on the peace treaties were under way in Paris, and Bulgaria was anxious to have Yugoslav support for its position there. Hence,

65

there was a desire to avoid any action which might antagonize Belgrade. At the same time, the Bulgarian leaders were facing strong opposition, both inside and outside the party, to surrendering Macedonian territory to Yugoslavia. The Bulgarian Central Committee, in an attempt to have its cake and eat it, passed the Yugoslav-desired resolution agreeing to eventual Macedonian unification, but did not make the resolution public. In the Pirin district, the party followed the same policy. Government and party organs were kept firmly under Bulgarian control, but at the same time the level of Macedonian national consciousness was being raised by Yugoslav Macedonians working in the Pirin district with Bulgarian approval.

Macedonian unification and federation were major issues at the Bled Conference between Tito and Dimitrov in July 1947. The communiqué on the meeting indicated that the two governments had signed a series of agreements which provided for close economic cooperation, the eventual establishment of a customs union, mutual assistance, and action against "frequent frontier provocations of the Greek Monarchist-Fascists."[37] The statement did not mention federation, and Dimitrov unequivocally declared that "a federation of South Slavs or a Balkan federation . . . was not a subject of discussion at the conference."[38] However, after the Cominform expelled the Yugoslav party, a resolution adopted by the Bulgarian Central Committee, and Dimitrov himself, clearly stated that the two governments "had agreed on a number of measures regarding the forthcoming establishment of federation."[39]

At the Bled talks, Dimitrov insisted that the unification of Macedonia could only be achieved on the basis of federation. He indicated that it had been agreed that the Pirin district and the Yugoslav People's Republic of Macedonia should eventually be united and also that Bulgaria should be compensated for the loss of the Pirin district by receiving areas which Bulgaria had ceded to Yugoslavia after World War I.[40] It has also been suggested that the Bled agreements involved the Greek communists, and that Yugoslavia was to receive Aegean (Greek) Macedonia in addition to Bulgarian Macedonia. Bulgaria was to be compensated for the loss of the Pirin district by being given western Thrace. In return, the Greek communists would receive extensive Bulgarian and Yugoslav support in the guerrilla struggle against the royal Greek government.[41] Although there is no documentary evidence to support this point of view, it is consistent with Yugoslav ambitions at that time. However, in public statements prior to the agreement the Greek party strongly opposed any such transfer of territory.[42] Despite numerous post–1948 revelations about other aspects of Bulgarian-Yugoslav relations during this period, neither Bulgaria nor Yugoslavia has disclosed detailed information about an agreement involving Greek Macedonia.

Although no agreement was reached at Bled on the immediate transfer of Pirin Macedonia, Tito did receive Bulgarian approval for Yugoslav Macedonian cultural workers to enter the Pirin Region. The Yugoslavs published a newspaper, *Pirinski Vjesnik,* for the Bulgarian Macedonians; the Bulgarian assembly passed a law calling for the teaching of the Macedonian language and Macedonian history in the Pirin Region schools; and many teachers from Yugoslav Macedonia were allowed to enter Bulgaria.[43] In November 1947 Tito visited Bulgaria and signed a treaty pledging consultation, mutual military support, economic cooperation, and the creation of a customs union.[44] Despite this apparent agreement at top government and party levels, however, problems developed between the Yugoslav cultural workers and local Pirin party officials and the population.[45] The Bulgarian party insisted upon federation before relinquishing its hold in Pirin Macedonia. No Bulgarian government could afford to give up Bulgarian Macedonia to a foreign country; hence, unification could take place only within a federation to which Bulgaria belonged.

At this point the Soviet Union announced its opposition to the establishment of any South Slav federation. In response to a statement made by Dimitrov in Bucharest suggesting customs unions for all the countries of the Soviet bloc, *Pravda* editorially denounced federation: "What these countries need is not a problematical and artificial federation, confederation, or customs union, but the consolidation and defense of their independence and sovereignty."[46] As differences between the Yugoslav and Soviet party leaders became more pronounced, Stalin reversed his opinion and attempted to force a Bulgarian-Yugoslav federation. In February 1948 Bulgarian and Yugoslav representatives were summoned to Moscow, where Stalin told them that "Bulgaria and Yugoslavia should create a federation tomorrow." When the Yugoslavs explained why they favored gradual federation, Stalin replied, "No, the federation should be proclaimed immediately, the sooner the better. The matter is ripe. First Bulgaria and Yugoslavia should unite, and then they should annex Albania."[47] Stalin's insistence on immediate union was simply an attempt to control the Yugoslav party. Since Moscow had the Bulgarian apparatus firmly in hand, Stalin hoped thereby to infiltrate and dominate the Yugoslav organization. Tito, aware of Stalin's intentions, told the Yugoslav party's Central Committee in March 1948 that federation must be carried out gradually, because if there were an immediate merger, "there would be a Trojan horse within our party." He gave as reasons for waiting for federation Bulgaria's weak economic position and the reparation payments she owed to Greece.[48]

In this confused situation the First Congress of the Bulgarian Fatherland Front (February 1948) avoided the Macedonian question entirely, but a local conference of Pirin Macedonian party members held at the end of April in Blagoevgrad took a hostile stand toward Yugoslavia's Macedonian initiatives. The Yugoslav break with Moscow came when the Yugoslav party was expelled from the Cominform on June 28, 1948, and this put a definite end to any prospect of a Balkan federation.[49]

Following the Cominform resolution a vicious anti-Yugoslav campaign was launched by the Soviet Union and the faithful communist regimes of Eastern Europe, in which the national question was used to attack the Yugoslavs. Yugoslav writers have denounced the Soviets and East Europeans for attempting to "exploit Yugoslavia's national minorities to create a special front intended to disrupt Yugoslavia from within."[50] Tito accused the Soviet Union of making "use of every vulnerable point in Yugoslavia, of every contradiction" in its postbreak propaganda: "In its broadcasts in Macedonian, Moscow Radio played upon the feelings of the Macedonians by alleging that Belgrade was oppressing them; that is, it played the old card in Yugoslavia, disunity among the people. On the other hand, in its broadcasts in Serbian it said the Serbs were being oppressed in Yugoslavia."[51]

There were also attempts to appeal to the anti-Serbian feelings of the non-Serbian population. A Hungarian communist, Andor Berei, castigated Tito for reviving great-Serbian chauvinism and inflaming the antagonisms among Serbs, Croats, and Slovenes. He accused the Yugoslav government of placing Serbs rather than members of the local nationalities in government positions in Bosnia-Hercegovina and Slovenia, but his strongest denunciations were reserved for ill-treatment of the Macedonians, Albanians, and Hungarians. He claimed the Serbian chauvinists were denying Albanians their rights and imposing forced labor and migration upon them.[52] Vasile Luca, one of the Rumanian party leaders, in a similar article claimed that the Yugoslav secret police were closing minority schools, confiscating property, and denying the right to travel to Rumanian and other minorities.[53] Hungary's Mátyás Rákosi accused Belgrade of Serbian chauvinism and denounced Serbian oppression of minorities in Montenegro, Bosnia, and the Vojvodina.[54] In addition to propaganda aimed at Yugoslavia, some of the faithful satellites pursued a policy of persecuting the Yugoslav minorities living within their borders, and the Yugoslav government delivered a number of denunciatory notes to the various communist states protesting the mistreatment of minorities.[55]

The most vicious nationality attack on Yugoslavia came from the Albanians.* Shortly after the expulsion of Yugoslavia from the Cominform in 1948, a resolution issued by the Albanian Communist Party's Central Committee called upon the Albanians of Kosmet and Macedonia to "fight against all pan-Serbs." The Cominform states apparently expected a split to develop within the Yugoslav leadership, and the Albanians exhorted their brethren in Kosmet to side with the pro-Cominform faction: "The only correct path for the Albanians of Kosmet and Macedonia to follow is that leading to firm unity with the brotherly people of Yugoslavia and with the healthy elements of the Communist Party of Yugoslavia."[56]

By the following year it was apparent that the Yugoslav leadership was not going to split. Addressing "the population of Kosovo," Enver Hoxha, the Albanian leader, said their salvation "will be ensured by their untiring struggle against Tito's fascist band and his spies in Kosovo."[57] The Albanian minority was also encouraged to struggle against Tito by Tuk Jakova, Vice-Premier of Albania

* The intense anti-Yugoslav feeling in Albania is more understandable when it is realized that almost one-third of all ethnic Albanians live within Yugoslavia. Also the Yugoslav Communist Party had dominated the Albanian party from the beginning and forced the Albanian communists to renounce their national claims against Yugoslavia. The complete annexation of Albania by Yugoslavia was narrowly averted by Yugoslavia's expulsion from the Cominform.

and a Central Committee secretary. Jakova claimed that the people of Kosovo "want to be free to realize their centuries-old aspiration—union with Albania." He added, "Our party has not neglected this question," and encouraged the Albanians in Yugoslavia to "rise up together with the Yugoslav peoples . . . to fight Tito's clique, to overthrow Tito, to win freedom, and then the question of Kosovo will surely be solved justly, and its future, in accordance with the principle of self-determination, will be incorporation into Albania."[58] This tactic also failed to bring about a successful revolt on the part of the Yugoslav Albanians.

The Albanian propagandists also took the line of publicizing the atrocities of the Tito regime in the hope of inciting the Albanians to revolt against the Serbs. In the new attack the Albanians claimed to have documents showing "that the Tito-Ranković clique is exterminating the 800,000 Albanian people in Yugoslavia . . . that the Titoists machine-gunned thousands of Albanians in Kosovo and Macedonia; that thousands of Albanians were killed by means of poison gas and by spreading typhus; that the fascist degenerates bury people alive and subject others to brutal torture before killing them."[59] This Albanian propaganda, however, appears to have been unsuccessful in producing any serious disorders among the Albanian minority in Yugoslavia. There was a serious uprising among the Albanians in 1944 and 1945, but by 1948 the Yugoslav secret police had a firm grip on the Albanian areas.

The Macedonians were the other major national minority to which the Cominform states made extensive appeals. After the Cominform resolution, the Bulgarian party directed a vicious attack against the Yugoslavs and took immediate steps to eliminate Yugoslav influence in Pirin Macedonia. Macedonian cultural workers from Yugoslavia were expelled from the Pirin region; "compulsory" instruction in the Macedonian language and "compulsory" subscriptions to Macedonian newspapers were stopped. Though strongly opposing Yugoslav annexation of its portion of Macedonia, the Bulgarian party continued to recognize the Macedonian nationality and advocate the unification of Macedonia. Dimitrov told the Fifth Bulgarian Party Congress in December 1948: "Our party has always advocated, and continues to advocate, that Macedonia belongs to the Macedonians." But he added that national unity was possible "only within the framework of a federation of South Slavs."[60] Both countries set up organizations of Macedonian refugees from the other country and from Greek Macedonia. There were frequent trials of alleged conspirators. Bitter polemical editorials were common to both sides. Much of the testimony at Traicho Kostov's trial in December 1949 related to his and the other defendants' alleged conspiracy to detach Pirin Macedonia from Bulgaria.[61] After the Cominform break, the Bulgarians talked vaguely and infrequently about a united Macedonia in a Balkan federation, but Sofia's propaganda concentrated on one of the sore spots of the Macedonian question, charging that the newly created Macedonian language and other Yugoslav attempts to create a Macedonian national consciousness were directed solely toward the Serbianization of the Macedonian population.[62]

Generally, the Cominform states' attacks on the Yugoslavs which used nationality appeals were limited to the national minorities and came from the ethnic homeland—Albanian appeals to the Albanians of Kosovo-Metohija and Macedonia, Hungarian appeals to the Magyars of the Vojvodina, and Bulgarian appeals to the Macedonian population. These attempts appear to have had little effect in inciting the minorities against the Yugoslav state.[63] There was no serious attempt to disrupt the balance between Serbs and Croats and the other Yugoslav peoples. The Croats, who had suffered under Serbian domination between the wars and were an independent German satellite during the Second World War, would have been the ideal nationality to incite against the Serbs in order to weaken Yugoslavia internally. However, the Croatians were Catholic and strongly anticommunist, and an upsurge in Croatian nationalism would hardly have helped Stalin. Perhaps the Cominform did not undertake a more vigorous campaign to incite nationality unrest because Stalin felt that Tito would be quickly overthrown and that, once the nationality cauldron began to boil, a pro-Soviet regime might be scalded. He may also have feared that inciting the national issue would rally Serbian national support to the Yugoslav leaders. Once it became clear to Stalin that the Yugoslav regime could not be easily toppled, he probably feared the effect a campaign based on inciting Yugoslavia's national minorities might have on the Hungarian and Rumanian irredentists. Since the communist propagandists were now proclaiming that the national question in Eastern Europe had been "solved," Stalin may have feared to put his solution to the test.

By 1948 the communist parties throughout Eastern Europe had

assumed complete control of their governments. But the local communist leaders, except in Yugoslavia, had such a limited base of local support that they were heavily reliant upon the support of the Red Army. With the Soviet military as their chief source of power, they had no choice but to follow Moscow's will on any question. Supporting the national claims and aspirations of the local population would not help them to gain or retain power. When Moscow made a decision favoring their national interests, the local communists were as nationalist as bourgeois politicians, in some cases even more so. But when the word from Moscow went against their national interests the local communists obediently carried out Soviet wishes. For example, when the Hungarian communists thought Moscow did not want changes in the Rumanian-Hungarian border in Transylvania, they resolutely opposed the claims advanced by the noncommunists in the Hungarian government. However, when Ferenc Nagy, accompanied by Rákosi and others, visited Moscow in April 1946, Stalin seemingly gave approval for Hungary to propose revisions of her border with Rumania. Communist spokesmen were quick to declare that the Communist Party had always been a true defender of Hungarian national interests and had consistently opposed the Trianon frontiers.[64] Soviet insistence upon leaving the border unchanged at the foreign ministers meeting in May 1946 forced the Hungarian party to drop this line.

With noncommunist ministers in the governments, it was often unavoidable that national questions would be raised and that they would become public. However, once the communist parties were firmly in control, these national issues were decided by the party and by Moscow. Discussion in public was completely eliminated. To raise a question publicly or use public channels of discussion was detrimental to one's case and actually dangerous for any individual who dared do so. Hence, there was the appearance of friendly relations between the states in the area because none of them brought up publicly the national issues that divided them. Absolute Soviet dominance ended overt conflict on the national question among regimes faithful to Moscow until after Stalin's death.

As communist influence came to dominate the East European states, laws and constitutions were established granting national equality. In Rumania, national equality was an essential condition for the return of northern Transylvania. In February 1945 a law was passed guaranteeing minority schools, use of the mother tongue, and national equality. The Rumanian constitutions of 1948 and 1952 guaranteed equal rights to the minorities as well as use of their mother tongue, education in the minority language, and use of that language in local administration.[65] Less than two months after the communist coup in Czechoslovakia in 1948, a government ordinance permitted persons of German and Magyar nationality resident in Czechoslovakia to become citizens through a naturalization process. However, all those over fourteen years of age were required to demonstrate a knowledge of the Czech or Slovak language. The Czechoslovak constitution of 1948 also guaranteed minority rights.[66] Yugoslavia guaranteed equal rights to all nationalities, and made it a criminal offense to incite national hatred or deny someone's rights because of nationality. This law was strictly enforced by the Yugoslav authorities.[67] However, the guarantees of equality were aimed principally at the "Yugoslav nationalities" and the national minorities—Albanians, Hungarians, Germans, Bulgarians—were treated worse than other Yugoslavs. In Yugoslavia— as well as Hungary and Czechoslovakia—members of the German minority were not allowed to become citizens or to have equal civil rights until 1948. It was not difficult for a communist government to grant paper rights to its national minorities. With a judiciary dependent upon party instructions in rendering its verdicts, the communist government could still exercise discrimination if it wished to do so. In many cases the laws against inciting nationality unrest were harshly enforced against members of the minority populations rather than against the predominant nationality of the state. Under the Stalinist regimes, even if the minorities were given the same treatment as the *Staatsvolk,* their rights were still very limited. In most communist countries, however, the situation of the minority was no worse than it had been under the ultranationalist regimes before and during World War II, and in many cases the minorities were better off under communism.

As communist power was consolidated throughout Eastern Europe, the states were bound to the Soviet Union and to each other by a series of bilateral treaties of friendship, cooperation, and mutual assistance.[68] States whose relations had been strained throughout the entire interwar period because of minority questions and conflicting territorial claims now pledged themselves to strengthen friendly relations and to increase cooperation. If the minority problems were mentioned in the speeches which accompanied the signing of the treaties, they were seen as a bridge uniting nations, not as a source of conflict dividing them. Though unfriendly relations resulting from unresolved nationality problems delayed the signing of some of these treaties (for example, the Hungarian-Czechoslovak treaty was not signed until April 16, 1949, almost a full year after all the others), by 1949 the treaty network was complete. Where previously national problems had caused bitter relations, now silence and treaties of friendship masked the conflicts.

With the communist parties in power, the official ideology was advanced that the national question had been solved in Eastern Europe. While "bourgeois nationalism"—according to the Soviets —was used by imperialist and reactionary regimes "as a weapon to achieve aggrandizement in the sphere of international relations," the communist regimes "have put an end to the [national] strife in central and southeastern Europe, and [this has] led to the establishment of enduring peace and friendship."[69] Communist ideology postulates that national problems are the result of the bourgeois system, and therefore, "after the capitalists' and landlords' regime has been overthrown and exploitation eliminated [that is, after the establishment of a communist regime] it becomes possible to solve the national question completely."[70] Solving the national question internally by establishing a communist government has as its corollary in the international sphere "the uniting of the proletariat, of all working people regardless of nationality, in the struggle to build a new life, to forge friendship among peoples in areas cleared of exploitation and exploiters."[71] Social and political problems are the enduring concern of the working people; hence, these issues unite the peoples of communist states, and the former divisive national questions which disrupted relations among the bourgeois states are no longer significant.

The Yugoslavs, since they had departed from the true faith, were condemned to nationality strife. "Tito and his underlings are trying to inculcate among the peoples of Yugoslavia national hatred for the peoples of the neighboring democratic countries and the Soviet Union."[72] As agents of imperialism and lackeys of Wall Street, the Yugoslavs were unable to solve the national question. However, the Yugoslavs themselves came to quite a different conclusion. As early

74

as 1945, Milovan Djilas maintained that the war had heightened national contradictions in Yugoslavia, but the example of the Yugoslav Communist Party and the realization during the war of the community of interest of all peoples had enabled the Yugoslav peoples to resolve the nationality question.[73] Thus, in the gray uniformity of the Stalinist system, all signs of national conflict were eliminated except in the relations between the redeemed Cominform states and the schizmatic Yugoslavs.

In postwar chaos and instability the national question was an issue among communists. The boundary settlements, transfers of population, and the Balkan federation were all involved. However, because local communists required Soviet support in order to seize power, they submerged their national desires and became pliant agents in carrying out Moscow's will. The national question in southeastern Europe was "solved" in that it was no longer publicly discussed. In the communist countries all resources were concentrated on carrying out extensive social and economic changes, and the national question became a secondary issue, though Moscow allowed the loyal parties considerable freedom to attack Belgrade. Among the first issues to be raised against Yugoslavia were the nationality-based claims of her Albanian, Bulgarian, and Hungarian neighbors. While the Soviet Union was firmly in control in Eastern Europe and the local communists were forced to rely on Moscow to retain their right to rule, the national divisions that had inflamed international relations in the past were submerged. But when Soviet control weakened, when the local communist leaders developed an indigenous base of power, national issues began to reappear.

Chapter 4

National Minorities and the Hungarian Revolution

The minority question was one of the first issues to reappear when Moscow's will could no longer be enforced in Eastern Europe. The most dramatic illustration of this was the breakdown of communist authority during the Hungarian Revolution of 1956. The fall of 1956 was critical for all East European communist states. The relaxation of Soviet control which began with the death of Stalin was given impetus by Khrushchev's de-Stalinization speech at the Twentieth Congress of the Communist Party of the Soviet Union in February 1956, and in the fall of that year Eastern Europe was shaken by serious crises. Popular pressure forced Moscow to accept major changes in the Polish government and party leadership. In Hungary the communist government tottered and then collapsed in the wake of a full-scale revolution against communist rule. Though Hungary and Poland were the most dramatic examples, communist authority in all of the East European states was threatened during October and November. In the wave of unrest that swept through the Soviet satellites at that time, the national question was one of the first issues to re-emerge.

The question of the Hungarian minorities in other countries was raised in Hungary, but it was not a primary issue during the uprising of 1956. The major concerns were internal affairs and relations with the Soviet Union, but the national question was another factor that alienated the Hungarian population from the Rákosi regime. At a gathering in Bem Square on October 23, Péter Veres, President of the Hungarian Writers' Union, read a seven-point resolution that had been adopted by the presidium of the Union. The second of these points demanded "an end to national minority policies that disturb the friendship between peoples. We want true and sincere friendship with our allies—the USSR and the people's democracies. This can only be realized on the basis of Leninist principles."[1] The Writers' Union resolution was drawn up before the revolution had really begun, and was, therefore, cautious and phrased in Marxist terms. But the fact that the status of the Magyar minorities outside Hungary was raised by the communist-dominated leadership of the Union indicates Hungarian concern for the minorities, despite official silence with regard to their treatment.

Once the fighting began, more immediate problems pushed the question of the minorities into the background. Nevertheless, during the uprising there were numerous references to the creation of a Danubian federation which would involve those states with Hungarian minorities. The problem of nationality has always been one of the major reasons for federation, even when Kossuth first suggested the idea in the nineteenth century. The attitude of the Hungarian communists toward a Danubian federation was inconsistent. Béla Kun supported the idea as a solution to the nationality problem and as a step to world revolution, but, with the collapse of Soviet Hungary and Moscow's loss of interest in the scheme, federation was quietly abandoned. Hungarian communists gradually adopted anti-Trianon nationalist slogans. With the coming of the Nazi threat the communist line shifted, and national independence began to be emphasized. When territorial changes were made in favor of Hungary, the Comintern instructed the Hungarian communists to advocate self-determination, including separation, for Ukrainians, Rumanians, and Slovaks. During the war the communists in Hungary again became interested in federation, but the Hungarian Muscovite group, reflecting the views of the Soviet leaders, saw anti-Soviet tendencies in these proposals. After the war

Hungarian communists paid lip service to the concept of Danubian cooperation, but at the same time they blocked attempts by the Hungarian government to achieve it. After 1948, when plans for the Bulgarian-Yugoslav federation were dropped at Moscow's insistence, the Hungarian communists openly abandoned the idea of a supranational federation.[2] Imre Nagy, however, despite Soviet disapproval, continued to favor some form of federation and advocated it in his writings.[3] During the revolution Nagy's tenure was so short and events so turbulent that federation did not come to play a role in his government programs. Had the revolution succeeded, or had Nagy remained in power, it would have become an issue.

Though it did not become part of any government program during the revolt, Danubian federation and concern for the Hungarian minorities outside the country were issues frequently raised on a local level. The student parliament of Miskolc, for example, at a meeting on October 26, 1956, demanded that Hungary "should become a member of a Danubian federation as proposed by Kossuth."[4] The Veszprém County revolutionary council felt the government "should pay more attention to the fate and situation of Hungarians living beyond our frontiers, and to our relations with them." In this context, "the Foreign Affairs Committee of the parliament . . . should raise the idea of a Danubian confederation."[5] The revolutionary daily *Magyar Szabadság* urged the Hungarian government "to strive for the establishment of a confederation of the peoples in the Danube basin." "This," said the newspaper, "is the most specific demand of our national foreign policy."[6]

With the Hungarian freedom fighters proclaiming that "all Hungarians are with us," with Hungarians in Rumania and Czechoslovakia crossing the borders to aid the insurgents, with restless Hungarian populations in Slovakia, Transylvania, and the Vojvodina, the communist governments of Czechoslovakia, Rumania, and Yugoslavia became concerned about a revival of Hungarian irredentism. The Hungarians—perhaps remembering that these three countries had allied themselves against Hungarian revisionism in the Little Entente—attempted to quiet the fears of the neighboring states. Radio Miskolc expressed regret in the Hungarian, Rumanian, and Slovak languages that "the Slovak and Rumanian nations attribute an irredentist and revisionist character to our proposal [for a Danube federation]. . . . We do not propagate irredentist slogans, and we do not want a revision of our borders. We wish to live in the most sincere friendship with our neighboring brother nations."[7] Other revolutionary stations broadcast similar statements.

During the Hungarian Revolution, communist authority in Hungary collapsed. An end to censorship of the mass media and the formation of power groups outside communist control permitted free discussion of Hungarian problems. Immediately, the question of the Magyar minorities in the neighboring states was raised, and changes were demanded—hardly an indication that the national question had been "solved" in the eyes of the Hungarians. But the period of free expression was short, chaotic, and preoccupied with the creation of a Hungarian government and with defining Hungary's relationship to the Soviet Union. In Czechoslovakia, Rumania, and Yugoslavia, however, the question of the Hungarian minorities became of prime concern. These minorities were the first to be affected by events in Hungary. There the issue of Hungarian irredentism was more serious and immediate.

In Czechoslovakia, government troops were reinforced in southern Slovakia—the area inhabited by the Hungarian minority. British and French embassy personnel in Prague were advised not to visit Slovakia because "public temper is very high as a result of the incidents in Egypt," and Slovakia was closed to all foreigners. Students demonstrated their sympathy with the Hungarians, and there were reports that Hungarians had been arrested for arousing "strife between different nationalities." Some Hungarians in Slovakia were apprehended by Czechoslovak authorities when they attempted to cross the border into Hungary and join the fighting.[8] Czechoslovak newspapers and radio accounts referred to the revolutionaries in Hungary as "chauvinists" and "bourgeois-nationalists" in the very first reports on the revolution. One writer, for example, declared: "A struggle will have to be waged [in Hungary] against bourgeois-nationalist slogans, including the ancient irredentist call for the creation of a greater Hungary."[9]

The Czechoslovak government also took steps to calm its Magyar citizens. The semiofficial Cultural Association of Hungarian Workers in Czechoslovakia (Csemadok)—with Prague's approval if not at its prodding—issued a call to Hungarians in Slovakia: "In these tragic days it is more necessary than ever that we loyally and firmly

79

support the National Front and its leading force, the Communist Party of Czechoslovakia, in decisively rejecting all attempts by foreign reactionaries to disrupt the unity among the nations of our country, to undermine the friendship between the Slovak and Hungarian peoples."[10] As if to reassure Prague of the loyalty of the Hungarian minority, the statement went on to cite the "enthusiastic effort" the Hungarian minority was making to fulfill its economic quotas. Other statements by Csemadok and resolutions by Hungarian workers were produced to quiet the minority.

The first comment by a high government official on events in Hungary was made in a speech by President Antonín Zápotocký on November 3. In a statement too relevant to be accidental, he expressed the concern of the government for the Hungarian minority: "The fraternal links between Czechs and Slovaks and all other nationalities in our country are constantly growing stronger. Our unity is the firm foundation on which our advance is based, and it cannot be menaced by any hostile incitement."[11] In a speech the following month, Oldřich Černik, then a secretary of the Czechoslovak party Central Committee, went even farther, implying that there had been disturbances but that these had not resulted in serious disruption. The solidarity in the East European bloc, Černik claimed, "has added to the unity and to the determination of our working class and all our working people to nip in the bud any attempt to destroy peace and hinder socialist construction in Czechoslovakia."[12]

Even a year after the events of 1956, a Swiss newsman on a visit to southern Slovakia wrote, "We met hardly anyone who did not spontaneously tell us about those 'terrible days' of the Hungarian uprising."[13] A further reflection of the seriousness of the situation in Slovakia in 1956 came to light twelve years later, when liberalization in Czechoslovakia had removed the restraints on the freedom of expression. As the Hungarian minority became more aggressive in demanding its rights to equality, Slovak polemics invariably brought up assertions of unfaithfulness on the part of Hungarians toward Czechoslovakia in 1956.

The memory of the struggle for the existence of the Slovak nation against the Hungarian majority, which lasted for a thousand years, cannot be erased by the 20-year-old friendship of the Hungarian people's state. This experience cannot be erased, particularly because more recent experience also exists—the experience of twelve years ago [1956]. From the very beginning of the Hungarian events, voices were raised on the Hungarian side demanding that southern Slovakia be annexed by Hungary, and those demands were supported by some Hungarians in this country. This is a fact which common decency cannot permit us to forget or to pass over in silence.[14]

In rebuttal to this and other Slovak articles, Hungarian writers admitted the unrest but claimed that instances of Hungarian irredentism were "isolated" and insisted that "one cannot generalize from them."[15] The fact that the events of 1956 became an issue in the polemics between Slovaks and Hungarians twelve years later leaves little doubt as to the seriousness of the problem in Slovakia at the time.

When the decision was made to crush the Hungarian revolt, it was justified to the people of Czechoslovakia on the basis of an alleged revival of Hungarian irredentism. After raising the specter of a revived fascist, Horthyite Hungary, Radio Prague asked: "Can anyone in this country accept the recurrence of a situation in which groups of spies infiltrated our country from Hungary, when Hungarian irredentist reaction was active in our country . . . ? No one in this country, and none of the socialist countries, can allow such a development."[16] In a report to the Czechoslovak National Assembly, Viliam Široký, head of the Czechoslovak government, emphasized the same point: "Fascist Hungary [the Hungarian government of Imre Nagy] was to have become an instrument [to be used] primarily against Hungary's neighbors, including Czechoslovakia."[17]

Because it was really afraid that a noncommunist Hungary would revive the nationality issue, the Czechoslovak government was generous in its aid to the Kádár government, advocated military intervention before November 4, and supported Soviet intervention after it occurred. On November 6 Prague announced that the workers of Czechoslovakia had created a "solidarity fund for the benefit of the Hungarian working people."[18] On November 15, Široký led a delegation of Czechoslovak government officials to Budapest to hold talks with János Kádár and his government, and in a joint statement the Prague delegation's support for the new, Moscow-installed government was indicated.[19] Aid and further statements of support came later. The prospect of a nationalist Hun-

81

gary advancing claims to Slovakia—particularly in light of the disturbances instigated by the Hungarian minority there—was not pleasing to Prague.

In Rumania the problem was perhaps more serious. The Hungarian minority—which had been integrated into Rumanian political life after 1945—became increasingly isolated after 1952. When the Hungarian revolt broke out, its impact on the Hungarian minority in Transylvania was immediate. Gheorghe Gheorghiu-Dej and other Rumanian leaders cut short a visit to Yugoslavia and returned to Bucharest as soon as fighting broke out in Budapest. Though student—and even some worker—demonstrations were reported in Bucharest and other cities, the focus of unrest in Rumania during the Hungarian uprising was the Hungarian minority. Meetings were organized, demonstrations took place (at least one of which could be broken up only by a volley fired by Rumanian troops) and leaflets were printed, all supporting the Hungarian cause. There were signs of unrest among the Hungarian units in the Rumanian army, which perhaps is the reason some Rumanian army troops were confined to barracks and forced to surrender their arms to the Soviet army. Many Magyars crossed over illegally from Rumania into Hungary to help the revolution. There were also reports that a Soviet train carrying Hungarians being deported to the USSR was stopped while passing through Rumanian territory. Rumanian police and army units, as well as Soviet troops, were heavily reinforced in the Hungarian-inhabited areas. In some Hungarian regions travel between villages was prohibited in order to prevent unrest from spreading. Foreigners were barred from Transylvania, and the Rumanian borders contiguous to both Hungary and Yugoslavia were closed. Many Hungarians were arrested, and it was later reported that eight were executed and forty-four others were given prison terms for "separatist plotting" at the time of the Hungarian uprising.[20] In order to strengthen its shaky position, the Rumanian government increased workers' salaries, children's allowances, and pensions on October 30. It was also announced during the Hungarian uprising that the government had decided to compensate for, or return to, the German minority property which the Rumanian government had confiscated after World War II.[21]

The first official Rumanian comment on the Hungarian uprising expressed the government's concern for the loyalty of the minorities by noting that the Rumanian working class would continue to promote "friendly relations between the Rumanian people and the minorities, in the conviction that this will guarantee progress."[22] To rally minority support, the government produced, and quoted extensively from, "spontaneous" resolutions supporting it and condemning Hungary, which were approved by Hungarian workers in the minority areas of Rumania.[23] Special meetings were also held among the Hungarians in Transylvania. The most important of these took place in Cluj at the Hungarian-language Bolyai University, under the slogan "Let Us Strengthen Fraternal Relations between the Rumanian People and the Minorities." Miron Constantinescu, member of the Rumanian party Politburo and first deputy chairman of the Council of Ministers, and CC members Alexandru Moghioroș and Iosif Chișinevschi were delegated to attend the session. During the meeting, which lasted for several days, liberal Hungarian intellectuals criticized Bucharest's rigid cultural policy which discriminated against the Hungarian minority. A resolution passed at the meeting condemned the "counterrevolutionaries" in Hungary, expressed support for the new government of János Kádár, and declared that all would work to "strengthen the fraternal relations between the Rumanian people and the Hungarian minority."[24]

In a speech to the conference, Constantinescu declared that the principal task for the working people of Rumania and of Cluj was "strengthening the unity among the people of Rumanian, Hungarian, German, and other nationalities." He also denied Hungarian and Western reports of demonstrations in Rumania.[25]

The concern of the Rumanian leadership was such that a special conference of the party organization of the Hungarian Autonomous Region was convoked in the provincial capital, Tîrgu Mureș. The main speaker was Gheorghiu-Dej, first secretary of the Rumanian Workers' Party. Most of Gheorghiu-Dej's speech was devoted to a Marxian, class analysis of the Hungarian revolt. He cited the rigidity of the Hungarian party leadership, careerists in the party, and the influence of the intellectuals as the major causes. However, when he indicated to his audience the lessons Rumanians could learn from the events in Hungary, his first point was unrelated to his Marxian analysis:

Our party calls on all the communists, on all the working people, to constantly strengthen the alliance between the working class and the working peasantry and the leading role of the working class in this alliance, to develop friendship and fraternal cooperation between the Rumanian people and all the minorities.

Each party organization has a duty to ruthlessly combat every manifestation of nationalism and chauvinism, to educate the working people in a spirit of socialist patriotism and proletarian internationalism....[26]

Gheorghiu-Dej appeared to be reciting not the lessons to be learned from the events in Hungary (where minority problems played an insignificant role in the revolution), but those to be learned from Rumania's experience during the uprising. This obvious concern with minority problems and with nationalism and chauvinism reinforces other evidence that there was serious unrest among the Hungarians in Transylvania, but it was not until the summer of 1957 that the Rumanian government acknowledged that demonstrations had indeed taken place in Hungarian areas of Rumania at the time of the Hungarian revolt.

In Rumania, the response to the possibility of a nationalist government in Budapest was similar to that in Czechoslovakia. Rumanian spokesmen not only condemned the Hungarian "counterrevolutionaries" as "fascist" and "Horthyite," but also advocated intervention by Moscow. In response to a Hungarian plea, the Rumanian government extended considerable aid to the government of János Kádár almost as soon as it was established.[27] Gheorghiu-Dej led a parliamentary delegation to Budapest which included Chairman of the Council of Ministers Chivu Stoica and Minister of Defense Emil Bodnăraş. In addition to expressing support for Kádár and praising the Soviet intervention, the Rumanians extended a loan of some sixty million rubles.[28] Soviet troops were permitted to enter Hungary through Rumania, and there were reports that Soviet deportation trains also left through Rumania. The reorganization of the shattered security forces in Hungary was apparently also made possible by the assistance of large numbers of Hungarian-speaking Rumanians and Slovaks. This may explain why Imre Nagy and other leaders of the revolution were taken to Rumania when they were arrested by the Soviets after leaving the Yugoslav embassy in Budapest.

With the approach of October 23, 1957, the Bucharest government took precautions against any anniversary demonstrations. A week before that date the party organization in Cluj held a meeting of intellectuals to discuss "strengthening the friendship between the Rumanian and Hungarian working people and the struggle against nationalism and chauvinism." The major performance at this conference was the self-criticism of Lajos Jordáky, a Hungarian intellectual and long-time member of the communist movement who had criticized the Rumanian party leadership in the Cluj meeting the previous November. Referring to the 1956 Hungarian revolt, Jordáky confessed: "As a consequence of my friendship with many Hungarian writers, on October 23, 1956, I sympathized with the actions carried on by Imre Nagy, the Hungarian Writers' Union, and the Petöfi circle. . . . I remained passive in the action to unmask the causes and aims of the Hungarian counterrevolution and I did not sign the appeal addressed by the Hungarian writers in Rumania to the writers in Hungary."[29] Speaker after speaker followed Jordáky all denouncing nationalism, calling for vigilance in the struggle against it, and citing the evil effects Jordáky's action had had on students and faculty the previous October. *Scînteia,* the daily of the Rumanian party Central Committee in Bucharest, published an extensive, two-part report on the affair on October 16 and 17, 1957. The government's precautions apparently prevented a repetition of the difficulties in 1957. The government, however, was badly shaken by the effect of the Hungarian revolt on the minority, and harsh measures were instituted against the Hungarian population afterward.

In Yugoslavia the problem of the Hungarian revolt was much more complex. The Soviet-Yugoslav rapprochement, which had brought new respectability to national communism, was a major factor in precipitating events in Poland and Hungary. The Yugoslavs approved Gomulka's assumption of power and favored Nagy and Kádár in Hungary. However, once events in Hungary had moved to the point where the power monopoly of the Communist Party was endangered, the Yugoslavs were caught on the horns of a dilemma. Either Hungary would be led by a noncommunist, or even an anticommunist, government, or the Soviet Union would have to intervene with military force to install a hard-line, pro-Soviet regime. Neither alternative was favored by Tito. The prospect of a nationalist Hungarian government, however, was especially unpalatable to the Yugoslavs. The Hungarian minority, which numbered half a million in the Vojvodina and Croatia, were linguistically and culturally susceptible to influence from Budapest. A noncommunist government advancing claims to the former Hungarian areas and championing the rights of the Hungarian minorities would not have been to Belgrade's liking.

Compared with their counterparts in Rumania and Czechoslovakia, the Hungarians in Yugoslavia were relatively quiet during the uprising, There were no reports of serious unrest, arrests, or demonstrations among the Hungarian minority.* The rumor of troop concentrations in the Hungarian areas of Yugoslavia began to circulate only after the Soviet forces had intervened in Hungary on November 4, and it probably was sparked by the presence of these troops in Hungary, rather than by unrest among the Hungarian minority. Refugees from Hungary who sought asylum in Yugoslavia were isolated from the Yugoslav Magyars, and a joint agreement was reached to permit those refugees who wished to return to Hungary to do so. There was some concern among the Yugoslav Hungarians that the repatriation was not completely voluntary, but there were no serious problems.[30] Though perhaps as many as twenty thousand Hungarian refugees left Hungary through Yugoslavia, this number is small in comparison with the number that fled through Austria.

The Hungarian minority in Yugoslavia remained relatively passive during the uprising, while the minorities in Slovakia and Rumania were more seriously affected, largely because of the lower level of discontent among the minority in Yugoslavia. In both Czechoslovakia and Rumania the Hungarians as a group were ac-

---

* Croatian students were much more severely affected by the events in Hungary than were members of the Hungarian minority. Several students in Zagreb and other Croatian universities were arrested for "Croatian nationalism" and for demonstrating solidarity with the Hungarian revolutionaries. In a speech at Pula in which he analyzed the Hungarian revolution, Tito's comments on the internal difficulties which it provoked were directed against Croatians and other Yugoslav nationalities rather than against the national minorities: "The events in Hungary have also somewhat stimulated various elements that still exist in this country. . . . I have never said that we have liquidated or re-educated all the Ustaši, Chetniks, and those bigoted Vatican adherents. I have always said that only the unity of the people will prevent them from attempting and achieving anything in this country." (*Borba,* November 16, 1956.)

tively discriminated against by the communist governments. Prague had attempted to expel its entire Magyar population after the war. When this failed, a policy of "re-Slovakization" was followed in the attempt to suppress Hungarian national consciousness. Distrust led Prague to appoint non-Hungarian and unsympathetic administrators in the Hungarian minority territories. Immediately after the war the Rumanian party had followed a liberal policy toward the Hungarian minority; many party and government officials were recruited from among the Magyars, and some rose to positions of leadership. After 1952, however, with the ascendency of Gheorghiu-Dej, the Rumanian government began to isolate the Hungarians. Rumanians replaced ethnic Hungarians in minority areas, while the Hungarian activists were dispersed throughout ethnically Rumanian territories. The repressive conditions and the low standard of living, which were felt by all nationalities living in Rumania, intensified the discontent of the Hungarian minority.

In Yugoslavia conditions were not so harsh. The attempts by neighboring communist states to disrupt Yugoslavia by creating nationality unrest after 1948 had forced the Yugoslav government to take steps to reduce minority grievances. Also, the Yugoslav party had from the beginning made a serious effort to recruit party activists from among the national minorities. Though in 1956 few of these minority party officials held high positions in the republic or federal party and state organs, the majority of activists remained in their home areas and supplied a needed link between the minority population and the Yugoslav regime. The necessity for the Yugoslav communists to increase their popular support in the face of Soviet and East European hostility after 1948 led the Yugoslavs to decentralize their economy, abandon rigid, Soviet-style central planning, end forced collectivization in agriculture, and give local citizens a greater voice in economic and political decisions. Thanks to both political administration and expanded educational opportunity in their own language, and also to party concern that serious national discrimination be avoided, the national discontent of the Hungarians in Yugoslavia was kept to a minimum.

Though the Yugoslav Hungarians were not as restless as Hungarian minorities elsewhere, Belgrade was still concerned about the prospect of a nationalist Hungarian government, even though it might be led by a good communist like Imre Nagy. Yugoslavia had lost territory to Hungary during the Second World War, and hence the revival of "fascists" and "Horthyites" meant only one thing—a revival of Hungarian claims to Yugoslav territorry. The foreign policy editor of Tanjug (the Yugoslav press agency), who wrote a major article supporting Soviet intervention on November 4, used the specter of a fascist Hungary to justify the decision to intervene: "During the past few days the Yugoslav public has followed with alarm both an increasingly strong tendency on the part of the re-actionary forces to gain a dominating role . . . and the proclamation of slogans which sounded more and more like a return to the times of Horthy and the times of the Nyilas [the Hungarian Arrow Cross Party]."[31] The analysis of the Hungarian revolution in Tito's Pula speech also justified the crushing of the revolution because "the reactionary elements got mixed up in this uprising and exploited it for their own ends." "Are there not plenty of Horthyites there?" he asked. Though Tito criticized the Soviet and Hungarian leadership in this speech, he supported the use of Soviet troops.[32] There was no question that a conservative, pro-Moscow government in Budapest was preferable to a nationalist one that would promote revisionist claims.

At the time of the Hungarian uprising, there were also reports of guerrilla activity in the Soviet Transcarpathian Ukraine (Carpatho-Ukraine), which had a population of over 146,000 Hungarians.[33] These may have been Ukrainian rather than Hungarian guerrillas, since the Carpathians were a center of Ukrainian opposition to Moscow. However, the Soviet government did feel compelled, when there were reports that Hungarians were being deported, to elicit statements of denial from members of the clergy of the Hungarian minority in that area.[34]

All communist states with Hungarian minorities eventually endorsed the Soviet intervention in Hungary, although the decision to support intervention was made only after considerable soul-searching in Belgrade. The Czechoslovak and Rumanian regimes were unequivocal, enthusiastic, and early in announcing their support of intervention. Both cooperated with the Soviet Union in suppressing the Hungarian uprising, and extended assistance to the newly installed Kádár regime. The new Hungarian party leadership expressed its fraternal appreciation for this aid by renouncing claims upon the neighboring Hungarian minority territories.

Conditions were sufficiently stabilized in Hungary to allow Kádár and other leaders to visit Rumania in February 1958. "The real object of our visit," explained Kádár upon his return to Budapest, "and we regarded this as our foremost moral duty, was to thank the working people of Rumania for their brotherly help to the Hungarian people in the days of their great ordeal."[35] These thanks took the form of public renunciation of claims to Rumanian territory. On several occasions Kádár and other members of the delegation denied irredentist claims to the former Hungarian territories, but they consistently reminded their Rumanian audiences that "if the counterrevolution had succeeded in Hungary . . . the counterrevolutionaries [would have] revived the so-called frontier question"[36] At the mass rally in Bucharest just prior to the departure of the Hungarian delegation from Rumania, Kádár reiterated his stand in the strongest terms: "The Hungarian People's Republic has no territorial or any other claim against any country. Anyone who makes such a claim is not only an enemy of the neighboring people's democracies which are living in fraternal friendship with us, but is above all a deadly enemy of the Hungarian People's Republic and of the Hungarian working people who have suffered so much under their [past] rulers."[37]

This visit was also used as an occasion to discourage nationalism in Hungary. All major speeches by members of the delegation to Rumania were broadcast at home in Hungary. On the day the delegation left for Bucharest, *Népszabadság* began publishing a series of articles on the evils of nationalism, "The Fight to Win over the Masses," by István Szirmai, a member of the Central Committee of the Hungarian party. He particularly condemned "anyone who seeks to make us abandon the fraternal ties by which we are linked to the neighboring Rumanian, Czechoslovak, and Yugoslav peoples, anyone who tries to sow discord and broach again the question of frontiers."[38] To quiet Hungarian fears, the members of the delegation toured extensively in the Hungarian minority region of Transylvania, and described the excellent treatment and rights enjoyed by the Hungarian population there.

The Hungarians repaid the visit of the Prague leaders and expressed their thanks to the Czechoslovak peoples in December 1958. In his first speech on arriving in Prague, Ferenc Münnich, chairman of the Hungarian Council of Ministers and leader of the delegation, confirmed the Czechoslovak-Hungarian boundary and denounced irredentism.[39] The theme of equal treatment for the minorities in Slovakia was also stressed in propaganda for home consumption. Though the major purpose of the Hungarian delegations' visits to Czechoslovakia and Rumania was to renounce territorial claims, trips were made to the Hungarian minority regions in both countries. Upon his return to Budapest from Czechoslovakia, Münnich cited the rights extended to the minority in Slovakia and emphatically declared, "Not once did we come across the slightest sign of discrimination."[40] The Hungarian regime apparently felt it necessary to take some steps to mollify Hungarian nationalism by showing concern for the Hungarian minorities.

The first major breakdown in communist authority in Eastern Europe occurred with the Hungarian revolt in 1956. Though this period was short and chaotic, the supposedly "solved" national question became an important issue. Unrest among the Hungarian minority populations and fear of a revival of Hungarian irredentism should a nationalist government come to power in Budapest were major factors which led Czechoslovakia, Rumania, and, reluctantly, Yugoslavia to counsel and support Soviet military intervention. Soviet occupation restored communist power in Hungary, and the show of military force quieted unrest in Rumania and Slovakia. Nevertheless, the Soviet grip on Eastern Europe had been weakened. Attempts to suppress any open discussion of the national question can no longer be enforced absolutely. The common ideology has been unable to erase all traces of national conflict, but it has had a profound impact on the framework within which national issues are now debated.

Chapter 5

Making Sense of the Census and New Nationalities

Manipulation of census figures has long been a technique used in Eastern Europe to strengthen ethnic claims to a particular disputed territory. While this practice predates the establishment of communist governments, certain features are peculiar to the post-1945 regimes. Noncommunist governments, for the most part, claimed legitimacy as the representatives of a particular nationality. One of the most valid claims such a nation-state can make to a contested territory is that the inhabitants of the area are of the same nationality as the majority of the state making the claim. Such governments have not hesitated to alter census data in order to "prove" their position. The 1910 Hungarian census in Transylvania and Slovakia shows far more inhabitants to be ethnically Hungarian than do the Czechoslovak and Rumanian government census data collected after these territories were detached from Hungary. This is not to imply that the Czechoslovak or Rumanian census figures were more correct. The Hungarian census maximized Hungarians while the Czechoslovak and Rumanian censuses maximized Slovaks or Rumanians but minimized Hungarians. The real number of Hungarians—the inhabitants of these areas who considered themselves to be Hungarian—probably lies somewhere between the two extremes. There is some truth to the Czechoslovak and Rumanian explanations that ethnic Hungarians left Slovakia and Transylvania after these areas were separated from Hungary, but the number is in all probability smaller than has been claimed. A comparison of the 1910 Hungarian census figures and those of the 1921 Czechoslovak census for Slovakia shows a significant divergence in the number and percentage of Czechs-Slovaks and Hungarians[1]:

	Czechoslovak census (1921)		Hungarian census (1910)	
Nationality	Number	Percent	Number	Percent
Czechs-Slovaks	2,010,295	68.1	1,697,552	54.5
Hungarians	635,981	21.5	901,793	30.5
Germans	139,242	4.7	198,887	6.7
Ruthenians	85,650	2.9	111,687	3.8

In addition to outright manipulation of census figures, governments frequently combined different nationalities to create a *Staatsvolk*. The interwar Yugoslav censuses combined Serbs, Croats, Serbo-Croatian-speaking Moslems, Montenegrins, the inhabitants of Yugoslav Macedonia (most of whom at that time considered themselves to be Bulgarian), and even Albanians into a single "Serbo-Croatian-speaking" population in order to give the appearance that the state had a majority core or *Staatsvolk*. The same thing was done in Czechoslovakia. In the 1921 and 1930 censuses, Czechs and Slovaks were enumerated together, giving the two nationalities a total of about 65 percent of the population. Czechs alone would have made up only half of the population, and the German minority would have outnumbered the Slovaks.

Communist governments also consider census statistics important. Differences of opinion and methods of manipulating statistics are seldom revealed in the controlled press of Eastern Europe. However, an indication of the seriousness with which statistics are regarded is shown in Yugoslavia, where liberalization has gone so far that a major controversy erupted over the methods of enumeration in the 1971 Yugoslav census. Although there were charges that various groups were being pressured to claim one nationality or another,[2] the major difficulty involved the instructions to the census enumerators for taking declarations of nationality. The original instructions of the Federal Institute for Statistics permitted a citizen to declare his nationality, to declare that he was a "Yugoslav" (which no one in Yugoslavia considers to be a nationality), or to declare himself as a member of a geographical region (that is, Serbian, Croatian, or Italian inhabitants of Dalmatia could declare themselves to be "Dalmatians"). The possibility of declaring regional rather than national identification caused particular concern in the Yugoslav republic of Croatia.[3] A number of Croatian groups feared that since regional identification was strong, many Croats would indicate a regional, rather than a national, affiliation. The result would be fewer Croats in the census totals. This would weaken the Croatian position vis-à-vis the Serbs in the Yugoslav federation and even in the Croatian republic, which had a substantial Serbian minority. The resulting controversy led to a change in the instructions. The new regulations permitted each of the six republican institutes of statistics to issue binding instructions on the way in which the nationality provisions were to be recorded in the census data gathered on the territory of the republic.[4]

The communist governments have not only manipulated their census figures; they have questioned each other about the accuracy and validity of such figures. The Hungarian government has been especially careful to prevent interest in the Hungarian minorities from giving rise to uncommunist-like problems in its relations with neighboring communist states. However, along with a reviving interest in the literature of the Hungarian minorities, there has also been criticism of the census data of neighboring states. The Hungarians did not openly criticize the Czechoslovak report on the number of Hungarians in Slovakia. But by citing with approval other sources which had criticized these figures, they clearly questioned the Czechoslovak census.

During the liberalization of 1968 the Hungarian leaders in Slovakia, emboldened by the removal of censorship restraints and by increased freedom of speech, criticized the Czechoslovak census: "It has been proved in a number of instances that the results of [the 1961] census—with regard to national composition—do not agree with the facts. I know, for example, not only of individual families but of a number of villages where, according to the census, the majority of the population is of Slovak nationality, but where no one—except the teachers and one or two officials—speaks the Slovak language."[5]

An article by a member of the Hungarian minority in Slovakia analyzed Czechoslovak census figures on people of Hungarian nationality from World War I to the present. He discussed the various ways in which "bourgeois" census data for 1921 and 1930 were manipulated to minimize the number of Hungarians, implying that some of these techniques were used by Slovak statisticians in the communist censuses. On the basis of a statistical analysis, he concluded that the number of Hungarians in Czechoslovakia was not the official figure of 560,000, but between 720,000 and 740,000.[6]

Although Slovaks upheld the original census figures Hungarians in Hungary agreed with the revised figures. Z. David, a deputy section chief in the Hungarian Central Statistical Office, cited the figures worked out by the Hungarians in Slovakia with approval: "We should certainly consider the results of the latest careful surveys—720,000 to 740,000 in 1968 (*Uj Szó,* April 12, 1968)—as correct, even if in the meantime some of the populations in the 'islands' which are located far from the cities and Hungarian mass settlements have been absorbed."[7] David went on to estimate the number of Hungarians in Rumania to between 1,800,000 and 1,850,000. Since the nationality data in the 1966 Rumanian census showed that the Hungarian population in Rumania had increased by less than 2 percent over 1956, to only 1,619,592 David's article certainly was intended as criticism of the Rumanian statistics.

Criticism of census data has been more widespread in Bulgaria and Yugoslavia. The Yugoslavs have maintained since World War II, when they recognized the separate existence of the Macedonian nationality, that the inhabitants of Pirin (Bulgarian) Macedonia are also of Macedonian nationality. Between 1944 and 1948 the Bulgarian communists agreed that a separate Macedonian nationality existed, and they admitted that most of the inhabitants of the Pirin district were Macedonians. The Bulgarians were in effect advocating an independent Greater Macedonia (which could then join Bulgaria) or a Balkan federation with a united Greater Macedonia as one federal unit which would have special links with Bulgaria. In line with this policy, the Bulgarian party encouraged the population of the Pirin Region, most of whom considered themselves to be Bulgarian, to declare themselves to be "Macedonians" in the

1946 census. Although precise figures were not published at that time, both Bulgarian and Yugoslav reports indicated that some 70 percent were listed as Macedonians. In a recent controversy over the existence of the Macedonian nationality which involved citing of census figures, a Yugoslav newspaper claimed that the 1946 census showed 169,544 Macedonians in Bulgaria.[8] The next Bulgarian census, in 1956, was taken just after the rapprochement between Yugoslavia and the USSR but before the Hungarian revolt strained relations between Yugoslavia and the Soviet bloc. Although the Bulgarian party was in the process of reversing its earlier policy of admitting the existence of a Macedonian nationality, the Bulgarian census again found that the majority of the Pirin district's population (187,729, or 63.7 percent) was Macedonian.

When the 1965 Bulgarian census was taken, the Bulgarians went to some lengths to appeal to Bulgarian national feeling, and apparently removed the former requirement that the Pirin district have a Macedonian majority. The results showed only 8,750 Macedonians living in all of Bulgaria. When the census data were made public, *Nova Makedonija,* the Yugoslav Macedonian party newspaper, and *Borba,* the leading Yugoslav party newspaper, denounced the Bulgarian figures.[9] Later, Krste Crvenkovski, first secretary of the Macedonian party organization, revealed that the Yugoslavs had approached Sofia on this question even before the census was taken: "Prior to the last census, we warned the People's Republic of Bulgaria, officially and on the highest level, that the requirement made of the Macedonians in Pirin Macedonia—that after 20 years they should change their declaration and call themselves Bulgarians—was unacceptable to us, and that this move was being viewed with alarm not only by the Macedonian public but by the entire Yugoslav public."[10] The Yugoslavs were concerned about the threat the Bulgarian census posed to their claim to the existence of a separate Macedonian nationality. Hence, they warned the Bulgarians before the census, and openly criticized the data when they were released, even though Bulgarian-Yugoslav relations were otherwise quite friendly at this time.

The radical decline in the number of Macedonians in Bulgaria, however, was apparently not due to pressure from the Bulgarian communists on the population of Pirin Macedonia to call themselves Bulgarians in 1965. In fact, the Bulgarians claim that the exact opposite was true. In an authoritative booklet setting forth the Bulgarian position on the Macedonian question published in November 1968, the Bulgarian party answered Yugoslav criticism of its census statistics:

Our party corrected the error that had been allowed to occur— namely, that the population of [the Blagoevgrad] region was forced to register as "Macedonians," in accordance with the decisions of the tenth plenum of the CC in 1946, decisions whose purpose was the supposed facilitating of what was then the forthcoming creation of a federation of southern Slavs. Later these people were granted full freedom to determine their nationality for themselves, in the most democratic manner. At the last census in 1965 only about one half of 1 per cent of the population in the Blagoevgrad district described itself as "Macedonian." At the same time, in the Socialist Republic of Macedonia not a single Bulgarian is allowed to claim that he is of Bulgarian nationality.[11]

Crvenkovski and other Yugoslavs have called these Bulgarian explanations an "incomprehensible and unacceptable assertion."[12] Nevertheless, the Bulgarian statement may be the truth. The fact that 8,750 inhabitants of Pirin Macedonia considered themselves to be of "Macedonian" nationality gives credence to the Bulgarian claim that free choice was permitted on the question of nationality. If the Bulgarian officials had forced the inhabitants of Pirin Macedonia to declare themselves to be Bulgarians, there would not have been 8,750 Macedonians. In the Yugoslav Macedonian Republic (with a population four times as great as the Blagoevgrad Region of Bulgaria), there were only 3,087 Bulgarians according to the 1961 Yugoslav census.

Although communist governments have on occasion padded statistics on the *Staatsvolk* and cut the numbers of ethnic groups linked with neighboring national states, the more common technique has been to maintain that the peoples of a contested territory are ethnically distinct from both nations that claim the area. Hence the Yugoslav census of 1948 found a Rumanian minority numbering 64,095. Of this number, 92.5 percent were in the Vojvodina, near the Rumanian border. However, to minimize the number of Rumanians, the Rumanian-speaking inhabitants of Macedonia and the mountainous areas of south Serbia (102,953 in number) were listed as "Vlachs." The term is actually derived from Wallachia, the name of one of the two historical provinces that were combined in 1859 to form the beginning of modern Rumania.* Not a single "Vlach" was to be found in the Vojvodina, and the number of "Rumanians" in southern Serbia and Macedonia was very small. In the 1953 census the number of Vlachs dropped to 36,728, and in 1961 they were not listed as a separate nationality. The Vlachs are a rather primitive people and had few links with Rumania. They inhabited the mountainous regions of the Balkan Peninsula but have gradually been assimilated culturally, as well as statistically, by their more numerous and advanced neighbors.

The classic examples of creating a third nationality to neutralize claims by another state are the "Moldavians" and the "Macedonians." The Soviets, beginning in 1924 with the creation of the Moldavian Autonomous Republic for a part of the Rumanian population on the Soviet side of the Dniester River, declared their Rumanian population to be "Moldavians." When Bessarabia was reannexed to the Soviet Union during World War II, the campaign to distinguish between "Moldavians" and Rumanians was pursued in earnest. The Soviets—in order to give their claim to Bessarabia greater validity—have distinguished between Rumanians and "Moldavians" in their nationality censuses. There were 2,214,139 "Moldavians" in the Soviet Union according to the 1959 nationality census. Of this number, 1,886,566, or 86 percent, lived in the Moldavian Soviet Socialist Republic and 241,650 or 11 percent, in areas of the Ukraine adjacent to the Moldavian SSR. The distribution of the population declared to be "Rumanian" follows an interesting pattern. There were 106,366 Rumanians recorded in 1959, but of this number only 1,663 were living in the Moldavian SSR. Most of them were living in two *oblasti* in the Ukraine— Chernovtsy had some 79,760 Rumanians (just over 10 percent of the population of the *oblast*), and Zakarpatskaya had a Rumanian population of 18,346. The interesting feature of this is that those territories with Rumanian populations were areas which had never been part of Russia or the Soviet Union until World War II. Chernovtsy is northern Bukovina, and Zakarpatskaya is the Carpatho-Ukraine. Apparently the official distinction is that Ruma-

* The Soviet Union, ironically enough, calls its Rumanian population in Bessarabia "Moldavians," after the other historical province.

nians living in Bessarabia and areas east of the Dniester are Moldavians, while those living in areas that were not under Russian control until World War II—northern Bukovina and the Carpatho-Ukraine—are Rumanian. The Odessa *oblast,* which includes the portions of Bessarabia along the Black Sea which have a predominantly non-Rumanian population, has a minority of 125,045 "Moldavians," but there are no Rumanians.

The Yugoslav communists declared the Slavic inhabitants of the Yugoslav portion of Macedonia to be "Macedonians," although the people considered themselves, and had been considered by most ethnographers for a hundred years, to be Bulgarians. In their census data the Yugoslavs have been very careful to show statistically that these "Macedonians" are not Bulgarians. In the 1948 census, the Yugoslav Republic of Macedonia had a population of 1,152,986. Of this number, 789,648 (68.5 percent of the republic's population) were "Macedonians" and only 899 (or less than 0.1 percent) were Bulgarians. The Yugoslavs have found a population of over 60,000 Bulgarians living in Yugoslavia in each of the three postwar censuses. However, about 55,000 of these live in the Serbian Republic, in territories along the Bulgarian border which were ceded by Bulgaria to Serbia after World War I. Part of the territory ceded in 1920 was the city of Strumica and its surrounding area, which is now part of the Macedonian Republic. The population of this area, since it is part of Macedonia, is overwhelmingly "Macedonian." Apparently the border regions which were ceded by Bulgaria in 1920 can have a Bulgarian population if they are in Serbia, but not if they are in the Macedonian republic. (The rest of the Bulgarian population in Yugoslavia consists of a group of some three thousand Roman Catholic Bulgarians who have lived in the Vojvodina for generations.)

Communist states have more often created a third nationality than resorted to radical distortion of statistics on the *Staatsvolk.* There are a number of reasons for this. First, the legitimacy of communist rule is generally based on ideology rather than on the national right of an ethnic group to its nation-state. Since ethnic or national claims to legitimacy have been less significant to the communist regimes, there is less direct threat to a government's legitimacy in having a state with many nationalities. Second, through historical developments during the communist seizure of power, the Soviet Union became a federal state with republics for its various ethnic groups. This Soviet practice has given the ideological imprimatur to the practice of creating autonomous regions and republics for various nationalities. Hence, it has become almost a status symbol for communist states to acknowledge more than one nationality and grant it limited territorial and administrative rights.[13]

When the Soviet Union was the only communist state, ideological arguments were a prime basis for claiming territory. In the case of Bessarabia, in particular, Soviet propaganda demanding the return of the territory was based upon ideological arguments that the workers and peasants of Bessarabia had been freed by the Great October Socialist Revolution, but when the Rumanian government annexed the area they were again enslaved by imperialists and capitalists. Little emphasis was placed on the historical or ethnic aspects. Stalin explained this in relation to the Russian border lands in a government statement on the national question in 1920:

The demand for the secession of the border regions from Russia as the form of the relations between the centre and the border regions must be rejected. . . . The seceded border regions themselves would inevitably fall into the bondage of international imperialism. . . . There are only two possible outcomes for the border regions:

Either they go along with Russia, and then the toiling masses of the border regions will be freed from imperialist oppression;

Or they go along with the Entente, and then the yoke of imperialism will be inevitable.[14]

As long as the question is whether a given territory should be part of a communist state or part of a noncommunist state, the communist state should unquestionably receive it. Ideological considerations take precedence over ethnic or historical ones.

However, when only communist states are involved the ideological question is no longer relevant. It is under these conditions that ethnic criteria again become important. Khrushchev, looking into the communist future, explained this to a German audience:[15]

With the victory of communism on a world-wide scale, state boundaries will become extinct, Marxism-Leninism teaches us. In all probability only ethnographical boundaries will remain for the time being, and even they will no doubt only be conventional. On these boundaries, if they can be called such at all, there will be no frontier guards, no customs officials, no incidents. They will simply record the historically evolved fact that this or that nationality inhabits a given territory.*

Therefore, since World War II the Soviet Union has tended to emphasize Soviet historical, ethnic, and cultural claims to Bessarabia because the ideological considerations are no longer valid. In principle, though not in practice, most communist parties admit the theory of self-determination, including secession, for nationalities, and thus ethnic identity assumes new importance. If the "Moldavians" are Rumanians, why should they not join their ethnic brothers in socialist Rumania? If the "Macedonians" are Bulgarians, why should they not become part of the fraternal People's Republic of Bulgaria? Hence, when the ideological question becomes irrelevant, the ethnic question assumes new importance in justifying a claim to contested territory. As a result communist states are eager to prove their ethnic claim to a territory they hold, or at least to negate the ethnic claim of a neighboring socialist state by showing the area to be inhabited by a third nationality different from the nationality of either of the contending parties.

Though in several instances communist governments have tinkered with their population statistics to create new nationalities, in two cases they have gone far beyond mere statistical manipulation. The Yugoslavs in the case of the Macedonians and the Soviets in the case of the Moldavians have expended great effort to establish a new nationality. The circumstances that led both Mos-

---

* In the same speech Khrushchev dealt with a number of the territorial disputes that involve communist states. He observed, "For us communists, the boundary question is not the principal one, and it cannot breed conflict among socialist countries." He also referred, however, to territory claimed by both Yugoslavia and Hungary: "After the Second World War, part of Hungary's territory, with a Hungarian population of about one million, passed to Yugoslavia." The Yugoslavs, less than a week after the text of Khrushchev's speech was published in *Pravda,* issued a rebuttal explaining that only 507,000 Hungarians—not a million—lived in Yugoslav territory. The article reviewed Yugoslavia's historical claims to the Vojvodina and corrected Khrushchev by explaining that the territory had passed from Austria-Hungary to Yugoslavia after World War I, not after World War II. (*Komunist,* April 2, 1959).

cow and Belgrade to do this were similar. The population that became the new nationality was large. Moldavians, according to the 1970 Soviet census, numbered over two and a half million. In 1948 Macedonians in Yugoslavia totaled 810,126, and by 1971 they had increased to well over one million. With a population of this magnitude, padding statistics is somewhat more difficult. In addition, the populations were more closely connected ethnically to groups in a neighboring state, and were too unlike the *Staatsvolk* of the state to which they belonged to be readily assimilated. The "Moldavian" population in the USSR speaks Rumanian, a Romance language, and is culturally unlike either the Russian or the Ukrainian Slavs. Although the Macedonians are Slavs, as are the Serbs, they are much closer ethnically to the Bulgarians. The Serbian attempt in the interwar period to assimilate the inhabitants of Macedonia was a complete failure, and it alienated the Macedonian population. Since the "Moldavians" had stronger ethnic links with Rumania and the "Macedonians" were more closely tied to Bulgaria, the Soviet Union and Yugoslavia created new nationalities to bolster their own claims to the territories in question and also to sever, or at least weaken, the link between the contested population and the neighboring state.

In Stalin's first major work on the national question, *Marxism and the National Question,* he gave four criteria for the existence of a nation: "A nation is a historically constituted, stable community of people formed on the basis of a common language, territory, economic life, and psychological make-up manifested in a common culture."[16] Both the Soviet Union and Yugoslavia have attempted to demonstrate that the "Moldavians" and the "Macedonians" satisfy these criteria and should therefore be recognized as separate nations.

The first criterion listed by Stalin is language, and this is probably the key element in creating a separate national consciousness. The Soviets were particularly anxious to distinguish the Moldavian language from Rumanian, and the first step was to change the alphabet in which "Moldavian" was written. Although Rumanian was written with a Cyrillic script in the Middle Ages, during the first part of the nineteenth century the Roman (Latin) alphabet came into general use for written Rumanian in Transylvania, Wallachia, and Moldavia. Therefore, the Soviets declared the

101

Russian Cyrillic as the proper alphabet for the "Moldavian" language. Although the Soviets claimed the Moldavians and their language were different from Rumanian before 1940, the real drive to differentiate Moldavians from Rumanians came only after the USSR annexed Bessarabia during World War II. The Soviets were willing to admit similarities between "Moldavian" and Rumanian, but made it clear that the two were to be considered separate languages. The second edition (1954) of the *Bolshaya Sovetskaya Entsiklopedia* declared that the Moldavian language is "a Romance language belonging side by side with Rumanian to the group of eastern Romance languages," and that "the Moldavian language is extraordinarily similar to the Moldavian dialect of the Rumanian language, which is spoken in Moldavia (Rumanian People's Republic)."[17] Though the encyclopedia clearly specified that Moldavian was separate from Rumanian, it did admit that "questions of the history and modern conditions of the grammatical system and the vocabulary of the Moldavian language, in addition to its dialects, have as yet been insufficiently studied."[18]

This state of affairs is being remedied by Soviet scholars. Numerous studies of the language have appeared. Although the "Moldavian" language is not generally specifically compared with Rumanian, it is obvious that a number of studies are calculated to show the distinctive features of Moldavian vis-à-vis Rumanian.* In addition to differences from Rumanian, there has been some attempt to link the Moldavian language more closely with other Soviet languages, particularly Ukrainian and Russian.[19] About the time that Rumania began advancing historical (though not linguis-

* At times the Soviets have slipped in distinguishing between "Moldavian" and Rumanian. For example, in 1959 a Russian-language translation of Rumanian historian Bogdan Petriceicu-Hasdeu's book *Ion-Vodă cel Cumplit* (Prince John the Terrible) was published in Kishinev. (B. P. Khashdeu, *Ion Voevoda Lyutii,* trans. by N. Romanenko [Kishinev: Gosudarstvennoe Izdatelstvo MSSR "Kartya moldovenyaske," 1959].) The introduction called the monograph a "classic of Moldavian and Rumanian literature," but the note on its translation indicated that the book had been "translated from *Moldavian.*" Although Hasdeu himself was born in Bessarabia, the book was written and published in Bucharest in the mid-1860s, after Hasdeu had left Russia permanently. It can hardly be said to have been written in "Moldavian" since no such language was recognized at that time. For a discussion of why this volume was published in the Moldavian SSR, see Ladis K. D. Kristof, "The Rumanian Ivan the Terrible and Some Problems of Communist Historiography," *Slavic Review* 20:4 (December 1961), 685–694.

tic or ethnic) claims to Bessarabia, the number of Soviet publications on the Moldavian language increased significantly.[20]

When the Yugoslav communists gained control of Macedonia, one of their first acts was to encourage the development of a Macedonian language. In August 1944 the communist-dominated Macedonian government declared Macedonian to be the language for Yugoslav Macedonia, and a commission was created to establish standards for the new language. The dialect chosen as the basis of the language was that of central Macedonia, which least resembles either Serbian or Bulgarian. Scholars working on the language were under instructions to replace foreign words and phrases with expressions based on the various Macedonian dialects, but the purging has been more rigorous with those borrowed from Bulgarian and Russian than with expressions from Serbo-Croatian. Closer links between Serbian and Macedonian are encouraged, but Serbianization is not pushed to the point of alienating the Macedonian population. Although there are still some problems with the language, Macedonian is widely used and generally accepted among the Yugoslav Macedonians.[21]

Language has been the main claim to separate existence for the "Moldavians" and the "Macedonians." Though some Soviet scholars have proposed revisions of Stalin's criteria for the existence of a nation, they continue to cite language as a major, if not the major, factor in nationality.[22] The Soviets and Yugoslavs, recognizing the importance of language, have been zealous in maintaining the existence of separate languages for their new nationalities. The Rumanians, who since 1964 have advanced cautious historical claims to Bessarabia, have not publicly claimed that the "Moldavians" speak Rumanian. Since a separate Moldavian language, implying a separate nationality, is probably more important to the Soviet claim than historical rights, the Rumanians have been cautious on this point.

The Bulgarian attitude on the Macedonian language has not been characterized by the same restraint that has prevailed in Rumania's treatment of the Moldavian language. Some of the most bitter Yugoslav-Bulgarian exchanges have been over the question of the Macedonian language. In 1958, when relations between Yugoslavia and the Soviet bloc were particularly bad, Dimitar Ganev, a member of the Bulgarian party presidium from Pirin

103

Macedonia, told a Bulgarian audience: "In Vardar [Yugoslav] Macedonia, neither Bulgarian papers nor Bulgarian books are allowed. The Macedonian population has been compelled to give up its mother tongue, the language which its fathers and grandfathers spoke, and one artificially molded, strongly Serbianized language—which the Skopje paper *Nova Makedonija* admits is not even known by clerks, students, and pupils—has been imposed by force."[23]

The Yugoslavs were quick to answer this challenge to the existence of the Macedonian language. The Yugoslav Macedonian party daily *Nova Makedonija* delightedly pointed out that Radio Sofia —after broadcasting speeches by Bulgarian leaders which denied the existence of the Macedonian language—continued to announce that broadcasts beamed at Yugoslavia were "in the Macedonian language." Radio Sofia promptly dropped all reference to a Macedonian language after this article appeared.[24] Numerous newspaper articles and speeches by party and government officials condemned the Bulgarians and insisted on the validity of the Macedonian language.[25]

Even in periods of friendship, the question of a Macedonian language has rippled the otherwise placid surface of Bulgarian-Yugoslav relations. At the Fifth International Congress of Slavists in Sofia in September 1963, some members of the Bulgarian delegation incurred the wrath of the Yugoslav delegation by denying the existence of a Macedonian language. The indignant response of the Yugoslavs was published in *Borba,* despite the warm relations with Bulgaria.[26] In late 1966 a meeting of Bulgarian and Yugoslav writers produced another crisis when the head of the Bulgarian delegation refused to recognize a Macedonian language. The Yugoslav responses were surprisingly harsh in view of continued good party and government relations between the two countries at the time.[27] When relations worsened in 1968, the existence of a Macedonian language became a major subject of polemic controversy. However, after a period of strained Bulgarian-Yugoslav relations, Soviet leader Leonid Brezhnev paid a visit to Belgrade in 1971, and polemics over the Macedonian question were gradually eliminated. The fact that a bilateral protocol on tourism written in the Bulgarian and Macedonian languages was signed by the Bulgarian representatives shortly after the Brezhnev visit seems to indicate that, under Soviet pressuure, Sofia has quietly altered its position on the existence of a Macedonian language.

Stalin's second criterion for determining the existence of a nation was territory. Both Macedonians and Moldavians have been granted their own national republics. Although the Rumanian-inhabited territory of Bessarabia was annexed to Rumania in 1919, there was a small Rumanian population on the east bank of the Dniester River which had been under Russian control for a much longer period. In 1924 the Soviet government created a Moldavian Autonomous Soviet Socialist Republic, within the Ukrainian Republic, which included the majority of the Rumanians living in the Soviet Union.* In August 1940, just a few months after Bessarabia was reannexed to the Soviet Union, the Moldavian ASSR was combined with the predominantly Rumanian areas of Bessarabia to form the Moldavian Soviet Socialist Republic, and the area was elevated to the status of a full union republic. In Yugoslavia the communist party advocated the creation of a Macedonian Republic as one of the six federal units of the new Yugoslavia as early as the Jacje conference in 1943, before any meaningful communist control had been established in Yugoslav Macedonia. This proposal was carried out in 1944, when party and government organs were created for the Macedonian republic. The boundary between Serbia and the new Macedonian republic followed almost exactly the line proposed earlier by Macedonian nationalists, and hence had some historical justification.[28] The Yugoslavs, however, in their desire to acquire all of Macedonia (Greek and Bulgarian as well as Yugoslav), defined the ethnic and historical territory of the new Macedonian nation as including the Bulgarian region of Blagoevgrad (Pirin Macedonia) as well as a large part of northern Greece (Aegean Macedonia).[29]

The third factor in Stalin's definition of a nation is a common economic life.† Once it became official policy that Moldavians

---

* An autonomous republic in the Soviet federal system is a special autonomous region within one of the union republics. A union republic is a constituent unit of the Soviet federation and is theoretically a sovereign entity similar to the states in the federal system of the United States. The union republics in the Soviet Union, with the exception of the Russian Federated Soviet Socialist Republic, are established in areas with predominantly non-Russian populations.

† This feature was probably included as a concession to Marxian ideology, which declares that economics is the foundation of history and the key moving

and Macedonians were distinct nationalities, historians attempted to demonstrate the historical economic links between each of these peoples that separated them from their neighbors and bound them together economically. Histories emphasized internal trade and commerce to show the development of an economic life on the territory of the nationality. All this, of course, was done within a Marxian historical context.[30]

The final essential in Stalin's definition of a nation was a "psychological make-up manifested in a community of culture." Both the Soviet Union and Yugoslavia have emphasized culture to differentiate their nationalities from their relatives across the border. The Soviets have permitted research and expressions of cultural distinctiveness, particularly folk dances and folklore and national (or quasi-national) histories and literatures. They have not been willing to grant the Moldavians any greater latitude than is allowed all other Soviet nationalities, however. History, art, literature, and folklore have been allowed to assume Moldavian form in order to demonstrate the community of culture and differentiate it from Rumanian, but the bounds are set.[31] Moldavian culture must emphasize those links that bind Moldavians to the Soviet Union and omit those that link it with Rumania.

The Macedonians have been allowed much greater freedom in terms of culture than the Moldavians. The Yugoslavs were sufficiently anxious to establish the Macedonian nationality that they granted the Macedonians somewhat greater freedom in the cultural sphere than was allowed other Yugoslav nationalities. Macedonian art, history, folk traditions, and other forms of culture have been encouraged. Since religion has long been a crucial factor determining nationality in the Balkans, Belgrade even went so far as to permit and even encourage the Macedonians to establish their own independent Macedonian Orthodox Church.[32]

Although the Soviet Union has done a great deal to create a nationality, the effort has been kept strictly within certain limits.

---

force of human existence. Actually, a common economic life is not an essential element in nationality. The Poles—split between Austria, Russia, and Prussia (later Germany)—had no common economic life, yet there is no doubt that they were a single nation. In Bohemia, Czechs and Germans worked side by side under a single economic system, yet, despite this common life, there existed two distinct and separate nationalities.

The new nationality is not being overtly assimilated by the dominant nationality, but its prerogatives do not include any real independence from the central government. National distinctiveness is limited principally to culture; political independence is not allowed. Those aspects of national consciousness that are permitted must weaken, not strengthen, ties with the ethnically similar group of the neighboring state. In Yugoslavia the fostering of the Macedonian nationality was initiated under similar controlled circumstances, but the evolution of the Yugoslav political system has brought about considerable political and cultural autonomy for the Macedonian republic. Despite these changes, however, the Macedonian leadership is still loyal to Belgrade and still limits any expression of local nationalism to that which favors Yugoslavia. The Macedonian cultural and political leaders continue to emphasize the distinctness of the nationality vis-à-vis Bulgaria and strongly protest any statement or action by Sofia which implies that the Macedonians are Bulgarians.

The extent to which the creation of new nationalities has reduced tension between communist states is difficult to determine. There is no doubt that permitting the local population to use a form of its own dialect—call it Macedonian rather than Bulgarian, Moldavian rather than Rumanian—and to exercise limited cultural autonomy has reduced the discontent of the populations in the border territory. This has probably prevented the neighboring states from using this discontent to intervene actively in order to protect their ethnic brethren across the border. The fact that the contested peoples are said to be a separate nationality theoretically eliminates the right of the neighboring states to interfere. However, the Bulgarians—at times when Yugoslavia's relations with the Soviet bloc are strained, and increasingly in recent years even when these relations are good—have not hesitated to deny the existence of the Macedonian nationality and to claim that the Macedonians are Bulgarians.

It is doubtful, however, that the creation of new nationalities by communist regimes has been a major factor in achieving the relative calm that has obtained in Eastern Europe with regard to the national question since World War II. The Soviet-imposed interpretation that the question has been solved and Moscow's insistence that the subject not be raised have been far more crucial factors.

Chapter 5

The new nationalities have been more useful as a propaganda technique to legitimize the retention of a certain territory and people. Its effectiveness is a function of how credible communist propaganda is along this line. For Russian citizens of the Soviet Union, the argument that Moldavians are not Rumanians but a separate people who belong, and should continue to belong, to the USSR is probably persuasive. Most Rumanians in Rumania probably dismiss the concept of a Moldavian nationality as a Soviet-invented fable. The opinion of the Moldavian inhabitants of the USSR about their own nationality is a key question, but one that cannot be answered—the Soviets will not permit any honest sampling of their feelings. The situation in Yugoslav Macedonia is much the same. No Macedonian would call himself a Bulgarian openly, regardless of his private convictions.

Whether a Macedonian or Moldavian national consciousness really does exist is a crucial but unanswerable question, therefore. There are more similarities in both culture and consciousness between Moldavians and Rumanians, between Macedonians and Bulgarians, than either the Soviet Union or Yugoslavia will admit. On the other hand, the differences between Macedonians and Bulgarians, and perhaps between Moldavians and Rumanians, are probably greater than Rumanians and Bulgarians claim. Whether these new nationalities have any significance beyond propaganda value can only be demonstrated if they are given some meaningful opportunity to exercise choice, which does not appear likely in the near future. However, as time passes the differences become greater and the separate national consciousness grows stronger.

Chapter 6

Territorial Autonomy and Cultural Rights: Slovakia

A key feature of Soviet nationality policy is that compact nationalities are entitled to some form of administrative autonomy, as well as the right to develop their national culture. The greatest autonomy and highest recognition in the Soviet Union is for a nationality to achieve the status of "union republic." Stalin, in a speech dealing with the national question and the Soviet constitution in 1936, listed three conditions for the establishment of a union republic. First, it must be "a border republic, not surrounded on all sides by USSR territory." Since a union republic has the right to secede from the Soviet Union, only one on the periphery of the USSR could secede. (Stalin quickly added, "Of course, none of our republics would actually raise the question of seceding from the USSR.") Second, a given nationality must form a "compact majority" on the territory in question. Third, a union republic must have a large population, which Stalin specified should exceed one million inhabitants.[1] In theory, union republics are entitled to their own constitution and government organs, and can carry on diplomatic relations and maintain an army. In actuality the republics are severely limited by the Soviet government in the exercise of any real power. Although the republics are granted extensive rights on paper, in practice the Soviet system is far more rigidly centralized than other federal states. Nationalities which do not qualify for union republic status or which are denied this status for political reasons may become autonomous republics, autonomous regions, or national areas. These categories represent declining forms of national recognition granted to various nationalities.

In Eastern Europe, Yugoslavia was the only state after World War II to follow the Soviet model and create a federation of constituent republics and autonomous regions for its various nationalities. Rumania later created a Hungarian Autonomous Region but has since abolished it. Czechoslovakia established a Slovak National Council (government) and separate Slovak party organs, but since there were no government or party units for the Czech Lands, it was not a federation of equal units. Czechoslovakia followed this asymmetric pattern until October 1968 when the first steps were taken to create a real Czech-Slovak federation. Since the Soviet-inspired "normalization" under Gustáv Husák, however, this federalism has been eroded. In setting up separate administrative units for nationalities, the communist countries of Eastern Europe have followed the general rule that no minority living on the border of the state with which it is ethnically identified should be given administrative autonomy. Hence, in the early postwar years the Czechoslovak government was unwilling to create a Hungarian autonomous region which would have stretched along the Hungarian border. Yugoslavia was unwilling to grant republic status to the Hungarian population of the Vojvodina or to the Albanian population of Kosovo. Although these two Yugoslav areas are autonomous provinces, they have remained a part of the Republic of Serbia and have been kept under central control. The Rumanian government was willing to create a Hungarian Autonomous Region in the Szekler areas in eastern Transylvania, far from the border with Hungary, but the regions along the Hungarian border, which also have a high proportion of Hungarians, were not given autonomous status. The exceptions to this rule are Macedonia and Moldavia. However, in these two instances the Soviet Union and Yugoslavia have not granted administrative autonomy to a minority linked with a neighboring state, but to a new nationality.

In addition to republics and autonomous regions, the boundaries of the nonnational administrative districts have a significant influence on national question and on relations between the East European communist governments. The linguistic, educational, and cultural rights granted to minorities are frequently a function of the proportion of the minority population in an administrative unit. The implementation of minority rights is often a responsibility of local administration. The question of gerrymandering administrative boundaries thus becomes not only a question of internal administrative policy but also an important indicator of minority treatment. Since the cultural rights of a minority are a matter of concern to the ethnically related national state, boundaries of internal administrative districts, as well as cultural rights, have at times become a source of friction between communist states.

No special nationality districts have been established in Slovakia for the Hungarian minority; however, administrative districts have played an important role in the treatment of the Hungarians.[2] As has been discussed above, the Slovaks attempted, with Stalin's approval, to expel their Hungarian minority, but British and American opposition coupled with strong Hungarian resistance resulted in a large Hungarian population remaining in Slovakia. The Hungarian communists suggested that an autonomous area be created for the Hungarian population, but this was strongly opposed by the Slovak communists. In fact, the communist-drawn administrative regions have attempted to minimize the proportion of Hungarians in any one area. The administrative divisions re-established in Czechoslovakia after World War II were those which had existed before September 1938, when the Munich agreement permitted Hitler to seize German-inhabited areas of Bohemia. The first communist administrative divisions were established by law in December 1948, just a few months after the coup d'état gave the communist party complete control of the Czechoslovak government. In Slovakia there were six *kraje*. The boundaries of these units generally ran north-south. Since the Hungarian population is concentrated on an east-west axis along the southern border and the Slovak population is more compact in the hilly areas of north and central Slovakia, the Hungarian minority was split among several *kraje*. Of the six Slovak units, four had Hungarian minorities. The most heavily concentrated Hungarian population, in the Dunajská

Streda and the Komárno areas, was split between the Bratislava *Kraj* and the Nitra *Kraj*.

Although the administrative districts established in 1948 did not make allowances for the Hungarian population, a gradual though uneven improvement in their situation began after the communist coup of 1948. A series of measures in 1948, 1953, and 1958 restored citizenship to some Hungarians. Those Hungarians who were deported to western Bohemia immediately after the war were allowed to return to Slovakia after 1948. In 1949 the Slovak Communist Party Central Committee began to publish a Hungarian-language daily, *Uj Szó,* and the same year Csemadok—the Cultural Association of Hungarian Workers in Czechoslovakia—was established. The cultural life of the Hungarians gradually improved during the 1950's. In 1955 Csemadok launched a weekly, *Hét,* and the Hungarian section of the Slovak Writers' Union began to publish a Hungarian literary journal, *Irodalmi Szemle,* in 1958. One of the Slovak publishing houses set up an autonomous branch to publish and promote Hungarian literature. Hungarian-language schools were established again in 1948–1949, and were expanded during the 1950's.

Despite these improvements, the granting of greater rights to the Hungarian minority was not always consistent. The second division of Czechoslovakia into administrative units, which was carried out in 1960, was not a favorable development for the Hungarian minority. The six Slovak *kraje* were combined into three—again with the boundaries running north-south. This further reduced the influence of Hungarians in any one *kraj*. The division of the *kraje* into *okres* (districts) was also carried out so as to minimize Hungarian influence. Although generally speaking the 1960 administrative reorganization combined smaller units, in all of Slovakia only two *okres* had a Hungarian majority—Dunajská Streda and Komárno, both located in the West Slovak Region. In the Central Slovak Region none of the districts had a Hungarian majority, though under the 1949 division three had Magyar majorities. In the East Slovak Region one district that had a large Hungarian majority after the 1948 reorganization was combined with two predominantly Slovak districts, which reduced the Hungarian population to 39 percent.

This is not intended to imply that reducing the influence of the

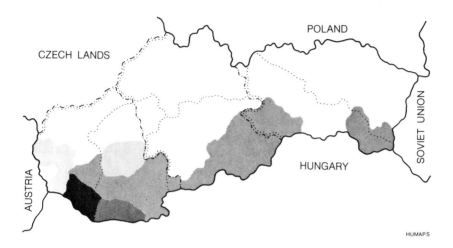

Slovakia (*percent Hungarian*)

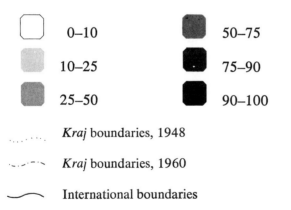

☐	0–10	▨	50–75
▨	10–25	■	75–90
▨	25–50	■	90–100

.... *Kraj* boundaries, 1948

⌐·−⌐~ *Kraj* boundaries, 1960

⌐~ International boundaries

Hungarian population was the only factor in establishing the administrative divisions in Slovakia. Certainly economic considerations, transportation links, geography, and other factors played a role. However, since the creation of a predominantly Hungarian region or administrative districts with Hungarian majorities would not have been difficult and could have been economically justified, there is little doubt that minimizing Hungarian influence in the administrative districts was a consideration in their establishment.[3] It must also be added, however, that the territorial divisions in Slovakia during Hungarian rule (before 1918) also ran north-south. This may have been because of the geography of Slovakia, but, on the other hand, there may have been a deliberate effort on the part of Hungarians to prevent the Slovak population from being heavily concentrated in a few northern territorial units.

In conjunction with the territorial reorganization, other steps were undertaken which must be considered setbacks for the Hungarian minority. Many Hungarian-language schools were amalgamated with Slovak schools and put under Slovak administrators. The number of subjects taught in Slovak was increased. In many districts with mixed populations, the use of Hungarian as well as Slovak in administrative affairs was delayed, even though this program of bilingualism had begun only in 1959.

The year 1964 marked the beginning of a new era for the cultural development of Hungarians in Slovakia. Apparently at a meeting of the Czechoslovak party Central Committee on December 19, 1963, in a still unpublished document, the nationality policy of 1945–1948 was condemned as a manifestation of anti-Hungarian nationalism. Although some Slovak communists who had earlier been tried for bourgeois nationalism (Clementis, Okali, Novomeský, Husák, and others) were specifically criticized, it was admitted that the entire party had agreed with this policy directed against the minority.[4] Following this party decision, *Irodalmi Szemle* published the first serious studies dealing with the treatment of the minority in 1945–1948. From this time on, the Hungarian press in Slovakia began to publish articles on the problems of minority life. Although the material published was very carefully chosen and edited, it was urged that the minority be fully absolved from the accusations of the early postwar years. Some articles emphasized the "bridge-building" role of minorities in relations between East

114

European states, and others expressed concern for the small number of minority intellectuals and the limited scope of their activities in Slovakia. Also, in 1964 an agreement was reached between Czechoslovakia and Hungary to purchase and use a number of schoolbooks published in Hungary for the Hungarian minority schools in Slovakia. By the mid-1960's there were some twenty-two Hungarian-language newspapers and journals, and the output of books published in Slovakia in the Hungarian language had doubled, totaling some eighteen to twenty books per year. The cultural activities sponsored by Csemadok, as well as the membership of this organization, had increased substantially.

Depite the progress achieved in improving the status of the Hungarian minority, their condition was still not entirely satisfactory. By the mid-1960's there were 310 kindergartens, 496 elementary schools, 36 secondary schools, 1 Hungarian teachers' college, 28 agricultural, and 22 professional schools giving instruction in the Hungarian language. The number of Hungarian students in these schools was between 90,000 and 100,000, and the size of the teaching force between 3,200 and 4,000. For the most part, however, these Hungarian schools were only sections of the local Slovak schools. While 35 percent of pupils in Slovak-language elementary schools continued their education, only 30 percent in the Hungarian-language sections did so. With secondary schools the discrepancy was even greater. Of all Slovak students who completed secondary schooling, some 60 percent went on to higher schools, but only 36 percent of Hungarians who completed secondary school did so. It was estimated that some 25 to 30 percent of Hungarian children were attending Slovak- or Czech-language schools.[5]

On the eve of the dramatic events that took place during 1968, the Hungarian minority still felt less than completely satisfied with its status, despite the significant improvements made since the early 1950's. However, it is unlikely that the full extent of these dissatisfactions would have become known without the removal of restrictions on free expression that accompanied the democratic revival in Czechoslovakia in the spring of 1968. As the Slovaks and Czechs began to consider ways to put their relationship on an equal federal basis under the Dubček regime, the Hungarian minority, which would be seriously affected by changes in the structure of the Czechoslovak state, began to make its voice heard in the debate between Czechs and Slovaks. The Central Committee of Csemadok drew up a resolution presenting its position on the issues being considered in formulating the Action Program of the Czechoslovak Communist Party. The Csemadok position was based on the concept that national minorities should be accepted as part of the state, not only as individuals but also as organized groups. As such, they should be entitled to manage their own affairs on the basis of self-government or self-determination. Their view of self-government was not a separatist one; rather, it was firmly integrated into the state structure and organization.

In order to ensure adequate consideration of minority interests Csemadok proposed that nationality committees and nationality agencies be organized on the level of the federal government in Prague, the Slovak national council (government) in Bratislava, and on the level of all local government organs. One of the basic proposals essential to carrying out the concept of self-government was territorial reorganization. The 1960 administrative districts were specifically criticized, and new districts were proposed:

We propose territorial reorganization of mixed-nationality districts:

The new districts established in the 1960 territorial reorganization are hindering rapprochement and fraternal coexistence between nations and nationalities. Rather than strengthening the unity between nations and nationalities, they are a cause of friction. They slow down the practical enforcement of the nationality policy and implementation of the resolutions of party and state organs. Experience has shown that districts inhabited predominantly by one nationality are more prosperous and successful in the political and economic fields.

The further improvement of political and economic life, and the settlement of the nationalities question and the guaranteeing of their equality, make necessary the establishment of compact units —homogenous from the point of view nationality—in areas inhabited by the nationalities, through reorganization of districts along appropriate geographical lines.

At the same time there must be a constitutional guarantee of equality of rights for minority groups among the nations and nationalities in these districts.[6]

Csemadok's call for territorial reorganization was echoed by a number of Hungarians in Slovakia who discussed the minority problem.[7]

In addition to demands relating to the administrative districts, Csemadok and various Hungarian groups and individuals raised a number of demands in the field of culture and education: Hungarian-language schools should have Hungarian administrations; Hungarian youth should be given equal opportunity for further study both in Czechoslovakia and in Hungary; cultural institutions should be established for the minority; use of Hungarian in the administrative affairs of ethnically mixed districts should be expanded; discrimination against Hungarians in the hiring policies of economic enterprises should be stopped.[8]

The initial response of the Slovaks to the Csemadok proposals came from a group of Slovaks who settled in southern Slovakia immediately after World War II. They criticized the Hungarian minority for ignoring the rights of Slovaks in areas of mixed nationality, and criticized Csemadok's activity as "nationalistic, chauvinistic, even more, irredentist."[9] Very quickly the Slovak press, and particularly the cultural papers, began to criticize the Hungarian minority program. The Slovak reaction almost immediately involved Hungary in the question of the Hungarian minority. One of the first attacks on the Csemadok program drew attention to the situation of the Slovak minority in Hungary and revived the principle of reciprocity as the only possible approach to the minority problem.[10] The principle of reciprocity was the nationality policy followed by the "independent" Slovakia set up under the leadership of Father Tiso after 1939. Under this policy concessions to Hungarians living in Slovakia would be granted only if similar concessions were granted to Slovaks in Hungary. This approach not only failed to solve the problem, but it also had unfortunate consequences for the minorities on both sides during World War II.

Articles in the Slovak press began citing mistreatment of the Slovak minority in Hungary. Claiming that 300,000 Slovaks still lived in Hungary, one article decried the decline in the number of Slovak schools, the lack of Slovak literature in Hungary, and the small number of teachers who spoke good Slovak.[11] Following the publication of such claims, other articles on the size and treatment of the Slovak minority in Hungary were published "almost simultaneously by nearly every Slovak paper," according to a Hungarian report.[12] Letters were published voicing concern for the rights of the Slovaks in Hungary and "expressing indignation over the demands contained in the [Csemadok] resolution."[13]

The response of the Hungarian minority in Slovakia was immediate. Several articles by Hungarians appeared in the Hungarian- and Slovak-language press rejecting the connection of Hungarian rights in Czechoslovakia to the situation of the Slovaks in Hungary. Some tried to justify the situation in Hungary by explaining that it was invalid to "compare the Hungarian minority living in a compact community in the southern part of Slovakia with the Slovak minority scattered all over Hungary."[14] However, the main argument of the Czechoslovak Hungarians was that the only valid comparison for Magyar minority rights was not treatment of Slovaks in Hungary but the rights of other citizens of Czechoslovakia. One Hungarian writer rejected the theory of reciprocity by explaining, "From the point of view of the Hungarians living in Czechoslovakia, it makes no difference what the relation between the Hungarian authorities and the Slovaks living in Hungary is."[15]

While some Hungarians apparently advocated that Magyar-inhabited lands be restored to Hungary, these were isolated cases, not a general demand.[16] The Slovaks, however, apparently feared that administrative autonomy and greater cultural-educational rights would be used by the Hungarians as a base for seceding from Slovakia. The Slovaks frequently recalled the events of 1938–1945 and expressed the fear that "Hungarians in Slovakia are to a considerable extent chauvinistic, and they would misuse autonomy only to break away from us and join Hungary."[17] The Csemadok demands for the establishment of separate youth organizations, schools, and Hungarian districts were said to "arouse distrust between the Slovak and the Hungarian populations and bring to mind the situation in 1939, when sections of the Hungarian population demanded the annexation of southern Slovakia to Hungary."[18]

The Slovaks not only feared that Hungarians would take advantage of autonomy to join Hungary; they also feared that the Hungarian minority would appeal to the Hungarian government and the Hungarian Communist Party for aid in their struggle for greater rights. One Slovak journalist warned that the Hungarian minority must not "ask the Hungarian communists to come and

help the Hungarians in Slovakia to settle their nationality problem."
The minority "must be made to realize, the sooner the better, that
they are Czechoslovak citizens living in Slovak territory and that
they are not entitled to try to consort with foreign nationals for
the settlement of our internal affairs, nor to call for the intervention
of a foreign state."[19]

The Czechoslovak Hungarians not only insisted upon comparing
their rights to those of other Czechoslovak citizens rather than to
those of Slovaks in Hungary; they also specifically denied any
desire for intervention by the government of Hungary on their
behalf. "To speak plainly," one Hungarian in Czechoslovakia
wrote, "the Hungarians have not so far tried to take a hand in
shaping the destiny of Hungarians in Czechoslovakia, and we do
not want them to do so. This is an internal affair in the strictest
sense of the word, and we should at least agree on that point."[20] In
an interview, Gyula Lőrincz, chairman of the Central Committee
of Csemadok and editor-in-chief on *Uj Szó,* reiterated this stand:
"Neither I, nor Csemadok, is a partner of the Hungarian party
leadership or the Hungarian government." He added, "In settling
our problems we have never demanded intervention or assistance
from Budapest. We have always proclaimed that we must settle
our problems within our fatherland." When pressed by the two
Slovak journalists who were interviewing him about the condition
of the Slovak minority in Hungary, Lőrincz repeated: "The Hungarian side carefully observes the principle of noninterference in our
affairs. We appreciate this and cannot therefore assert that our side
should interfere [in Hungary's treatment of its Slovak minority]."[21]

While the Hungarian government did not involve itself directly
in the affairs of the Magyar minority in Slovakia, both the government and the Hungarian people were concerned with the affairs
of the minority. Even before the democratization process began
in Czechoslovakia, the Hungarian party and government had
relaxed the restrictions on intellectuals concerned with Hungarian
minorities in neighboring countries. In the fall of 1967, for the first
time since the communist seizure of power, public expressions of
interest in the affairs and literature of the Magyar minorities in
neighboring countries were permitted. The minorities were discussed at a congress of the Patriotic Peoples' Front in April 1968,[22]
and the literature of the Hungarian writers in neighboring states

was the subject of a number of articles and later a series of discussions in the Hungarian Writers' Union.[23] With this greater latitude for public discussion of the minorities, the reassertion of rights by the Hungarian minority in Slovakia was followed with considerable interest in Hungary.

Shortly after the exchanges between Slovaks and Hungarians in Czechoslovakia began, a letter from Prague by Pál Fehér, a leading Hungarian journalist and commentator on events in Czechoslovakia, was published in Budapest. Fehér rejected the principle of reciprocity, and he criticized Slovak articles which compared the Hungarians in Slovakia with the Slovaks in Hungary, as well as Slovak opposition to the Hungarian minority's demands for equal rights. At the same time Fehér praised the rebuttal of a Czechoslovak Hungarian and claimed that an exchange of ideas on the national question "is needed by the Czechoslovak socialist democracy . . . as well as by the whole of socialist Central Europe."[24] Although the Hungarian government did not officially comment on the situation of the minority in Czechoslovakia, Hungarian news media frequently reported on their affairs. In Hungarian interviews with Czechoslovakia officials, questions were always asked about the Magyars of Slovakia.[25]

In June 1968 representatives of the Hungarian and Czechoslovak governments signed a treaty of friendship and mutual alliance in Budapest. In a speech delivered at the signing of the treaty János Kádár, first secretary of the Hungarian party, spoke of the ties between Czechoslovakia and Hungary resulting from their common history and geographic proximity. "Some [undesirable] remnants of this past," he said, "have survived to this day, and their elimination is possible only on the basis of socialism and a Leninist nationality policy." Though he strongly advocated solution of the nationality problem, Kádár advised the Hungarians in Czechoslovakia to look toward Prague and not toward Budapest.[26] In a speech on the same occasion, Czechoslovak party first secretary Alexander Dubček replied to his Hungarian host: "We are constantly applying the principles of socialist internationalism, according to which members of other national minorities will be citizens of our socialist republic with equal rights."[27] Dubček, himself a Slovak, was generally sympathetic to the Hungarian minority's desire for greater rights, as were many of the liberal Czech and Slovak reformers.

After the August invasion of Czechoslovakia, the Hungarian press became more critical of the handling of the national question in Slovakia. *Népszabadság* discussed an article in *Rudé Právo* on the nationality question, and particularly criticized attacks made earlier in the spring on the Hungarian government's treatment of its Slovak minority. In referring to the "nationality excitement" in Slovakia a few months earlier, the official organ of the Hungarian party condemned the "sharp attacks" and "violent protests" as "irresponsible accusations against the Hungarian People's Republic —in matters shaping the internal affairs of our country."[28] Little more than a week later another article appeared in *Népszabadság*. While declaring that "there is no tension in the country between Hungarians and the minorities," the article went on to justify Hungarian minority policy on those very points which Slovak writers had criticized earlier. The article reasserted interest and concern for the situation of the Hungarian minorities living beyond the borders of Hungary:

No people ever cuts the peculiar bonds by which it is tied to those who speak the same language, share the same historical past, and enjoy an identical culture. . . . Neighboring countries have the same feelings toward their own people living in Hungary as minorities, and this is quite natural—we have the same regard for the Hungarian minorities in neighboring countries. We believe that to cultivate and safeguard these bonds is our everlasting duty. At the same time, we always maintained—and adhere strictly to this principle—that the destiny of Hungarians living beyond the frontier is entirely in the hands of those nations with which history has, in various periods and in various ways, united them.[29]

The Hungarian article also admitted that Budapest had responsibilities toward its own minorities, and improvement in their treatment was urged.

Throughout the period before the August invasion, the Hungarian leaders in Slovakia supported the Csemadok proposals for the creation of predominantly Hungarian districts, for the creation of a separate representative body and a separate Slovak government ministry with Hungarian officials to deal with the Hungarian minority. The Slovaks were just as adamant in resisting these Hungarian proposals. When the Action Program of the Slovak Communist Party was drafted, the problems of the minorities were recognized. How-

121

ever, the specific changes proposed in the Action Program to safeguard minority rights included only the creation of nationality committees which would be attached to the existing government and party organs. The Hungarian proposal for the creation of compact Hungarian administrative districts was completely ignored.[30] Meetings of the Slovak National Council's subcommittee on nationalities were held several times during June and July in an attempt to reconcile differences on the best way to ensure protection of Hungarian rights. However, at these meetings the Hungarians consistently supported Csemadok's proposals, and the Slovaks just as consistently opposed them.[31]

The problems of cultural rights and territorial autonomy continued to be discussed even after the Soviet invasion had begun to dampen the brief effervescence of Czechoslovak democracy. However, the Soviet-imposed limitations and the process of normalization postponed resolution of the minorities' status. Gustáv Husák, at the time first secretary of the Slovak Communist Party, delivered a frank and understanding speech to Csemadok shortly after the invasion. He praised the "tremendous majority of the Hungarian population" for their loyalty and patriotism toward Czechoslovakia during the difficult period. Although he expressed considerable sympathy for the demands of the minority for improvement of their situation, he appealed for patience because of the difficult circumstances and explained the necessity of delaying some measures.[32] Despite the delays, a special bill on national minority rights was submitted for public discussion in early October 1968. The bill declared that the minorities were entitled to be educated in their respective languages, to develop their cultural life, to use their own languages in administrative affairs, to develop cultural and social organizations, and to have mass media in their own languages, as well as other rights. In October 1968 it was also reported that the Commission on National Committees (local government units) of the Slovak National Council was considering changes in the boundaries of local administrative units. During 1968 the commission had received requests for the re-establishment of thirty-nine districts abolished in the 1960 reorganization. The proposals to create Hungarian districts were postponed, however, and have apparently died an administrative death. A constitutional amendment generally outlining minority rights was passed in October 1968, but the law which was to define these rights in detail was never approved.

The process of normalization has been pursued in earnest since the removal of Dubček from Czechoslovak party leadership; hence, the ability of the Hungarian minority to make its dissatisfaction known has decreased. There are some signs that the situation of the minority has deteriorated. The number of students in Hungarian-language schools is said to have declined from some 90,000 to 100,000 in the mid-1960's to only 71,000 in 1970.[33] However, there is a Hungarian-language publishing house in Slovakia which produces an average of thirty-five to forty books per year, and, under the terms of an agreement with Hungary on the joint production of books and teaching materials, some 200,000 copies of books printed in Hungary are brought into Slovakia annually for use of the minority.[34] The most serious setback since 1968 is to be found in the personnel changes in the leadership of Csemadok. In May 1970 the secretary-general and another secretary of Csemadok's Central Committee were removed from their posts, and a member of the Central Committee was expelled from the organization. Csemadok and its leadership came under public criticism, and in March 1971 the chairman and twenty-seven members of the Central Committee were purged. Although the government and communication media in Hungary have refrained from commenting on these changes in the organization, the fact that the information concerning the purges came from Budapest and that it has not been published in Czechoslovakia indicates Hungary's serious interest in this matter.[35]

Chapter 7

Territorial Autonomy and Cultural Rights: Yugoslavia

Yugoslavia was the only East European communist state after 1945 to follow the Soviet Union in establishing a federal system. Six federal Yugoslav republics were created. Five were for a single nationality—Serbia, Croatia, Macedonia, Slovenia, and Montenegro —and the sixth, Bosnia-Hercegovina, was for an area of mixed Serbian, Croatian, and Serbo-Croatian speaking Moslem population. Each of the nationalities entitled to its own republic plus the Serbo-Croatian speaking Moslems were classed as "Yugoslav nationalities." These "Yugoslav nationalities" live primarily within Yugoslavia, although there are a few small groups living in neighboring states.* Those nationalities which live in Yugoslavia but are the irredenta of a neighboring nation were classed as "national minorities" and were not given their own republics. Denial of re-

---

* The Macedonians are the exception. Yugoslavia claims there is a Macedonian population of over 200,000 in Bulgaria and a Macedonian population of 200,000 to a million (depending on the time and the individual making the estimate) living in northern Greece. Greece and Bulgaria both deny the existence of a Macedonian nationality and maintain that there is no Macedonian population within their borders.

public status to these minorities is not purely a question of size, since two of the national minorities are larger in number than the Montenegrins—one of the "Yugoslav nationalities." The 1948 census reported that there were 425,703 Montenegrins in Yugoslavia, with 342,009 of them living in the Montenegrin republic. The same census enumerated 750,431 Albanians with 498,703 in Kosovo-Metohija, and 496,492 Hungarians, of whom 428,932 were living in the Vojvodina. Although the principal areas in which these two nationalities live were established as autonomous regions in 1945, they were retained as parts of the Serbian Republic.

The "national minorities" have not been granted territorial autonomy through being given republican status, but the cultural and self-governing rights which they have been permitted in recent years are extensive. Immediately after the communist party assumed power in Yugoslavia the rights given to any nationality were limited, and the minorities were generally given even fewer privileges. However, there has been a real attempt to satisfy, at least to some extent, the national desires of the various peoples. Yugoslavia was forced to take a more generous position toward its minorities because of its foreign policy and its internal diversity. The open hostility of the Soviet Union and the other states of Eastern Europe after 1948, and in particular their attempt to weaken Yugoslavia by appealing to national antagonisms, forced the communist regime to undertake a policy of granting national concessions in order to reduce the vulnerability of the minorities to external attempts at disruption. In addition, because Yugoslavia is a state in which no nationality has a decisive superiority in numbers, tolerating diversity and granting national rights have been essential for the continued existence of the federation. The minorities have benefited from these policies.

The Yugoslav government has made a serious effort to give the minorities an opportunity for education in their own languages. In most cases the proportion of students studying in minority-language schools approaches the minority's proportion of the total population. However, in the higher grades the number of minority-language students falls off. This is largely due to the fact that many advanced subjects are not taught in minority languages because of the lack of trained teachers and materials, and also because the demand for persons with such training in the minority languages is not great. Frequently children of mixed marriages and even children whose parents are both of a minority nationality go to Serbo-Croatian language schools because of the increased economic and educational opportunities available to those who speak the major Yugoslav language. Although students in the minority-language schools have always been required to study the language of the republic in which they live, students of the "Yugoslav nationalities" living in areas with a substantial minority population have recently begun to study the minority languages. In the Dimitrovgrad *opština,* which is the major area inhabited by the Bulgarian minority in Yugoslavia, all pupils regardless of nationality are now required to study the Bulgarian language.[1]

The statistics on Albanian minority schools indicate the growing equality with which the nationalities receive education in minority languages. The 1961 census indicates that Albanians made up 3.85 percent of the Yugoslav population. Although the proportion of students in Albanian-language elementary schools has consistently been higher than the Albanian proportion of the population, the number in high schools has been much lower until recently:

Students in Albanian-language schools as a
percentage of total Yugoslav students[2]

Year	Elementary	General secondary (*Gimnazije*)
1953–54	5.90	0.97
1958–59	4.85	1.42
1964–65	5.69	2.07
1968–69	7.33	3.88

This is due to the very high birth rate among the Albanian population—the highest of any Yugoslav nationality. The greater proportion of elementary and secondary pupils in Albanian-language schools in recent years also reflects the policy of the Yugoslav government to improve the situation of the Albanian minority, which is the least advanced group in Yugoslavia.

Another reflection of the generous cultural rights granted to the minorities is the number of minority-language publications. In 1969 there were twelve newspapers and eleven journals printed in the Hungarian language, and eleven newspapers and seven journals in Albanian. Though the Albanian minority is more than twice as large as the Hungarian, the latter are educationally and culturally further advanced. The other minorities also have newspapers and journals in their own languages,[3] which generally operate under the same conditions and restrictions in force for the major-language publications.

The Yugoslav political system has also provided for the minorities to be represented in the leading party and government organs and has given them some opportunity to influence local government agencies. The Yugoslav concept of self-management of the economy as well as of government was introduced in the early 1950's and has been seriously implemented since the mid-1960's. Under this system the minorities, as is true for all citizens of Yugoslavia, are given a greater voice in managing their own affairs. The right to use one's native language in affairs of government administration in areas with mixed populations has become a general practice throughout the country. In addition, the party and government have deliberately recruited activists from among the national minorities. There is a serious effort to secure officials who are loyal to Belgrade but who are also of the same nationality as the people with whom they deal. Granting proportional equality to nationalities in government legislative and administrative bodies has been a principle of the Yugoslav constitution since 1963, and it was practiced before that date.

In the early days of communist rule there was real concern about the loyalty of certain minorities, and, hence, restriction of their rights. Their treatment has significantly improved in recent years, however.[4] While there is still some anxiety for minority irredentism, the Yugoslavs are more open and realistic about their minorities than other communist governments. In large part this is because Yugoslavia is multinational, and some tolerance for national differences and respect for national rights is an essential condition for the continued existence of the state. This is not to say that serious national differences do not still exist, as the current revival of nationalism shows. However, despite these difficulties, the minorities have received better treatment under Tito than they have received under other communist governments.

Except for the special problems of Macedonia and of the Albanian minority, Yugoslavia's policy toward those of its minorities that have links to other communist states has been a factor contributing to good relations with these states. The treatment of its

Czech and Slovak minorities has been a source of satisfaction to the Czechoslovak government in Prague and to Slovak authorities in Bratislava. While this question is not the prime element in their relations, it does help to strengthen relations between Czechoslovakia and Yugoslavia when other conditions are favorable. The Bulgarian minority in Yugoslavia has generally been well treated in Belgrade. This is largely because the Yugoslavs frequently contrast the rights enjoyed by the Bulgarians in their country with the denial of rights to the Macedonian population living in Bulgaria. Although authorities in Sofia are no doubt pleased at the national rights given to the Bulgarian minority in Serbia, the question of Macedonia is such an important and disruptive element in Yugoslav-Bulgarian relations that the Bulgarian minority is regarded as a minor affair.

The Albanian and the Hungarian minorities are the most interesting and most important in their effect on Yugoslavia's relations with its communist neighbors. These two are numerically the largest of the minorities, and they inhabit contested areas that have frequently changed hands. Because of the size and location of these two populations, they play an important role in Yugoslavia's relations with Albania and Hungary as well as in internal Yugoslav affairs.

Currently both the Albanians and the Hungarians enjoy essentially the same cultural, educational, and linguistic rights that the other minorities in Yugoslavia enjoy. This has not always been true, however. The Albanian minority was less willing than the others to return to Yugoslav control at the end of World War II. An uprising in Kosovo in 1944–1945 was ruthlessly suppressed, but limited Albanian resistance to Yugoslav rule continued for some time. Although there has been a continuous attempt to enlist party and government officials from among the Albanian minority, Kosovo has largely been dominated by Serbs. Special technical and financial assistance for the economic development of poorer regions was given to Bosnia-Hercegovina, Montenegro, Macedonia, and southern Serbia. However, the assistance given to Kosovo until the late 1950's was minimal, despite the fact that Kosovo was the poorest region in Yugoslavia. Since the early 1960's, however, economic and technical assistance for Kosovo has increased considerably.

One of the major factors in the development of greater rights for the Albanian minority was the removal, in the summer of 1966, of Aleksandar Ranković as Vice-President of Yugoslavia and heir apparent to Tito. Ranković lost his party and government positions because he and his Serb-Montenegrin entourage in the bureaucracy of the federal government and party and of the Serbian Republic were opposed to the economic and political-social reforms which the party had attempted to implement for some years. Although the immediate excuse for Ranković's removal was the finding of hidden microphones in Tito's homes and office, the real reasons were his opposition to economic reform and serious irregularities in the Yugoslav secret police for which he was responsible. During the purges of Ranković's entourage, which followed his "resignation," numerous instances were revealed of Serbian officials' violating the rights of the Albanian and Hungarian minorities.[5] However, the social and political changes in Yugoslavia since 1966 have largely eliminated the differences between the Albanians and the other Yugoslav minorities.

Despite the extensive cultural, educational, and administrative rights granted the Albanians and Hungarians, neither minority has received full territorial autonomy as a constituent Yugoslav republic. Both, at least according to criteria of size and compactness, would seem to be qualified for republic status. The reason they have been denied this privilege appears to be largely political. Of the Hungarians in Yugoslavia, 87 percent live in the Vojvodina. They make up only one quarter of the total population of that region, but they do form a fairly compact mass. The Serbs, who make up about half the population of the Vojvodina, are concentrated in the southern portion, while the Hungarian poplulation is concentrated in the north and north-central areas near the Hungarian border. A republic with a Hungarian majority and a populalation equal to Montenegro could be formed if the southern, predominantly Serbian, areas were not included. There could be some question about the economic and geographic rationality of such a move, however.

Creating a republic in the Kosovo Region is better justified from the standpoint of population than creating one in the Vojvodina. The population of Kosovo, according to the 1971 census, is almost three-quarters Albanian. Of the twenty-eight *opština* in Kosovo at the time of the 1961 census, twenty-three had an absolute majority

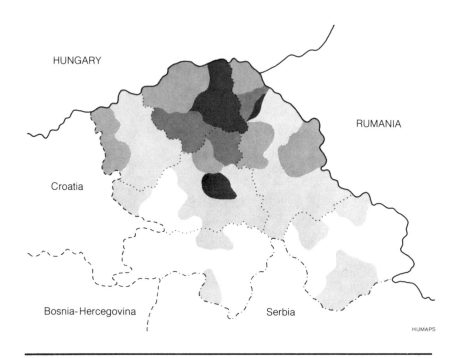

HUNGARY

RUMANIA

Croatia

Bosnia-Hercegovina

Serbia

HUMAPS

Vojvodina (*percent Hungarian*)

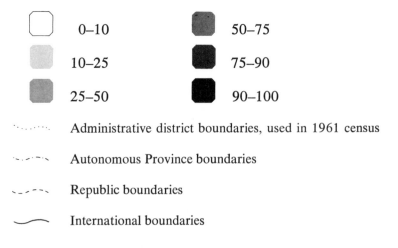

	0–10		50–75
	10–25		75–90
	25–50		90–100

Administrative district boundaries, used in 1961 census

Autonomous Province boundaries

Republic boundaries

International boundaries

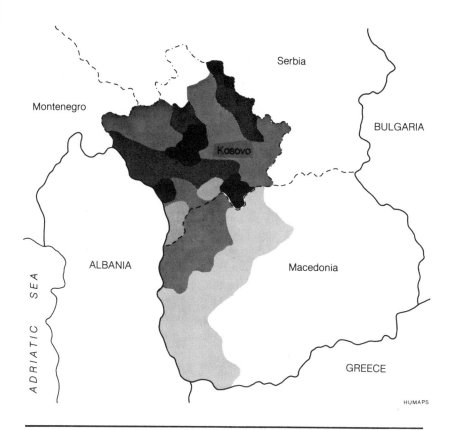

Kosovo and Macedonia (*percent Albanian*)

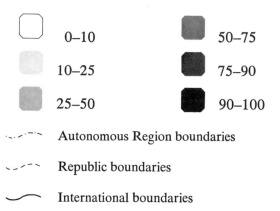

☐	0–10	▨	50–75
▨	10–25	▨	75–90
▨	25–50	■	90–100

⌐·-¯   Autonomous Region boundaries

⌐--¯   Republic boundaries

⌐¯   International boundaries

of Albanians. Of the five remaining districts, two had just under 50 percent Albanians, one was a third, and the remaining two about 5 percent Albanian. These last *opština* are both on the Serbian border and have Serbian majorities. The areas of the Republic of Macedonia adjacent to Kosovo are also heavily populated with Albanians, and almost 200,000 Albanians live in Macedonia itself, where they made up 13 percent of the population in 1961. The Tetovo region is 55 percent Albanian; in the Ohrid area, Albanians make up 22 percent, and in the Skopje region 13 percent of the population. The Albanian areas of the Macedonian Republic were not included in the Kosovo Autonomous Region after World War II because of geography and politics. The Šar Mountains form a physical barrier between the two areas that makes communication between the Kosmet and the Tetovo regions difficult. But, perhaps more important, the Albanian-inhabited areas were historically part of Macedonia. In order to go as far as possible in accommodating Macedonian nationalism, the Yugoslav communists were quite willing to divide the Albanian minority in the Tetovo area from those in Kosovo in order to appeal to the Macedonian population. In addition, separating the Albanian population was certainly desirable from the Yugoslav point of view since it would make it easier to control this minority, particularly in light of the Albanian uprising in 1944–1945. The boundary of the Macedonian Republic established in 1945 followed that advocated by Macedonian revolutionaries in the interwar period.[6] Even without those parts of Macedonia inhabited by Albanians, however, an Albanian republic could be created that would be larger in population and almost as large in territory as the Montenegrin Republic.

The creation of republics inhabited chiefly by Hungarians in the Vojvodina and by Albanians in Kosovo would have been undesirable from the Yugoslav communist point of view in 1945 for two reasons. First, the Hungarian and Albanian minorities are most concentrated along the borders of the neighboring states which lay ethnic claims to the areas they inhabit. The fact that republics are theoretically entitled to the right of self-determination and secession* and the somewhat greater autonomy given to republics might

* The Yugoslavia constitution of 1946 declares that the peoples of Yugoslavia "on the basis of the right of self-determination, including the right of secession, have expressed their will to live together in a federative state." (*Con-*

encourage the Hungarians and Albanians to attempt to join their ethnic homelands. Although Belgrade could prevent the Hungarians or Albanians from seceding, the safest policy was to avoid encouraging any kind of separatist sentiment by keeping the two areas under the control of the Serbian Republic.

A second reason for not granting Kosovo and the Vojvodina republican status was Serbian nationalism. The Hungarian and Albanian areas had been recently acquired by Serbia. Kosovo was part of Turkey prior to the First Balkan War (1912–1913), but during that conflict Serbian armies conquered large parts of northern Albania and Kosovo. The great powers insisted on the creation of an independent Albania in order to block Serbia from reaching the Adriatic, and required that Serbia give up a large part of Albanian-inhabited territory. However, the Serbs were permitted to retain Kosovo. The Vojvodina, which was part of Austria-Hungary after it was retaken from the Turks in the seventeenth century, had a mixed population with many Serbs, a large number of Hungarians, and Rumanians, Slovaks, Ruthenians (Ukrainians), and others. Novi Sad, the largest city in the territory, became a leading Serbian cultural center in the last half of the nineteenth century. After the disintegration of the Austro-Hungarian Empire at the end of World War I, Serbian troops occupied the Vojvodina and southern Hungary, claiming the area because of its Serbian population.[7] Since Serbian troops had conquered both Kosovo and the Vojvodina before Yugoslavia came into existence, Serbia's claims to the areas were closely linked with Serbian nationalism. After 1945 the Yugoslav communists were particularly anxious not to antagonize the Serbian population. As the largest single ethnic group in prewar Yugoslavia, Serbs had dominated the kingdom. The creation of federal republics in Macedonia (which Serbia acquired in the First and Second Balkan Wars) and in Bosnia-Hercegovina (which Serbia occupied and annexed at the end of

---

stitution of the Federal People's Republic of Yugoslavia [Washington, D.C.: Embassy of the Federal People's Republic of Yugoslavia, 1946], Article I.) The constitution and the principle of self-determination for union republics are based on the Soviet constitution of 1936. As in the USSR, however, no real exercise of that right would be willingly permitted. The 1953 constitutional law did not refer to self-determination or secession; however, the 1963 constitution again included these terms, but only in the preliminary statement of principles, not in the actual text of the document.

World War I) no doubt led many Serbs to conclude they were losing out in the new Yugoslavia. To avoid intensifying that feeling, Kosovo and the Vojvodina were not detached from Serbia. Since Tito's partisans lacked popular support among the ethnic Serbs of Serbia during the war,[8] the Yugoslav communists were anxious not to weaken their appeal in Serbia by further offending Serbian nationalism.

In a compromise move, the Albanian and Hungarian regions were given the status of autonomous areas within the Serbian Republic. The status of the two areas under the terms of successive Yugoslav constitutions, however, became a declining concern of the Yugoslav central government before 1966. The 1946 federal constitution specified that Yugoslavia was composed of six republics and that the Serbian Republic included "the Autonomous Province of Vojvodina and the Autonomous Kosovo-Metohija Region." The distinction between "autonomous region" and "autonomous province" was not significant, but indicated a slightly higher status for the Vojvodina. The province was entitled to twenty delegates in the Chamber of Nationalities of the Federal Assembly, the autonomous region to only fifteen. The legislative branch of the autonomous province's government was called the People's Assembly of the province, while the autonomous region had a Regional People's Committee. These differences were probably a reflection of the fact that the Vojvodina, which had been part of Austria-Hungary, was further advanced educationally, culturally, economically, and politically than Kosovo, which was the least developed area in all of Yugoslavia.

The key sentence in the constitution of 1946 was in Article 103: "The rights and scope of the autonomy of autonomous provinces and autonomous regions are determined by the constitution of the [Serbian] Republic."[9] The Yugoslav federal system as it operated after 1946 permitted the federal republics only a very limited degree of self-government,[10] but the "autonomous" regions were allowed even less autonomy. The Serbian constitution of 1947 and the statutes of the autonomous areas adopted in 1948 kept them firmly under Belgrade's tutelage. Jovan Djordjević, a leading Yugoslav authority on the federal system, admitted that in the constitution of Serbia and the statutes "some points were not elaborated clearly enough, namely, the concept of autonomy and the relationship between the federation, the republic, and the autonomous units."[11]

The 1953 constitutional law, which was drawn up to reflect the reforms introduced in Yugoslavia after 1949, specified that local units of government were to be given a greater voice in their affairs. However, "neither the constitutional law of Yugoslavia [1953], the constitutional law of the [Serbian] Republic, nor the statutes [of the autonomous units] altered the substance and the status of the Autonomous Province or the Autonomous Region. They did not even remove certain differences which from the beginning existed among them with regard to their names and to some organizational features."[12]

The Yugoslav constitution of 1963 went even further in downgrading the status of the autonomous provinces, although it did eliminate the formal inequality between the Vojvodina Province and the Kosovo Region by calling both areas autonomous provinces. The new constitution specified:

A republic may found autonomous provinces in accordance with the constitution in areas with distinctive national characteristics or in areas with other distinguishing features, on the basis of the express will of the population of these areas.[13]

The only limitation on republics is that "the foundation or dissolution of an autonomous province shall take effect when this is sanctioned by the constitution of Yugoslavia"—that is, under a constitutional amendment or constitutional law approving the republic's action. Although Professor Djordjević maintains that this did not change the position or the rights of the autonomous units, he does say, "Unlike the 1953 constitutional law the present [1963] constitution is no longer the legal document which created the autonomous units."[14] The fact that this change in the constitution was at least seen as a downgrading of the autonomous units is evidenced by the subsequent demands of Kosovo and the Vojvodina that their autonomous position be specifically established in the federal constitution. One Albanian leader in Kosovo saw a regressive trend to restrict the autonomy of the autonomous provinces which culminated in the 1963 federal constitution, which, he said, "eliminated the provinces' state judiciary, autonomy, and sovereignty."[15]

The declining status of the autonomous regions in the Yugoslav federal constitutions was not necessarily an indication of declining rights of self-government. From the very beginning the autonomous areas were under Serbian domination, and were given little, if any, real autonomy. A reversal of this situation came about only after the removal of Aleksandar Ranković. Before that, a strong Serbian element in the federal government and party had a disproportionate amount of influence in Yugoslavia. After it, there was a resurgence of the non-Serb nationalities. In addition to the Croats, Slovenes, and Macedonians, the minorities also began to assert their rights. Part of this renaissance included a demand for greater autonomy for Kosovo and the Vojvodina. Among the Albanian minority there developed a movement to establish a separate republic for Kosovo. Among the Hungarians of the Vojvodina, however, the desire for a separate republic was not as strong. There are a number of reasons for this difference of attitude toward republic status in the two areas.

First, Kosovo is more solidly non-Serb than is the Vojvodina. The number of Albanians in Kosovo approaches one million, while the number of Hungarians in the Vojvodina is only about half that number. In Kosovo, according to the 1961 census, twenty-three of twenty-eight *opština* had an Albanian majority, and Albanians made up 67 percent of the autonomous province's population. Serbs made up only 23.6 percent. By contrast, in Vojvodina the Hungarians were in the majority in only ten of fifty-seven *opština,* and made up only 23.6 percent of the total provincial population; 54.9 percent of the area's population was Serbian, and well over half of the *opština* had Serb majorities. Republic status for the Vojvodina, therefore, would hardly increase the Hungarian minority's voice in the affairs of the province.

Also, while the proportion of Hungarians in the Vojvodina is declining, the proportion of Albanians in Kosovo is growing, due to migration of Serbs and Montenegrins from Kosovo. The 1971 census revealed that, during the ten-year period since the last census, the Albanian population of Kosovo had increased by 42 percent. In 1971 Albanians made up 73.8 percent of the province's population, while in 1961 they were only 67.1 percent. At the same time the number of Serbs in Kosovo increased by only 0.67 percent, but their proportion in the region declined from 23.6 percent of the total population in 1961 to 18.4 percent in 1971. The Montenegrin population declined by 16 percent, and the proportion of Montenegrins in the province's population went from 3.9 to 2.5 percent.[16] To a great extent this migration is due to economic factors. Per capita income in Kosovo is the lowest in all of Yugoslavia. For Serbs and Montenegrins there are no cultural or linguistic barriers to discourage them from migrating to Belgrade or the more prosperous areas of Serbia. Albanians, on the other hand, face linguistic and cultural difficulties in other parts of Yugoslavia, as well as a certain amount of discrimination against them.

Economic motivations, while a major factor in the Serb-Montenegrin migration from Kosovo, are not the only explanation, however. There is also some concern on the part of the Serbs that the Albanians are taking over the province and will discriminate against them. The president of the Kosovo Provincial Committee of the League of Communists expressed concern over the problem of migration and called upon the Albanians in Kosovo to work "to enable the Serbs in Kosovo to feel at home, and not to have the impression that they now represent a minority surrounded by Albanians."[17] But the growing proportion of Albanians is likely to bolster Albanian nationalism and strengthen the demand for the creation of a Kosovo republic. The latest census results have already given rise to open concern among the Serbs in Kosovo and in Serbia, and the increase in the number of Albanians is likely to continue as a source of friction between Albanians and Serbs.[18]

Another reason the Hungarian minority has been less insistent upon republic status than the Albanians is that the Hungarians are better developed educationally, culturally, politically, and economically than the Albanians. Hence, Hungarians have been better able to adjust to changing social conditions in Yugoslavia, while the Albanians, who are still largely traditional in outlook, have been less able to do so. These social changes are linked in the minds of many Albanians to nationality—the economic changes are Serb-inspired to undermine the Albanian way of life. The greater assimilation rate of the Hungarians attests to their greater ability to adjust to the Yugoslav system. The Hungarian population in Yugoslavia increased from 496,492 in the 1948 census to only 504,398 in 1961, and declined from 3.2 percent of the total population in 1948 to 2.2 percent in 1961. Over the same period the Hungarian population in the Vojvodina declined from 25.8 percent to 23.9 percent.* The Albanians, as we have seen, have significantly in-

* Although the small increase in the Hungarian population since World War II can be partially explained by the movement of Hungarians from Yugoslavia

creased in both numbers and in proportion to the total population.

The Albanians in Yugoslavia constitute a much larger proportion of the total number of Albanians in the world, and this may also be an explanation for their greater concern to be accorded republic status. While the Hungarians in Yugoslavia equal only 4.4 percent of the population of Hungary, the Albanians in Yugoslavia represent 38 percent of the population of Albania.[19] Since the Albanians in Yugoslavia form such a large proportion of the world's Albanian population, they are a much more crucial element in Albanian culture and consciousness. In fact, after the disturbances that upset Kosovo in the fall of 1968, the fear was expressed that the Albanians in Yugoslavia were attempting to become the new center of the Albanian nation. They were accused of advancing theories that "the Yugoslav self-management society becomes a sort of 'Piedmont' of the Albanian population, no matter where the population may be."[20] For the Yugoslav Hungarians, their culture is obviously centered in Hungary proper, and the Vojvodina Hungarians are only a small fragment of a much larger nation.

Once Ranković and his followers had been removed from leading positions in the party and government, the movement to give the autonomous areas greater rights began in earnest. It started quietly, but quickly gained momentum. In June 1967, less than a year after the beginning of the Ranković affair, a symposium was held in Novi Sad on the status of the Vojvodina and Kosovo-Metohija autonomous provinces, and numerous proposals for reform were made.[21] That same month an Albanian-language journal published in Priština, the capital city of the Kosovo province, advocated republican status for that area.[22] By early 1968 commissions in both autonomous provinces were considering specific proposals to amend the Yugoslav federal and the Serbian republican constitutions, as well as the statutes of the autonomous provinces, in order to give them greater self-governing powers.

The League of Communists was willing to permit extensive constitutional revision in order to grant the autonomous provinces almost the same powers as those which the republics enjoyed; however,

---

to Hungary, the number who have left is small, and most of them did so before the 1948 census. The number is still too small to account for the discrepancy between the actual and expected census figures, calculated on the basis of birth and death rates.

it was not willing to permit these provinces to become separate republics. During the discussions in the Vojvodina this apparently caused no difficulty, but in Kosovo there was opposition to this limitation even among responsible leaders. The Kosovo Provincial Prosecutor, Rezak Šalja, called "categorically and unambiguously for a separate republic for the Albanians in Yugoslavia and constitutional legislation permitting the right of self-determination up to secession."[23] Despite the much greater interest in republic status for Kosovo, the final proposals for constitutional reform from the Vojvodina and Kosovo were almost identical.[24]

Although the changes enhanced the powers of the autonomous provinces, there was still discontent in Kosovo over the issue of republic status, and in late October Tito met with the Kosovo provincial leadership. While he fully supported the proposals for constitutional reform that had been approved, he was equally adamant in opposing the establishment of a republic for the Albanians. The very fact that he had to comment on the question indicates the persistence of the idea among Albanian leaders. According to one of the participants in the meeting, Tito said:

> The Autonomous Province must enjoy all the rights provided by the system of self-government. These rights must be complete, and they must be assured through constitutional changes. Republican status alone will not solve all the problems. If the rights under autonomous status are properly expanded, for which maximum efforts must be made, then this status too can solve all the social, economic, and cultural problems of the territory in question.[25]

The consistent opposition of the Yugoslav League of Communists to granting full republic status to the autonomous provinces was due to Serbian opposition to complete autonomy for these territories. Since the Brioni Central Committee session had removed Ranković from his leadership positions, Yugoslavia had undergone a renaissance among non-Serb nationalities, and this had developed many anti-Serb aspects. At the fourteenth plenum of the Serbian League of Communists in May 1968 the April proposals of the Kosovo leadership for constitutional reform came under harsh attack by two Serbian Central Committee members. The harshest and longest of these was made by Dobrica Ćosić, who denounced the "irredentist and separatist aspirations among certain strata of

139

the Šqiptar [Albanian] national minority" and declared that the proposals for constitutional change "have seriously alarmed the socialist public of the country." After criticizing the Albanian proposals Ćosić "referred to the situation in the Vojvodina, noting that in the description of the political situation in the Vojvodina there was no mention of Hungarian nationalism and separatism." The two speeches opposing the assertion of Albanian rights ran counter to the enunciated policy of the League of Communists and provoked a vigorous discussion in the Serbian plenum.[26] Although the Central Committee in the end endorsed the leadership's policy, the fact that such a public outburst occurred indicates the depth of Serbian feeling on the issue.

Despite the numerous improvements in Kosovo since the removal of Ranković, or perhaps precisely because the improvements had been made at last, violent demonstrations broke out in Priština and several other cities in Kosovo during the 1968 celebrations of November 28 (the day on which the Albanian Republic was proclaimed in 1912) and November 29 (the Yugoslav national holiday). A proclamation drawn up in Priština demanded that Kosovo be made a full republic and be given its own constitution and the right of self-determination.[27] A similar violent demonstration broke out on December 23, 1968, in Tetovo, in the Macedonian Republic. Among the demands of the Tetovo demonstrators was the annexation of Albanian areas of Macedonia to Kosovo to form an Albanian national republic in Yugoslavia.[28]

Serbian opponents of greater Albanian self-government used the demonstrations as evidence of the unpreparedness of the Albanian minority for greater autonomy, but the amendments to the constitution were approved on schedule in December 1968. The autonomous provinces became the Socialist Autonomous Province of Vojvodina and the Socialist Autonomous Province of Kosovo. (Metohija was dropped from the name when "Socialist" was added.) The federal constitution specified greater rights for the autonomous provinces and restricted the Serbian Republic's ability to abolish the provinces or change their boundaries without their consent. Provincial delegations to the Chamber of Nationalities were henceforth to be chosen by the provincial assembly rather than by the Serbian Assembly. Each province was entitled to a "constitution" as its supreme law instead of a "statute," an independent court system, and a people's assembly with the right to pass "laws." The provinces were given much greater control over allocation of their own financial resources. Both provinces adopted new constitutions taking advantage of the new rights permitted them.[29]

Although the amendments to the federal and Serbian constitutions and the writing of provincial constitutions gave the autonomous provinces almost the same rights as those to which republics are entitled, the Yugoslav League of Communists made it quite clear that republic status was out of the question. At the 12th session of the LCY Central Committee in February 1969, the party declared:

> For principled reasons the League of Communists resolutely opposes every tendency to present, in one or another way, either openly or surreptitiously, the problem of equality of nationalities in our community as a problem of separate state constitutions, or the creation of separate republics.
>
> Such an attitude on the part of the LCY in no way restricts the real rights of nationalities . . . nor does it affect the equal status of every people and nationality in our country. It represents the only possible way to resolve in a democratic manner the problem of internationality relations in the areas in which our peoples have been living together for centuries, i.e., in the communities of mixed nationalities. Precisely for this reason, the tendencies we are speaking about [demands for republic status] necessarily lead to raising the question of territorial changes, and by this very fact not only to an artificial sharpening of relations among the peoples and nationalities in respect to the question of state boundaries, but also to the complication of general international relations, and to a continuing danger of conflict.[30]

The increased rights granted to the autonomous provinces and the statement of the League of Communists temporarily pushed the question of republic status for Kosovo into the background. Although the issue was occasionally revived, it remained dormant until the fall of 1970, when Tito proposed a series of constitutional amendments designed to give the republics greater powers and to encourage decentralization of the Yugoslav government system. The discussion of these new proposals led to serious reconsideration of the status of the autonomous provinces. As before, the

Vojvodina, with its large number of Serbs, reaffirmed its unity with Serbia. Although the leaders in the Vojvodina approved the granting of greater autonomy to the republics, the autonomous provinces, and local units of government, they emphatically reiterated that "the socialist autonomous provinces are part of the Socialist Republic of Serbia and express their sovereignty and statehood through it. This very fact makes it impossible to conceive of constitutional and legal equalization of the republic and the provinces."[31] The authorities in the Serbian Republic supported this view that the "socialist autonomous provinces are component and inseparable parts of the Republic of Serbia" and that "the sovereignty and statehood of these parts of our republic can be put into effect only through the sovereignty and statehood of our republic as a whole."[32] As before, the Albanian leaders in Kosovo, encouraged by a continuing crescendo of Albanian nationalism, called for greater autonomy for the provinces, which, the Albanians argued, should "be more or less fully independent from Serbia" and should "become practically new republics, retaining only their present names."[33]

The constitutional amendments as approved on June 30, 1971, further served to strengthen the autonomy of the provinces. The amendments specified the rights to be given to the federal government and in all but a few relatively minor instances treated the autonomous provinces in the same manner as they did the republics. There were implicit indications in the documents that the provinces were not fully equal to the republics, but the differences between the two are minor.[34] Basic changes in the constitutions of the autonomous provinces, which were drawn up after the federal constitutional amendments were approved, have further expanded the rights of the provinces. Albanian leaders in Kosovo consider the province a constituent federal unit on exactly the same level as the republics.[35] Although leaders in the Vojvodina have not emphasized their de facto republican status, they are exercising their new sovereign rights fully. (In keeping with the policy of granting equal rights to the Hungarians, the Serbian-dominated provincial assembly of the Vojvodina elected a Hungarian as the head of the provincial government administration in 1971.) The greatly expanded autonomy Kosovo has gained since 1966 is a source of satisfaction to the Albanian population, but the element of prestige involved in being recognized, de jure as well as de facto, as a fully equal republic will probably encourage the Kosovo leaders to continue to struggle for full republican status.

The extent to which the question of republic status for Hungarian and Albanian minorities has affected the relations of Yugoslavia with Hungary and Albania is difficult to determine. The problem has not been of major significance in Yugoslav-Hungarian relations. Hungary, which has adhered to the Soviet position in questions of foreign policy, is far more strongly influenced by Moscow's attitude toward Yugoslavia than by Belgrade's treatment of its Hungarian minority. On the other hand, Budapest is concerned about the rights granted to the Hungarian minorities. The Yugoslav Hungarians are the smallest of the three major groups of the Hungarian diaspora, however, and they enjoy far more extensive rights than do the Magyars in Rumania or Czechoslovakia, and in recent years Hungary has in general been pleased with the cultural rights enjoyed by the minority in Yugoslavia. There are opportunities for exchanges of writers between the minority and Hungary, and Yugoslav-Hungarian government agreements have facilitated the flow of Hungarian-language materials between the two countries. The Hungarian government has imposed certain restrictions on Hungarian-language materials from Yugoslavia which are considered politically unacceptable, but the Yugoslav authorities have not restricted material coming from Hungary. Yugoslavia's treatment of its Hungarian minority has been a significant element in strengthening Yugoslav-Hungarian relations when other factors have been favorable for good relations. The question of the Yugoslav government's granting republic status to the Vojvodina, in view of the other rights the minority enjoys, has not been a factor in Yugoslav-Hungarian relations.

In the case of relations with Albania, however, the question of Kosovo has been much more significant. As noted above, the Yugoslav Albanians represent over one-third of the population of Albania. In addition, Albanian relations with Yugoslavia have been far less influenced by external factors and far more by local national concerns than has been the case with Hungary. When relations between Yugoslavia and the Soviet bloc improved after the death of Stalin in 1953, Albania was the last of Yugoslavia's neighboring states to stop advancing ethnic claims to Yugoslav territory. Again, after the Hungarian Revolution Albania began voicing ethnic concern and denouncing Belgrade some time before the open Soviet-Yugoslav break came in early 1958. Once relations began to deteriorate, it was obvious that the question of the Albanian minority in Yugoslavia was a matter of serious concern to the Albanian leadership. Mehmet Shehu, head of the Albanian government, made this clear in a statement in the fall of 1958:

> Had we not raised our voice in defense of our Albanian brothers in Kosovo, Montenegro, and Macedonia, we would have betrayed Marxism-Leninism. We are not chauvinists. We are not at present asking that Kosovo join with Albania. But the same mother that gave birth to us gave birth to the Albanians in Kosovo, Montenegro, and Macedonia. . . . We demand and we shall continue to demand that the Yugoslav government grant the Albanians of Kosovo, Montenegro, and Macedonia all the rights pertaining to them as a national minority.[36]

The concern expressed by the Tirana leadership for the Albanians in Yugoslavia probably represents a sincere interest in the treatment of their ethnic brothers. However, since the Albanian leaders are still somewhat paranoic about the Yugoslav attempt to annex Albania just after World War II, propaganda about the mistreatment of the Albanians in Kosovo is a useful way to maintain anti-Yugoslav sentiment at home and to counter any future attempts at Yugoslav imperialism.

Albania's fear that to further Soviet-Yugoslav rapprochement Moscow might approve annexation of Albania by Yugoslavia was an important factor in Albania's break with the Soviet Union in 1960–1961. Yugoslavia's treatment of its Albanian minority was one of the themes used in anti-Yugoslav propaganda by Tirana after its break with the Soviet bloc. Belgrade responded with an anti-Albanian line in foreign policy during this period, although some gestures were made toward improving relations. After the removal of Ranković, however, the Albanian minority in Yugoslavia began to call for improved relations with Albania.[37] The response from Albania, while indicating a willingness to provide the minority with Albanian-language materials on Albanian culture and other topics, was highly critical of Yugoslavia and its treatment of the minority.[38]

The fear of Soviet aggression in the Balkans provoked by the invasion of Czechoslovakia softened Albania's attitude toward Yugoslavia, but it continued to attack Yugoslavia's policy toward the minority. Just a few months after the Czechoslovak invasion and on the eve of the disturbances in Kosovo, the chief Albanian newspaper criticized Belgrade for failing to give the Albanians republican status. A parallel was drawn between Macedonia, with "a population of 1,800,000, of whom 300,000 are Albanians," and Kosovo. Macedonia was granted republican status, but the Albanians in Kosovo, "who are in the same position as the Macedonians," have been denied this right.[39]

Despite occasional polemics, however, Albanian-Yugoslav relations have gradually improved since 1968. A long-term trade agreement calling for a significant increase in trade between the two countries was announced in the spring of 1971, and in February of the same year the two countries agreed to raise their legations to the embassy level and both appointed ambassadors—the first since 1958. One significant feature in improving Albanian-Yugoslav relations has been the cultural exchanges between the two countries, which have focused primarily on Kosovo. Delegations of writers, as well as folk song and dance groups, have come to Kosovo from Albanian-language schools and universities. The real progress being made in Yugoslavia toward granting equal rights to the Albanians and the greatly expanded autonomy now enjoyed by Kosovo have not been a major cause of improved relations between the two countries, but at least the problem of the Albanians in Yugoslavia is becoming less of an impediment to improved relations.

Chapter 8

Territorial Autonomy and Cultural Rights: Rumania

In the first years after the Second World War, Rumania was probably the most generous of the East European states in the treatment of national minorities. Under Stalinist rule no part of the population was entitled to extensive rights, but in Rumania the minorities were generally accorded the same privileges which the Rumanian population received, and in addition they were granted relatively liberal linguistic and cultural rights. Although there were differences in the way in which the Hungarian, German, and Jewish minorities were treated from time to time, initially, with the exception of the German minority in the immediate postwar period, they were better treated under the communist than under previous Rumanian nationalist regimes.

Minority policy in Rumania was not so much a function of enlightened leadership as it was of Soviet tactical considerations. As a condition for the return of Transylvania, Stalin insisted that the Rumanian government must guarantee full rights to the minority populations. By doing so he hoped to mitigate Hungarian anger over the loss of northern Transylvania and to minimize the reaction against the Soviet Union. Stalin decided to follow a minority strategy in seizing and holding power in Rumania. In Czechoslovakia, Bulgaria, and to some extent in Poland, *Staatsvolk* nationalism and historic pro-Russian or pan-Slav sentiment had been utilized to increase Russian influence, but in Rumania such strategy would have brought little success. Traditional anti-Russian feeling had been reinforced by the fact that the Soviet Union had taken Bessarabia and northern Bukovina from Rumania in 1940, and Bulgaria had retained southern Dobruja with Soviet assistance. Also, because the Rumanian Communist Party was composed of sizable non-Rumanian elements, it was hardly capable of appealing to Rumanian national sentiment. Therefore, the Soviet Union pursued a policy in Rumania that gave preference to non-Rumanian ethnic elements. Since non-Rumanian leaders would be less able to develop support among ethnic Rumanians, they would be more dependent on Soviet power, and Rumanian nationalism, with its anti-Soviet overtones, would have less opportunity to develop. This strategy involved giving a disproportionate number of leading positions to non-Rumanians* and granting relatively generous privileges to the minorities.

This generally favorable treatment of the minorities, however, was not unanimously approved by either the Rumanian leadership or the party membership. Lucrețiu Pătrășcanu, one of the communist leaders and Minister of Justice from 1944 to 1948, was apparently strongly anti-Hungarian. When he was purged in 1948, a resolution of the Rumanian Central Committee noted that "the struggle against the anti-Marxist national-chauvinism of Pătrășcanu has helped to establish fraternal relations between the Rumanian people and the other nationalities living on the same territory."[1]

---

* The Rumanian party has not published a biographical dictionary of its postwar leaders, and therefore it is somewhat difficult to determine the nationality of early party and government members. However, the nationality of a number of prominent postwar non-Rumanian communists is known. Vasile Luca, Alexandru Moghioroș, Leontin Sălăjan, and probably Iosif Rangheț were Hungarian; Ana Pauker and Gheorghe Stoica were Jewish; Emil Bodnăraş's father was Ukrainian, and his mother was German. Many other less prominent persons were also non-Rumanian, and many had spent long periods in the Soviet Union, which weakened their ties with Rumania. For a more detailed consideration of this problem, see D. A. Tomasic, "The Rumanian Communist Leadership," *Slavic Review,* 20:3 (October 1961), particularly pp. 477–480, 485–487.

Pătrășcanu's nationalism was echoed by other ethnic Rumanians in the party who were anxious to improve communism's mass appeal.

The nationality policy followed in Rumania was neither consistently formulated nor consistently applied. In the immediate postwar years the German minority was under a cloud of suspicion because some of its members had supported the Third Reich, and measures directed at those who collaborated with Germany were sometimes applied against the minority as a group. However, Rumania did not attempt to expel its *Volksdeutsche,* and as a result the largest German minority in Eastern Europe today is in Rumania. Although the worst of the laws directed against this minority were revoked after the communists seized power in 1948, the question of compensation for property confiscated from ethnic Germans was not completely resolved until 1956.

The restoration of rights to the Jewish population, who had lost most of their civil rights and property under the regime of Marshal Ion Antonescu, was an uneven process. They were initially well treated, but, shortly after the communists consolidated their power, Stalin launched an anti-Zionist campaign which soon turned into overt anti-Semitism. In December 1948 the Rumanian party Politburo issued a resolution on the national question which praised the Marxist-Leninist-Stalinist nationality policy but criticized nationalism and its negative manifestations among the minorities. The harshest criticism was leveled at Zionism and "Jewish bourgeois nationalism." Thus the situation of the German minority gradually improved while the Jewish population fell under increasingly rigid restrictions.[2]

Between the end of the war and the Hungarian revolt of 1956, the Hungarian minority in Rumania fared consistently better than other minorities. Despite some anti-Hungarianism among the party leadership, Hungarians were essentially accorded the same rights as those enjoyed by other Rumanian citizens. Hungarian-language schools, theaters, and folklore groups, as well as newspapers, periodicals, and books, were available. Hungarians were even permitted to have their own political association—the Hungarian National Democratic Union (MADOSZ), later the Hungarian People's Union (UPM)—which was a member of the National Front and represented their special interests.

The creation of the Hungarian Autonomous Region was one of

the most symbolic indications that the Hungarian minority was being given special recognition by the Rumanian government. However, despite the fact that communist-dominated governments had ruled Rumania since March 1945 and a new, communist-inspired constitution had been adopted in 1948, the Hungarian Autonomous Region was not established until 1952. The first communist administrative divisions were created after Rumania was proclaimed a republic and a new constitution adopted (in April 1948), which specified that Rumania would be divided into regions, counties, districts, and communes.[3] The guiding logic behind the administrative divisions was to rationalize the local government units along economic and geographic lines, and apparently no ethnic criteria were followed in establishing the regions. The area with the greatest concentration of Hungarians (which in 1952 became the Hungarian Autonomous Region) was divided between two of these regions. The regions along the Hungarian frontier all included territory stretching away from the border, so that none of them was predominantly Hungarian. However, there was economic, geographical, and historical justification for the administrative boundaries to follow these lines, and there is no evidence to indicate that they were set up to reduce the proportion of Hungarians in any one district.

MADOSZ, which had considerable influence among the Hungarians in Transylvania, had been pressing for the establishment of some kind of autonomous status for the Hungarian minority. Although Rumania had agreed to protect the Hungarians' rights, no special territorial provisions had been made for the minority as a whole. Rather unexpectedly, the draft of the 1952 constitution, which was published on July 18, 1952, included provisions for the creation of the Hungarian Autonomous Region, although no mention of such a region had been made previously. Shortly before the new constitution appeared Vasile Luca, a party leader and an ethnic Hungarian, was purged. This apparently caused concern among the minority in Transylvania, so the autonomous region may have been included in the new constitution to quiet Hungarian fears. On the other hand, the way in which the provisions for the creation of the region were made public also indicates that word may have come from Moscow insisting upon the minority provisions. It is possible that Stalin acted at the suggestion of the communist leaders in Hungary, since Budapest had always showed particular interest in the idea of an autonomous region.

The new constitution provided that the autonomous region should be created in "the territory occupied by the compact Hungarian Szekler population," and listed the specific districts to be included in it.[4] The territory in question involved only a small part of Transylvania, but did include the most heavily concentrated group of Hungarians. In the 1956 census the region had a population of 731,387, of whom 565,510, or 77 percent, were Hungarian. However, this was only about one-third of the Hungarian population in Rumania. Sizable Hungarian settlements contiguous to the region were to be found in the neighboring regions of Cluj (257,-974 Hungarians) and Stalin, later Brașov (108,751). The reason for not including these Hungarians in the region was that the minority population in neighboring regions was less concentrated. Also, the Rumanian government, making concessions to the Hungarian population (in all probability at Moscow's insistence), was anxious to keep the Hungarian region as small as possible. In addition there were economic considerations that would justify limiting the area.[5] It is significant that, in establishing a Hungarian national region, the Rumanians did so in eastern Transylvania—the area farthest from the border shared with Hungary and completely surrounded by areas containing a preponderance of Rumanians. If ethnic composition had been the principal criterion, another autonomous region for Hungarians could perhaps have been set up along the Hungarian border. However, the Hungarians are most heavily concentrated in a north-south line along this border, while the river valleys and transportation lines run east-west. The hinterlands of the cities along the Rumanian-Hungarian border tend to follow the geographic-transportation pattern, generally running east-west and including ethnically diverse populations.

The constitution specified that the Hungarian Autonomous Region would have "an autonomous administration elected by the population of the autonomous region," but in fact the region functioned much the same as other territorial administrative divisions. The constitution of 1952 declared:

The laws of the Rumanian People's Republic, as well as the decisions and directives of the central organs of the state, are binding on the territory of the Autonomous Hungarian Region.

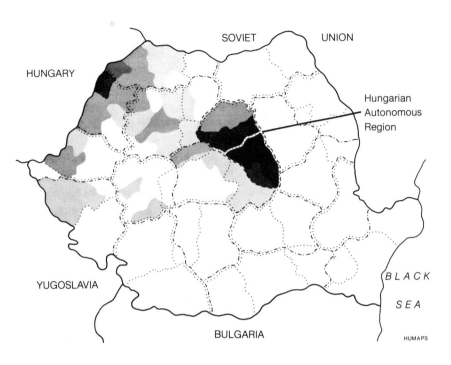

Rumania (*percent Hungarian*)

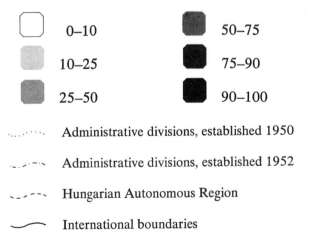

☐	0–10	▧	50–75
▨	10–25	■	75–90
▦	25–50	■	90–100

.... Administrative divisions, established 1950

_. .-~ Administrative divisions, established 1952

_.-~ Hungarian Autonomous Region

⌣ International boundaries

The statute of the Hungarian Autonomous Region is drawn up by the people's council of the autonomous region and submitted for approval to the Grand National Assembly of the Rumanian People's Republic.[6]

Although the secretary of the people's council in the region stated that there was no essential difference between the autonomous region's government and the local administration of other districts in Rumania,[7] the fact that most of the officials were Hungarians was an important concession to the minority. As late as 1958 some 80 percent of the deputies to the people's councils and some 78 percent of the civil servants in the autonomous region were members of the national minorities, principally Hungarians.[8]

The year 1956 marked a turning point in the treatment of the Hungarian minority in Rumania. The impact of the Hungarian revolt upon the Hungarians in Transylvania demonstrated their isolation from Rumanian life and emphasized their close association with developments across the border. This led Gheorghiu-Dej to conclude that the minority must be integrated into Rumania and its links with Hungary weakened. At approximately the same time, the Soviet Union began to follow a different policy in controlling its satellites in Eastern Europe and in maintaining the local client regimes in power. The demise of the Stalinist system of domination brought about important changes in the relationship of the Rumanian party with the population. Although events in Hungary showed that force could always be relied upon should it be required, emphasis was increasingly placed upon more subtle means of maintaining communist power. There was greater emphasis on improving the links between the party and the population and on ending the party's non-Rumanian image. The purging of Ana Pauker and Vasile Luca and their followers in the party in 1952 eliminated a portion of the non-Rumanian ethnic element in the leadership. Although the purge was primarily a move by Gheorghiu-Dej to consolidate his position as the sole leader, it prepared the way for a "Rumanianization" of the party. The party's attempt to appeal to Rumanian nationalism was a gradual development that became evident only in the early 1960's, but it was one that worked to the disadvantage of the minorities.

Shortly after the Hungarian revolt, the Rumanian party began to pursue in earnest its policy of integrating the Hungarian and other minorities. Since intellectuals and students had been most affected by the events in Hungary, it was to these groups that the party first turned its attention. The first anniversary of the revolution was used as an occasion to call a meeting of Hungarian intellectuals to denounce nationalism and chauvinism among the minority and to pledge loyalty to Rumania. The minorities—and the Hungarians in particular—hitherto had schools in which instruction was given in their native languages and which were largely under their own control. As the policy of integration proceeded, however, Hungarian-language instruction was increasingly carried out in special classes attached to Rumanian-language schools. In the 1955–1956 school year there were 1,022 four-year basic schools in which instruction was given solely in Hungarian, but by 1958–1959 there were 915. The number of basic four-year schools offering instruction in both Rumanian and Hungarian increased over the same period from 38 to 124. In the 1955–1956 school year there were 493 seven-year basic schools teaching only in Hungarian, and in 1958–1959 there were 469. Again, the number of similar schools offering dual-language instruction increased from 10 to 77 over the same period. Although the government has not published statistics on minority-language schools since 1959, the trend to merge Hungarian-language with Rumanian-language schools continued. There were unofficial reports that by the mid-1960's separate Hungarian-language schools no longer existed.[9]

The most serious blow to intellectuals among the Hungarian minority was the merger of the Hungarian-language Bolyai University in Cluj, the cultural center of the Hungarians in Transylvania, with the Rumanian-language Babeş University in the same city. Gheorghiu-Dej initiated the merger in a speech to a conference of the Union of Student Associations in Rumania in February 1959 in which he criticized "tendencies toward national isolation and remnants of national hostility." The Rumanian party leader also quoted two lengthy statements in which Lenin strongly opposed separate nationality schools.[10] Gheorghiu-Dej's clear instructions were later echoed even more explicitly in the student association conference. Lajos Takas, rector of Bolyai University, called for a struggle against "manifestations of national isolationism" and questioned the policy of having separate Hungarian- and Rumanian-language universities. The rector of Babeş University declared at the same session that "the line between Rumanians and Hungarians, between Rumanian and Hungarian professors and students, is an anachronism."[11] At a meeting of the teaching staffs of the two universities in July the merger was completed. Published reports on the action and speeches by members of the faculty approving the measure condemned "national chauvinism" and "national isolation" and viewed the merger as a step toward strengthening "the unity between the Rumanian people and the national minorities."[12] There was serious, but of course officially unreported, opposition, however, and some Hungarian intellectuals who refused to accept the merger reportedly committed suicide.[13]

The "Rumanianization" of the unified university was gradually carried out. When the merger was announced, it was stated that instruction would be given in both Hungarian and Rumanian, but it was not specified which courses would be taught in which language. From the original announcement it appeared that the lower-level courses would be taught in both languages, but that advanced courses would be in Rumanian only. It was reported in 1967 that about 30 percent of the classes were being taught in Hungarian, and theoretically any class can be taught in Hungarian if the students so desire. However, there are indications that the study of the Hungarian language is falling far behind the study of Rumanian. Between 1960 and 1965, the number of graduates in Hungarian language and literature rose from 29 to 39, but the number of those majoring in Rumanian language and literature increased from 40 to 218. Although at first there was an attempt to give Hungarians adequate representation in the administration of the merged university, gradually Rumanians have come to play an increasingly dominant administrative role. When the merger was announced the rector was Rumanian but two of the three prorectors were Hungarian. By 1967 the number of prorectorships had been increased to five, but three were Rumanian. Also, seven of the eight deacons of the university and 61 percent of the teaching faculty were Rumanian.[14] At the time Babeş and Bolyai Universities were merged, the Dr. Petru Groza Agricultural Institute in Cluj was "reorganized," and separate language instruction was dropped. The Hungarian medical school in Tîrgu Mureş has also undergone a process of "Rumanianization."

Most of these first steps against national isolation were directed at the intellectuals rather than at the Hungarian minority as a

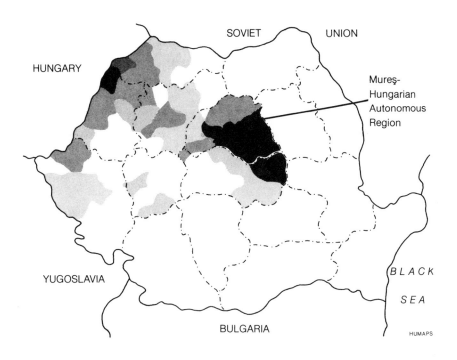

Rumania (*percent Hungarian*)

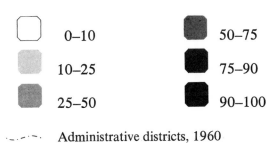

⬜	0–10	◼	50–75
▨	10–25	◼	75–90
▨	25–50	◼	90–100

⋅_⋅_⋅⋅ Administrative districts, 1960

⌣⌣ International boundaries

whole. However, in late 1960, when the boundaries of the Hungarian Autonomous Region were altered, the Rumanian government's policy affected the entire minority. Although there was a strong movement among Rumanian nationalists to eliminate the separate Hungarian region entirely, the territorial changes of December 1960 took two districts from the region but added three new ones. The name was changed from the "Hungarian [or Magyar] Autonomous Region" to the "Mureş-Autonomous Hungarian [or Magyar] Region." Adding the Rumanian word "Mureş" to the name of a Hungarian region was an indication that the Hungarian character of the region was being changed. At the time the regional alterations were made, Article 19 of the Rumanian constitution was amended, and the passage describing the autonomous region as "the territory occupied by the compact Hungarian Szekler population" was deleted.[15]

The changes significantly altered the Hungarian proportion of the population in the Mureş-Autonomous Hungarian Region. The districts of Sfîntu Gheorghe (85.3 percent Hungarian) and Tîrgu Secuiesc (90.2 percent Hungarian) were removed and added to the Braşov Region. The three districts added were Luduş, (22.1 percent Hungarian) and Sărmaş (13.7 percent Hungarian), located in the Cluj Region, and part of the Tîrnăveni district (25.6 percent Hungarian), located in the Braşov Region. The change had the effect of splitting the Hungarian population so that their concentration in any single region was reduced:*

| | RUMANIANS | | | |
| | Before 1960 | | After 1960 | |
Region	Number	Percent	Number	Percent
Hungarian Autonomous Region and Mureş-Autonomous Hungarian Region	146,830	20	266,403	35
Cluj	963,748	77	883,172	76
Braşov	616,220	68	587,628	60

* The sources used in establishing the data were *Recensămîntul Populaţiei din 21 Februarie 1956: Rezultate Generale* (Bucharest: Direcţia Centrală de Statistică, 1959), pp. 558–559; and *Anuarul Statistic al R.P.R., 1961* (Bucharest: Direcţia Centrală de Statistică, 1961), p. 74.

HUNGARIANS

Region	Before 1960		After 1960	
	Number	Percent	Number	Percent
Hungarian Autonomous Region and Mureş-Autonomous Hungarian Region	565,510	77	473,154	62
Cluj	257,974	21	236,858	21
Braşov	108,751	12	222,248	23

Not only was the proportion of Hungarians in the autonomous region reduced from 77 to 62 percent while ethnic Rumanians increased from 20 to 35 percent, but Rumanians also began to assume a greater number of administrative positions, and Hungarian culture was put under increasingly severe restrictions.[16]

There is little doubt that the territorial reorganization was a matter of concern in Hungary and caused friction in the relations between Bucharest and Budapest. It was carried out in December 1960, and within one month *three* members of the Hungarian party Politburo visited Rumania—Ferenc Munnich, then premier; György Marosán, who was known to be interested in the Transylvania Hungarians; and Sándor Rónai, speaker of the Hungarian parliament. Ostensibly they were vacationing in Rumania, but who goes to Bucharest in December or January for a vacation? No doubt they came to question the Rumanian leadership about the territorial changes, and it is possible that pressure from Hungary prevented even more drastic alteration of the Hungarian Autonomous Region at that time.

The nationality policy pursued by Gheorghiu-Dej during his last years was a continuation of that adopted after 1956. Although there were no further drastic actions like the merging of the universities in Cluj or the gerrymandering of the Hungarian Autonomous Region, Rumanian nationalism was allowed to reappear under official guidance, and, on occasion, it assumed certain aspects detrimental to the Hungarian minority. When Nicolae Ceauşescu became party leader on the death of Gheorghiu-Dej in early 1965, there was no alteration in the basic nationality policy, but the situation of the minorities improved. Ceauşescu continued to oppose and restrict links between the Hungarian minority and Hungary, but he was more willing than Gheorghiu-Dej to permit the use of the Hungarian language and the development of Hungarian culture. As a result, cultural exchanges are still generally restricted: book exhibits and theatrical groups from Hungary appear in Bucharest but not in Cluj. Nonpolitical Hungarian books are purchased for the minority, and agreements have been reached on joint publication of certain types of book. However, periodicals and newspapers from Hungary are only available in very limited numbers in Transylvania.

At the same time Ceaușescu has indicated a willingness to permit greater national rights than his predecessor, as long as it is clearly emphasized that the minorities are Rumanian citizens and their first loyalty is to Rumania. Ceaușescu's first domestic visits after he came to power were to areas with a substantial Hungarian population. In his speeches on these occasions he emphasized the role of the minorities in the development of Rumania, stressed that they should receive equal treatment and that they have a right to their own culture and language, but was adamant in condemning any indications of "nationalism and national chauvinism."[17]

Although Ceaușescu was willing to permit the nationalities to exercise their constitutional rights, he was also anxious to break down the sense of minority isolation. Under him the Mureș-Autonomous Hungarian Region was completely eliminated. Although it was abolished when the entire country underwent a major local administrative reorganization, the fact that no autonomous region was designated can be attributed to his interest in emphasizing that the minorities are an integral part of the Rumanian state. Although the elimination of the autonomous region had a serious psychological effect upon the Hungarian population, the territorial changes were carefully carried out in order to avoid difficulties with the minority or with Budapest.

The draft program on the creation of new administrative units which was announced in October 1967 called for the creation of between 40 and 50 counties (*judeţe*) and the abolition of the 16 regions and 150 districts that had constituted the administrative system since 1952. The proposals for territorial reorganization were considered at a National Party Conference on December 6–8, 1967. Ceaușescu outlined to the conference the reasons for the change, specifying the need to bring economic management closer to the units of production. As a concession to the minorities he explained that "the national composition of the population" would be taken into consideration in establishing the new territorial units, and to placate the Hungarians he stressed that the new county administrative bodies "will see to it that the provisions of the country's constitution regarding the use of the mother tongue in state administration, in schools, and in cultural institutions are strictly observed in those localities in which the cohabiting nationalities live."[18]

An indication that Ceauşescu's rhetoric was to be put into practice came later in the National Party Conference when Deputy Premier Janoş Fazekaş, an ethnic Hungarian who had been elevated to full membership in the Rumanian party executive committee just one week before the conference, announced that as part of the reorganization a "powerful county" which would include the most heavily Hungarian areas would be created. In addition to the districts of Gheorgheni, Odorhei, and Miercurea Ciuc, which had the highest percentage of Hungarians in the Mureş-Autonomous Hungarian Region, the county was to include Tîrgu Secuiesc and Sfîntu Gheorghe, the two heavily Hungarian districts which were part of the former Hungarian Autonomous Region from 1952 to 1960 but were detached and put into the Braşov Region in the latter year. Fazekaş stressed the role the people's councils of the new counties would have to play in guaranteeing the rights of the minorities.[19]

The proposal of the party and state commission entrusted to work out the territorial divisions was published in Scînteia on January 14, 1968. With a few minor changes, this was the division into counties which was adopted. For the most part the old regions were divided into two, and in a few cases into three, new counties. The western districts of the former Mureş-Autonomous Hungarian Region, including its capital, Tîrgu Mureş, plus the area of Sighişoara, which had been in Braşov Region, became part of Mureş County. The eastern half of the autonomous region was joined with the Szekler areas which had been in the Braşov Region after 1960 to create a large Hungarian county, as Fazekaş had announced.

The divisions proposed by the commission in January were adopted by the Grand National Assembly in February, except that four new counties were added to the 35 the commission had suggested, and the Szekler area was divided into two counties rather

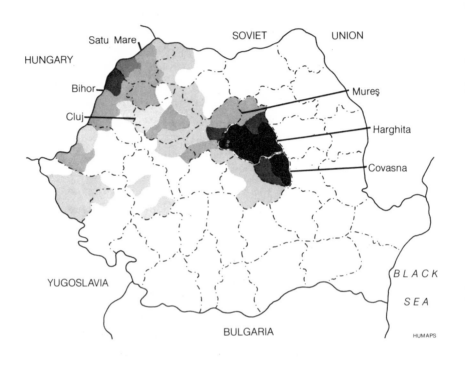

Rumania (*percent Hungarian*)

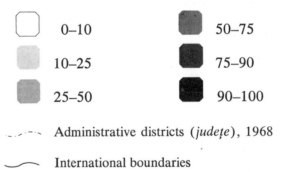

0–10	50–75
10–25	75–90
25–50	90–100

⌐·—··⌐ Administrative districts (*judeţe*), 1968

⌐—⌐ International boundaries

than a single large one. In presenting the territorial reorganization to the assembly, Ceaușescu proposed that Covasna County be created out of the former Sfîntu Gheorghe and Tîrgu Secuiesc districts. This would establish a separate county for the two heavily Szekler districts which had been severed from the Hungarian Autonomous Region in 1960. Ceaușescu explained that this change would "guarantee a more appropriate economic and social development for all localities in this county, and ensure better conditions for the organization of Harghita County."[20] This did not alter the ethnic situation in either county, since both Covasna and Harghita Counties had Hungarian majorities. Both were also earmarked, in addition to seven other counties, to receive special investments to encourage economic development. Apparently the division was made for administrative purposes. Uniting Harghita and Covasna Counties would not result in too large a unit. Their combined population (1966 census) would number only 459,250 and, according to Ceaușescu, "the average population of a county is over 450,000 inhabitants."[21] Ten counties in the country had populations of over 550,000; so far as population was concerned, Covasna was the smallest county and Harghita was fifth from the bottom. If nationality considerations were involved in the decision, it must have been decided that it was better to fragment the Hungarians, even though they still represented a majority in both counties, than to have one large, predominantly Hungarian, county. In his report to the assembly, Ceaușescu again emphasized the necessity of granting full rights to the national minorities and cited progress in non-Rumanian participation in local and national government and in the party.[22]

In many cases the new counties have a greater proportion of Hungarians than the old regions. However, the organizational reforms approved at the National Party Congress strengthened the party control of the central and local governments. Thus, although the proportion of Hungarians increased in several counties, there was no doubt that these areas would remain under strict central party control. The nationality data of the 1966 census indicate the ethnic composition of the new counties: *

* The source for these figures was *Recensămîntul Populaţiei şi Locuinţelor din 15 Martie 1966* (Bucharest: Direcţia Centrală de Statistică, 1969).

161

County	Total Number	Rumanians Number	Percent	Hungarians Number	Percent
Bihor	586,460	377,837	64.4	192,948	32.9
Cluj	631,100	457,169	72.4	164,768	26.1
Covasna	176,858	34,099	19.3	140,472	79.4
Harghita	282,392	31,272	11.1	248,886	88.1
Mureş	561,598	278,386	49.6	249,675	44.5
Satu Mare	359,393	203,780	56.7	147,594	41.1
Sălaj	263,103	194,790	74.0	63,850	24.3

The proportion of Hungarians in those areas in which most of them live is greater in the new counties than it was in the old regions. Although none of the counties along the western Rumanian frontier (adjacent to Hungary) has a Hungarian majority, in areas populated by Hungarians their proportion has increased. Satu Mare County is 41 percent Hungarian, while the old Maremureş (or Baia Mare) Region was only 28 percent Hungarian. Bihor County is 33 percent Hungarian, while the region of which it was formerly a part was 28 percent Hungarian.

In the Szekler areas and the former Mureş-Autonomous Hungarian Region, two overwhelmingly Hungarian counties were created. The proportion of Hungarians in Harghita and Covasna Counties (88 percent and 79 percent) is much higher than it was in the Hungarian Autonomous Region. The western part of the Mureş-Autonomous Hungarian Region became Mureş County, with the addition of part of the Sighişoara district. The territory added was predominantly Rumanian and German, which left the Rumanian and Hungarian populations about evenly balanced. Sighişoara may have been added to Mureş to reduce the ratio of Hungarians in the county, since this gives the county a strange geographical shape reminiscent of gerrymandering. On the other hand, even without Sighişoara, the population of Mureş would have been about 45 percent Rumanian and 49 percent Hungarian, which is not all that different from its current 50 percent Rumanian and 45 percent Hungarian population.

The Rumanians kept Budapest informed of their plans to eliminate the Mureş-Autonomous Hungarian Region and create new territorial divisions. Ceauşescu visited Hungary in mid-May 1967, and although questions of foreign policy were apparently the major topic of conversation, the impending territorial changes were surely a secondary topic. In September 1967—less than a month before the decision to carry out a territorial reorganization was publicly announced—Rumanian Vice-Premier Janoş Fazekaş went to Hungary "on vacation." The Hungarian government was apparently reassured since no Politburo members came from Budapest after the reorganization was carried out. Although eliminating the Mureş-Autonomous Hungarian Region had a symbolic significance which caused some concern among the Hungarians, the fact that two of the new counties had Hungarian majorities somewhat softened the blow.

A major concern of the Rumanian government and an important factor in the treatment of the Hungarian minority is the question of Rumania's relations with the Soviet Union and Hungary. Since Budapest (with the brief and disastrous exception of the period of the Hungarian revolt in 1956) has closely adhered to Soviet wishes in questions of foreign affairs, Budapest's attitude toward Bucharest is most often a reflection of Moscow's policy rather than of Hungarian national considerations. The question of the treatment of the Hungarian minority in Transylvania is not raised by the Hungarian government without Soviet approval. Until the late 1950's Rumania was a loyal adherent of Moscow, but since the Rumanian party started to pursue its own interests and began cautiously appealing to Rumanian nationalism, there have been occasions when the question of the Hungarian minority has been raised—in many cases only by implication, but increasingly in explicit terms—with the intention of warning the Rumanian leadership to limit its independent policies.

In the mid-1960's Hungary became the primary critic of Rumania's independent foreign policy. Explicit disagreement with specific Rumanian policies and strong criticism of nationalism, which implied criticism of Bucharest, was voiced at the highest levels in Budapest.[23] A debate between Hungarian historians and their Rumanian and Slovak colleagues on the national question in the Austro-Hungarian Empire before World War I was permitted by Budapest as a further reminder that the national question was lurking in the background and could still be raised.[24] Although the Hungarian government did not publicly and officially pose the question of the Hungarian minority, in a number of instances the issue was clearly, though implicitly, raised. In an interview with a UPI correspondent Hungarian party leader János Kádár stated that

163

Hungary had no territorial claims against its neighbors, but he also referred to the Treaty of Trianon, which established the current Rumanian-Hungarian boundary, as "an imperialist *diktat* which dismembered the territory of Hungary."[25] In addition to quoting official statements, Western correspondents in Hungary reported unofficial expressions of concern by Hungarian leaders for the Hungarian minority in Rumania.[26]

Rumania's response to these Hungarian attempts to apply pressure was to reassert Rumania's right to conduct its own policy and to oppose any attempts to interfere in the country's internal affairs. When writers in Hungary expressed an interest in and a responsibility for the literature of the Hungarian minorities in the neighboring countries, a member of Rumania's Hungarian minority was chosen to criticize specific Hungarian journals and to emphasize that this concern on the part of writers in Hungary "can only be considered a violation of the tenets which should govern the relations between friendly and fraternal states."[27] Rumania's veiled historical claims to Bessarabia, first advanced during this time, also appear to have been part of Bucharest's reaction. (There were other reasons for the claims as well, however.) The fact that the Rumanian Communist Party permitted the publication of historical works implying that Rumania had claims to that Soviet-held territory would remind the Soviet Union that raising the issue of Transylvania might lead to Rumania's raising the problem of Bessarabia more openly. Bucharest was in a good position to remind Moscow that manipulating ethnic minorities is a game two can play.[28]

When Ceauşescu took over the leadership of the party he sought to improve relations with the minority in order to make it less vulnerable to Hungarian and Soviet attempts to put pressure on Bucharest, but during his first years in office there was no crisis serious enough to test the loyalty of any of the minorities. When the real crisis came, at the time of the Soviet-led invasion of Czechoslovakia (which Ceauşescu strongly condemned), the Soviet Union and Hungary were extremely harsh in criticizing Rumania. The visit of Hungarian Politburo member and nationalities specialist Dezső Nemes to Bucharest just five days after the invasion indicated that the minorities question had been revived in private discussions in order to threaten Rumania, although it was not publicly used. The Rumanian leadership, however, considered the problem a serious one, and embarked on a series of steps to mobilize the minorities in support of the regime. Ceauşescu made a quick tour of the Hungarian minority areas less than a week after the invasion, and other party leaders visited various concentrations of minorities in Transylvania during the following days. The unity between the minorities and the party was emphasized by widely publicizing two telegrams from groups of Hungarian and German intellectuals supporting the party's position on Czechoslovakia and pledging loyalty to Rumania. At the end of October the party decided to establish a new national front organization as part of a campaign for national unity and, as elements of the front, organizations of the national minorities were also created on both a country-wide and an individual county basis. The fact that influential party leaders from among the minorities assumed the leading role indicated a serious interest in making the new organizations meaningful.[29]

Having weathered the immediate aftermath of the Czechoslovak crisis, the Rumanian party began a policy of bettering the conditions of the minorities. Improvements were made in the publication of books, newspapers, and periodicals, and in radio and television programs, and by increasing opportunities for education—all in the minority languages. However, despite these improvements it was clearly stressed that the minorities were citizens of Rumania, and efforts were made to encourage the development of Hungarian and German culture in Transylvania as distinct from the cultures of Hungary and Germany.

The most overt attempt by the Soviet Union and Hungary to use the national question as a means of exerting pressure on Rumania came during the summer of 1971. However, earlier events probably increased Bucharest's vulnerability to such pressure. The Polish government's decision to permit ethnic Germans to emigrate to West Germany following the signing of the Polish-West German nonaggression treaty on December 7, 1970, led ethnic Germans in Rumania to ask why Bucharest did not permit more of its Germans to emigrate.* The Rumanian government vigorously opposed such

* Between 1950 and early 1971, some 17,290 ethnic Germans were permitted to emigrate from Rumania to Western countries, a large portion having left for West Germany after 1967, when Bonn and Bucharest established diplomatic relations (*Nürnberger Nachrichten*, February 24, 1971). The German

ideas. The leading newspaper of the German minority published a number of articles stressing that "Rumania is our fatherland," and that the minorities were an integral part of Rumania. They also began a campaign to discourage emigration by publishing negative reports from ethnic Germans who had returned to Rumania after living in West Germany. A special meeting of the German nationality council was addressed by Ceaușescu, who declared, "There is not now, nor will there ever be, any agreement or understanding with anyone on the removal of the population of German or any other nationality."[30]

The Rumanian party's opposition to German emigration was based on the difficulties which the loss of this well-educated and numerous minority would be to the Rumanian economy. However, any sizable migration of Germans would also have a serious effect upon the Hungarian minority, many of whom might emigrate to Hungary if there were a possibility to do so. The vigorous opposition to any mass migration and the subsequent improvements in the situation of the minorities indicate the importance which the Rumanian party attached to retaining these populations. In order to mobilize the minorities, to discourage the desire to emigrate, and to strengthen them against possible foreign influence, a series of meetings was held by the nationality councils of each county with a minority population. The party also made a number of improvements in the cultural situation of the minorities, though at the same time renewing the emphasis on their links to Rumania.[31]

During this period Hungary, with the assistance and at the instigation of the Soviet Union, raised the minority problem in an effort to put pressure on Rumania because of the USSR's serious concern at Bucharest's foreign policy. A much-publicized state visit by Ceaușescu to Peking after the granting of a sizable Chinese loan to Rumania came at a time when Yugoslavia was improving relations with China after a long period of strain. At the same time Albania began to emerge from its international isolation and to improve relations with its Balkan neighbors. These events led Moscow to fear the creation of a pro-Peking axis in the Balkans which might beome a threat to Soviet policy in that area and in Eastern

minority in Rumania numbers nearly half a million, and it has been reported that as many as 60,000 of these have relatives in Western countries.

Europe generally. In the Soviet-inspired campaign against Rumania and Yugoslavia that began in June, Hungary assumed the role of primary critic of Belgrade and Bucharest; the Soviet Union criticized both countries indirectly, while leveling its principal verbal attacks on China.

In the polemics with Rumania, the question of the Hungarian minority was raised publicly for the first time since the establishment of the communist regimes in Eastern Europe. On June 24, 1971—the day Ceauşescu returned to Bucharest from his visit to China and other Asian communist states—Zoltán Komócsin, a member of the Hungarian Politburo, discussed Hungary's foreign relations and noted that there were differences in the foreign policies of the two countries which made relations difficult from time to time. He continued, "We are fundamentally interested in having the inhabitants of both our country and Rumania—including those of Hungarian nationality living there—come to understand that the fate and destiny of our peoples are inseparable from socialism."[32] Komócsin's reference to the Hungarian minority was ambiguous, and it was probably intended to be so. However, any reference to the Hungarian minority in a speech delivered by a leading Hungarian official is highly unusual. It is also most unlikely that such a reference would have been made without instructions from the Soviet Union.

The Rumanians regarded this statement as an attempt by Hungary to interfere in their internal affairs and responded vigorously. In an article by Paul Niculescu-Mizil,[33] Komócsin's counterpart in the Rumanian party's Standing Presidium, the statement to the Hungarian parliament was quoted in full and specifically criticized. Niculescu-Mizil rejected interference in Rumanian internal affairs and praised the fact that in Rumania there "is equality of rights for all working people, irrespective of nationality." An even stronger statement was contained in a speech to the party Central Committee in which Ceauşescu launched a campaign for cultural-ideological revitalization. Although he did not mention Komócsin by name, the Rumanian party leader explained that "the party has been able to solve the national question in the spirit of the Marxist-Leninist teaching," and went on to criticize in the harshest terms any attempt, internal or external, to utilize national antagonisms for any purpose:

Anyone who tries to pursue a policy fostering national hatred is pursuing a policy against socialism and communism—and consequently must be treated as an enemy of our socialist nation. We must fight for national advancement. We observe the rights of the nationalities and work to ensure these rights. We wish to advance together toward communism. Therefore, we cannot permit any attempts at nationalism- or chauvinism-mongering, no matter where they come from. This should be treated as an activity inimical to the cause of socialism and communism.[34]

The Hungarians did not reply directly to the vigorous criticism of Niculescu-Mizil and Ceaușescu, but Hungarian newspapers reiterated the correctness of Komócsin's assessment of Hungarian-Rumanian relations. Later that summer a Budapest newspaper highly praised the Austrian-Italian settlement for the German minority in South Tyrol, but phrased the discussion in such a way that the similarity between South Tyrol and Transylvania was quite clear.[35]

The Soviets did not question Rumania's treatment of the Hungarian minority directly, but various public statements contained clear, though implicit, references to Rumania. In a Radio Moscow broadcast in Rumanian[36] commemorating the first anniversary of a new Soviet-Rumanian twenty-year treaty of friendship, the listeners were told that it was only thanks to close reliance upon the Soviet Union that Rumania's territorial integrity had been preserved after World War II, when Hungary advanced claims to parts of Transylvania. The current implications of this message for Rumania were clear. Another criticism, directed at China, was also an implicit criticism of Rumania. An article in *Sovetskaya Rossia* accused Peking of chauvinism toward its minorities and denounced Chinese administrative territorial changes which reduced the proportion of minority peoples in their autonomous regions. The similarity between this and the boundary alteration and elimination of the Hungarian Autonomous Region in Rumania in 1960 and 1968 was obvious, but to make sure that the Rumanians knew the criticism was also intended for them, Radio Moscow broadcast a Rumanian-language program based on this article.[37]

In the face of these threats, the Rumanian party followed its earlier program in an attempt to appeal to the minorities—party leaders made visits to minority areas, further concessions were granted to the minorities in the cultural and educational fields, and statements of support from non-Rumanian groups were publicized.[38] At the same time it was stressed that the minorities were an integral part of Rumania, and it was only after the crisis in relations with the Soviet Union had passed that the Rumanian government considered it safe to emphasize this point by insisting that the minority-language press use Rumanian spelling and Rumanian names for cities in Rumania.

The Rumanian regime is facing an unpleasant dilemma. The pursuit of its independent foreign policy requires the support of a generally united population, and the sizable non-Rumanian minorities represent a potential threat to that unity. If it denies rights to the non-Rumanian sections of the population, their discontent will increase, which in turn will give outsiders greater opportunities to influence the minorities. On the other hand, granting greater rights to the national minorities may result in their identifying more closely with their ethnic homeland, and may encourage them to seek still greater national rights from Bucharest. The Rumanian party seems to be following a middle road: granting greater rights but at the same time emphasizing the common links between ethnic Rumanians and the minorities. However, the party's cautious revival and encouragement of Rumanian nationalism has made minority rights a domestic political issue, and recent Soviet and Hungarian attempts to use the nationality question have complicated the regime's task.

Chapter 9

"Historical" Debates:
The Hungarian Successor States

Though the Soviet Union is no longer in a position to enforce silence on national questions, the common communist ideology has given a special form to public discussion of nationality problems among the communist states. Between the two world wars, bourgeois politicians and scholars in Eastern Europe openly and publicly advocated border revisions and championed the rights of national minorities in other states. Communist spokesmen and scholars, however, write under the restraints imposed by party censorship and must maintain the appearance of proletarian internationalism. Factionalism is anathema to communists, and, if there are differences, they are concealed from public view. Therefore nationality debates are carried on by means of "ideological" and "historical" discussions which have a second level of meaning.

Deciphering these esoteric communications (content analysis, or "Kremlinology" as it is sometimes called) has been acknowledged by both communist officials and Western scholars as essential for understanding communist meaning. East Europeans who have held important party positions have reported that the communist *ap-*

paratchiki study key speeches and articles in *Pravda* in order to attune themselves to current trends in Soviet policy, and communist publications have admitted the validity of this kind of analysis.[1] Soviet literature, which frequently provides useful insights into the Soviet system, contains references to content analysis. In the novel *Cancer Ward,* for example, Alexander Solzhenitsyn reveals the thoughts of a middle-level party *apparatchik:* "He regarded newspapers as a widely distributed instruction, written in fact in code; nothing in it could be said openly, but a skillful man who knew the ropes could interpret the various small hints, the arrangement of the articles, the things that were played down or omitted, and so get a true picture of the way things were going."[2] Western scholars have found deciphering esoteric communications useful in arriving at an understanding of interparty and intraparty conflict. Though this approach is not without its methodological pitfalls, it does provide information on policy disagreements which is not available from other sources.[3]

Discussions of history and the interpretation of history have been particularly suitable vehicles for expressing differences on the national question. History has been made the principal basis for territorial claims in southeastern Europe, and to debate the interpretation of the history of certain areas is to debate the validity of the current claim. Also, national consciousness is closely linked with history in Eastern Europe, and therefore takes on emotional and patriotic overtones. Serbs still celebrate June 28th as their national holiday (Vidovdan)—the anniversary of the defeat of the Serbian armies by the Turks in 1389, which marked the end of a Serbian state until the nineteenth century. Rumanian nationalism is deeply colored by historical claims of ethnic descent from prehistoric Dacian tribes and the later Roman conquerors, which sets them apart from their Slavic neighbors. Few areas are as history-minded as Central and Eastern Europe. There history is perhaps the most important foundation stone of national consciousness; the past is not a subject for harmless small talk.

History is not only especially relevant in the setting of Eastern Europe, but it also has particular significance in communism, which makes historical polemics more relevant as a means of carrying on nationality conflicts. According to the Soviet handbook on ideology, Marxism has discovered the scientific laws of history, a discovery which "makes it possible to foresee . . . the general direction of historical development." This places on Marxists a special obligation to make "a thorough study . . . of historical data, of historical facts. Only in this way can one discover the internal connection between events and explain each one, so as not only to understand the past and the present but also to foresee the future scientifically."[4] One enthusiastic Soviet historian in the early 1920's went so far as to equate Marxism with history: "Marx is historical to the core. Marxism is historicism. We must be historians because we are Marxists. . . . Materialism is primarily a historical outlook."[5] With this Marxist emphasis upon the correct interpretation of history, historical debates are particularly useful in expressing differences among communists on the national question.

Before we examine some of these historical debates, a framework for evaluating them should be established. First, major statements in the debates are usually made on the anniversary of some historic occasion. However, the significance of the occasion is not necessarily commensurate with the political importance of statements made. Lazar Koliševski, first secretary of the Macedonian Republic party and president of the assembly of the Yugoslav Macedonian Republic, once delivered an important address denouncing Bulgaria's claims to Macedonia and reiterating the Yugoslav stand. The occasion was the centennial of the founding of the first high school in the town of Titov Veles.

Second, such statements are not important for their contribution to the understanding of history, but for their relevance to current events. Communists have always stressed that "historical science not only explains the past but provides the key to a correct understanding of contemporary political events."[6] The communist concept of history also views the historian as a partisan in the class struggle. A communist historian must "stand clearly and unambiguously on the side of progress against reaction, on the side of revolution against counterrevolution, on the side of democracy and socialism against imperialism."[7] With the concept of history as the key to current events and historians as partisans in a struggle, it requires no change in method to use historical interpretations to support a national point of view in an interparty conflict.

Third, historical debates always center on the correct Marxist interpretation of events. Since "the materialist concept of history"

—that is, the Marxist-Leninist interpretation of history—is "an accurate compass that will give . . . a true understanding of historical events,"[8] communists always focus on a class analysis of history with emphasis on the underlying economic forces. Forcing interpretations of history to conform to a Marxian historical framework, however, does not mean that all communists arrive at the same conclusion, or that only one interpretation is correct. On the contrary, "the dialectical-materialist method encourages people to make a concrete analysis of every given situation, of the special features existing in their country . . . at any given time." Since each party operates "in special circumstances, under specific national conditions,"[9] diametrically opposed points of view can be and are advocated, but all are based on Marxian historical materialism.

A fourth feature of these historical debates is the use of frequent citations from the writings of those who originated the ideology. Just as medieval scholastics "proved" their analyses with quotations from scripture or the early Church fathers, communists bolster their claims and demonstrate their orthodoxy by citing Marx, Lenin, Engels, and others. Though the founders of communism left voluminous writings from which statements proving almost any point of view can be extracted, those engaged in historical debates have not been above tearing sentences out of context to "prove" their points of view. Frequently, some significance is also attached to citing a particular authority. Failure to quote a leading communist prophet who is associated with a specific stand on some question is a subtle way of voicing disagreement with his point of view.

A fifth fundamental in examining historical polemics is the source of a statement or article. With few exceptions, everything printed in a communist country must pass official censors and must be approved by publishers or editors who are often stricter than the censors in judging manuscripts that may provoke party criticism. However, some statements and articles are more official than others.[10] The two key factors to consider in evaluating the significance of a historical analysis are the medium through which it is made public, and the individual making the pronouncement or analysis. The daily, weekly, and theoretical journals of the Central Committee of the party are closely attuned to the will of the party leadership. Hence, statements in these central party organs are more significant than those in provincial party and government organs.

The organs of nongovernment, nonparty organizations—the trade unions, the writers' unions, the Academy of Sciences, and other groups—are kept under party scrutiny, but are not as immediately responsive to the official position. Books are carefully edited by censors and publishers, but unless they appear with the party imprimatur or are written by leading party officials, they represent the author's point of view expressed within party guidelines. Radio broadcasts are generally closely controlled. The most official stations are those broadcasting from the capital; stations in major cities and provincial and local stations descend in importance.

The person who makes a historical analysis is a key consideration in assessing its worth. The acknowledged leader of the country, members of the party Politburo, and high government officials are clearly spokesmen for official policy. Party leaders have, on occasion, used subelites and academicians to prepare the way for changes in the party line or to advocate a point of view that would be difficult for the leadership to announce directly. Historians as well as party officials are aware of the technique of using historical esoteric communications as a means of voicing nationality claims that would otherwise be banned. Though the party has control over the press and thereby ultimate control over what is published, this does not prevent historians from drawing esoteric inferences to go beyond what the party officially allows. Party leaders in almost every communist state have struggled with historians who, under the guise of historical studies, have discussed national questions which the leadership has proscribed. In examining historical debates one must keep in mind that historians sometimes move beyond the limits of the party's general line. Nonetheless, historians also are frequently used by party leaders to express ideas which the leadership cannot openly voice and which they must later criticize, though they may initially have approved them.

One of the most extensive historical debates, which involved a large number of East European states, began in the spring of 1964. It centered on the question of nationality and the collapse of the Habsburg Empire, and ultimately involved communist historians from Hungary, Czechoslovakia, Rumania, and Yugoslavia. The major issue was whether or not the creation of national states in the Danube basin was a progressive step. The positions taken by the various communist historians and defended with Marxist arguments were those of their own states. The debate began in May 1964 at a conference of historians in Budapest on "The Historical Problems of the Austro-Hungarian Monarchy 1900–1918." One of the five major sections of the conference dealt with the national question in Austria-Hungary. The opposing points of view were expressed in the papers presented.

On the one side was the Hungarian position, presented by László Katus, who analyzed the economic and social basis of the national question. His conclusion was that bourgeois-democratic elements dominated the national movements and sought to align the peasantry and workers with their bourgeois-national aims, with the result that the proletarian movement was separated and isolated. The obvious implication was that the national movement and the division of Austria-Hungary into separate national states was regressive and detrimental to the cause of socialist development.[11] During the discussion that followed the presentation of papers, Erik Molnár, a leading Hungarian historian, compared the Russian and Austrian Social Democratic solutions of the national problem. He praised the Russian solution because it established a federation and condemned the creation of separate national states on the territory of the Austro-Hungarian Empire.[12]

The opposing point of view was presented by a group of Rumanian historians led by Miron Constantinescu. They concluded that the Habsburg Monarchy was socially, economically, politically, and ideologically moribund, and that the creation of separate national states was a logical and progressive step after the demise of the empire.[13]

After the conference the progressiveness of national states remained a major issue in discussions among East European historians. The positions adopted by the various national historians reflect the viewpoint of their nationalities and of the communist leadership in their states. The Hungarians have continued to advocate the position that federation of the former Austro-Hungarian peoples would have been preferable to the creation of national states.[14] This position is championed by Hungarian nationalists and is made to appear consistent with the Hungarian party's position on nationalism. The creation of a federation would have left Hungary intact. Although nationalities would have been given greater rights than they enjoyed under the Hungarian monarchy, there would

have been no Trianon Hungary, no absolute separation of historical
and ethnic Hungarian territory from the Hungarian heartland. The
justification for such a federation is not national but primarily
economic. According to Hungarian party pronouncements, economic and social considerations take precedence over the national
question. Hungarian historians advocate a Hungarian national
cause but support it with nonnational arguments, in keeping with
the current party line.

Rumanian historians have continued to be the most vocal in
championing the national state.[15] Rumanian nationalists have been
obsessed with the idea of uniting ethnic Rumanians into a single
Rumanian state. By 1964 the Rumanian party had become an
outspoken advocate of national sovereignty and independence
within the Soviet bloc. The emphasis of Rumanian historians on
the progressiveness of creating national states represents the party
line in Rumania.

Slovak historians, particularly in the debate over Ludovít Štúr
(see below), were almost as adamant as the Rumanians in
championing national rights. The economic difficulties in Czechoslovakia, as well as Slovak national discontent, began to revitalize
Slovak national consciousness in the mid-1960's. Slovak nationalism later reached the point where it became one of the major factors
in the removal of Antonín Novotný and in precipitating the Czechoslovak liberalization of 1968. Slovak nationalism has traditionally
been strongly anti-Hungarian, and the debate over the desirability
of a Danube federation after 1918 gave Slovak historians a target
for their national fervor. To some extent the Hungarians may have
served as a surrogate for the Czechs, whose domination and discrimination Slovaks opposed. While anti-Czech sentiments could
not be overtly expressed, anti-Hungarianism was a popular aspect
of Slovak nationalism and one more readily permitted by Prague.

The debate between Hungarian and Slovak historians over
Ludovít Štur* was one of the most vigorous and interesting of the

---

* Štur was a Slovak born in Zay-uhrovec on October 29, 1815. He studied
in Bratislava (Pressburg, Pozsony) and later at the German University of Halle.
When he returned to Bratislava he became a leading spokesman for Slovak
national rights and an opponent of the theory then popular among some
Slovak intellectuals that Czechs and Slovaks were of the same ethnic stock.
Though a Slovak literary language, based on western Slovak dialects, had been
codified by Bernolák, it was Štur and some of his associates who began to

exchanges on the question of the Hungarian successor states. The debate is sufficiently illustrative of the kind of historical debate that is carried on between communist historians to merit closer examination. The occasion was the sesquicentennial of Štur's birth. However, the articles that appeared devoted little space to an evaluation of Štur's significance; the primary focus was on the revolution of 1848–1849 and the role of Slav nationalism in thwarting the Magyar uprising. Since the whole question is one of Slovaks opposing the Hungarian revolt in order to preserve their own national identity, the debate was clearly centered on nationality.[16]

There can be no doubt that both sides saw the debate not merely as a historical exercise but as a discussion of questions relevant to current Hungarian-Slovak relations. Vladimír Mináč, a Slovak writer involved in the debate, asked:

Should one touch healed wounds? Are the wounds really healed? National antagonism is a tough flower; if we do not talk about it, that does not signify that it does not exist. Our relationship to the Hungarians not only molded our national fate but also formed our way of thinking, it formed the soul of our nation. For many decades we existed simply as a reflex to the Hungarians, as people who would not give in, who lived outside them and against

---

publish a journal in the central Slovak dialects that became the foundation of modern Slovak.

When the Hungarian revolt of 1848 broke out, Štur was convinced that a Hungarian victory would destroy the Slovak nation. His activities in 1848–1849, therefore, were aimed at frustrating the Hungarian uprising. He and a number of other Slovak nationalists drew up a petition to the emperor demanding that Slovaks have full equality with Magyars. Štur maintained contact with other Slavs in the Habsburg Empire, participated in the All-Slav Congress in Prague, and aided the Slovak and other Slav uprisings against the Magyars. Despite the fact that he assisted the Austrian imperial government against the Hungarians, he was declared a traitor and forced to retire from political life after 1849. He was killed in a hunting accident in 1856.

Štur's best-known work, *Das Slawenthum und die Welt der Zukunft,* was written in German and first published in Russia in 1867; it advocated the union of all Slavs under Russia. For evaluations of Štur, see J. M. Kirschbaum, "Ludovít Štur and His Place in the Slavic World," *Slavistica* (Proceedings of the Institute of Slavistics of the Ukrainian Free Academy of Sciences), No. 32, 1958, pp. 1–34; Michael B. Petrovich, "Ludovít Štur and Russian Pan-Slavism," *Journal of Central European Affairs,* 12:1 (April 1952), pp. 1–19; and Ludovít Holotík, *Ludovít Štur und die Slawische Wechselseitigkeit* (Vienna: Verlag Herman Böhlau, 1969).

them. . . . I have not yet acquired an objective view of the matter; I am prevented from doing so by my personal experience, for I have witnessed irredentism in action.[17]

The principal spokesman for the Hungarian position, Erzsébet Andics, agreed that the lessons of 1848 were particularly relevant today:

> The evaluation of Marx and Engels, as well as of Lenin, of the 1848–1849 revolutions, and of the minority struggles at that time have ceased to be purely historical questions and have turned into urgent present day tasks. . . . Nationalistic mistrust and stirring up differences among peoples are still the favored instruments of the enemies of socialism.
>
> The danger of nationalism lies not only in external and openly hostile factors. It also exists within ourselves, if we are unable to overcome the shadows of the past and to forget the wounds mutually inflicted.[18]

For the Slovaks, however, the debate was not merely a question of the relation of nationalism to socialism or even of Hungarian irredentism. In 1966 the Hungarian minority offered no serious threat to Slovak rule. Although scholars in Hungary were supporting a historical point of view that could be considered irredentist, the party leadership in Budapest had renounced claims to Slovakia and was discouraging any Hungarian nationalist revisionism. The vehemence of the Slovak polemics was due to the then current revival of Slovak nationalism and to increasing dissatisfaction with Czech rule. Mináč was not silent on this issue. He not only championed Slovak national rights against the Hungarians, but he also praised Štur's role in the struggle to gain recognition for Slovak national identity vis-à-vis the Czechs and referred to historical "Czech indifference to Slovak matters." He also added, "To interpret the coexistence of our [Czech and Slovak] nations as an idyll is neither historically correct nor useful and safe for the future."[19]

At the heart of the Štur debate lay the correct Marxist interpretation of the role of Ludovít Štur and the Slovak revolt of 1848–1849. One of the prime questions was the nature of the classes involved in the struggle, because "only on the basis of this theory [of the class struggle] is it possible to explain the hidden, motivating springs of all the important events and changes that take place in a society based on exploitation."[20] The Slovak point of view—expressed by all three Slovak writers who participated in the debate, Mináč, Rapant, and Mésároš—was that while in 1848 "the Slovak-Hungarian conflict was *not always* identical with plebe versus aristocrat . . . *this was the general trend*."[21] The Slovaks claimed that the revolution in Hungary was no more than a struggle between the German (Austrian) and Hungarian ruling classes. The issue "was not freedom but nationality, and in this guise the national, economic, political, and social privileges of the ruling section of the Hungarians and Germans."[22] In 1848–1849, Mináč claims, in Hungary "there was no need for a countermovement, for any kind of reaction or restoration which would deny [the uprising]. The revolution grew together with the aristocracy . . . and this aristocracy swallowed the revolution."[23] Rapant went further, attempting to show that Marx and Engels had acknowledged that the events in Hungary could not be classified as a revolution. He cited a letter from Engels to Marx dated April 3, 1851, in which Engels used the term "uprising" rather than "revolution" in referring to Hungary in 1849.

Andics, on the Hungarian side, admitted that the Slovak programs "contained a strong plebian, democratic element and these masses in many respects made more far-reaching and more radical endeavors than those that characterized the policy of the liberal Hungarian nobility." However, the Slovak movement became a counterrevolutionary factor when it aligned itself with the Habsburgs against the Hungarians because there could be no doubt, said Erzsébet Andics, that "the 1848–1849 struggle of the Hungarian people was also the battle of the opposing classes of Hungarian society. This struggle was not only pursued against Habsburg absolutism, which suppressed the country, but it was also a life-and-death struggle against the Hungarian aristocracy of big landowners, which defended the feudal institutions to the last."[24] To bolster her point of view on the class character of the struggle, she quoted Marx and Engels as having firmly rejected "the groundless allegation that the Hungarian events of 1848–1849 were caused by Hungarian feudal lords and magnates" and also as having pointed out that "this accusation was the favorite slander used by the reactionary forces to discredit the leaders of both the Hungarian and the Polish revolutions."[25] Since the class struggle is the "guiding thread" which leads Marxists to a correct interpretation of history, the nature of the class struggle is crucial to the correct interpretation of the events of 1848.

One of the key ideological issues in the debate was the merit of national as opposed to social revolution. The Slovaks, of course, were strong advocates of the value of the national revolution. The Hungarians, who claim the Hungarian revolution was a bourgeois-democratic one, were firmly in favor of the superiority of social over national uprisings. Julius Mésároš claimed that the revolution had three objectives: "1) to destroy as thoroughly as possible the economic bases of feudalism; 2) to secure the broadest possible degree of democratization of political life; 3) to give all the nations of the monarchy equal rights."[26] These objectives, Mésároš said, "are absolutely equal in importance, and none of them can be subordinated to the others." The Slovak revolt, even if it had only national goals, was just as important as the Hungarian revolt, even if the latter was bourgeois-democratic in character. According to Rapant, the Slovaks did not choose between democratic and national goals—they had both. "The endeavor of the Slav nations was primarily aimed at safeguarding their national existence as a premise for, or as an additional element of, complete freedom."[27] Hence the Slovaks were progressive no matter how one looked at them. The Slovak revolution was as significant as the Hungarian revolution.

From the Hungarian point of view (which is also the view of Marx and Engels, who ignored the national aspects of revolution or considered them reactionary), the only issue was the antifeudal bourgeois struggle. "Whatever important and essential role may be played by individual national endeavors, they must always be subordinated to the general interests of universal progress," which in 1848–1849 "meant subordination to the antifeudal bourgeois" Hungarian revolt.[28] Mésároš, whose article was written in answer to the Andics article, was particularly critical of Miss Andics's argument. It could be true, he said "only as long as the interests of a single nation are not given priority over the interests of the whole under the guise of revolution and struggle for general progress; only as long as the interests of the smaller nations are not ignored, especially when their efforts are more progressive than those of the nation proclaiming itself to be the main bearer of the revolution."[29]

The final ideological question is to determine who is progressive and who is reactionary, not only with regard to Štur personally but also in regard to the Slovak revolutionary movement. The Slovaks, of course, conclude that Štur "was progressive in the social sense, more progressive than many of his contemporaries, including the leaders of the Hungarian revolution."[30] "Štur's nationalism was definitely progressive," as his social program "caught up in its entirety and in detail with the most progressive Hungarian program of that time." The "Slovak political program . . . was far more radical than the Hungarian freedoms,"[31] Not only was Štur exonerated as a progressive, but the Slovak historians condemned the Hungarian revolution as "not a struggle for world or even for European independence, but only for its own narrow aims,"[32] thereby justifying the Slav-Habsburg alliance. The conclusion: "Whether, under these circumstances, the leaning of the non-Hungarian nations toward Vienna, when they fought for their very life, can be described as a service to the counterrevolution is problematic, to say the least."[33]

The Hungarians were just as adamant in labeling Štur a counterrevolutionary as the Slovaks were in honoring him as a progressive. The movement of Štur and his friends became a counterrevolutionary factor, despite subjective good intentions, "at the very moment when it expected the fulfillment of democratic and national objectives from a political and military alliance with reaction, and not from a joining of forces with the progressive elements."[34] Although Erzsébet Andics declared that "the unfortunate move on the part of Štur and his friends could be justified," she was extremely critical of the Slovak historians "who, more than one hundred years after the events and fully aware of all the consequences of Štur's action, are trying to make a virtue out of this fatally mistaken policy and to glorify it as brilliant foresight."[35]

One of the most interesting features of the debate was the attitude of both sides to Marx and Engels. The Slovaks openly rejected the Marx-Engels analysis of the Slav movements of 1848, while the Hungarians staunchly defended it. Rapant began his article by declaring his intention to "revalue" the importance of the Slovak uprising of 1848 and to eliminate the "slur of 'reaction' [which] was put upon this most glorious period in Slovak history due to erroneous political and historical conclusions and criteria." He claims that, thanks to the "particularly weighty" and "well-known" article by "Marx" in the *Neue Rheinische Zeitung*,[36] critics of the Slav position had elevated this anti-Slav analysis to the level of "the official view in the socialist and people's democratic countries. Opposite views have been described as bourgeois nationalism, although it would be relatively easy to demonstrate that the source of the official view was actually the Hungarian bourgeois nationalism which, thanks to the above-mentioned article, was able to elevate its narrow view to the official pedestal." Rapant not only accused the Hungarians of using Marx to support their bourgeois nationalism, but claimed that Marx and Engels "were not altogether free of German arrogance" on the national question and therefore, by implication, were anti-Slav. He also attempted to show that Marx "subsequently changed his opinion on the Hungarian revolution, and on its leader Kossuth, substantially, and in certain points even radically, to his own disadvantage."[37]

Pál Fehér, the second Hungarian involved in the debate, considered the Slovak articles "emotionally understandable but in reality anti-Marxist."[38] Erzsébet Andics accused the Slovaks by implication of being "scholars of bourgeois historiography" and observed that "bourgeois historical trends . . . can be noticed quite frequently in our own [communist] historiography." She went on to deny that Hungarians use Marx to support their narrow nationalism by claiming that Marx and Engels had emphasized that "the Hungarian revolution was of European significance." As for the charge of German arrogance, the founders of communism were "against reaction, not against Slavs." Hence, they opposed tsarist Russia as counterrevolutionary but favored the revolutionary Poles, who were Slavs. She did admit that Engels' judgment "on the 'nonviability' of the Slav peoples . . . was not proved by history." They were saved from absorption because they later came to expect "the fulfillment of their just national demands from the democratic and socialist development, not from the dynastic forces." Miss Andics was particularly adamant in maintaining that Marx and Engels did not revise their opinion of the true revolutionary character of the Hungarian uprising of 1848. She did admit, however, that they turned against Kossuth and the Hungarian revolutionaries who aligned themselves with Napoleon III against Austria "for the same reason for which they condemned the minorities of the Habsburg Empire, above all the Slavic minorities in 1848–1849—that is, for their alliance with reaction."[39]

The Slovaks gleaned a few statements from the prophets of communism to support their case, while the Hungarians supported almost every point with a citation. Since the opinions of Marx and Engels did not support their cause, the Slovaks openly questioned the conclusions reached by the founders. The author of one of the most authoritative of the Slovak articles in the debate observed, "To try to prove that . . . Marx and Engels never changed their views on the evaluation of the fundamental questions of the bourgeois revolution, and the Hungarian revolution in particular, is no way to prove the correctness or incorrectness of the view itself."[40] When the choice was between a Marxist text and the national existence of the Slovaks, the Slovak communist historians unhesitatingly chose the latter.

To evaluate the position of the Hungarian and Slovak parties on the issues raised in this debate regarding the role of Ludovít Štur, the individuals involved and the media they used to make their positions public should also be considered. The Slovak authors who were attacked in the Hungarian polemics were only two of several Slovak intellectuals who had written articles on the anniversary of Štur's birth. Rapant, a leading Slovak historian,* wrote his article for *Slovenska Literatura,* the bimonthly published by the Slovak Academy of Sciences. Mináč, a well-known Slovak author,† had his evaluation of Štur published in three successive issues of the Slovak Writers' Union weekly, *Kulturny Zivot.* While

---

* Daniel Rapant, a respected Slovak scholar, published historical works in prewar, as well as postwar, Czechoslovakia. His major work is a multivolume history and collection of documents on the events of 1848–1849 in Slovakia. The first volume appeared in 1937, and succeeding volumes have been published between 1947 and 1967. (Daniel Rapant, *Slovenské povstanie roku, 1848–49: Dejiny a dokumenty,* 5 vols. [Turčianskom sv martine: Vladala Matica Slovenská, 1937, 1947–1950; and Bratislava: Vydavatelstvo Slovenskej académie vied, 1954–1967]. He has also published a number of other historical studies and collections of documents dealing with Slovak history.

† Vladimír Mináč's fictional works (all published since 1948) include the trilogy *Dlhý čas čakania* (1956); *Živí a mŕtvi* (1959) and *Zvony vzonia na deň* (1961), as well as *Prielom* (1950), *Na rozhraní* (1954), *Cas a knihy* (1962) and *Kriminálny príheh* (1964). Mináč became a member of the Czechoslovak Writers' Union Central Committee and presidium in May 1956 and served a term on the latter body. He has been a member of the presidium and Central Committee of the Slovak Writers' Union since June 1956. In June 1964 he was elected to the Czechoslovak National Assembly. His contributions to the Štur debate did not hamper his rise in Czechoslovak politics; he was elected to candidate membership on the Central Committee of the Czechoslovak Communist Party in June 1966.

the Academy of Sciences and the Writers' Union, as well as their publications, would have been under ultimate party control, the fact that Rapant's and Mináč's articles were published would imply, but not necessarily prove, party approval of their revised interpretations of the Slovak role in 1849, with its implications for Slovak-Hungarian relations. However, considering Mináč's later election to candidate membership of the Central Committee of the Czechoslovak party and his membership on the presidium of the Slovak Writers' Union, the articles could not have been considered too far out of line.

The best evidence that Mináč and Rapant were not deviating from the party line is the last article in the debate, which came from the Slovak side. It was written by the Slovak historian Julius Mésároš* and was published in *Predvoj,* the weekly of the Slovak Communist Party and the most official publication in which any of the articles in the debate appeared. Since it was the last to be published, it certainly indicates party support for the positions taken by Rapant and Mináč. Mésároš expressed regret that the complete Andics article had not been published in Slovak. (However, the complete text was republished in Hungarian by *Irodalmi Szemle,* the scholarly journal of the Hungarian minority in Slovakia; hence it is possible that Mésároš's rebuttal was intended as much for the Hungarian minority intellectuals in Slovakia as for historians in Hungary.) Mésároš declared, "It is our duty to study Andics's polemic carefully, lest we be tarnished again by nationalist and revisionist deviation." Mésároš supported Mináč and Rapant and openly questioned the correctness of Marx's and Engels' interpretation of the events of 1848 in Hungary.

The principal Hungarian protagonist was Erzsébet Andics, Hungarian historian and long-time member of the Communist Party of Hungary,† whose article was published in *Valóság,* the

---

*Mésároš is a Slovak historian whose works appear to follow accepted Marxist interpretations closely. He has written *K problematike prezitkov feudalismu na Slovensku v druhej polovici xix storicia* (Bratislava: Vydavatelstvo Slovenskej akadémie vied, 1955) and has edited two volumes: *Matica slovenska v nasich dejinach* (Bratislava: Vidavatelstvo Slovenskej akadémie vied, 1968), and *Slováci a ich národný výnin: Sborník materiálov z.V. sjazdu slovenských historikov v Banskej Bystrici* (Bratislava: Vydavatelstvo Slovenskej akadémie vied, 1966).

† Miss Andics and her husband, Andor Berei, were members of the Rákosi circle, and both held high party and government positions until 1956. She and

184

monthly publication of the Society for the Propagation of Social and Natural Sciences. Miss Andics's ties with the party, the fact that her articles were subject to party censorship, and the publication by *Valóság* six months later of an article supporting a similar Hungarian nationalist point of view[41] would imply tacit party approval of her position in the polemics. Her article was the most pungent in the entire Štur debate. Perhaps her sarcastic, biting tone was one of the reasons why a second article was published. Possibly at the suggestion of the party, Pál E. Fehér† wrote an article on nationalism and international cooperation for *Élet és Irodalom,* a literary and political weekly. Though Fehér did not deny any of Miss Andics's conclusions and accused the Slovaks of holding anti-Marxist views, he took a much more conciliatory line and soft-pedaled the differences of interpretation. He balanced condemnation of Slav aid to the counterrevolution with an admission of Kossuth's failure to recognize just Slovak rights and added, as if trying to bring both sides together, "We still do not believe that . . . only those events are important which separate these nations from each other."[42] He called for greater understanding and cooperation on both sides.

The Ludovít Štur debate is a classic example of historical debates on a current sensitive national issue. Slovak nationalism has always been strongly anti-Hungarian, and the events of World War II and at the time of the Hungarian uprising in 1956 kept the issue alive. This debate is only one manifestation that it continues to fester beneath the surface. At the time it took place, Slovak nationalism was increasing because of growing discontent with

---

her husband fled to the Soviet Union at the time of the Hungarian revolt and remained there until the summer of 1958. Since then she has been a member of the Social and Historical Section of the Hungarian Academy of Sciences and apparently on the staff of the Institute for Historical Science. Miss Andics has written a number of historical studies of the Hungarian revolt of 1848–1849, including *A nagybirtokos arisztokrácia ellen forradalmi szerepe, 1848–1849-ben,* 2 vols. (Budapest: Akadémiai Kiadó, 1952); and *A habsburgok magyarországi cári intervenció diplomáciai előtörténete* (Budapest: Akadémiai Kiadó, 1961).

† Fehér, a critic and literary historian, has a special interest in Czechoslovakia and the Slovak population there. During the 1968 Czechoslovak liberalization several articles by him appeared in the Hungarian press, dealing with the Hungarian minority in Slovakia and with Czech-Slovak relations. See *Élet és Irodalom,* May 11, 1968; *Népszabadság,* June 1, 1968; *Magyar Hirlap,* May 29 and July 16, 1968.

Czech tutelage. The sesquicentennial of Štur's birth provided an opportunity for the Slovaks to reassert their national individuality. Štur had not only been a champion of the Slovak nationality in the face of Magyarization, he had also been an early spokesman for the ethnic distinctness of Slovaks vis-à-vis Czechs. At the same time the Hungarian party, with the Soviet leadership's approval if not at its request, had become the chief advocate of "internationalism" in Eastern Europe. It was the Hungarian party leadership which openly criticized the nationalist position taken by the Rumanian party, and Hungarian historians were the principal opponents of the Rumanian historians' emphasis on the sovereignty and independence of the national state. The internationalism which it became Hungary's role to stress coincided to some extent with the Hungarian national position. When the Slovak communist historians became spokesmen for Slovak nationalism, which they did more and more openly as Slovak discontent increased, the Hungarians supported their own national position and attempted to chide their Slovak comrades for nationalism. The anniversary of the birth of Ludovít Štur was the spark which touched off the debate, but the question at issue was Slovak and Hungarian nationalism. In the exchange both used Marxist arguments, but advocated their own national positions.

Chapter 10

"Historical" Debates: Macedonia

The root of the Macedonian problem has been the question of the nationality of its inhabitants. In the nineteenth century, disinterested ethnographers generally were in agreement that the Slavic inhabitants of Macedonia were Bulgarians. The Serbs, who gained autonomy from the Ottoman Sultan in 1829 and were anxious to expand their borders, maintained that they were Serbs. The Greek Kingdom, which had gained its independence in 1832 and was expanding northward, claimed Macedonia for ethnic as well as historical reasons. The establishment in 1870 of the Bulgarian Exarchate, whose territory included all of Macedonia, Dobruja, and western Thrace, as well as present-day Bulgaria, advanced the Bulgarian claim, particularly in light of the close connection between nationality and religion in the Balkans. This claim was further enhanced by the Treaty of San Stefano (1878) which gave newly independent Bulgaria most of the area under jurisdiction of the Exarchate, including all of Macedonia. Although the treaty was nullified at the Berlin Conference later that year and Macedonia was returned to Turkish rule, re-establishment of the San

Stefano boundaries became a Bulgarian national goal. The rise of Balkan nationalism in the last half of the nineteenth century pitted Bulgaria against Serbia and Greece in a struggle for Macedonia. Each contender established a different ethnographic make-up of the area to support its own claims.

In the immediate post-World War II years, Bulgarian and Yugoslav communists were in agreement on the existence of a separate Macedonian nationality. However, they followed the same policy for conflicting reasons. Yugoslav communists favored the creation of a Macedonian nationality as a means of reducing Bulgarian influence and as a basis on which to deny Bulgaria's claims to Macedonia. Also, since the Macedonians had become alienated from Yugoslavia by the attempts to Serbianize them during the interwar period, calling the population "Macedonians" and recognizing some of their national peculiarities had the effect of reducing their opposition to Belgrade's rule. The Bulgarian communists realized that a defeated Bulgarian state could make no acceptable claim to Yugoslav Macedonia, and therefore they "recognized" a separate Macedonian nationality in the hope that an independent Macedonia would be created which, thanks to its historical and ethnic links, would gravitate toward Bulgaria. Because a united Macedonian Republic within a Balkan federation could also accomplish this goal, the Bulgarian communist also favored this idea.

After Yugoslavia's expulsion from the Cominform in 1948, the Bulgarian communists continued to advocate a separate nationality for Macedonians, but at the same time they eliminated the traces of linguistic, historical, and ethnic differences between Macedonians and Bulgarians which Yugoslav teachers had been permitted to implant in the population of Bulgarian Macedonia before 1948. Between 1948 and 1956 the Bulgarian communists continued to advocate a separate Macedonian nationality in their propaganda in the attempt to win over the population of Yugoslav Macedonia.[1]

Before 1956, however, there were changes in attitude that presaged a change in policy. Under Dimitrov's leadership, the Bulgarian party's recognition of a Macedonian nationality was unequivocal; at his death, the Bulgarians were only willing to admit that the process of forming a separate Macedonian nationality had begun in 1918, and later they moved the date of the beginning of Macedonian national consciousness to 1944.[2]

Apparently the decision to no longer recognize the existence of a separate Macedonian nationality was taken at the April 1956 plenum* of the Bulgarian party Central Committee.[3] At the same session there were a number of changes in Bulgaria's internal political situation that were related to the changed policy on Macedonia. The chairman of the Council of Ministers appointed at the plenum was Anton Yugov, who was born in what is now Greek Macedonia. Being a Macedonian, Yugov was more interested in the Macedonian issue than his predecessor, Vulko Chervenkov, who was born not far from Sofia. The de-Stalinization drive, as well as the approval given to national roads to communism after the first Soviet-Yugoslav rapprochement in 1955, had led to a limited revival of Bulgarian nationalism, which is closely linked with the Macedonian issue. At this time the Bulgarian party was badly split. Todor Zhivkov, its first secretary, was obviously the leading contender for power. Chervenkov, who had been the unquestioned leader of Bulgaria before de-Stalinization, was removed from his post as head of government in April 1956, but he still had a sufficient following on the lower and middle levels of the party to prevent his complete removal. He retained his seat on the Politburo, but was demoted from chairman to deputy chairman of the Council of Ministers. Yugov, the new chairman of the council, used his position to gather around him a recognized faction. Since none of these factions was strong enough to risk alienating Bulgarian nationalism, none opposed a nationalist position once the Macedonian question was broached.

Although the change in Bulgaria's policy on the Macedonian question was apparently decided upon in April 1956, international conditions were not appropriate for this position to be openly expressed for nearly two years. The primary reason was the good state of Soviet-Yugoslav relations from before 1956 until the

* The Bulgarian census which was taken on December 1, 1956, several months after this meeting, was carried out on the basis of the earlier decision that the majority of the population of Pirin Macedonia were Macedonians. Despite the April plenum's change in policy, the published statistics indicated that there were some 187,789 "Macedonians" in Bulgaria, and that "Macedonians" constituted the majority of the population of the Blagoevgrad Region (Pirin Macedonia). The 1959 edition of *Statisticheski godishnik* (the Bulgarian statistical yearbook) listed these data, and it was not until the 1960 and subsequent editions of the yearbook that the table entitled "Population by Nationalities" was omitted.

end of 1957. These relations had been hostile since the expulsion of the Yugoslav party from the Cominform on June 28, 1948, but after the death of Stalin the Soviet leaders entered on a cautious program of improvement. The high point of the rapprochement was the Khrushchev-Bulganin visit to Belgrade in June 1955, which was followed one year later by Tito's visit to Moscow. The Hungarian revolution and the USSR's violation of the Hungarian-Yugoslav agreement on the protection of Imre Nagy, however, temporarily strained relations between Yugoslavia and the Soviet bloc, and at the time of the conference of world communist parties in Moscow during November 1957 Soviet-Yugoslav relations grew much worse. The Soviet leaders, pressed by the Chinese to assert the Soviet Union's leading role in the international communist movement more strongly, decided to use pressure against Tito, hoping to force him into a closer alignment with the bloc. But they had miscalculated, and the Yugoslav delegation to the Moscow conference, from which Tito withdrew at the last minute due to "illness," refused to sign the declaration drawn up at the conference. Shortly after this, the Yugoslav party published the draft program for its seventh congress. In early April the Soviet party announced it would send no delegation to the forthcoming Yugoslav congress and two weeks later *Kommunist,* the official organ of the Communist Party of the Soviet Union, published a lengthy "comradely party criticism" of the Yugoslav party's draft program. The announcement of Imre Nagy's execution on June 16, 1958, plunged relations to an even lower level.[4] The states of Eastern Europe faithfully followed Moscow's lead and attacked the Yugoslav revisionists. Thus in 1958 the Bulgarians were at liberty to revive claims to Macedonia since this was consistent with the current state of Soviet bloc relations with Yugoslavia.

The first Bulgarian claims were advanced under the guise of the celebration of the eightieth anniversary of the liberation of Bulgaria from Turkey in 1878. The occasion was used to emphasize Bulgarian-Russian friendship, since it was the Russian conflict with Turkey in 1877–1878 that had led to Bulgarian independence. The highlight of the celebrations was a meeting in Sofia on March 3, 1958, the eightieth anniversary of the Treaty of San Stefano. All party and government leaders were present, as well as representatives from the Soviet Union. The main speech was given by Encho

Staikov, member of the Politburo of the Bulgarian party and chairman of the Fatherland Front. The bulk of his speech dealt with the sufferings of the Bulgarians under Turkey, the mass revolutionary uprisings, and the crucial role played by Russia in the liberation. However, there were two statements relevant to the Macedonian issue.* First Staikov declared, "In accordance with this treaty [of San Stefano] the Bulgarian people were liberated and united in one state . . . but at the Berlin Conference, Bulgaria was torn to pieces . . . destroying the just cause of the peace of San Stefano"—a clear assertion that the Treaty of San Stefano had been a proper settlement for Bulgaria and that it included those areas which were Bulgarian. The population of Macedonia, though not singled out for specific mention, had been among the peoples liberated by the Treaty of San Stefano and united with the new Bulgarian state. Second, Staykov praised Bulgaria's policy toward its national minorities and discussed the rights which were enjoyed by the Turkish minority, though he did not mention a Macedonian minority.[5]

Staikov's speech was made in March, when Soviet-Yugoslav relations had not yet reached their low point; hence, Yugoslav

* At the same time as the Bulgarians revived the question of Macedonia in the campaign against Yugoslavia, they sought to improve relations with Greece. Normal relations between the two countries had not been re-established since the end of the Second World War. Shortly after Staykov's speech, *Rabotnichesko Delo* (March 25, 1958) carried an article on the 137th anniversary of the Greek rebellion against the Turks, in which hope for an improvement in Greek-Bulgarian relations was expressed. Todor Zhivkov's opening speech to the seventh Bulgarian party congress in June 1958 also stressed the desire for rapprochement with Greece, and other articles and speeches continued to repeat this theme. The Bulgarian shift on the Macedonian question made such a rapprochement easier. The Greek position had always been that there was no Macedonian nationality but that the territory of Macedonia was inhabited principally by Greeks (although some who lived in Greece spoke Slavic), Bulgarians, and Serbs. The Greeks opposed the Yugoslav concept of a distinct Macedonian nationality split between the three countries and claimed that the Greek-held part of Macedonia was inhabited solely by Greeks. The Yugoslav claim that a Macedonian nationality existed was a direct threat to Greek territory. Now that Bulgaria no longer acknowledged the existence of the Macedonian nation, both countries were in opposition to Yugoslavia, which in effect claimed the parts of Macedonia which both held. Although the Bulgarian party's reassertion of the ethnically Bulgarian character of Macedonia also posed some threat to Greece, since 1945 the Yugoslavs had been the most vigorous in advancing claims against both Bulgaria and Greece, and hence there were grounds for a Greek-Bulgarian understanding on Macedonia.

commentary on his remarks was cautious. The first statement appeared in *Nova Makedonija,* the party organ of the Macedonian People's Republic. However, it did not appear until three weeks later, and it was mild in tone. Emphasizing Yugoslavia's interest in the Bulgarian anniversary, the paper questioned Staikov's failure to mention the Macedonian minority: "An impartial observer has no choice but to conclude that either Macedonians . . . do not exist in Bulgaria, or if they do exist, officials are unable to report any progress" in their development. "Our public," *Nova Makedonija* concluded, "is deeply interested in the explanation of this silence, which inevitably and justly causes doubts about the character and aims of such a national policy." *Nin,* in its March 30 issue, also questioned Staikov's silence on the Macedonians.

As Yugoslav-bloc relations deteriorated, Bulgaria pushed its offensive throughout the spring and summer, utilizing historical occasions to question the Yugoslav thesis on Macedonian nationality. An article on the Balkan wars in the BCP's theoretical journal quoted statistics of the Bulgarian Exarchate to show that there were no Macedonians and to prove that Bulgarians were the most numerous nationality in Macedonia.[6] On the fifty-fifth anniversary of the death of Macedonian revolutionary Gotse Delchev, *Rabotnichesko Delo*[7] published an article which criticized Yugoslavia's "revisionist" policy, ignored the Yugoslav Macedonian People's Republic, and linked Delchev with Bulgaria. The seventh Bulgarian party congress in June provided a major forum for criticizing Yugoslav revisionism and the Yugoslavs' "incorrect bourgeois and nationalistic positions . . . in regard to the Macedonian problem."[8] The fifty-fifth anniversary of the Ilinden Uprising was commemorated in Sofia on August 1 with speeches criticizing the Yugoslavs for "claiming that the Macedonian question is their question."[9]

At this time Bulgarian commentary on Macedonia was always linked to some historical occasion, did not directly respond to Yugoslav commentary on Macedonia, and was generally moderate in tone. Most Yugoslav commentary, on the other hand, was not linked to specific historical events but was in direct response to statements and articles by Bulgarians. While the Yugoslav parries were generally more strongly worded than the Bulgarian thrusts, they were not as bitter or antagonistic as they were to become. Most Yugoslav commentary on Bulgaria's treatment of the Macedonian question originated in the Macedonian Republic, with Belgrade's response often limited to merely reprinting articles or speeches from Skopje.[10] Most of the Yugoslav articles were attacks on Bulgarian officials and authors for ignoring or denying the Macedonian nationality and degrading or criticizing the Yugoslav Macedonian Republic, and they contained accusations of Bulgarian bourgeois nationalism and chauvinism.

The Yugoslavs, who had limited their commentary on the Macedonian question to answering Bulgarian initiatives, went over to the offensive in September. A major celebration was staged on September 16 to commemorate the fortieth anniversary of the Battle of Dobropolje, in which Serbian troops spearheaded an allied attack that led Bulgaria to appeal for an armistice at the end of World War I. The Bulgarian newspapers *Rabotnichesko Delo* and *Zemedelsko Zname* immediately and simultaneously published editorials attacking the Yugoslav campaign, "which by its chauvinistic character rivals all those carried out so far."[11] The debate was not left to newspapers, however. The Bulgarian government delivered a note to the Yugoslav government protesting the "recent tendencies of an anti-Bulgarian character" in the Yugoslav celebrations.[12] Both the diplomatic note and the editorials emphasized that involvement in World War I was opposed by the Bulgarian Socialist (later Communist) Party which "was the only party in the Balkans to take a correct international stand toward World War I." Not to be outdone on historical occasions, the Bulgarians announced that they would celebrate the fortieth anniversary of the Vladaya soldiers' rebellion and the proclamation of the Radomir Republic. "How distant—in sense and aim" observed *Rabotnichesko Delo,* "are the celebrations of the two fortieth anniversaries by our western neighbor and by our country! How great is the difference between the correct, Marxist-Leninist attitude to the events of the First World War manifested by our party and country, and the national-chauvinistic attitude of the Yugoslav League of Communists."[13]

The following day *Borba* asked why the Bulgarian papers opposed honoring the courageous Serbs who were fighting for the liberation of their country. The Belgrade daily continued: "Either the Bulgarian press generally abhors historical facts and the truth, or the writers of the editorials in the Sofia papers . . . associate themselves with Bulgaria's policy of 1915 and 1943 and now feel hit."[14] *Borba* also recalled that "Lenin emphasized the liberating character of Serbia's struggle against Austria, notwithstanding the generally imperialistic character of World War I."[15] The Bulgarian response accused the Yugoslavs of association with French fascists (that is, with the French World War I veterans' organizations, which had sent representatives to the celebrations at the invitation of the Yugoslavs) and reminded them that the Entente armies had suppressed the Bulgarian uprisings against the Sofia monarchy.[16] The Yugoslav counterresponse accused Bulgaria of territorial pretensions against Yugoslavia and criticized the Bulgarians for discriminating against their Macedonian minority.[17]

The Bulgarian counterattack came on September 21, in a speech by Dimitar Ganev—member of the Bulgarian party Politburo, secretary of the Central Committee, and a former leader in Pirin Macedonia. The occasion was the thirty-fifth anniversary of the September uprising, which was instigated by the Bulgarian communists on September 23, 1923, and the place was Razlog, a town which had been one of several centers of the uprising but which was also in Pirin Macedonia. Ganev stressed that the Bulgarians were commemorating "a brilliant deed of the working people," but characterized the Yugoslavs as "panting with chauvinistic madness." "Yugoslav leaders are digging into the trash heap and are displaying and praising the bloody butchery in which hundreds of thousands of sons of the Bulgarian and Serbian peoples perished for the benefit of the imperialists and the ruling capitalist cliques." Ganev went on to make the strongest anti-Serb indictments uttered by any Bulgarian official up to that time. He denounced "the great Serbian chauvinists and their Skopje agents" who "demand that the Macedonian population break relations with all that is Bulgarian and give up its past *which is in common with the history of the Bulgarian people.*"[18] On the question of a Macedonian nationality, Ganev was even more explicit: "The Macedonian population [in Yugoslavia] is compelled to give up its mother tongue, the language used by its fathers and grandfathers, and to use an artificially molded, strongly Serbianized language. . . . Today in Vardar Macedonia no one has the right or dares to call himself a Bulgarian, although there are many who possess Bulgarian national consciousness."[19] There is no doubt that

Ganev's speech represented official party policy. Not only was Yugov on the stage at Razlog when Ganev delivered it, but other Bulgarian leaders continued to denounce the Yugoslavs in similar terms.[20]

The Yugoslav response to Ganev's speech was immediate. *Politika* observed that if the Bulgarian Tsar Boris were still in power, "he would not give better wording to Ganev's ideas and would even congratulate him with all his heart."[21] *Borba* declared that the Ganev speech confirmed that the "manifestations of greater Bulgarian chauvinism" were not isolated outbursts, but a calculated policy of the Bulgarian leadership. The paper also published portions of an article from *Rabotnichesko Delo* of January 16, 1947, and the text of a 1944 letter written by Georgi Dimitrov which declared "that one of the main causes of all misfortunes and catastrophes which have assailed our people during the last decades lies in greater Bulgarian chauvinism."[22] A panel of Yugoslav radio commentators agreed that the Bulgarians were acting under Soviet direction, and the Yugoslav government delivered a strong note of protest on Ganev's speech to the Bulgarian government.[23] The head of the government of the Macedonian People's Republic claimed that the Bulgarians had gone beyond the anti-Yugoslav campaign conducted by the Cominform after 1948 and declared Ganev's attack to be without parallel.[24]

The Yugoslav response to the Bulgarian claims was not limited to verbal exchanges on "historical" occasions. The Yugoslav government also parried the Bulgarian attack by creating the Macedonian Orthodox Church. The purpose was not to further the spiritual welfare of the Macedonians, but to establish the national individuality of the Macedonians more securely. Religious identification, as was mentioned earlier, is a key element of Balkan national consciousness. The Orthodox Church in Macedonia was placed under the jurisdiction of the Serbian hierarchy when that area became part of Serbia in 1913. When the Macedonian nationality was recognized by the Yugoslav communists and given its own republic at the end of World War II, there was a movement to create a separate Macedonian Orthodox Church. The Yugoslav government, after considering the issue, opposed the action in an effort to gain the support of the Serbian church. During the 1950's attempts were made at various times to create a Macedonian church, but these were successfully opposed by the Serbian clergy. The Bulgarian denial of the existence of the Macedonian nationality in 1958, however, gave Skopje the trump card in a renewed bid to create a Macedonian church. Less than two weeks after Ganev's speech (October 4, 1958), a church council of laymen and clergy met at Ohrid, the ancient seat of a Macedonian archbishopric, and established the Macedonian Orthodox Church. The council elected a Macedonian as Metropolitan Bishop of Ohrid and Skopje to head the church, and in a move to soothe ruffled Serbian feelings, declared that the new church would remain "in canonic unity" with the Serbian Patriarch.[25]

The Yugoslavs responded to the Bulgarian challenge by staging a major celebration in honor of the seventeenth anniversary of an October 11, 1941, uprising against the Bulgarian occupation of Macedonia. Numerous articles were published in honor of the occasion, most of which also denounced the territorial aspirations of Sofia and reaffirmed the existence of the Macedonian nationality.[26] A commemorative meeting was held in Skopje with Lupčo Arsov, chairman of the Macedonian Executive Council, as the main speaker. He discussed the Bulgarian Communist Party's attempt to gain jurisdiction over Yugoslav Macedonia during World War II, and drew a parallel between Bulgarian actions in 1941 and the current claims against Macedonia.[27] *Nova Makedonija* and *Borba* both published the text of a long interview with Lazar Koliševski, secretary of the Macedonian League of Communists and chairman of the Macedonian National Assembly. He claimed that the uprising of October 1941 was "a war against the Bulgarian occupation authorities," and that it pitted "the Communist Party of Yugoslavia and the Macedonian people" against "the Central Committee of the Bulgarian Communist Party." Citing Bulgarian opposition to the creation of a Macedonian Republic throughout the entire war as evidence of irredentist designs by the Bulgarian party, he then praised the Yugoslav communists who during World War II "did not wait for the Red Army to reach its frontiers" before acting— a slap at the Bulgarian party which had waited until Soviet troops entered Bulgaria before staging a coup d'état.[28] The Yugoslavs kept up the barrage of anti-Bulgarian articles throughout the remainder of October, and the Yugoslav Macedonian party leadership was even more adamant than Belgrade in pursuing the campaign and defending the Macedonian nationality. However, Tito himself criticized the Bulgarians, questioning the relevance of the territorial claims to the ideological differences supposedly separating Yugoslavia from the rest of the bloc.[29]

The Bulgarian party leadership ceased making inflammatory public statements after the speeches of Ganev and Yugov. Perhaps Khrushchev insisted that the Macedonian question be quieted to prevent reviving other national emotions. It is also possible that the vehemence of the Yugoslav response led the Bulgarians to fear that continuation of the polemics might lead to the use of force. At the same time, the decision to take a Bulgarian "great leap forward" was sufficiently unsettling to the economy and the party that it absorbed much of the energy of the leadership. Though the Bulgarian party leaders were no longer directly involved in exchanges on the Macedonian question, however, articles continued to appear denying the existence of a Macedonian nation. One of the strongest of these was published by the Institute of History of the Bulgarian Communist Party. It underlined the Bulgarian position on the events of 1877–1878, criticized Yugoslav newspapers, and concluded with one of the strongest official Bulgarian statements:

> There is no reason to grant the status of national minority to the population of the [Pirin] Region. Such separation would be artificial and would amount to the creation of differences that do not exist. . . . Between the population of the Pirin Region and the Bulgarians there are no differences in language, culture, economy; there are no legal or national differences. To transplant the semi-Serbian literary langauge, which is fabricated in Skopje, to the Pirin Region would be tantamount to exerting pressure on the inhabitants of that region.[30]

The single most important statement from the Yugoslav side in the 1958 "historical" debates was a speech by Lazar Koliševski on November 2, 1958, on the occasion of the centennial of the founding of the first high school in Titov Veles. Koliševski's speech was divided into two main sections. The first was a review of Macedonian history, which became a key to the correct interpretation of the history of that area written in Yugoslavia thereafter. His thesis was that a separate Macedonian national consciousness had begun to develop during the nineteenth century. While admitting that "we

197

are still faced with many major tasks in the field of our national history," he blamed the failure to acknowledge a Macedonian nationality in the nineteenth century on the imperialistic aims of the Serbian, Greek, and Bulgarian bourgeoisie. He criticized "the progressive socialist movements in the Balkans" as being "disoriented with respect to the genuine national essence of the Macedonian movement," and he accused the Bulgarian communists of having committed the "fundamental error," during the interwar period, of assuming that Macedonians were "essentially Bulgarians."

The second part of Koliševski's speech was a specific refutation of Bulgarian statements dealing with the Treaty of San Stefano. The thrust of his argument, which he bolstered with citations from Marx, Lenin, Dimitar Blagoev (founder of the Bulgarian Communist Party) and the Soviet encyclopedia, was that the Russians were not concerned about Bulgarian liberation or Bulgarian national interests, but merely intended to use the Bulgaria of San Stefano to further their imperialist designs on the Balkans. He ended with a criticism of Blagoev and a denunciation of the current Bulgarian party leadership for its failure to recognize the historical existence of the Macedonians.[31] Koliševski's speech was considered of such importance that it was not only published in many Yugoslav newspapers but also printed separately in Macedonian, Serbo-Croatian, and several non-Yugoslav languages.

Bulgaria's reply to Koliševski's speech came in the form of a verbal protest to the Yugoslav government on November 19, 1958. The Bulgarians not only protested Koliševski's speech but also statements by Tito and Svetozar Vukmanović-Tempo and articles in Yugoslav newspapers. The Bulgarian government admitted "the existence of the People's Republic of Macedonia and the Macedonian problem," but the note did not use the term "nation" or "nationality" in relation to the Macedonians. The Bulgarians did, however, accuse the Yugoslavs of carrying on an "anti-Bulgarian campaign for the purpose of taking over territory from the People's Republic of Bulgaria." The note accused the Yugoslavs of producing inaccurate history and geography texts which claimed that "the population of Pirin Macedonia . . . wants to join Yugoslavia" and that "during World War I Bulgaria annexed Pirin Macedonia," making it "seem that Bulgaria had taken territory from Yugoslavia when history proves just the opposite." The Yugloslavs were also accused of inciting "chauvinistic passions" by bringing up the difficulties between the parties in 1941–1944 instead of "stressing the joint struggle of the two peoples against fascism."[32]

After delivering the note of protest the Bulgarians quietly allowed the Macedonian issue to drift into the background, although occasional articles still appeared questioning the existence of a Macedonian nationality. The celebration of the eighty-first anniversary of the Treaty of San Stefano was low-keyed and was not used for verbal attacks on Yugoslavia. However, the Yugoslavs, particularly the Yugoslav Macedonian leadership, continued to publish articles and make speeches denouncing Bulgaria. Lazar Koliševski's speech commemorating the fortieth anniversary of the founding of the Yugoslav Communist Party and his address to the Third Congress of the League of Communists of Macedonia both contained lengthy and bitter denunciations of the Bulgarians.[33] Finally, even the Yugoslavs gradually allowed the issue to slip into the background. Periodically, however, the press in Yugoslav Macedonia denounced Bulgaria on the basis of "new evidence" that minority rights were being denied to the inhabitants of Pirin Macedonia. In Bulgaria, although the issue remained relatively quiet, the party and government continued to deny the existence of a Macedonian nationality and took steps to prove their point.

By 1961 there were signs of a Soviet-Yugoslav rapprochement. Koča Popović, the Yugoslav Foreign Minister, visited the Soviet Union in July 1961. Soviet Foreign Minister Gromyko returned the visit in April 1962, and the following month Khrushchev, in Bulgaria, declared that Soviet-Yugoslav relations were no longer "strained" but were "normal" and even "good."[34] Despite the improvement in Soviet-Yugoslav relations, however, the Bulgarian party was slow to alter its position on the Macedonian question. The Yugoslavs, whose fighting spirit had been roused in a dispute with Greece over the existence of the Macedonian nation,* revived

* The Greeks have maintained that there is no Macedonian nationality and that Slavic-speaking inhabitants of Greek Macedonia have Greek national consciousness. In the interest of good Greek-Yugoslav relations after 1948, Belgrade played down the differing views. However, after 1960 the issue came into the open, at a time when Soviet-Yugoslav relations were improving. Some Greek government officials, including George Papandreou, speculated that the motive behind the reappearance of the differences was to further improve relations with the USSR by deliberately damaging Yugoslav relations with a NATO coun-

the historical polemics with the Bulgarians, hoping to force Moscow to reprimand Sofia in the interest of good relations with Yugoslavia.[35]

The Bulgarian government, however, continued to follow its own policy on Macedonia, ignoring the Belgrade-Moscow rapprochement. The Bulgarian chargé d'affaires in Athens requested a meeting with a leading Greek opposition politician on April 2 and assured him of Bulgaria's support for the Greek position in the Greek-Yugoslav differences over Macedonia. It is difficult to believe that a Bulgarian diplomat would have made such a statement without instructions from Sofia. The move was obviously part of an apparent attempt to improve Greek-Bulgarian relations at a critical time. (A Bulgarian trade delegation was to arrive in Athens shortly to negotiate an increase in trade between the two countries as well as to consider other aspects of their relations, including the sensitive issue of Bulgarian reparations, which had been owed to Greece since 1947 and had not yet been paid.)

Bulgaria's insistence upon publicly voicing its views on the Macedonian question forced Moscow to make the Soviet position clear. Patriarch Alexis of Moscow, head of the Russian Orthodox Church, was sent, with Khrushchev's blessing, to visit Yugoslavia and Bulgaria. His last stop before going to Sofia was in Skopje, to visit the Archbishop of the Macedonian Church. Moscow could not have chosen a better way to demonstrate Soviet recognition of the Macedonian nationality, and the Yugoslav Macedonians, now with Soviet approval, continued their "historical" polemics with Bulgaria.

Bulgarian success in quieting internal dissension over Macedonia

---

try. While this may be a partial explanation, there are indications that Skopje was forcing Belgrade in the campaign. In Yugoslavia there was a resurgence of internal nationality conflict which was exacerbated by serious economic problems. The accusations against Greece of failing to acknowledge its "Slavophone" minority as Macedonians and an almost simultaneously renewed campaign against Bulgaria were strongly motivated by this resurgence of nationalism. There is evidence that Belgrade was interested in keeping good relations with Greece despite differences over Macedonia. A Greek correspondent claimed that the Yugoslav ambassador in Athens was instructed by Tito personally that Yugoslavia desired good relations with Greece. (*Acropolis,* April 22, 1962.) Also, although the Greek government suspended its border agreement with Yugoslavia, the Yugoslav government did not suspend the agreement and continued to allow border traffic under terms of the old agreement.

came only after the Eighth Bulgarian Party Congress in November 1962. At this congress Todor Zhivkov succeeded in eliminating his rivals for power. The party expelled Chervenkov, who had been removed from the Politburo a year earlier. Yugov was removed as premier and his entourage was eliminated from leading positions. Zhivkov was only able to do this, however, by relying heavily on Soviet support. Though he assumed leadership of the government in addition to remaining first secretary of the party, his reliance on Soviet support in some ways increased his subservience to Moscow. Now that the various factions in the Bulgarian party had been decapitated, it became somewhat easier to enforce silence on the Macedonian question. At a meeting between Zhivkov and Tito in January 1963 the Bulgarian leader apparently told the Yugoslavs that "the Bulgarian leadership and party would pursue and develop Dimitrov's line with respect to the Macedonian National Question."[36] To the Yugoslavs this implied Bulgarian recognition of the existence of a Macedonian nationality, since Dimitrov was the Bulgarian party leader who had first acknowledged this. The Bulgarian party did attempt to silence historical and linguistic denials of Macedonian nationality, but there was no official declaration recognizing its existence. Although both countries attempted to keep the issue of Macedonia in the background, neither side was completely successful. However, the periodic outbursts by academicians and local officials were not allowed to escalate, and commentary by the central press organs was conciliatory rather than polemical.[37]

The high point during this period of good relations came at the time of Tito's visit to Bulgaria in September 1965. That Macedonia was a key item on the agenda of the discussions is emphasized by the fact that the second-ranking man accompanying Tito was Vidoe Smilevski, chairman of the Assembly of the Macedonian Republic. Upon his return to Yugoslavia, Tito stated: "As a result of our talks, all that made it impossible to maintain good relations earlier [that is, Macedonia] has been overcome." He went on to criticize historians "who write and interpret the history of our peoples according to their own desires,"[38] and implied that agreement had been reached with the Bulgarians on the Macedonian question. However, since the Bulgarian position was the direct antithesis of that of the Yugoslavs, the most that was agreed upon was that both sides would use restraint in discussing the issue. Apparently Zhivkov gave assurances that the question "would not be treated polemically in the press, but would be left for expert discussions among scholars."[39] Krste Crvenkovski claimed that the basic disagreement had not been resolved at the meetings, but apparently Tito and Zhivkov criticized "the attitudes of individual historians who falsified the past, thus hampering neighborly and friendly relations." Both sides insisted on "more restraint during public polemics and on shifting the research of the past onto a scientific level with more scientific and moral responsibility."[40]

After the 1965 meetings specific steps were taken to improve economic cooperation between Bulgaria and the Macedonian republic, and the head of the Macedonian government spent several days in Bulgaria at the invitation of Todor Zhivkov. Despite these improvements, however, the "historical" polemics continued. *Istoricheski Pregled,* the publication of the Institute of History of the Bulgarian Academy of Sciences, was a leading protagonist of the Bulgarian national position. In late 1965 and throughout the following year a number of articles appeared, usually in the form of reviews of recently published works on history, which consistently held to the thesis that "Macedonians as a separate nationality do not exist."[41] Articles also occasionally appeared in Bulgarian publications which provoked Yugoslav responses because they listed "Macedonian" historical figures among "the glorious host of sons of the Bulgarian people."[42] The Yugoslav responses to these articles were generally restrained in tone and appeared several weeks after the Bulgarian articles were published. They emphasized the current good state of Bulgarian-Yugoslav relations, and called on both sides "to do everything in their power to avoid the repetition of similar statements."[43]

In January 1967, after a conflict with Bulgarian writers over the existence of a Macedonian language just two months before, the Yugoslavs became more polemical in responding to Bulgarian articles. A Yugoslav Macedonian writer criticized articles in Bulgarian newspapers commemorating the ninety-fifth anniversary of the birth of Gotse Delchev, which he said referred to Delchev as "a Bulgarian national hero." The author concluded that "views previously presented by individuals have now been elevated to the position of a general view."[44] While the Bulgarian articles did refer to Delchev as a "Bulgarian patriot," however, they were otherwise cautiously worded and did not signal a change in the Bulgarian party line.[45] The Yugoslavs not only responded harshly to the articles on Delchev's anniversary, but the following week, contrary to previous practice, they took the initiative in attacking Bulgaria, and *Nova Makedonija* and *Borba* published articles criticizing the 1965 Bulgarian census, which listed less than 10,000 Macedonians in Bulgaria, some 180,000 less than in 1956.[46] Nevertheless, though historical debates on Macedonia continued to disturb Yugoslav-Bulgarian relations periodically, there was still a strong desire on the part of both governments to maintain good relations. Bulgarian-Yugoslav relations were not significantly upset by the Macedonian question between the fall of 1962 and December 1967. Periodic outbursts from local party officials and academicians were not permitted to escalate the dispute, even though the leaders were not willing to drop the issue entirely.

In the fall of 1967, however, the Bulgarian party changed its line on Macedonia. This was not due to any decline in Soviet-Yugoslav relations; in fact, Yugoslavia's relations with the USSR between June 1967 and March 1968 were in general excellent. The Arab-Israeli war so perturbed Tito that Yugoslavia became an outspoken advocate of bloc unity in order to support the Arab governments, and differences over events in Czechoslovakia did not introduce a note of discord into Yugoslav bloc relations until April. Although Belgrade was opposed to the conference of communist parties which Moscow had long been advocating, neither side permitted this question to disturb their relations until disagreements over other issues became apparent in April and May 1968.*

Despite good Soviet-Yugoslav relations in the fall of 1967, the Bulgarian leadership permitted the Macedonian question to upset its relations with Yugoslavia. The reasons behind this policy change were primarily internal. Although in 1962 Todor Zhivkov, with Soviet assistance, was able to decapitate other factions by removing his chief rivals and their entourages, he did not succeed in

---

* The Yugoslav party, since it had not been a participant in the 1960 Moscow conference of communist parties, was not invited to the consultative meeting in Budapest from February 26 to March 5, 1968. The Hungarian party, as host to the next (April 24–28, 1968) meeting on the communist conference, did invite the Yugoslavs. Though the latter declined to attend, their reasons for not doing so were not made public until after the conference (*Borba*, May 5, 1968), when relations with the bloc had already begun to cool.

extending his influence over his rivals' followers on the lower levels of the party. He was in the position of balancing groups rather than dominating the party. The abortive coup d'état in April 1965 showed the weakness of his grip on the party and again pointed up his dependence upon Soviet support, and after the April conspiracy Zhivkov gradually took steps to strengthen his hold over the party through a number of personnel changes. However, neither the party nor its leader was particularly popular with the Bulgarian population, particularly the youth. Therefore Zhivkov launched a campaign to encourage Bulgarian patriotism in order to weaken the appeal of Western influences upon youth and to identify the communist party with Bulgarian nationalism. The new patriotic campaign was initiated in the fall of 1967, when Zhivkov presented a series of theses on the party's youth activity to the Politburo. These theses, which were adopted as the guidelines for education and youth work, emphasized, among other things, patriotic education:

> Behind our motherland Bulgaria there is a dramatic and heroic history . . . but there is hardly any other state which allows such an underestimation and even belittling of its historic past. . . .
> Our young people must be educated in a spirit of love for the Bulgarian state, which for thirteen centuries has resisted all trials of history and stood up to all storms and hardships, in a spirit of love for their native land. . . . We must be proud of our history, our past, and our glorious revolutionary traditions.[47]

This revival of emphasis on Bulgarian patriotism could hardly avoid exacerbating the Macedonian question since Bulgarian nationalism and history for over a century have been closely linked with Macedonia.

Moreover, reviving the Macedonian question in the fall of 1967 had further value. Although Zhivkov's theses and other articles on Bulgarian patriotism were careful to emphasize that "patriotism is inseparable from our love and respect for the Soviet Union and its great communist party,"[48] there was some discontent both within the party and among the Bulgarian population about Zhivkov's slavish adherence to Soviet policies. The resurrection of the Macedonian issue at a time when Soviet-Yugoslav relations were obviously good would demonstrate Bulgarian independence vis-à-vis Moscow.

With the new emphasis on Bulgarian history and patriotism, commemoration of the ninetieth anniversary of the liberation of Bulgaria from Turkey and of the Treaty of San Stefano began early. Over two months before the anniversary *Rabotnichesko Delo* published an article by Professor Khristo Khristov which dealt mainly with events of the Russo-Turkish War of 1877–1878.[49] The opening paragraph, however, claimed that "the Treaty of San Stefano decreed the setting up of an autonomous Bulgarian principality which included all those lands in which the majority of the population was recognized as Bulgarian." The author also quoted letters written in the 1870's by people living in what is now Yugoslav Macedonia in which they called themselves Bulgarians, demanded liberation from Turkey, and favored national unification with Bulgaria.

The Yugoslav response, following the pattern of similar exchanges over the past five years, was restrained. *Nova Makedonija* replied to the article nine days after it was published. A much sharper response was published still later, after the Yugoslavs had been convinced by "articles published in other Bulgarian newspapers" that the article in *Rabotnichesko Delo* "was not merely a passing reference to the Bulgaria of San Stefano, but a deliberate political act having clear implications." The responsibility for the revival of the Macedonian issue was placed squarely on the Bulgarian party, but the Yugoslavs also declared their willingness to let the polemics cease in order to maintain good relations with Bulgaria.[50]

The Bulgarian leadership, however, had apparently decided to pursue its revival of Bulgarian nationalism even at the expense of relations with Yugoslavia. The same day the strong Yugoslav response appeared, *Rabotnichesko Delo* published the text of Todor Zhivkov's speech to the Bulgarian communist youth organization's congress. Following the line he had announced earlier, his speech was filled with appeals to Bulgarian patriotism. In listing five "summits in our country's history, of which we are justifiably proud," Zhivkov included the Ilinden Uprising of 1903.[51] The center of the uprising and its most noteworthy events occurred in what is now Yugoslav Macedonia, and since 1944 Yugoslav historians have maintained that the uprising was a revolt of the Macedonian nationality against the Turks. Claiming that this was a key Bulgarian historical event was bound to upset the Yugoslavs.

Although Zhivkov's statement indicated a fundamental change of policy on the Macedonian question, Belgrade still exercised restraint and made conciliatory gestures. An editorial in the Yugoslav party daily noted that the campaign was "obviously assuming the nature of a political action on the part of Bulgarian propagandists," but it also cautioned that the statements on Macedonia "grossly contradict both the friendly relations that have developed between socialist Bulgaria and socialist Yugoslavia and the Marxist-Leninist approach to history and internationalism."[52] Despite *Borba's* conciliatory tone, the Bulgarian articles and Zhivkov's speech produced a flood of Yugoslav articles in late January and early February 1968.[53] *Nova Makedonija* and the mass media in Yugoslav Macedonia were the most vocal and vigorous in denouncing the Bulgarians. Since the last historical polemics ended in 1962, the Yugoslav national republics had considerably enhanced their autonomy from Belgrade. Though the central government and party apparently preferred to play down the Macedonian question in the interest of Bulgarian-Yugoslav relations, Belgrade was forced by Skopje to be more vigorous in defending Macedonian interests. Numerous articles were published in Belgrade and in other republics defending the Yugoslav position on Macedonia, and the vigorous verbal attacks eventually led to an exchange of diplomatic protests by both sides.[54]

As in the 1958 polemics, the Bulgarians took the initiative by including phrases in historical articles that denied the existence of the Macedonian nationality. Although such claims were at times implied in historical journals and unofficial popular publications between 1962 and 1967, denials of the Macedonian nationality in a historical context now appeared in articles in *Rabotnichesko Delo,* the official central committee daily, *Trud,* the official trade union newspaper, *Narodna Mladezh,* the youth journal, and other leading newspapers and journals. The Bulgarians did not dwell upon this point of view exclusively; nor did they draw conclusions about the current situation from the history they discussed. The majority of the Yugoslav articles, by contrast, were specific attacks on Bulgarian articles which dealt not only with past history but also with current implications of Bulgarian statements.

The Soviet role in this revival of historical polemics in early

1968 is not clear.* The Yugoslavs felt that the USSR was obviously behind the campaign. A Slovene journalist observed that "Bulgarian nationalism could not become expressly anti-Yugoslav to such an extent if its authors did not enjoy at least the tacit agreement of their most powerful allies."[55] At the time, plans were being worked out to hold conferences to prepare for a meeting of the communist parties of the world, and the Soviets could have used the Macedonian issue to remind the Yugoslavs that pressure might be brought to bear if Belgrade refused to attend. However, Khrushchev's failure to coerce Tito into agreement prior to the 1957 Moscow conference was not a promising precedent for the use of pressure tactics in this situation.

Contrary to some Yugoslav statements, the Soviets at this point in the polemics apparently insisted that the Bulgarians mute their stand on Macedonia. Soviet Foreign Minister Andrei Gromyko paid a visit to Sofia from February 12 to 16. There was no statement of Soviet support for "Bulgaria's peaceful policy in the Balkans"—a stock phrase usually included in Soviet comments on Bulgarian foreign policy—in published speeches by the Soviet minister and in the joint communiqué issued at the conclusion of his visit. Although the communiqué did not indicate that Balkan (that is, Yugoslav) relations had been discussed during Gromyko's meetings with Bulgarian officials, after the Soviet minister's departure *Otechestven Front* noted that "the Bulgarian-Soviet talks in Sofia are an important, constructive element in the atmosphere in the Balkans" and their "favorable significance is beyond doubt."[56]

After Gromyko's visit there was a significant drop in the intensity of Bulgarian polemics. Sofia's celebration of the anniversary of San

* At the height of the January-February polemics, *Politika* (February 12, 1968) reviewed the third volume of a series of documents on the 1877–1878 liberation of Bulgaria published by the Soviet Academy of Sciences in which there were documents alluding to the "Bulgarian population" of Macedonia. (See *Osvobozhdenie Bolgarii ot Turetskogo Iga* [Moscow: Izdatelstvo "Nauka," 1967], III.) The review stated that the volume was "just off the press," implying that the appearance of the publication at that time showed Soviet support for the Bulgarian position. Although the book became available to the public in early 1968, it had actually been compiled and gone to press much earlier, at a time when Soviet-Yugoslav and Bulgarian-Yugoslav relations were good. It is doubtful that it was intended by the Soviet government to be a part of the polemics, since even the Yugoslavs had difficulty in finding really irredentist statements in the documents.

Stefano on March 2 and 3 was surprisingly mild. The principal speaker was Georgi Traykov, chairman of the presidium of the National Assembly and a native of Macedonia. Although he mentioned the Turkish but not the Macedonian minority in Bulgaria, his comment on the Treaty of Berlin was bland in comparison with other recently published Bulgarian statements on the subject. To reassure the Yugoslavs Traykov emphasized that "the inviolability of existing borders between European states is the basis of a lasting peace in Europe."[57] *Nova Makedonija* observed that Traykov had said little about the Treaty of San Stefano, but noted the special stress in his speech on improving relations among the Balkan countries.[58]

The Macedonian issue remained relatively calm for two months, but by the end of April there was growing tension in the relations between Yugoslavia and the orthodox members of the Soviet bloc. The Yugoslavs did not attend the Budapest consultative conference of communist parties held on April 24–28, and during the Budapest meeting the Yugoslav press began criticizing the conference. Growing Soviet opposition to the liberalization in Czechoslovakia and the increasingly vocal Yugoslav defense of the Prague Spring further heightened tensions. As Soviet-Yugoslav and Yugoslav-Bulgarian relations began to cool, the historical polemics on the question of Macedonia again grew more intense.

The sixty-fifth anniversary of the death of the Macedonian revolutionary Gotse Delchev in May was the occasion for a number of Bulgarian articles which referred to Delchev as "a great Bulgarian patriot" and declared that his deeds "are in the consciousness of every Bulgarian and must be retained as an element of Bulgarian national merit."[59] Belgrade openly accused the Bulgarians of attempting "to deny Macedonia's existence, culture, and history; to appropriate its historical heritage, traditions, and literature; to arrogate its freedom fighters; and to degrade its struggle for national freedom to pro-Bulgarian movements." This, claimed *Komunist,* "is neither science nor history, but a systematic, deliberate, and intrinsically harmful political action."[60]

The Bulgarians then escalated the exchange by specifically admitting the existence of differences. The reply was made by Khristo Khristov, director of the Institute of History of the Bulgarian Academy of Sciences. Khristov, who had written numerous articles supporting the Bulgarian position on Macedonia since 1958, noted: "There are differences between us and some of our Yugoslav colleagues concerning the interpretation of medieval and modern Bulgarian history." After citing a number of instances of historical distortion by the Yugoslavs, he observed, "Friendship between peoples does not require the falsification of history."[61] Two days after the Yugoslavs attacked Khristov's article, the Bulgarian embassy in Belgrade prohibited ten Bulgarian singers from performing in an opera written by a contemporary Macedonian composer. The embassy declared that the opera "Emperor Samuilo," which deals with a medieval Balkan ruler who was said to be a Bulgarian by Bulgaria and a Macedonian by Yugoslavia, "hurts Bulgarian national feelings."[62]

As differences over the Czechoslovak liberalization became more acute, the conflict over Macedonia escalated. During June, *Nova Makedonija* kept up an amost constant flow of articles on the subject, while the press in Belgrade and Zagreb commented frequently. Although the Bulgarians generally refrained from direct criticism of the Yugoslavs, the polemics intensified in July with the publication of a terse Bulgarian response to a number of *Nova Makedonija* articles.[63] *Borba* in turn responded that the Bulgarian campaign "is obviously officially approved and encouraged and has been intentionally planned for a long time."[64]

The sixty-fifth anniversary of the Ilinden uprising produced another polemical exchange. *Rabotnichesko Delo's* treatment of the event was considered "relatively moderate" by the Yugoslavs, though one of its articles quoted foreign journalists, writing at the time of the uprising, who referred to "Macedonian Bulgarians" and the "Bulgarians in Macedonia."[65] Other articles published a few days later spoke of the uprising as "the greatest event in the history of the Bulgarian people after the April 1876 uprising" and called Gotse Delchev and other Macedonian revolutionaries "loyal sons of the Bulgarian people."[66] The Yugoslavs staged a major commemoration at Kruševo, the city in which a short-lived republic had been established during the uprising. The celebration was reportedly attended by some 30,000 people, and mass media in Belgrade and in all the Yugoslav republics gave it generous coverage. The Ilinden controversy was given official Bulgarian sanction when *Otechestven Front* reprinted an unsigned article published in the leading Pirin

Macedonian newspaper harshly criticizing the Yugoslavs for their historical interpretation, and when Georgi Kulishev, deputy chairman of the Bulgarian National Assembly presidium, delivered a commemorative speech on the Bulgarian nature of the Ilinden uprising on August 17—two weeks after the anniversary.[67]

When the armies of the Soviet Union, Poland, East Germany, Hungary, and Bulgaria invaded Czechoslovakia, the Yugoslav party denounced the invasion and undertook measures to defend their own country against the Soviet Union. Relations between Yugoslavia and the invading Warsaw Pact states were bad, but the invasion made them worse. The historical polemics over Macedonia became more bitter than at any time since the end of World War II. The same issue of *Rabotnichesko Delo* that announced Bulgaria's participation in the invasion of Czechoslovakia also contained an unsigned article on the Macedonian question, which criticized an interview given by Krste Crvenkovski, head of the Macedonian League of Communists.[68] This was the first time in recent years that the Bulgarians had made an extensive personal attack on a Yugoslav leader. The article explained that, historically speaking, there had never been a Macedonian nationality, and it listed a number of medieval rulers of the territories that are now Bulgaria and Macedonia who were, it was emphasized, Bulgarians, not Macedonians.

To show the Bulgarians that claims to Macedonia were considered a threat to all of Yugoslavia, the first response to this stepped-up Bulgarian attack came from Zagreb. "The outright negation of the Macedonian nation and of everything that is Macedonian, including its territorial integrity," was considered "nothing but an attempt to impose a dictatorship of violence and a threat to resort to arms." Lest there be any misunderstanding, the article emphasized that any attack would be met with "the strongest possible resistance," and that "any onslaught on the Socialist Republic of Macedonia is also an attack against the Socialist Federal Republic of Yugoslavia." Though its criticism of Bulgaria was harsh, the article did conclude by calling on Sofia to abandon its anti-Macedonian campaign "in the interest of Yugoslav-Bulgarian relations."[69]

The direct response from Skopje to the *Rabotnichesko Delo* article appeared a few days later and was given wide publicity in

Yugoslavia.[70] It reviewed Yugoslav-Bulgarian relations over the Macedonian question since 1963. The frequent deviations of scholars from the declared policies of the Bulgarian party on the Macedonian question, *Nova Makedonija* said, resulted from the fact that the anti-Yugoslav campaign "reflects the general orientation of present official Bulgarian policy." For Macedonians "the great-Bulgarian claims do not represent a debate about peripheral historical questions, but rather a defense of our national freedom and independence and of the right to national and socialist development unhindered by anyone." The article also observed: "When Bulgarian bourgeois historiography disputed the historical past of the Macedonian people, it did so for the purpose of making territorial claims," but "we are asked to believe that, when Bulgarian Marxist historiography does the same thing today, it does so in the interest of friendship and cooperation."

The bitter polemics continued through September, and all were still very much concerned with history.[71] Numerous articles and speakers in Yugoslavia compared the situation since August 1968 with the crisis of 1948. In mid-September the thesis, since called the "Brezhnev Doctrine," was enunciated that orthodox socialist states have an international duty to intervene in the internal affairs of another socialist country to ensure ideological orthodoxy. This caused serious concern in Yugoslavia because the deterioration of Yugoslav bloc relations after the invasion of Czechoslovakia was accompanied by denunciations of Yugoslav ideological revisionism in the Soviet and East European press. In late September it appeared that Yugoslavia and Bulgaria might become involved in a military conflict, and both countries strengthened the troops stationed along their common border. Albania declared that there were concentrations of Soviet troops in Bulgaria and delivered a note to the Bulgarian government asking that they be requested to leave.[72] The Yugoslav press continued to claim that Bulgaria nurtured territorial pretensions vis-à-vis Macedonia.

After initially assuming an aggressive posture in order to forestall any military reaction to the invasion of Czechoslovakia, the Soviet Union cautiously began to repair the damage to its own international prestige, to the world communist movement, and to détente with the West. One of the first steps in this process was a lessening of tension in the Balkans, and particularly in relations with Yugoslavia. On September 28 the Bulgarian news agency released an officially authorized statement that the Bulgarian government "has not had and does not have territorial claims with regard to any other country" and that Bulgaria accepted "the inviolability of the frontiers established after World War II." The statement also declared that the Bulgarian government would "continue in the future to make all necessary efforts to improve relations among the Balkan countries, the Socialist Federal Republic of Yugoslavia included, and to consolidate peace and security in the Balkans."[73] Macedonia's reception of this announcement was cautious. Although the statement was welcomed, *Nova Makedonija* called on Sofia to demonstrate its intention with deeds as well as declarations.[74] The reply of the Yugoslav government, which came in the form of a Tanjug release, echoed the sentiments of *Nova Makedonija*. It called upon the Bulgarian government to "confirm" its intentions "in practice" by "strictly respecting the sovereignty and territorial integrity of Yugoslavia, by refraining from interference in its internal affairs," and "above all by abandoning its anti-Macedonian and anti-Yugoslav campaign."[75]

Despite the expressed desire of both countries to improve relations, however, the polemics continued. The historical observances which had been a part of the 1958 polemics were repeated. The Yugoslavs celebrated the Serbian victories of 1918, while the Bulgarians commemorated the Radomir Soldiers' Rebellion which had taken place at the same time in Bulgarian-occupied Vardar Macedonia. The army newspaper *Narodna Armiya* made exaggerated claims about the Bulgarian army's participation in the liberation of Macedonia and Serbia in 1944, and Yugoslav newspapers, as well as Tito himself, spoke up to assert the Yugoslav position.[76] The Yugoslavs celebrated the anniversary of the first resistance to the Bulgarian occupation of Macedonia in 1941 with speeches affirming the existence of the Macedonian nationality, while the Bulgarians celebrated the Kresna Razlog uprising of 1878 against the Treaty of Berlin with appropriate speeches and articles denying the existence of a Macedonian nationality.[77]

Both sides professed a desire to improve relations, yet both continued to engage in polemics. In a speech on November 2, 1968, Todor Zhivkov, head of the Bulgarian party and government, said that although "we have no illusions about the serious differences and contradictions in our part of the world, we are absolutely convinced that good-neighborly relations are in keeping with the basic interests of our people."[78] Nevertheless, just a few weeks later the Bulgarians took the offensive with the publication of a pamphlet setting forth in explicit terms the Bulgarian position in the historical controversy. The pamphlet, published by the Historical Institute of the Bulgarian Academy of Sciences in November 1968, was apparently at first distributed only to party officials. It did not become generally available until a few months later, after its contents had been broadcast by Radio Sofia and it had been published in the newspaper of Pirin Macedonia.[79] The pamphlet was the most extensive exposition of the Bulgarian position in the Macedonian debate yet to appear.

Most of the material it contained consisted merely of stronger and more detailed restatements of previous Bulgarian arguments, but a few new and significant arguments were advanced. The Bulgarian communists for the first time openly justified Bulgaria's nationalist policy in the First World War. The pamphlet repeated the historical fact that during World War I the Bulgarian armies were welcomed by the people of Macedonia "as proper and wanted liberators, and the Bulgarians of Vardar [Yugoslav] Macedonia deserted *en masse* to join the ranks of the Bulgarian Army."

The most interesting feature of the Bulgarian booklet, however, was its commentary on socialist and communist treatment of the Macedonian question. It quoted part of the resolution of the Third Conference of the Communist Party of Yugoslavia, held in January 1924, which denounced the Serbian bourgeoisie for having forced the "nationally conscious sections of the Bulgarian, Turkish, and Albanian populations" to emigrate from Macedonia. The desire was obviously to embarrass the Yugoslav party by accusing it of pursuing and inconsistent policy on Macedonia. Dimitar Blagoev, the leading figure in early Bulgarian socialism and communism, was praised for his own and the party organization's progressive attitude toward the "Bulgarians of Macedonia."

In a highly significant step, the Bulgarian booklet also clearly, though implicitly, declared the Macedonian policy of Georgi Dimitrov to be incorrect. The fact that Dimitrov admitted the existence of a separate Macedonian nationality in the immediate postwar years has caused the Bulgarian party considerable embarrassment.

213

The Yugoslavs constantly raise the "Dimitrov line" on the Macedonian question in polemics with the Bulgarian communists. Although Dimitrov's stand on the Macedonians was apparently abandoned in 1956, the party had never publicly admitted that Dimitrov's position was wrong. Although he was not specifically criticized, there are references in the booklet that clearly imply that his policy on Macedonia was incorrect. It is emphasized that Dimitrov's parents were from Macedonia, but that both he and his parents declared themselves to be Bulgarians. At another point it is admitted that the Bulgarian Communist Party "did allow some incorrect, non-Leninist positions on the national question, including the Macedonian problem, to slip in." The specific examples of error were all cases of party slogans denying the ethnically Bulgarian character of the Macedonian population. Even more specifically, the booklet explains that only after the Fifth BCP Congress in 1948 (at which Dimitrov rejected Macedonian unification under Yugoslav aegis), and particularly after the April plenum of the Central Committee of the Bulgarian party in 1956 (at which the party apparently decided it would no longer support the existence of a separate Macedonian nationality), was the party "finally able to eliminate the weak points in its stand on the Macedonian problem." The implication that Dimitrov pursued an incorrect policy on Macedonia could not have been made by the Historical Institute of the Bulgarian Academy of Sciences; approval of the top party leadership would have been essential for the publication of such a claim.

Once Radio Sofia began to broadcast the contents of the pamphlet, the Yugoslavs issued the most vigorous protests, including a diplomatic note to the Bulgarian government on February 12 objecting to the dissemination of the booklet.[80] A further exchange of notes between Sofia and Belgrade apparently cleared the way for improved relations, and the booklet was withdrawn from circulation.[81] Despite the improvement in relations which followed this move, there were still flare-ups on historical occasions. The sixty-sixth anniversary of the Ilinden uprising and the twenty-fifth anniversary of the founding of the Macedonian Republic, which were celebrated on the same day, produced another, though somewhat milder, exchange.[82] In November the anniversary of the liberation of Macedonia and the Yugoslav national holiday provoked a spirited exchange over Bulgaria's role in the liberation of Yugoslav

Macedonia and parts of Serbia.[83] The Yugoslavs, meanwhile, attempted to give greater credibility to their interpretation of "Macedonian" history through the publication by the Institute of National History in Skopje of a three-volume *History of the Macedonian People*. The work goes into great historical detail in an attempt to show that elements of a separate Macedonian nationality began to develop as early as the Middle Ages.[84]

In the fall of 1970 there was another flare-up, but most of the commentary was from the Yugoslav side.[85] In the atmosphere of détente that followed the signing of the West German-Soviet and West German-Polish treaties in August and December, Belgrade apparently kept the Macedonian issue alive in the hope of getting Bulgaria to make concessions by recognizing the Macedonian nationality and denying any territorial claims to Macedonia. As the blush faded from the West German *Ostpolitik* in the course of negotiations over Berlin and the delay in the ratification procedure in Bonn, Yugoslavia also muted its campaign. During the summer of 1971, following the visits of the Yugoslav foreign minister and the Rumanian president and party leader to Peking, the Soviet Union became concerned about the possibility of a pro-Chinese Belgrade-Bucharest-Tirana axis in the Balkans. After the announcement that President Nixon intended to visit Peking, the Soviet Union and its faithful Warsaw Pact allies began a campaign of pressure against Yugoslavia and Rumania. Although Bulgaria, which had been involved in a Soviet-approved campaign to improve relations with its Balkan neighbors, did not participate in the verbal attacks as actively as did the other Warsaw Pact states, there was an increase in the historical polemics.[86] Although a visit by Soviet party leader Brezhnev to Belgrade in September marked the beginning of a new Soviet effort to improve relations with Yugoslavia, the Bulgarians intensified the polemics after his visit by publishing two poems, written by a father and son who had both formerly lived in Yugoslav Macedonia and then established residence in Sofia,[87] and also by distributing, at joint Yugoslav-Bulgarian border rallies on the Macedonian border, copies of the booklet by the Bulgarian Institute of History which had been a major source of controversy in early 1969.[88] It was somewhat unusual that before Brezhnev's visit to Belgrade and before tension in Soviet-Yugoslav relations was relaxed, Sofia was quite mild in its treatment of the Macedonian polemics. However, after Brezhnev's visit and the improvement of relations that followed, the Bulgarians launched a new anti-Yugoslav attack over the Macedonian question. Within a few weeks this exchange quieted down, however, and relative calm was again restored.

The historical debate over Macedonia has not again reached the bitter, vehement levels of the 1968 and early 1969 exchanges. Nevertheless, the quiet periods have not been as tranquil as 1963–1967. Since 1968 both Belgrade and Sofia have been less able to control the Macedonian polemics. In Yugoslavia the constituent republics have increased their autonomy since the fall of Ranković in 1966, and, as Belgrade no longer has the sole right of determination, the Macedonian Republic is anxious to assert itself under these new conditions. In Bulgaria the party's attempt to increase its popular support by mildly encouraging Bulgarian nationalism has made it more difficult and more disadvantageous to enforce compliance on the Macedonian question.

Macedonia has been the indicator of the state of Yugoslav-Bulgarian relations since the communist parties of both countries came to power during World War II. While Macedonia is still very much a current issue between them, it is not the only cause of bad relations. The problem has been more than merely an indicator of the state of relations, however. Macedonia was the primary cause of bad Bulgarian-Serbian (later Bulgarian-Yugoslav) relations between 1870 and 1944. The communist seizure of power in both countries did not alter the essence of the conflict, though it did place it in a different context. Because Bulgaria has been one of the East European regimes most faithful to Moscow, Sofia cannot allow the Macedonian conflict to vary significantly from the current Soviet line on relations with Yugoslavia. However, there are indications that the question has had a life of its own that even the Bulgarian communists have been unable or unwilling to control completely. In fact, some Bulgarian communists have been among the most outspoken advocates of Bulgarian claims to Macedonia. After the death of Stalin and the decision of the Soviet Union to improve relations with Yugoslavia, Bulgaria was one of the last of the communist states to follow suit. In 1958 Bulgaria raised the Macedonian question only after relations had begun to decline between Yugoslavia and the Soviet Union. But in 1962, when Soviet-Yugoslav relations were improving, the Bulgarian party had difficulty in cutting off the Macedonian debate. Between 1963 and 1967, when Soviet-Yugoslav relations were good, the Bulgarians were not successful in suppressing nationalist outbursts despite the fact that Tito and Zhivkov had agreed to prevent the issue from harming the relations between their respective countries. In late 1967 and early 1968, however, at a time when Yugoslav-Soviet relations were good, the issue reappeared in a campaign to foster Bulgarian patriotism. It appears that the Bulgarian Communist Party has only to loosen its grip slightly and the issue immediately flares up. Though Macedonia is no longer the prime factor in Bulgarian-Yugoslav relations, it remains an important element.

In the historical polemics between Bulgaria and Yugoslavia, the Yugoslavs have almost always been on the defensive. Until the Second World War few ethnographers or historians were willing to admit the existence of a Macedonian nation. Even the Yugoslav Communist Party did not acknowledge it as a nationality to which full rights, equal to those of the Serbs and Croats, should be granted until the Second World War. With so little historical background behind an obviously political decision to create a Macedonian nationality, the Yugoslav party and government, as well as the Macedonian communist leaders, have been extremely defensive on the question of that nationality. The internal structure of Yugoslavia also makes the party more sensitive to nationality problems. The federation is composed of Serbs, Croats, Slovenes, Macedonians, Montenegrins, Albanians, Hungarians, and several other nationalities, and there is no *Staatsvolk* around which the state can coalesce. Yugoslavia is unique among communist states in that it has become a truly federal state with centers of power in the republics. Thus there is give-and-take in the relations between federal party and government organs and those of the republics. In the face of nationality differences throughout Yugoslavia, Belgrade has been forced to support what the Macedonian communist leaders consider their vital interests, even though at times these may conflict with what Belgrade would consider to be in its own best interest.

The Bulgarian government, on the other hand, has retained far greater central control and is faced with no internal nationality conflict. Although in the past (1923–1934) Macedonians have dominated the central government and followed a regain-Macedonia-at-any-price policy, this has not been the case under communist rule. Individual Macedonians have held high positions in the BCP, but there has been no Macedonian group with enough power to dominate the party structure. The party, for the most part, has been more concerned about developing the economy than about devoting itself to the risky task of fulfilling Bulgarian national goals. However, in its attempt to gain popular support by fostering Bulgarian patriotism, it has opened a Pandora's box on the Macedonian question.

The Bulgarian-Yugoslav polemics over Macedonia have been the most extensive and most bitter of any of the nationality debates between communist parties. Among the reasons for this one can cite the nature of Macedonia and the Balkans. The nationalism of the Balkan peoples is a recent development. Bulgarian national consciousness dates back little more than a century, and throughout most of this period nationalism has been linked with the struggle to unite all Bulgarians in a single state. Many Bulgarians can still remember the struggle for Macedonia waged against the Turks and Serbs between 1900 and 1914, and no Bulgarian is far removed from those who were involved in the events of that period. Macedonian nationalism is an even newer phenomenon. It is probably reasonable to say that before World War II most of the Slavic inhabitants of Macedonia considered themselves to be Bulgarians, although they were aware of differences between themselves and the inhabitants of Bulgaria (just as Texans are conscious of differences between themselves and New Yorkers). Now, some thirty years after the Macedonians were made a nationality, with their own republic, language, history, and culture, it is difficult to say what the Slavs of Macedonia really consider themselves to be. There are probably some who still think of themselves as Bulgarians, while others have adopted a Macedonian consciousness. Because the nationality is not yet firmly established and fully accepted, there is some degree of national insecurity. Those who fully accept Macedonian consciousness, and this would include all the leaders of the government and party of the Macedonian Republic, are anxious to show to themselves and to those who may be wavering the validity of the Macedonian national existence. To them the Bulgarian denial of the Macedonian language and history represents the most serious challenge. The relatively young Bulgarian nationalism and the insecurely established Macedonian nationalism are ingredients for an extremely volatile situation.

Another reason for the extensive "historical" polemics on Macedonia derives from the status of Yugoslavia in the communist world. Since the Cominform resolution of 1948 Yugoslavia has not really been a member of the Soviet sphere, though at various times Belgrade has had very close relations with Moscow. Yugoslavia, which professes the same Marxist-Leninist ideology that inspires the rest of the Soviet bloc, is either a fraternal socialist state or a schismatic capitalist wolf in communist sheep's clothing. This love-hate relationship makes the variations in Yugoslav-bloc relations much more pronounced. Just as in the Soviet-Chinese polemics, the fact that Yugoslavia is a communist country adds a bitter sense of betrayal and treason to the communist cause when Yugoslavia and the Soviet bloc are on unfriendly terms.

Not only has the Macedonian debate been the most extensive and most bitter, it has also been the least esoteric of the nationality debates between communist parties. Although both sides have generally stayed within the framework of historical debate, they have gone farther by specifically accusing each other of making territorial claims. The other historical debates between East European communist states have generally stopped short of this. One of the reasons is Yugoslavia's position as a state that is not fully a member of the bloc, which means that there is no Moscow-imposed necessity to maintain a facade of good relations. East European states can accuse Yugoslavia of territorial claims, a charge they cannot explicitly make against other members of the bloc. And Yugoslavia, of course, is under no external restraint to maintain an appearance of unity with other members of the Soviet sphere.

Chapter 11

"Historical" Debates: Bessarabia

Bessarabia, and to a lesser extent northern Bukovina, both of which were taken from Rumania by the Soviet Union in 1940, have also been the subject of a fascinating historical debate.[1] But while the debates over Bessarabia and Macedonia follow the pattern of other historical controversies, there are a number of differences between the Rumanian-Soviet debate on Bessarabia and that between Yugoslavia and Bulgaria about Macedonia. Arguments about Macedonia are carried on in the daily press, with both sides attacking specific articles and authors. The scholarly publications and the academicians defend their own national points of view, but this is not the major field of engagement. The Bessarabian debate is far more subtle. Most of the articles are scholarly, and the daily newspapers and mass circulation journals are not usually involved in the exchange. Rumanian and Soviet sources have generally avoided direct attacks against specific individuals or articles, and, although charges are answered and countercharges are advanced, this is done without direct reference to the other party. Responses in the debate are ostensibly tied to a "historical" occasion rather than appearing as direct answers to a thrust from the opponent. The stridently polemical tone of the Macedonian debate has not been a feature of the Bessarabian exchanges.

There are a number of reasons why the Soviet-Rumanian controversy over Bessarabia has been more restrained than the Macedonian dispute. First of all, the Soviet Union is a great power, Rumania is a small state, and the two share a frontier some five hundred miles long. Rumania may succeed in advancing veiled, pseudohistorical claims to Bessarabia, but if these were to become overt or provocative the Soviet Union could resort to economic sanctions that could be detrimental to Rumania's program of economic development. Military pressure, in the form of a remote but ever-present threat of invasion, keeps Rumania's protests from being too blatant. As the dominant power throughout Eastern Europe, the Soviet Union demands and receives a certain amount of deference, even from an independent-minded Rumania. By contrast, Yugoslavia and Bulgaria (or for that matter, Hungary and Slovakia and Rumania and Hungary, which have also carried on historical debates) are small nations more or less equal in size and strength. The imposition of economic sanctions by one small state against another would not be serious, and any military measures undertaken would be of questionable success against an enemy of roughly equal strength. Hence, the disputants have neither the economic nor the military power to frighten their opponents into caution or restraint. Although the Soviet Union has been unwilling to permit the development of hostilities and has generally opposed even the appearance of enmity, this restraint is less rigidly enforced when Moscow is not directly involved.

Secondly, the framework of these historical debates is a communist one. Both Rumania and the Soviet Union consider themselves and each other to be members of the communist camp. Although Rumanian foreign policy has at times diverged from that of the USSR, there has never been any doubt about Rumania's status as a communist state. Though participation in joint military maneuvers has been limited, Rumania remains a member of the Warsaw Pact; though Rumania refuses to cooperate in certain aspects of East European economic integration, participation in Comecon continues. Yugoslavia's status as a communist state has, however, been less secure. In 1948 the Yugoslavs were expelled from the communist movement, and in 1949 they were branded as "spies and murderers, mercenaries of imperialism." Although in 1955 and again in 1962 Yugoslavia was acknowledged to be a full-fledged member of the communist community, when the Macedonian debate has been most intense her communist status has been questioned. In 1958, when the Macedonian issue was resurrected, the Soviet Union branded Yugoslavia revisionist and questioned her commitment to Marxist ideology. And again in 1968, when Macedonia was being openly debated, Belgrade's refusal to support an international communist conference and its outspoken opposition to the invasion of Czechoslovakia raised the question of Yugoslavia's fidelity to communism. Because Yugoslavia has at times been considered an ideological renegade and not subject to Moscow's control, the debate over Macedonia has not been greatly affected by Moscow's calls for unity. Because Russia and Rumania retain their status as faithful communist states, the necessity to give an appearance of bloc unity has required that the historical debate over Bessarabia be conducted more circumspectly.

Another factor that differentiates these two debates is the internal political situation. Yugoslavia is a federation whose constituent republics have limited independence from Belgrade. Since the leadership of the Yugoslav Macedonian Republic is vitally concerned about Bulgaria's historical claims to its territory and denials of the Macedonian nationality, Skopje has apparently put pressure on Belgrade, particularly since 1966, to respond strongly in the debate with Bulgaria. In addition, Yugoslav mass media are under less rigid control than those of most other communist states; issues and arguments are raised that would not arise elsewhere in the Soviet sphere. In Rumania and the Soviet Union, the restraining hand of the party has prevented the Bressarabian debate from becoming as passionate and vehement as that over Macedonia.

Time may also have been a factor in the Bessarabian and Macedonian disputes. Yugoslavia was expelled from the communist movement as the result of a sudden cathartic move in 1948, and Macedonia has been an issue in Bulgarian-Yugoslav relations, debated with varying degrees of intensity, since that time. Rumania's differences with the Soviet Union developed over a number of years, only becoming obvious in 1963 and 1964.

The Rumanian political leadership probably did not expect the Soviet Union to return Bessarabia;[2] nor does it nurture any illusions about its ability to regain the region by force. While there is no simple explanation for Rumania's having initiated claims against the Soviet Union, two major factors seem to be responsible. The Rumanian communist leadership has sought to expand its popular support, particularly since 1958, when Soviet troops were withdrawn from Rumanian territory and the party could no longer depend upon the Soviet Union to retain power. Although the party had achieved control over most aspects of Rumanian life, there was little popular enthusiasm for the regime; it was tolerated because there was no real alternative. The party, in an attempt to reduce this hostility and to win the active support of the Rumanian people, began consciously to link itself with popular national traditions. Placing emphasis on Rumanian interests, of course, meant giving priority to Rumanian rather than Soviet (usually described as "proletarian international") interests. There is an element of anti-Russianism in Rumanian nationalism that has its roots in Russia's domination over Rumanian principalities throughout much of the nineteenth century and in the annexation of Bessarabia in 1812 and again in 1940. In an attempt to appeal to this sentiment, during the late 1950's and early 1960's Russian names of streets, shops, and theaters were replaced by Rumanian names; Russian was dropped as a compulsory second language in Rumanian schools; greater emphasis was placed on Rumania's role, and less on that of the Soviets or the Russians, in Rumanian history. As part of this campaign, veiled, pseudohistorical claims were advanced to Soviet Bessarabia.

Raising claims to Bessarabia also furthered Rumanian foreign policy aims. In addition to seeking popular domestic support, the Rumanian party also embarked on a policy of greater autonomy from the Soviet Union in foreign affairs. The first indication of this policy was the opposition to Soviet-inspired integration under Comecon. The Soviet leadership was anxious to promote economic integration of the East European communist states in order to reduce the economic demands on the Soviet Union, to strengthen the weak economies of the bloc states, and to supplement the USSR's political hold over Eastern Europe. For both ideological and national reasons, the Rumanian party sought to develop Rumania's industrial base apart from those of other communist states, and, in addition to winning its struggle for economic independence from Comecon, Rumania has found political and economic reasons to expand her trade relations with the United States and the countries of Western Europe. She has followed a policy of neutrality in the Sino-Soviet dispute and has established much closer relations with China than Moscow would like. The establishment of diplomatic relations with West Germany in 1967, the state visit paid by President Nixon to Bucharest, and Ceaușescu's visit to the United States are notable successes in Rumania's drive to improve relations with noncommunist nations independently of, and at times in opposition to, Soviet desires. Rumania's historical claims to Bessarabia have served to accent her independence in foreign policy and have perhaps been a useful way of putting pressure on the Soviet Union in order to gain concessions in other areas.[3]

Before beginning an examination of the historical claims to Bessarabia advanced by Rumania, it is necessary to summarize the manner in which Bessarabia and northern Bukovina were treated in Rumanian historiography between 1945 and 1964. Generally speaking, there was no mention of either Bessarabia or northern Bukovina, and the few references to these territories were short and inconsequential. One book on Rumanian history, for example, discusses at length events in Transylvania and *southern* Bukovina in 1918, but does not mention what was happening in Bessarabia or *northern* Bukovina—even though at that time Bukovina was a single province under the jurisdiction of Austria, and later Rumania, and even though neither Bessarabia nor northern Bukovina was annexed to the Soviet Union until 1940.[4] In the effort to silence discussion of the lost provinces after World War II, the Rumanian government officially banned a number of books dealing with Bessarabia and prohibited the publication of literary anthologies that contained poetry mentioning the areas.[5] The loss of Bessarabia was a highly unpopular issue about which the Rumanian communists could do nothing since they depended heavily on Soviet support. Alienating Soviet leaders by raising territorial questions was not only dangerous but futile, and silence was the safest policy.

In a few instances when Bessarabia and Bukovina were discussed in Rumanian works, the validity of the Russian or Soviet claim was acknowledged. The successive annexations by Russia and the Soviet

Union were declared to be a more progressive fate than dominance by either Turkey or Rumania, and union with Russia was always described as being in accord with the will of the people. For example, a 1956 history text which described Bessarabia's "liberation from the barbarian Turkish yoke" and its annexation by tsarist Russia in 1812 explained that thanks to "the influence of the more advanced Russian state, the decline of feudalism was speeded up, along with the development of capitalism, a fact which, in spite of the backward character of tsarist policy, represented a step forward."[6] Treatment of Rumania's annexation of Bessarabia after World War I presented "the bourgeois-landowner regime of Rumania" as the agent of an imperialist plot to weaken the newly established Soviet state. It was said to have been carried out "with the approval of the Anglo-American and German imperialists," to have supported "the internal counterrevolution in Russia," and to have been "in the interest of the international counterrevolution."[7] The description of the USSR's annexation of Bessarabia in 1940 did not mention the ultimatum from Molotov and treated it as a mutually approved transfer: "Thanks to an understanding between the government of the Soviet Union and the government of Rumania Bessarabia and northern Bukovina were liberated, and thus the territorial conflict which developed after the counterrevolutionary intervention of the Rumanian army against the Soviets in 1918 was brought to an end."[8] The Rumanian interpretation of historical events involving Bessarabia and northern Bukovina paralleled Soviet historiography. However, much less was said about these questions in Rumania, which was trying to forget the problem, than in the Soviet Union, which was trying to justify Soviet citizenship for the Rumanians of Bessarabia.

In the early 1960's, as the process of de-Russification and reemphasis on Rumanian nationalism got under way, Rumanian historiography began to deal differently with the question of Bessarabia. This new treatment—in the light of both Soviet and earlier Rumanian historiography—represented nothing less than a resurrection of Rumania's claims to Bessarabia. The process began very subtly, within the framework of party directives on the rewriting of Rumanian history in order to emphasize its national aspects. References to Bessarabia and its annexation to Russia no longer acclaimed that annexation was a progressive step. New histories recounted the facts from a Rumanian point of view, frequently with an anti-Soviet twist. Whereas the Treaty of Bucharest (1812), by which Turkey ceded Bessarabia to Russia, was previously considered a progressive action, a 1964 Rumanian history merely recounted that, after the treaty had been concluded, "the Rumanian principalities, which had been occupied again from the beginning of the [Russian-Turkish] hostilities, were evacuated by Russia, except for the territory between the Dniester and the Prut [Bessarabia], which was incorporated into the Russian Empire."[9] No favorable evaluation was given of the Russian annexation. In general, since 1964 Rumanian statements on Bessarabia have all been directed toward eliminating the previous pro-Soviet interpretations.

The year 1964 was significant not only for the new treatment of Bessarabia in general historical works, but this was also the year in which the Rumanians published works by the Marxist prophets giving ideological sanction to Rumanian national positions. Obscure writings of both Marx and Engels were published which supported Rumania's claim to Bessarabia. An 1888 letter from Friedrich Engels to a Rumanian socialist journal published in London was reprinted in a volume on the socialist press in Rumania before 1900. Engels' strongly anti-Russian letter referred to the "twice-over snatching of Bessarabia" by Russia. He told the Rumanians, "Tsarism baits you, showing you Rumanian Transylvania in Hungarian hands, whereas it is tsarism that keeps it away from Rumania."[10]

The most widely heralded event in the Bessarabia debate was the publication of four manuscripts found in the archives of the International Institute for Social History in Amsterdam. These consisted of notes taken by Marx on political, social, and economic conditions in Rumania. Three of the four manuscripts were from a French volume on Rumania published in 1855.[11] Although Marx's notes dealt only peripherally with Bessarabia, his statements quite clearly indicated his acceptance of Rumania's claim to the area. On the Russian annexation in 1812, he wrote:

The Treaty of 28 May 1812. The Porte surrenders Bessarabia. Turkey could not surrender what did not belong to it, since the Ottoman Porte had never owned the Rumanian countries. The Porte itself avowed this at Karlowitz, when, pressed by the Poles to give up Moldavia-Wallachia, it answered that it was not entitled to make any cession of territory inasmuch as the capitulation had not conferred on it any rights of *suzerainty*.[12]

Not only did the Rumanian volume quote Marx's denial of Turkey's right to cede Bessarabia to Russia, but the introduction mentioned the principles of international law on which Marx's judgment of the issue was based, and the book also included two other references to the fact that Turkey could not legally cede Bessarabia to Russia. Marx also apparently accepted the French volume's figures on the Rumanian character of the population of Bessarabia since he copied statistics it presented showing 896,000 Rumanians in Bessarabia.[13]

The Rumanians not only issued the Marx manuscripts which supported their claim to Bessarabia, but they also published reviews which praised his judgments, "both implicit and explicit."[14] Although Marx's evaluation of the Transylvanian problem was praised, Bessarabia was not specifically mentioned. The praise of Marx's support for Rumanian national unity and the failure to criticize the passages dealing with Bessarabia, however, leave little doubt that the Rumanian leadership approved the implied claims to Bessarabia. Articles began to appear openly referring to territory annexed by the Soviet Union as being Rumanian.[15] The appearance of this material represented more than a lapse in the censor's office. In his report to the Rumanian party congress in July 1965, Nicolae Ceauşescu, the new head of the party, quoted from Engels' letter of 1888 which criticized Russia's annexation of Bessarabia. Although Ceauşescu merely cited one brief excerpt praising the Rumanian socialists and did not allude to territorial claims, the fact that he quoted from it at all indicates his awareness of its contents and his approval of it.[16]

The concern of the Soviet Union was heightened when the issue was raised not only by the Rumanians but also by the Chinese communists at about the same time. In an interview with a group of Japanese socialists, Chairman Mao Tse-tung was questioned about Soviet annexation of the Kuriles. The chairman of the Chinese Communist Party observed that "the places occupied by the Soviet Union are too numerous," and then he denounced the USSR's retention of the Kuriles and Mongolia. Mao went on to comment on the situation in Eastern Europe: "[The Soviets] *have appropriated part of Rumania.* Having detached part of East Germany, they drove the local inhabitants into the western part. Having detached part of Poland, they incorporated it into Russia, and as compensation gave Poland part of East Germany. The same thing happened in Finland."[17] Mao's reference to Rumanian claims to Soviet Bessarabia at about the time the Rumanians first began cautiously to revive the issue raises a number of interesting questions. Although the Chinese leader's statement and the revival of Rumanian claims may have been pure coincidence, this seems unlikely. Just a few months prior to Chairman Mao's statement, the Rumanian party sent a high-ranking delegation to Peking and Moscow in a futile attempt to reconcile the Soviet and Chinese parties. In his interview with the Japanese socialists Mao may have raised the question of territorial claims by other states against the Soviet Union (including Bessarabia) to show the Soviet leadership that a number of states had territorial claims against the Soviet Union, in an attempt to pressure Moscow to accede to some Chinese demands. It may also have been a bid to create an anti-Soviet coalition. In any case, Mao's endorsement of Rumania's claims to Bessarabia was hardly reassuring from the Soviet point of view.

The first intimation of Rumanian claims to Bessarabia provoked a counterresponse. The Soviet Union had been justifiably concerned about its hold over Bessarabia, and Rumania's claims posed a serious threat to that control. The Moldavian SSR is the only Soviet republic whose population is of the same nationality as a sizable population beyond the borders of the USSR. While control in the Baltic republics of Estonia, Latvia, and Lithuania has been a matter of major concern to the Soviets, the Baltic peoples do not represent the irredenta of some other state. Although some Armenians live beyond the Soviet borders, it is the Soviet Armenian Republic which attracts the non-Soviet Armenians. On the other hand, the Rumanian population of Soviet Moldavia, which numbers about two million, is clearly the irredenta of the Rumanian state with its population of over twenty million, sixteen million of whom are ethnic Rumanians. The obvious concern of Moscow to win the loyalty of the Moldavian population is shown by the fact that in 1963 only 44 of 159 members (27.6 percent) of the Moldavian

Communist Party's Central Committee were of Moldavian origin, but 72.4 percent were Slavs, despite the fact that Slavs constitute only 27.3 percent and Moldavians 65.4 percent of the total population of the republic. The percentage of ethnic Moldavians who are members of the communist party and the percentage of Moldavians who are members of the Moldavian Communist Party's Central Committee are considerably lower than the percentage of membership of the local nationality in any other Soviet republic.[18]

Given these indications of difficulty in controlling Moldavia, it is not surprising that the Soviet response was quick. Although the Soviet-Rumanian debate has remained far more circumspect than the Yugoslav-Bulgarian debate over Macedonia, there is no doubt that the Soviet Union has vigorously supported its own position. Its first response was to reiterate more loudly and more emphatically its traditional historical position on Moldavia. The Rumanian historical interpretations implying claims to Bessarabia were advanced in 1964, and the following year the first volume in a multivolume history of the Moldavian SSR was published. The number of monographs and articles supporting Soviet historical claims to Bessarabia also increased after 1964.

All of these works emphasized the progressive and permanent nature of the Russian annexation of Bessarabia: "The annexation of Bessarabia to Russia had a progressive significance for the population of this region. It was an important turning point in the life of the Moldavian people, who as a result of this historic act forever [*navsegda*] linked their future with the fate of their friends the Great Russian people."[19] The emphasis on the progressiveness of annexation to Russia, the uncovering of extensive links with Russia in earlier historical periods, the descriptions of cultural development, and the stress on the friendship of the non-Russian peoples for their Russian big brothers—traditional themes in Soviet treatment of the history of the non-Russian peoples—were all reasserted in Soviet writings in the Bessarabian debate.[20]

One point strongly emphasized by the Soviets was the position of the Rumanian Communist Party during the interwar period. Although the Yugoslavs have emphasized the Bulgarian party's previous position in certain cases during the Macedonian debates, they did not do so as extensively or as consistently as the Soviets have in the Bessarabian debate. Ivan I. Bodyul, first secretary of the

229

Moldavian party organization, emphasized this in a speech in Kishinev (capital of the Moldavian SSR) on the fortieth anniversary of the founding of the Moldavian Communist Party. The liberation of Bessarabia in 1940, he said, was "also welcomed with satisfaction by the working people and the Communist Party of Rumania." Bodyul then quoted a manifesto of the Rumanian Central Committee, which had been issued in 1940: "Now, when the gigantic force of the socialist state has liberated Bessarabia and northern Bukovina from the heavy yoke of Rumanian imperialism, there is a real possibility for friendship between the Rumanian people and the Great Socialist State."[21] A book review in the Moldavian party's theoretical-political journal praised the fourth congress of the Rumanian Communist Party because it declared that "the Rumanian Communist's responsibility is to support with all possible means the struggle of the working masses of Bessarabia to achieve unification with Soviet Moldavia."[22]

The celebration of the twenty-fifth anniversary of the reunion of Bessarabia with the Soviet Union on June 28, 1965, was also used as an occasion to emphasize past Rumanian party statements. *Kommunist Moldavii,* in addition to an article on the reunification, published a series of "Documents on International Proletarian Solidarity." The introductory commentary emphasized the Rumanian party's interwar position favoring the return of Bessarabia to the Soviet Union, and the documents published included articles from interwar Rumanian communist publications supporting the return of Bessarabia.[23] Frequent Soviet repetition of the Rumanian party's interwar statements was probably a factor in Ceauşescu's strong criticism of his party's previous stand on the national question in his speech of May 7, 1966. Since communist parties claim to follow the correct historical line, the party is infallible even though individual party members may err. Hence, by frequently reminding the Rumanians of their former position, the Soviets hoped to embarrass their Rumanian comrades into silence on Bessarabia.

The Soviets also quoted Marx and Engels, but it proved difficult to find statements as compelling as those the Rumanian academicians could produce. In justifying the annexation of Bessarabia in 1812, the best that the compilers of the authoritative *Istoria MSSR*[24] could claim was that "the Balkan peoples, in the just observation of K. Marx, saw in Russia their only support, 'their natural liberator and protector.' "* With little from the prophets that could be cited to support their cause, Soviet historians manufactured their own ideological justifications for the Soviet position. They explained that the annexation of Bessarabia in 1812 was correct because it joined "the people of Bessarabia with the all-Russian revolutionary movement, headed by the Marxist-Leninist party."[25] In other words, because in the next century the Soviet Communist Party would control that area as well as the rest of the Russian Empire, the annexation was justified and progressive.

The Soviet Union did not stop at giving historical responses to Rumania's implied claims. During September 1965 Ceauşescu led a delegation of Rumanian leaders to the Soviet capital, and the joint communiqué issued at the end of the visit declared that "both sides uphold the inviolability of the existing frontiers in Europe, including the state frontiers between the GDR [German Democratic Republic] and the German Federal Republic."[26] This formula, while applicable to Germany, also applies to other state boundaries. Communiqués issued by the Soviet Union and other East European states at that same time specifically opposed German boundary revisions, but they did not generally include statements on boundaries applicable to countries other than Germany. Obviously the Soviet Union considered the Rumanian reinterpretation of the history of Bessarabia to have more than academic interest.

At the congress of the Moldavian party in March 1966 condemnation of territorial revisionists and expressions of concern about the loyalty of the Moldavian masses indicated that the historical debate was having an undesirable effect. Dmitriy S. Kornovan, a secretary of the Moldavian Central Committee, admitted

* *Istoria MSSR*, I, 346. The footnote cites Marx and Engels, *Sochineniya* (Moscow, 1957), IX, 32. According to the note in *Sochineniya*, the article is by Engels, not Marx, and was written for the *New York Daily Tribune*. The article is entitled "What Will Become of European Turkey?" Two statements similar to the quoted phrase condemn the foreign policies of the West European states: "Thus that diplomatic system, which was devised to prevent Russian seizure of Turkey, forced ten million orthodox Christians in European Turkey to appeal to Russia for assistance"; "As long as the traditional policy of maintaining at any price the *status quo* and an independent Turkey in its current condition is the guiding principle of Western diplomacy, nine-tenths of the population of European Turkey will see in Russia their only support, their liberator, their messiah." Engels' article hardly represents approval of Russia's role as a protector of the Balkan Christians, however. The leitmotiv of his article is that Russia's expansion into the Balkans is reactionary and should be prevented.

231

that although that committee had "recently improved its ideological work," there were still deficiencies. He went on to specify that these deficiencies included "in the first place, education of the people in the spirit of Soviet patriotism and of proletarian internationalism."[27] In other words, anti-Soviet or anti-Russian sentiment was strong. Bodyul, in his speech to the congress, indicated that "bourgeois propaganda about the historical past of the Moldavian nation" was giving rise to "unhealthy influences." He went on to condemn "bourgeois apologists," and from his enumeration of their sins he obviously intended to include Rumanian historians: "The bourgeois apologists are striving to discredit and denigrate the conquests of the Soviet Union, sow hostility between the socialist countries, fan nationalism and chauvinism, make territorial claims against the Soviet Union and other socialist countries, and demand revision of the results of World War II."[28]

In its early stages the historical debate had received obvious but only implied support from government and party leaders in Rumania. The strongest and most official Rumanian statement was a speech of Nicolae Ceaușescu on May 7, 1966. Rumania's claim to Bessarabia had been advanced with increasing boldness for almost two years, and Soviet response had for the most part been limited to replies couched in historical terms. Although links with the bloc remained, Rumania's policy of autonomy in foreign affairs was bringing international prestige and economic benefits which could not have accrued with a pro-Soviet policy. Ceaușescu's authoritative assertion of Rumania's claim to Bessarabia was made in part because of the increasing confidence of the Rumanian leadership in its ability to pursue a course independent of the Soviet Union. However, there are also indications that Hungary—with Soviet knowledge if not at Soviet request—was pressuring Rumania on the question of the Hungarian minority in Transylvania. The policy of integrating the Hungarian minority into Rumania, which was pursued after 1957, had led to the taking of a number of steps against the Hungarian minority. On various occasions since 1959 the Hungarian leadership had expressed concern to the Rumanian leaders about their conationals in Transylvania, and there were some reports in early 1966 that the Hungarians had again raised the issue with the Rumanians. It is also possible that the Soviet leadership itself had raised the issue of Transylvania as a threat to Rumania if Bucharest should continue to pursue its independent foreign policy line and continue to press the Bessarabian issue. The Rumanians, undaunted, voiced their Bessarabian claims more vigorously. In his speech on May 7, 1966, Ceauşescu advanced the strongest and most official claim Rumania had thus far made to Bessarabia.

All the elements of a classic historical debate were evident in Ceauşescu's speech. The occasion for the speech was historical—the forty-fifth anniversary of the founding of the Rumanian Communist Party. The speech was important, not for its contribution to history but because of its relevance to relations with the Soviet Union and the current debate on Bessarabia. The most controversial comments were on the correct Marxist interpretation of certain party congress resolutions during the interwar period, and the communist prophets were cited—Marx, Engels, Lenin, the Rumanian progressive N. Bălcescu. The text of the speech, which was delivered by the leading Rumanian communist, was widely distributed; five days after it was given, it was available in English, Russian, French, and Italian translations.

Ceauşescu never mentioned Bessarabia, yet his implications were so clear as to leave no doubt that he was in effect justifying Rumania's claim to that territory. The Rumanian first secretary criticized resolutions of the third, fourth, and fifth Rumanian party congresses, held during the interwar period, in which "Rumania was mistakenly called 'a typical multinational state' created on the basis of 'the occupation of certain foreign territories.'" He continued, "The introduction into the party documents of the slogan of self-determination up to the severance from the unitary state, *the indications given the party to fight for the severance from Rumania of some territories which were overwhelmingly inhabited by Rumanians,* did not take into account the concrete conditions in Rumania—a unitary state."[29]

An examination of the congress resolutions referred to by Ceauşescu indicates clearly that a major element in these documents was the insistence upon the return of Bessarabia to the Soviet Union. The resolution of the third congress in 1924 declared that the workers and peasants of Bessarabia, "who lived in liberty in the first period of the Russian Revolution and at present groan under the boot of the Rumanian military dictatorship," are "striving for national revolution and union with the Union of Soviet Social-

233

ist Republics."[30] The party then pledged to support the principle of self-determination, including separation from Rumania, so the oppressed peoples could express their will. The resolution on the national question which was approved by the fourth congress indicates that as early as the 1920's the Soviet Union had adopted the position that the Moldavians were a nationality separate from the Rumanians. The Rumanian bourgeoisie was accused of "advancing the claim that Moldavians, who constitute a relative majority of the population of Bessarabia, are Rumanians, even when the population of Moldavia considers itself in reality an independent nationality with a culture of its own." The Rumanian party declared that it was "obligated to support by all possible means the struggle of the masses of workers of Bessarabia for unification with the MASSR [the Moldavian Autonomous Soviet Socialist Republic]" and to encourage "by all possible measures, in agitation and daily activity, the tendency toward unification of the masses of workers of Bukovina with the Soviet Ukraine."[31] Ceauşescu's statement that these resolutions on the national question were "erroneous" clearly implies rejection of the thesis that Bessarabia and Bukovina should have been annexed to the Soviet Union.

Not only did Ceauşescu declare that the Rumanian party line at that time was incorrect, he also observed that this was a "consequence of the practices of the Comintern which laid down directives that ignored the concrete realities of our country, gave tactical orientations and indications which did not accord with the economic, sociopolitical, and national conditions prevailing in Rumania."[32] In the early years of the Rumanian party, non-Rumanian ethnic elements (Hungarians and Jews) dominated the organization. The interparty disputes, including differences over the national question, were resolved by appealing to the Comintern for a declaration of the correct policy.[33] During the 1920's the Comintern supported Soviet claims to Rumanian territory, and, since it controlled the conferences and congresses of communist parties, it always succeeded in having its position on Bessarabia and the national question in Rumania adopted. At the sixth conference of the Balkan Communist Federation, for example, the conference resolution declared that "the laboring classes, workers, and peasants of Bessarabia" constantly expressed "their firm national-revolution-

ary desire to unite with the Union of Soviet Socialist Republics."
In view of this desire, the Communist Party of Rumania was instructed to support "the efforts of the workers and peasants of the
various nationalities on the basis of the principle of the right to
self-determination, including complete separation from the existing state organism."[34] The resolution on the national question
adopted by the fifth Comintern Congress in 1924 declared its support for "the slogan that the communist party is fighting against
the annexation of Bessarabia by Rumania and the slogan that this
country has a right to self-determination."[35] In 1929 the Balkan
Communist Federation supported the unification and independence
of Macedonia, Thrace, and Dobruja, but "in regard to Bessarabia
and Bukovina, they set up the slogan of union with Soviet Moldavia
and the Soviet Ukraine."[36] These formulations about self-determination, including separation from Rumania, were not applied to
Bessarabia alone. At various times the Rumanian party, under
tutelage of the Comintern, advocated that the same principle be
applied to Transylvania and Dobruja. However, in any statement
on the Rumanian national question the Comintern invariably called
for Soviet annexation of Bessarabia, while the less explicit statements about Transylvania and Dobruja did not specify that these
territories should be annexed to Hungary and Bulgaria.

The reaction of the Soviet leadership to Ceaușescu's speech was
swift. Brezhnev made a sudden unofficial trip to Bucharest only
three days after it had been delivered. (The visit was reported in
Soviet news media only after the Soviet party leader was back in
Moscow.)[37] There were other issues in Soviet-Rumanian relations
that may have prompted Brezhnev's trip—Chou En-lai was sched-
uled to visit Bucharest the week after Brezhnev left, and reports
were circulating that the United States had approached Rumania
to mediate in the Vietnam conflict. Whether Ceaușescu's speech
reviving claims to Bessarabia was the prime cause of Brezhnev's visit
or not, it was certainly a major topic of conversation between the
Rumanian and Soviet first secretaries. Other Soviet reaction to the
speech was curiously mixed. *Pravda* published excerpts and a summary of Ceaușescu's speech, carefully omitting his criticism of the
Comintern and of past Rumanian party resolutions on the national
question.[38] But at the same time an article by a Rumanian communist leader was published in the Soviet party's theoretical jour-

nal, *Kommunist,* which criticized leaders of the Comintern in the 1920's for "certain evaluations which were based on a lack of knowledge of the situation in Rumania."[39]

Advantage was taken of the twenty-sixth anniversary of the reincorporation of Bessarabia into the Soviet Union, in June 1966, to restate Soviet historical claims. The occasion was not used to engage in ostentatious reaffirmation of the Soviet position throughout the USSR,[40] but articles on the event published in the Moldavian Republic strongly re-emphasized previous historical arguments.[41] *Kommunist Moldavii* published another interesting collection of documents which included a July 6, 1940, Rumanian party resolution praising the annexation of Bessarabia, a Rumanian Komsomol resolution of July 1940 on "the liberation of Bessarabia and northern Bukovina," and an article from the Rumanian communist journal *Moldavia Roșie* of July–August 1940 lauding the Soviet annexation.[42] A pamphlet published for the occasion, subtitled "The History of the Revolutionary-Liberation Movement in Bessarabia, 1918–1940," appears to have been written in direct response to Ceaușescu's speech. It was published by the Moldavian Communist Party's Central Committee, and strongly reaffirmed the Soviet historical, ideological, and national claims to Bessarabia.[43]

A high-level conference of party first secretaries and heads of governments of member states of the Warsaw Pact was held in July 1966, and the question of territorial claims was explicitly discussed in the conference communiqué. Although the main emphasis was on German territorial revisionism, the statement on boundaries was so worded that its applicability in the case of Rumania's claim to Bessarabia may well have been more than coincidence. Among other things, it declared: "One of the main requisites for guaranteeing European security is the inviolability of the existing frontiers between the European states." The communiqué then went on to add, "As far as they are concerned, the Warsaw Treaty member states declare that they have no territorial claims in relation to any European state."[44]

The Rumanians, although not abandoning their historical claim to Bessarabia, did not voice it as explicitly or as authoritatively as Ceaușescu had in his speech of May 7. However, because of Moscow's difficulty with Moldavian nationalism, the Rumanian revival of historical claims to the area certainly aggravated the problems faced by the Soviets. By the end of 1966 it had become obvious that the Soviets were concerned about Moldavia. Under the auspices of the Moldavian party and government, a "Scientific Conference on Problems of the Development and Reconciliation of Soviet Nations and Peoples" was held in Tiraspol on December 15–17, 1966.[45] In February 1967 Shelepin, a member of the Politburo from Moscow, toured Moldavia with Bodyul. A few days later, at a plenum of the Moldavian Central Committee called to discuss preparations for the fiftieth anniversary of the Russian Revolution, Bodyul delivered a report in which the nationality question was prominently discussed. He recited the standard Soviet version of Moldavian history, justifying its position within the Soviet Union. However, he then went on to indicate that this interpretation was not seeping into the consciousness of the masses. The historical facts about Moldavia, he declared, "are little known among the broad masses." As a result, "individuals easily fall under the influence of disorienting propaganda." Bodyul was critical of "bourgeois falsifiers of history who deliberately avoid mentioning in their works all positive influences on the fate of the Balkan peoples earlier attributed to Russia; they suppress facts and events which characterize the age-old aspirations of the Moldavian people for union with Russia." He also noted that "in the West" there had appeared "attempts to deny the fact that Bessarabia was amputated from the Soviet Union; attempts to prove that the region was not occupied but united with bourgeois-landlord Rumania supposedly with the people's consent." To remedy these defects, Bodyul called upon Moldavian scholars "resolutely to expose the old and newly arrived 'specialists' on Bessarabia and to champion the indissoluble friendship which has long existed between the Moldavians and the other peoples of the Soviet Union." The mass media were called on to launch a campaign "to elucidate in depth the question of the real history of the Moldavian people."[46]

The intensified campaign called for by Bodyul was quickly begun. A letter to *Sovetskaya Moldaviya* from a worker asked "to hear in greater detail about the struggle of Bessarabia's workers against the occupation regime set up by royalist Rumania . . . and about the historical situation in which the significant act of resurrection of Soviet power on the long-suffering land of Bessarabia occurred." The newspaper kindly obliged by publishing a lengthy article on Bessarabian history.[47] The republic's newspapers and journals published increasing numbers of articles on Moldavian history. The anniversary on June 28 was the occasion for a flurry of propaganda emphasizing the earlier links of Moldavia with Russia and citing interwar Rumanian communist documents which supported Soviet annexation.[48] In a series commemorating the fiftieth anniversary of the October Revolution, Radio Moscow broadcast a special program in Rumanian setting forth its historical claim to Bessarabia. The broadcast emphasized very early Bessarabian links with Russia. The Rumanians were informed that the "lands between the Dniester and Prut even in the tenth, eleventh, and twelfth centuries were part of Tsarist Russia." In 1812, "as a result of the Bucharest Peace Treaty between Russia and Turkey, Bessarabia was liberated from the Turkish yoke and was *reintegrated* into the Russian state."[49] The broadcast also included the more frequently cited justifications for Soviet possession of Bessarabia—the revolts in Bessarabia after 1919 and the interwar Rumanian Communist Party resolutions.

One Soviet goal in the debate has been to paint a particularly dark picture of the era of Rumanian rule in Bessarabia. Not only does this implicitly criticize the current Rumanian regime for accepting the Rumanian claim to the territory, but it also tends to discourage Moldavian nationalists who might prefer Rumanian to Soviet rule. On most historical occasions this tactic is repeated. In October 1966, when Kishinev celebrated the five hundredth anniversary of its founding, officials of the city and of the Moldavian Republic attacked the period of Rumanian rule between 1918 and 1940 as one of the worst in the city's history, but at the same time the Rumanian communists were praised for having supported Soviet annexation in 1940.[50] In January 1968 a celebration was held in honor of the fiftieth anniversary of Soviet rule in Moldavia, and since the anniversary came only a short time before the fiftieth anniversary of the Rumanian annexation of Bessarabia, the main speaker at the celebration, Moldavian head of government Aleksandar F. Diorditsa, described the "bloody regime, terror, and repression," as well as the collapse of the Bessarabian economy, which followed the "perfidious seizure of Bessarabia by royalist Rumania."[51] In addition to speeches by public figures on historical occasions, scholars have also been encouraged to produce works which adopt this theme.[52]

During the first period of the polemics, Soviet historians generally limited themselves to emphatically restating the Soviet position on Bessarabia, to publicly reminding the Rumanian party of its earlier pro-Soviet stand on the question, and to showing the period of Rumanian dominance of Bessarabia to have been particularly repressive. Although very early in the debate Rumanian historians were criticized only implicitly for their position, specific criticism of individual historians was a later development that marked an intensification of the polemics from the Soviet side. The Rumanians have done little more than restate their previous positions, and they have avoided criticizing Soviet historians directly. In 1969 a volume was published in Kishinev dealing with Rumania from 1918 to 1940; it questioned the reinterpretation of the Bessarabian problem by Rumanian historians, quoting specific passages and citing page references.[53] The Rumanian *Dicționar Enciclopedic* was among the works criticized. Passages in the first volume (published in 1962, before the change in the Rumanian position on Bessarabia) were contrasted with comments on the same subject in the fourth volume (published in 1966). So that there would be no doubt that this criticism was voiced with official sanction, both the Moldavian government-party daily and the theoretical journal of the Moldavian Communist Party praised the book and singled out the authors' "friendly remarks" addressed to "some historians" in the Socialist Republic of Rumania who were guilty of "unsubstantiated, subjectivist interpretations of the events between 1918 and 1940."[54] A later article in Moldavia's leading daily added new Rumanian historical works to the criticized list.[55] The *Istoria Poporului Român* (History of the Rumanian People) by Andrei Oțetea was attacked, specific criticism being directed against the use of a single word in one sentence, but it is interesting that Oțetea was the editor of *K. Marx—însemnări despre români,* the volume of Karl Marx manuscripts published in 1964 which supported the Rumanian claim to Bessarabia. Other works criticized included a history text which, in a revised 1965 edition, had changed the treatment accorded the Soviet annexation of Bessarabia in the earlier 1960 version. As part of the intensified campaign, historians in the West, as well as prewar and émigré Rumanian historians, were attacked with increasing vigor.[56]

The apparent reasons for the USSR's intensification of the polemics were the growing concern in the Moldavian Republic about nationalism and the increasing irritation with Rumania for refusing to yield on its interpretation of the history of Bessarabia. During 1970–1971 there were indications that nationalism in Moldavia was a continuing, if not a growing, problem. In January 1970, at a conference of Moldavian party ideological functionaries at which there was a discussion of the problem of nationalism, a secretary of the Moldavian party Central Committee pointed out that "the remnants of nationalism are extremely deep-seated and tenacious." *Kommunist Moldavii* admonished that the "struggle against the remnants of nationalism is not a short-term campaign."[57] At the party congress in February 1971, Ivan Bodyul, first secretary of the Moldavian party, implied that Rumania's position on Bessarabia was making it more difficult to control Moldavian nationalism. He noted that imperialism "and its flunkeys" were "whipping up nationalism and encouraging so-called special roads to socialism and [a special program] in international relations"—a clear reference to Rumania. He called for "strengthening the struggle against the vestiges of the past," and criticized the intelligentsia for "glorifying and poeticizing long-outdated customs and traditions of national life."[58] In his address to the Soviet party congress shortly thereafter, Bodyul again criticized the Moldavian intelligentsia for its "enthusiasm for ancient times" and accused such attitudes of "encouraging harmful remnants of the past, particularly among young people, and preparing the way for the penetration of views and attitudes which are alien to us."[59]

Throughout the debate Rumania has continued quietly to maintain its position on Bessarabia in historical books and articles, but these have not gone so far as to criticize Soviet historical interpretations or to enter a defense against Soviet attacks. The Rumanians have also refused to make plain the current implications of their position in the historical debate. Ceaușescu, in a speech on the fiftieth anniversary of the Rumanian Communist Party, repeated his statement that during the interwar period Rumania was a "unitary national state," without going further on the point, and he again criticized interwar party documents on the national question. In an interview, however, he refused to reply to a question about Bessarabia and Bukovina which would have required him to comment on the meaning of his own statements.[60] Without seriously escalating the polemics and further angering the Soviet leaders, the

Rumanians continue to stress their position. They have not limited themselves only to revising their history textbooks; the Rumanian government replaced a 50-kilowatt radio transmitter with a powerful 1000-kilowatt transmitter in Iași, an important Rumanian city only a few miles from the border shared with Soviet Moldavia. The radio, which is easily heard in the Moldavian Republic as well as in countries much farther away, broadcasts programs on Rumanian culture, literature, and history.

The debate over Bessarabia has remained an irritant in Soviet-Rumanian relations. Since the Soviets would prefer that the question be dropped completely, the Rumanians clearly have the initiative. However, the Rumanian leadership is too cautious to pursue Rumanian claims to the point of provoking Moscow to action, and it is too wise to expect that the Soviets will voluntarily relinquish their claim to Bessarabia and cede the area to Rumania. The Bessarabian debate has not intensified because Ceaușescu's anti-Soviet image has been fairly well established and the consolidation of his position in the party and government does not make it necessary for him to court popular support by assuming a more nationalistic position on Bessarabia. Also, there is a limit beyond which Rumanian claims to Bessarabia will provoke a violent Soviet response, which was reaffirmed by the invasion of Czechoslovakia. Though Rumania has considerable support from Western states, as well as China and Yugoslavia, the Soviet Union is a neighbor too near and too powerful for Bucharest to flout openly. Bessarabia remains a potential point of further conflict in Soviet-Rumanian relations. Whenever it proves useful to the Rumanian leaders to demonstrate their independence of the Soviet Union, to claim for the Rumanian party some measure of popular support, to counter Hungarian pressure with regard to the treatment of the Hungarian minority in Transylvania, or to further the cause of a sizable faction in the Rumanian party leadership, the dispute over the Bessarabian question could intensify.

Chapter 12

National Identity in the Future

The national question has not been solved in Eastern Europe. Even under the repressive totalitarianism of the Stalin years, communists disagreed with their comrades in neighboring states over the national minorities, and, since de-Stalinization, these disputes have become sharper and more open. National conflict has, however, been altered by the communist seizure of power. Good interstate relations are no longer disrupted by the open, violent national disputes of the past. Instead of mobilizing troops on the frontier, issuing irredentist proclamations, and encouraging terrorist guerrilla raids, national disagreements are now discussed in private meetings of communist leaders and do not become public knowledge until later, and then only in part. The communist states of Eastern Europe still utilize and have further refined the subtler techniques formerly used by bourgeois East European states in nationality conflicts: manipulating census records, gerrymandering territorial subdivisions, and conducting pseudohistorical debates. A distinctively communist contribution has been added: the technique of creating a new nationality as a means of denying the claims of another state. Although many of the tactics used by communist states now are much the same as those used by governments in power before World War II, the level of conflict is much lower.

Under the Stalinist system some national conflict occurred, but for the most part nationalism played a minor role in the interstate relations of the Soviet bloc states. Since the de-Stalinization under Khrushchev, however, the forces which emphasized internationalism in Eastern Europe have declined while tendencies which encourage nationalism have increased. The change has been gradual, and, though it is neither consistent nor irreversible, the trend clearly favors increased nationalism. The Soviet Union has been the chief opponent of indigenous nationalism in the bloc, basing its claims for hegemony on ideology—as the mother country of socialism and the fountain of the revolution, the Soviet Union leads the sphere of socialist states. For this claim to remain valid, the states of Eastern Europe must adhere to Marxist-Leninist ideology wherein victory of the proletariat brings an end to national conflict. Soviet legitimacy in Eastern Europe requires the elimination of such conflict.

Ideology may legitimize Soviet hegemony, but it was established and is maintained by Soviet power, which is still the chief force preventing nationalist outbursts in the bloc. Under Stalin, Soviet troops and Soviet agents dominated the local governments and parties of almost every East European country, and there was little reluctance to use force to gain compliance with Moscow's wishes. Once Soviet control was established, nationalism was more or less effectively suppressed. Because the use of overt military force deepened internal divisions within the Soviet leadership and hampered Soviet relations with other states, the Soviet leadership has, since 1953, sought to avoid it and has attempted, instead, to rely on nonviolent means to hold its empire. This reluctance to use force has provided the East European states with somewhat greater latitude to express national concerns. It is ironical that the post-Stalin Soviet leadership has been forced to resort to military intervention on a much larger scale—Hungary in 1956 and Czechoslovakia in 1968—than Stalin ever did. The lessening of control over the daily affairs of the East European states has meant that, when Soviet intervention is required, it comes only after serious deviation; it must, therefore, be massive.

In place of overt military threats, Khrushchev and other post-

Stalin leaders have attempted to use the integration of the East European and Soviet economies as a means of control. Even though the Soviet Union is the single largest trading partner of each of the East European states and supplies them with essential raw materials and capital goods, economic influence has proved inadequate in preventing nationalist deviation. This can be ascribed partially to Stalin's economic policies, under which each state followed a program of developing a self-sufficient economy, but monetary exchange problems and rigid central planning limit economic integration as well. Rumania's initially successful opposition to such integration under Comecon has also hampered the achievement of Soviet goals. Although joint planning and Soviet persistence have led to increased trade and economic cooperation, integration is still far from an effective means of Soviet control in Eastern Europe.

The Communist ideology that discourages nationalism has also influenced East European communists. Marxism's internationalism has no doubt had some effect on the thinking of present-day communist leaders. Since communist governments of Eastern Europe derive their legitimacy to rule from ideology, they represent the proletariat of all nationalities, not all classes of a particular nationality; theoretically they pursue the class interests of all workers, not the national interests of a *Staatsvolk*. The post-Stalin drive to make communism popular and to reduce the necessity of relying on terror in order to maintain communist regimes in power has forced local communist parties to seek increased popular support, some of which comes from appealing to *Staatsvolk* nationalism. The Rumanian party has gone farthest in this direction. After Soviet troops were withdrawn in 1958, the party began to play on the traditional anti-Russian sentiment of the Rumanian people. Russian and Slavic names of streets, shops, movie theaters, and buildings were changed to historical Rumanian names; Russian was dropped as a compulsory second language in Rumanian schools; historical claims to Bessarabia were subtly advanced. The Rumanian party generally follows Moscow on most important issues and communist ideology remains the state religion; however, because the Rumanian Communist Party has made concessions to Rumanian nationalism and pursued Rumanian national interests, it is clearly identified in the popular mind as a Rumanian national party. To a lesser degree other communist regimes of Eastern Europe have made similar concessions to the nationalism of their *Staatsvolk*. The parties' attempts to link themselves with nationalism, or at least not to pursue policies contrary to strong national feelings, have encouraged nationalism and devalued the internationalism of communist ideology.

Another factor, which in the past contributed to submerging nationalism but now is a reason for the re-emergence of conflicting nationalism, is the cohesion of international communism. Under Stalin most ruling and nonruling communist parties were under Moscow's tutelage, and differences between parties and within parties were resolved in Moscow. De-Stalinization cracked, and the Sino-Soviet dispute destroyed, the facade of international unity. During the 1960's competition between Moscow and Peking for the allegiance of smaller parties permitted East European communists to use support for Moscow as justification for seeking special privileges. The East European parties have been increasingly able to adapt their policies to suit conditions in their own states, which in turn has permitted and encouraged them to follow a more nationalist path. The invasion of Czechoslovakia, while it has certainly indicated the Soviet will to keep change within limits, has slowed but not halted this trend.

The terror tactics employed during the Stalin era forced ruling parties and ruled populations into silent compliance with Moscow's directives. The post-Stalin period has, however, been marked by a gradual though uneven loosening of the requirement for uniformity of views. This limited liberalization, even though it has frequently been reversed, has permitted the expression of some degree of nationalism. For example, the Hungarian Communist Party, which has been vigorously antinational ever since it came to power after World War II, has recently permitted the Hungarian Writers' Union to discuss the literature of the Hungarian minorities in neighboring states, a subject which was previously banned. In Yugoslavia, the purge of Aleksander Ranković in 1966 and the concomitant blow to the central Serb-Montenegrin bureaucracy's power over economic and political life have produced a renaissance among non-Serb nationalities. This increased assertiveness on the part of the Macedonians and the Albanians in Yugoslavia has in turn affected Yugoslavia's relations with Bulgaria and Albania.

Ethnic animosities roused in struggles for national liberation and kept alive by nationalist conflict until the end of the Second World War are recent memories in Eastern Europe. Feeling against American or West European imperialism is far less emotional and intense than enmity between the fraternal working-class Serbs and Bulgarians, Serbs and Croats, Slovaks and Hungarians, Hungarians and Rumanians, or Rumanians and Russians. Forces operating in the communist world today tend to permit, and in some cases to encourage, the revival of nationalism. The role that national minorities have played in the relations among communist states is merely one aspect of the revival.

Although this nationalism has been tempered and molded by communist ideology as enforced by the Soviet Union, it has also affected ideology as the states have sought ideological justification for the national paths they have pursued. Theoretical debates on the elements composing a nation and its fate under socialism have become increasingly frequent in the communist world. As one would expect, those parties which have identified themselves most closely with the national interests of their states (Yugoslavia and Rumania) have been the staunchest defenders of the progressive role of the state and the nation. Although the Hungarian party leadership has faithfully adhered to its nonnational policy and played down the significance of nation and state, there has been extensive debate on questions of nationalism, socialist patriotism, and proletarian internationalism in Hungary. The Soviet Union is also witnessing a number of divergent views on the nature of the nation under socialism.

The Soviet debate has revealed some interesting contradictions in Marxist theories of the nation. The debate has revolved around two theoretical questions: What is a nation? What will be its fate under socialism? The points of departure for these debates have been the writings of Lenin and the early writings of Stalin on the national question. Attempts at defining "nation" begin with Stalin's brief statement: "A nation is a historically constituted, stable community of people, formed on the basis of a common language, territory, economic life, and psychological make-up manifested in a common culture."[1] At this point Soviet writers divide into two camps: one group emphasizing the economic aspects; the other, the linguistic-cultural aspects of Stalin's definition. Their differences on the nature of the "nation" are not merely theoretical arguments but justification for a policy that will either encourage or oppose the merging of nationalities.

Those favoring the amalgamation of nationalities in the near future have emphasized the economic-territorial aspects of the definition. According to this point of view, since the most important characteristics of a nation are its external features, change in the economic system changes the nationality. Those who hold this view see the precapitalist ethnic forms as having little connection with "nations," which developed only under capitalism; hence, the assimilationists consider the class links binding the proletariat to be stronger than national links. They see the proletariat, at least in the Soviet Union, as rapidly approaching the merging of nations. Lenin is the prophet most frequently cited by assimilationists. Although Marx implied that the merging of nations would occur and declared class to be more important than nation, Lenin was more explicit in declaring nations to be a transient phenomenon: "Marxism advances internationalism, the amalgamation of all nations in a higher unity." The proletariat, therefore, "supports everything that helps to obliterate national distinctions and remove national barriers; it supports everything that makes the ties between nationalities closer and closer, or tends to merge nations."[2] Some of the recent participants in the Soviet debate see events leading toward the merging of nations occurring already in the USSR, and they confidently predict that this merger will come about within the Soviet Union before it occurs in the world at large.

Because Marx implied and Lenin specified that it would come about, even those participants in the Soviet debate who oppose the merging of nations cannot oppose ultimate national amalgamation. However, they avoid the problem by explaining that the merging of nations will occur only in the distant future, when communism has been achieved on a world-wide scale. They emphasize the language-cultural-ethnic aspects of Stalin's national definition as characteristics which give the nation a deeper, more permanent significance. The assimilationist writers in the debate have been critical of Stalin's inclusion of language and "psychological make-up manifested in a community of culture" in his definition of nation because these elements make nationality more permanent and merging more distant. One author explained that the psychological-cultural aspect of Stalin's definition forces one "to view the nation as a naturalistic and eternal, not a social-historical community. With such an understanding of the essence of the nation, it would turn out to be not a transient but an eternal category."[3] However, one of the more recent and more authoritative contributions to the Soviet debate insists that psychological make-up is an essential element in the defining of nationality.[4]

It is ironic that Stalin—who in practice sought to eliminate all elements of prerevolutionary tradition among the non-Russian nations, minimized the precapitalist derivation of non-Russian national culture, saw non-Russian nationalism as an anti-Soviet conspiracy, and generally followed a policy of Russian chauvinism—should become the ideological patron saint of those who favor the continued existence of separate nationalities. During the early years of his rule in the Soviet Union, Stalin seems to have accepted Lenin's conclusions on the merging of nations though he explained that this merging would only occur after the victory of communism on a world scale. In the last few years of his life he went even further in giving the nation a more permanent significance. He denied that language was part of the superstructure or even of its economic base. Language is created, Stalin said, "by the entire historical development of society . . . not by any one class but by the whole society, by all classes of society, by the efforts of hundreds of generations." Because it "is the product of a great many epochs, during which it assumes shape, grows rich, and develops," language "lives incomparably longer than any base or any superstructure."[5] Since the roots of language go even deeper than the economic base, nationality by implication is also something more permanent. Stalin's new assessment of language required some intricate ideological gymnastics to reconcile it with earlier communist national theory.[6] After his death, however, these later views on the national question were dropped. Since the de-Stalinization of the 1950's, it has been generally unacceptable to quote any but Stalin's early writings. His later theoretical expositions, which would give further authority to the antiassimilationist position, are not cited.

Recent official Soviet policy has been somewhat ambiguous on the question of the merging of nations. The party program adopted at the Twenty-second CPSU Congress in 1961 reaffirmed the belief that under "full-scale communist construction . . . nations will draw still closer together until complete unity is achieved." But at the same time the party declared that "under socialism nations flourish and their sovereignty is strengthened."[7] The post-Khrushchev leadership has not publicly repeated the "complete unity" phrase, but there has been no questioning of the ultimate merger of nationalities. However, praise for the increasing friendship and rapprochement of the nationalities in the Soviet Union is counterbalanced by praise for the continuing development of the national life of all nationalities.

The national debate in the Soviet Union has focused primarily on the internal national problem, and only to a much smaller degree has it dealt with the implications of policy on the national question for Soviet foreign relations. The size of the Soviet Union, the number of its national minorities, and the revival of non-Russian nationalism have made the internal question of more immediate concern. The Soviet debate has been followed with interest by the East Europeans,[8] however, since Soviet policy toward its own nationalities may be a clue to future relations between the Soviet Union and the states of Eastern Europe.

The generally rigid Soviet interpretation of the character of the nation and its future was first theoretically attacked in Yugoslavia, where the party has not hesitated to revise ideology to satisfy its needs. In the 1950's, as the Titoist reforms were being cautiously implemented, the ideological justifications being given for the reforms eventually were felt in the theory of national relations. The primary work on this topic was Edvard Kardelj's discussion of the development of the Slovene national question, which was first published in 1938 and was reissued in 1958 in a revised edition which included a long introduction on Marxism and the national question.[9] Kardelj added to Stalin's definition of the nation the thesis that the nation arose "on the basis of the social division of labor in the epoch of capitalism." In the context in which he applied this phrase, it referred not only to the importance of economic elements in national development but also to the role of the nation in the development of economic relations. Kardelj also saw nation and nationality as more than a capitalist phenomenon because he asserted that they would continue to exist even under socialism. Although he did not condemn national feeling, he considered it to be

249

on a lower level than Yugoslav nationalism, which he designated "Yugoslav socialist consciousness" or "Yugoslavism." Despite Kardelj's favorable assessment of national feelings, however, he harshly criticized nationalism. Although he did not explicitly detail his views on the question of the merging of nations, those concerned with national prerogatives saw his views on "Yugoslavism" as an attempt to denigrate the role and significance of the Yugoslav republics.[10]

In Yugoslavia the merging of nations has been identified with Serbian dominance and Serbian chauvinism. To Serb nationalists, the integration of nations meant "the realization of the privileges of the Serbian language and the assimilation of lesser nationalities."[11] Therefore any attempt at unification of nations was strongly opposed by Croats, Slovenes, Macedonians, and other non-Serb nationalities. As the nonassimilationists in the Soviet debate, the non-Serbs emphasized that the economic components of the nation were not the only important features. In an exchange on Yugoslav culture, a Slovene Marxist maintained that nation and nationality are not only capitalist or bourgeois phenomena, but rather "are above class, or at least nonclass, categories." Recognition of the nation and of nationality "means recognition of the wholesomeness of the human personality. . . . A nation is more than a number of particular economic, geographical, and cultural characteristics. It cannot fulfill itself if only these elements are emphasized."[12]

Opposition to the concept that socialism will bring an end to the existence of separate nations has come not only from nationalist intellectuals but also from Yugoslav party leaders as well. In a speech to the eighth party congress Tito referred to "certain people, including even some communists," who "feel that the nationalities have become obsolete in our socialist social development and should wither away." He criticized them for fostering "the confused idea that the unity of peoples means the elimination of nationalities and the creation of something new and artificial, that is, a single Yugoslav nation."[13] In a later speech he declared unequivocally, "It is impossible to create a single nation here."[14] Lazar Koliševski, a leading Macedonian communist and a member of the federal party leadership for a number of years, also denied that a merging of nationalities was possible in Yugoslavia. He specifically criticized Stalin's earlier statements on the merging of nations, explaining that nations would continue to exist under socialism. He declared that "the working class . . . must of necessity become the champion of positive national interests and national progress, since its own development and its general socialist objectives and international obligations make this imperative."[15] The Yugoslavs have almost reversed orthodox Marxist national theory. To Lenin, nationality was a negative inheritance from the capitalist stage of development which would be superseded by international proletarian unity once socialism was established. To the Yugoslavs, the nation is more than an economic result of capitalism, and it will continue to play a postive role even under socialism.

There have been public disagreements over the relative importance of class versus national interests, particularly since 1966, when the purge of Aleksandar Ranković opened the way for the assertion of the rights of the nationalities. In general, the Serbs, who have tended to play a greater role in the federal party and government bureaucracies, have maintained the ideological position that class should take precedence over national interests. This implies limiting the powers granted to the nationalities and the various national republics in the interest of a stronger, unified Yugoslavia. Croats, on the other hand, have assumed the leading role in expressing the non-Serb nationalities' position that national interests must have priority over class interests. Although these divisions are generally accurate, one must be cautious because there are considerable shades of difference on ideological issues within both camps. Not all Serbs have been consistent centralists, and not all non-Serbs have favored greater autonomy for the national republics. Nijdan Pasić, editor of the party's monthly, *Socijalizam,* has attempted to maintain a middle ground between the extremes of the Serb centralists and the Croatian autonomists. In an interesting article he argues that ignoring national interests in favor of class interests is unacceptable, but at the same time he considers equally reactionary the point of view which uncritically places national above class interests and which claims that the working class is becoming a national class.[16] Despite Pasić's moderate position, Serb theoreticians have used his arguments for maintaining the pre-eminence of class interests in criticizing their Croatian counterparts. The Croats have in turn been critical of their Serbian comrades and have opposed the priority of class interests. Tito's assertion that the class spirit or character is the important element did little more than change the semantics of the debate.[17] The Croatian leaders refer to a national class spirit and Serbs to an international class spirit. (The Croats interpret this Serbian phraseology as a camouflage for Serbian nationalism.)[18] Although the crackdown on nationalism in Yugoslavia following Tito's criticism of the Croatian leadership has muted the debate, the essential differences still remain.

The Rumanian view of the significance of nation and state is similar to that of the Yugoslavs. While Yugoslavia's revised national theory is necessary because of the delicate internal nationality balance, Rumania's interpretations are motivated by its foreign policy. The merging of nationalities and the "internationalist" duties of communist parties and states imply subservience to the Soviet Union. Hence, the Rumanian emphasis on the continuing importance and progressive role of the nation and state is a part of the Rumanian campaign to strengthen its independence from the Soviet Union.

The Rumanian position on the theory of the state and nation has generally been formulated by the party leadership and only later was it taken up by the theoreticians and academicians. One of the most frequently cited assertions of the importance of the nation under socialism is Ceaușescu's speech to the Rumanian eighth party congress in July 1965. He maintained that "for a long time to come the nation and the state will continue to be the basis of socialist society." He anticipated critics who might accuse him of nationalism: "Not only does this not run counter to the interests of internationalism, but on the contrary, it is in full harmony with the international solidarity of the working people." In fact, "the development and flourishing of each socialist nation, of each socialist state —equal in rights, sovereign, and independent—is an essential requirement upon which depends the strengthening of the unity and cohesion of the socialist countries."[19] In his speech on the forty-fifth anniversary of the founding of the Rumanian Communist Party, Ceaușescu criticized "a number of theoreticians" who advocate "the idea that nations are an obsolete social category, left behind by history, which can no longer play an important role in social development during the contemporary epoch." He observed that "the nation will continue to be the basis for the development of our society for a long time to come, during the whole period of building socialism and communism." Again he reiterated that "it is incorrect and unscientific to present the socialist nation, the socialist homeland, as being opposed to socialist internationalism."[20]

Theoretical treatment of the national question in Rumania has generally been limited to embellishing Ceauşescu's pronouncements on the subject. However, Rumanians have attempted to brand the Soviets, by implication, as bourgeois nationalists because of their theories about the amalgamation of nations and their emphasis on proletarian "internationalism." One author, for example, criticized "ideas advocated by the ideological representatives of the *bourgeoisie*" concerning the "allegedly obsolete character of the nation."[21] Rumanian scholars have given theoretical justification to the Rumanian party's attempt to link itself with Rumanian nationalism. Not only have they proclaimed that "the nation in our era fulfills an immensely progressive role,"[22] but they have claimed that the pursuit of national interests is true "internationalism"!

Under conditions of socialism, national interests acquire a new content, they really belong to the entire nation, headed by the working class. To look after these interests is at the same time to fulfill significant international obligations. The economic and cultural development of each particular country, in line with its national interests, is not contrary to the interests of socialist internationalism; quite the opposite, it fully corresponds to these interests.[23]

The debate on nationalism in Hungary has produced some interesting differences between the party leadership and some of the more nationalist intellectuals. The party has generally opposed nationalism of any type. Zoltán Komocsin, a member of the Politburo and secretary of the Hungarian party Central Committee, for example, called for party concentration on the problem of "traditional" nationalism, which "continues to raise its head to this day." He singled out "a certain minority of the population in general and the intelligentsia and petty *bourgeoisie* in particular" as being the guilty groups. Although explaining that the main task of the party in every country is to fight nationalism within its own borders, he declared that "since the birth of the Soviet Union, hostility to the

Soviets has been a world corollary of nationalism." He also directed specific criticism at the Rumanians for their nationalism and anti-Sovietism.[24] Komocsin's negative assessment of nationalism was reiterated by János Kádár, the first secretary of the Hungarian party. In an interview he observed that "nationalism had a definitely negative role in the case of the socialist countries. . . . It is my conviction that, in our era, the best guarantee for the prosperity and friendship of the peoples and the safeguarding of peace is the mastering of nationalism."[25]

In contrast to the antinational position taken by the party and its leaders, a number of Hungarian intellectuals have come out with interpretations of nationalism that are very similar to the Yugoslav and Rumanian positions. István Sőtér, a professor of literature and history, for example, stressed the importance of encouraging national differences to prevent impoverishment of society. He began by declaring that the disappearance of nations under communism is a development for the distant future. But in order to avoid the social leveling and equalizing of nations resulting from the technological society, he called for consideration of "the constructive new possibilities of national awareness."[26] Another Hungarian intellectual, Aladár Mód, echoed Sőtér's views. He argued that socialism could compete with capitalism successfully only if socialist states show that "socialism involved not the uniformization of peoples, not the mechanical liquidation of national differences . . . but the beginning of a new and higher order of development, elevating nations into socialist nations."[27] The same author in another article almost went as far as the Rumanians in asserting that "as long as nations exist, we can only fight for the great international issues as sons of a specific nation." Although admitting that "the trend of development is toward internationalism," he declared that under present conditions "the point of departure is national and the development must have its source there."[28] These nationalist positions have been severely criticized by Hungarians who follow the party line more closely. Although official policy continues to oppose even a cautious revival of Hungarian nationalism, the length and vigor of the debate on the issue leaves no doubt about its continued relevance.[29]

These debates reflect the still-strong influence of nationalism on communist parties and states. The relationship of "nationalism" and "internationalism" to communism is complex. During Marx's lifetime socialists had stronger loyalties to their own nationality than to their class comrades in other nations. World War I found socialists for the most part supporting the interests of their own nationality. Once the communist party came to power in the Soviet Union, the continued existence of the Soviet state under the rule of the party took precedence over ideology. For the parties that aligned themselves with the Soviet party in the Third International, "internationalism" came to mean preservation of the Soviet state and the primacy of Soviet interests. This in turn meant that foreign communist parties became agencies of Soviet policy. The ability of the local parties to appeal to the electorate in their own states assumed a secondary position. Yet communist parties not in power have been most successful in cases when they have supported specific national causes of either minorities or the *Staatsvolk*. The ideology of internationalism, of the primacy of class-economic interests, has never been successful in attracting mass support.

In the states where Soviet power established and maintained communist rule after World War II, "internationalism" remained the euphemism for putting Soviet interests first. However, the desire of the local party organizations to establish their own base of support led some of these communist regimes to make alliances with local nationalism. The Soviet-Yugoslav break occurred largely because Belgrade refused to put Soviet interests first. Since the Yugoslav communists came to power by themselves and were not maintained in authority by Moscow, it was necessary for them to put Yugoslav interests ahead of Soviet interests. The Soviet threat of invasion and bloc harassment after Yugoslavia was expelled from the Cominform in 1948 made it still more expedient for the Yugoslav communists to develop even stronger links with the Yugoslav nationalities. In recent years, parties which have sought to rely more on their own popularity and less on Soviet support (e.g., Rumania) have made alliances with local nationalism, while those parties that rely most heavily on the Soviet Union (Hungary, East Germany, Bulgaria) have been the most outspoken supporters of "internationalism." The irony of this is that although communist ideology emphasizes that economic-class solidarity is superior to national solidarity, those communist parties which have pursued the national interest of their *Staatsvolk,* who have linked their party with nationalism, are generally the strongest parties. There is little doubt that nationalism has a much deeper and more profound influence on men than do class interests.

Nationalism will continue to play an important role in relations among communist states, but, as long as Soviet power remains supreme, there will be limits. Nationalism will not produce the disruption that it engendered in Eastern Europe between the world wars when the competition of great powers for the allegiance of the various independent states permitted rival nationalisms to reach a vehemence that has not been achieved since then. Today, and for the foreseeable future, Soviet influence will be dominant in Eastern Europe, and the Soviet Union will not allow nationalism to threaten its empire. Since the states of Eastern Europe will remain communist so as long as Soviet might maintains the local parties in power, the ruling elites will be influenced and united by a commonly accepted ideology. Although the tie of ideology is weak and frequently violated, it does provide a nonnational justification for communist rule that was absent during the interwar period.

The communist "solution" of the national question will continue to appear in the rhetoric of East European communism, though in practice nationalism will continue to be disruptive. Just as the Reformation left Europe divided along state boundaries into national churches, communism will probably continue splintering into separate national communisms. The pace at which this nationalism grows will be determined by the willingness of the Soviet leadership to tolerate it, and the extent of Soviet involvement in other areas of the world. If Soviet power in Eastern Europe should decline as a result of a serious confrontation with China or a serious internal crisis, nationalism would undergo a renaissance in the communist states of Eastern Europe.

Appendix, Notes,
Bibliography, Index

Appendix

Population by Nationality of East European Communist States

The data presented are official government statistics, and no attempt has been made to correct figures on the basis of unofficial or Western estimates. When population by nationality has not been given in official census returns or in statistical yearbooks, journal and newspaper articles have been used. At the time this appendix was prepared, official returns for most of the 1970 series of censuses had not been published, hence preliminary data published in newspapers and periodicals have been used. For purposes of comparison, data from one of the interwar censuses are also given. An attempt was made to include the census nearest the year 1930, but in some cases it was necessary to use census figures from other years.

I. Albania

Statistics on the Albanian population by nationality have been sketchy from the beginning of Albania's existence as a separate state. For various estimates of the interwar nationality composition of the population, see Wilhelm Winkler, *Statistisches Handbuch der europäischen Nationalitäten* (Vienna and Leipzig: Wilhelm Braumüller, 1931), pp. 234–238. In the 1955 census, which gave the total population of Albania as 1,391,499, the following percentages for nationality were given:

Nationality	Percent
Albanians	97.0
Greeks	2.5
Slavs	0.4
Others	0.1

Source: *Vjetori Statistikor i Republikës Popullore të Shqipërisë 1964;* and *Ekonomia Popullore,* 4:5 (1957).

II. Bulgaria

Statistics on the nationality composition of the Bulgarian population in the censuses of 1926, 1956, and 1965 are as follows:

Nationality	1926[a] Number	1926[a] Per-cent	1956 Number	1956 Per-cent	1965 Number	1965 Per-cent
Bulgarians	4,557,706[b]	83.2	6,506,541	85.5	7,259,147	88.2
Turks	557,552	10.5	656,025	8.6	746,755	9.1
Gypsies	—	—	197,865	2.6	—	—
Macedonians	—	—	187,789	2.5	8,750	0.1
Others	363,483	6.3	65,489	0.8	211,912	2.6
TOTAL	5,478,741		7,613,709		8,226,564	

Source: *Annuaire statistique du Royaume de Bulgarie 1929/1930* (Sofia, 1930); *Prebroiavane na naselenieto b Narodna Republika Blgariya na l. XII. 1956 godina* (Sofia, 1959); and *Rezultati ot prebroiavane na naselenieto na l. XII. 1965 g.* (Sofia, 1967).

[a] The figures for 1926 are for Bulgarian territory as it was then—i.e., excluding southern Dobruja, which became part of Bulgaria in 1940.

[b] The figures for "Bulgarians" include "Pomaks," although this group was listed separately in the census returns for 1926. "Pomaks" are Bulgarian-speaking Moslems, while the classification "Bulgarians" in 1926 was applied to Bulgarian Christians.

III. Czechoslovakia

Statistics on the nationality composition of the Czechoslovak population in the censuses of 1930, 1950, 1961, and 1970 are as follows:

Nationality	1930[a] Number	Percent	1950 Number	Percent	1961 Number	Percent	1970 Number	Percent
Czechs	9,688,943[b]	66.9	8,383,923	67.9	9,069,222	66.0	9,341,208	65.0
Slovaks			3,240,549	26.3	3,836,213	27.9	4,192,892	29.2
Hungarians	692,121	4.8	367,733	3.0	533,934	3.9	572,568	4.0
Germans	3,231,718	22.3	165,117	1.3	140,402	1.0	85,582	0.6
Poles	81,741	0.6	72,624	0.6	67,552	0.5	66,777	0.5
Ukrainians and Ruthenians	549,043	3.8	67,615	0.6	54,984	0.4	58,667	0.4
Jews	186,474	1.3	—		—		—	
Others	49,465	0.3	40,889	0.3	43,270	0.3	40,000[c]	0.3
TOTAL	14,479,505		12,338,450		13,745,577		14,362,000[c]	

Source: *Statistická Ročenka ČSR, 1934; Statistická Ročenka ČSR, 1957* and *1963; Prager Volkszeitung,* No. 17 (April 30, 1971).
[a] The 1930 figures are for Czechoslovak territory as it was at that time— i.e., including Ruthenia, which was annexed by the Soviet Union in 1945.
[b] Czechs and Slovaks were not enumerated separately in 1930.
[c] The 1970 figures are preliminary returns and these two figures are only approximate.

IV. Hungary

The 1930 census was taken on the basis of *native language* rather than nationality. The results of this census are as follows:

Language	Number	Percent
Hungarian	8,001,112	92.1
German	478,630	5.5
Slovak	104,819	1.2
Croat	27,683	0.3
Rumanian	16,221	0.2
Serbian	7,031	0.1
Bunievac, Chokac, etc.[a]	20,564	0.2
Others	32,252	0.4
TOTAL	8,688,319	

Source: *Recensement Général de la Population de 1930* (Budapest, 1933), part 1.

[a] These are apparently Serbian-speaking Roman Catholics who do not consider themselves Serbs. They are, however, of Serbian ancestry, and thus do not consider themselves to be Croatian.

In the postwar years exact figures on the population by nationality have not been generally available. Estimates of the size of the non-Hungarian population have varied considerably. *Népszabadság* (November 22, 1970) estimated that 2 to 3 percent of the population were minorities, while *Magyar Hirlap* (July 18, 1970) estimated the proportion at 4 to 4.5 percent. The Hungarian news service (MTI, April 15, 1971) gave the number of minorities in 1960 as 175,000, or 1.8 percent of the population. The latter figure seems to be the most accurate. The same source gave the following figures for the minorities:

| | Number | |
Nationality	1949	1960
Germans	22,455	32,196
Slovaks	25,988	30,690
South Slavs (Serbs, Croats, etc.)	35,054	37,597
Rumanians	14,713	—[a]

[a] The 1960 figure for Rumanians was not clearly received from the MTI transmission.

The MTI report gave no statistics on other nationalities, so the breakdown is not complete. Of a total Hungarian population in 1960 of 9,961,044, the number of non-Hungarians is insignificant.

V. Poland

Statistics on the nationality composition of the population of Poland on the basis of the 1921 census are as follows:

Nationality	Number	Percent
Poles	18,814,239	69.2
Ukrainians	3,898,431	14.3
Jews	2,110,448	7.8
Belorussians	1,060,237	3.9
Germans	1,059,194	3.9
Others	234,168	0.9
TOTAL	27,176,717	

Source: *Annuaire statistique de la République Polonaise 1925–1926* (Warsaw, 1927).

The considerable shifting of the Polish boundaries following World War II, the expulsion of the German population from postwar Polish territory, and the population exchanges with the Soviet Union left Poland after 1945 with a relatively homogeneous, ethnically Polish population. No official statistics on nationalities have been made available from the postwar censuses. Reliable, but unofficial, figures place the number of non-Poles at 400,000 to 450,000 (*Kultura i społeczeństwo,* No. 4, 1963, gives 453,000; *Życie Literackie,* May 28, 1966, gives 400,000; and *Słowo Polskie,* June 2, 1968, gives 442,000.) Of the total population of Poland in 1960, this represents only 1.4 percent.

On the basis of the above articles, the number of minorities in Poland can be estimated as follows:

Nationality	Number
Ukrainians	185,000
Belorussians	165,000
Czechs and Slovaks	22,000
Russians	20,000
Gypsies	12,000
Lithuanians	10,000

VI. Rumania

Statistics on the nationality composition of the population of Rumania in the censuses of 1930, 1956, and 1966 are as follows:

Nationality	1930[a] Number	Percent	1956 Number	Percent	1966 Number	Percent
Rumanians	12,981,324	71.9	14,996,114	85.7	16,746,510	87.7
Hungarians	1,425,507	7.9	1,587,675	9.1	1,619,592	8.5
Germans	745,421	4.1	384,708	2.2	382,595	2.0
Jews	728,115	4.0	146,264	0.8	42,888	0.2
Ukrainians	582,115	3.2	60,479	0.4	54,705	0.3
Russians	409,150	2.3	38,731	0.2	39,483	0.2
Bulgarians	366,384	2.0	12,040	0.1	11,193	0.1
Gypsies	262,501	1.5	104,216	0.6	64,197	0.3
Turks	154,772	0.9	14,329	0.1	18,040	0.1
Găugăuzi (Tartar)	105,750	0.6	20,469	0.2	22,151	0.1
Others	295,989	1.6	124,425	0.6	101,809	0.5
TOTAL	18,057,028		17,489,450		19,103,163	

Source: *Anuarul Statistic al Romîniei 1939* (Bucharest, 1939); *Recensămîntul Populaţiei din 21 Februarie 1956* (Bucharest, n.d.); and *Recensămîntul Populaţiei şi Locuinţelor din 15 Martie 1966* (Bucharest, 1969).

[a] These figures for 1930 are for the territory of Rumania as it was at that time. Bessarabia, northern Bukovina, and southern Dobruja were taken from Rumania during World War II.

VII. Union of Soviet Socialist Republics

Statistics on the nationality composition of the Soviet population in the 1926 census are as follows:

Nationality	Number	Percent
Russians	77,791,000	53.1
Ukrainians	31,195,000	21.3
Belorussians	4,739,000	3.2
Kazakhs	3,968,000	2.7
Uzbeks	3,905,000	2.7
Tartars	2,917,000	2.0
Jews	2,672,000	1.8
Georgians	1,821,000	1.2
Turks	1,715,000	1.2
Armenians	1,568,000	1.1
Mordovians	1,340,000	0.9
Germans	1,239,000	0.8
Chuvash	1,117,000	0.8
Tadzhiks	979,000	0.7
Poles	782,000	0.5
Turkmenians	764,000	0.5
Kirgiz	763,000	0.5
Bashkirs	714,000	0.5
Votyak (Udmurt)	504,000	0.3
Others	6,535,000	4.2
TOTAL	147,028,000	

Source: *Recensement de la population de l'U.R.S.S. 1926* (Moscow, 1929).

268

Following World War II there were major changes in the western frontiers of the Soviet Union. These changes were a factor affecting the national composition of the Soviet population. In 1959 and 1970 the nationality composition was as follows:

Nationality	1959		1970	
	Number	Percent	Number	Percent
Russians	114,114,000	54.6	129,015,000	53.4
Ukrainians	37,253,000	17.8	40,753,000	16.9
Uzbeks	6,015,000	2.9	9,195,000	3.8
Belorussians	7,913,000	3.8	9,052,000	3.7
Tartars	4,968,000	2.4	5,931,000	2.5
Kazakhs	3,622,000	1.7	5,299,000	2.2
Azerbaidzhani	2,940,000	1.4	4,380,000	1.8
Armenians	2,787,000	1.3	3,559,000	1.5
Georgians	2,692,000	1.3	3,245,000	1.3
Moldavians	2,214,000	1.1	2,698,000	1.1
Lithuanians	2,326,000	1.1	2,665,000	1.1
Jews	2,268,000	1.1	2,151,000	0.9
Tadzhiks	1,397,000	0.7	2,136,000	0.9
Germans	1,620,000	0.8	1,846,000	0.8
Chuvash	1,470,000	0.7	1,694,000	0.7
Turkmenians	1,002,000	0.5	1,525,000	0.6
Kirgiz	969,000	0.5	1,452,000	0.6
Latvians	1,400,000	0.7	1,430,000	0.6
Peoples of Dagestan	945,000	0.5	1,365,000	0.6
Mordovians	1,285,000	0.6	1,263,000	0.5
Bashkirs	989,000	0.5	1,240,000	0.5
Poles	1,380,000	0.7	1,167,000	0.5
Estonians	989,000	0.5	1,007,000	0.4
Others	6,269,000	2.8	7,652,000	3.1
TOTAL	208,827,000		241,720,000	

Source: *Chislennost, razmeshchenie, vozrastnaya struktura, uroven obrazovaniya, natsionalny sostav, yazyki i istochniki sredstv sushchestvovaniya naseleniya SSSR* (Moscow: Statistika, 1971).

Appendix

The nationality composition of the population of the Moldavian Soviet Socialist Republic according to the two postwar censuses is as follows:

Nationality	1959		1970	
	Number	Percent	Number	Percent
Moldavians	1,887,000	65.4	2,304,000	64.6
Ukrainians	421,000	14.6	507,000	14.2
Russians	293,000	10.2	414,000	11.6
Gagauz	96,000	3.3	125,000	3.5
Jews	95,000	3.3	98,000	2.7
Bulgarians	62,000	2.1	74,000	2.1
Others	31,000	1.1	47,000	1.3
TOTAL	2,885,000		3,569,000	

Source: *Chislennost, razmeshchenie, vozrastnaya struktura, uroven obrazovaniya, natsionalny sostav, yazyki i istochniki sredstv sushchestvovaniya naseleniya SSSR* (Moscow: Statistika, 1971).

VIII. Yugoslavia

The 1931 Yugoslav census did not give statistics for nationality. However, on the basis of the figures on language and religion, it is possible to give a very accurate estimate of the nationality composition of the Yugoslav population in 1931. Unless otherwise specified, the figures are those for native language:

	1931	
Nationality	*Number*	*Percent*
Serbs, Montenegrins, Macedonians, and Bulgarians	6,577,398	47.2[a]
Croats	3,186,295	22.9[b]
Moslems	908,167	6.5[c]
Slovenes	1,135,410	8.2
Albanians	505,259	3.6
Germans	499,969	3.6
Hungarians	468,185	3.4
Rumanians and Vlachs	137,879	1.0
Turks	132,924	1.0
Slovaks	76,411	0.6
Gypsies	70,424	0.5
Czechs	52,909	0.4
Others	182,808	1.1
TOTAL	13,934,038	

Source: *Definitivni rezultati popisa stanovništva od 31 marta 1931 godine* (Belgrade, 1937–1940).

[a] Figures are for Serbo-Croatian-speaking population who are of Eastern Orthodox religion.

[b] Figures are for Serbo-Croatian-speaking population who are of Roman Catholic religion.

[c] Figures are for Serbo-Croatian-speaking population who are of Moslem religion.

Statistics on the nationality composition of the Yugoslav population in the censuses of 1948, 1953, 1961, and 1971 are as follows:

Nationality	1948		1953		1961		1971	
	Number	Percent	Number	Percent	Number	Percent	Number	Percent
Serbs	6,547,117	41.5	7,065,923	41.7	7,806,213	42.1	8,432,524	40.5
Croats	3,784,353	24.0	3,975,550	23.5	4,293,860	23.1	4,803,497	23.1
Slovenes	1,415,432	9.0	1,487,100	8.8	1,589,192	8.6	1,718,096	8.3
Moslems[a]	808,921	5.1	—[a]	—	972,954	5.3	1,218,732	5.9
Yugoslavs[a]	—[a]	—	998,698	5.9	317,125	1.7	408,903	2.0
Macedonians	810,126	5.1	893,247	5.3	1,045,530	5.6	1,202,761	5.8
Albanians	750,431	4.8	754,245	4.5	914,760	4.9	1,243,451	6.0
Hungarians	496,492	3.2	502,175	3.0	504,368	2.7	515,012	2.5
Montenegrins	425,703	2.7	466,093	2.8	513,833	2.8	608,071	2.9
Turks	97,954	0.6	259,535	1.5	182,964	1.0	221,947	1.1
Vlachs	102,953	0.7	36,728	0.2	—	—	—	—
Other	532,616	3.3	497,279	2.8	408,492	2.2	433,543	1.9
TOTAL	15,772,098		16,936,573		18,549,291		20,806,537	

Source: *Konačni rezultati popisa stanovništva od 15 marta 1948 godine* (Belgrade, 1951–1956); *Popis stanovništva 1953* (Belgrade, 1958–1962); *Popis stanovništva 1961* (Belgrade, 1965–1967); *NIN*, July 4, 1971.

[a] In the 1948 census Yugoslav citizens were permitted to declare their nationality as "Moslem," but there was no category entitled "Yugoslavs of unspecified nationality." In the 1953 census "Moslem" was omitted as a category but "Yugoslav, unspecified" was added, hence most Serbo-Croatian-speaking Moslems of Bosnia-Hercegovina declared themselves to be "Yugoslavs." In the 1961 census the "Moslem" category reappeared, and as in 1948 the majority of Moslems in Bosnia-Hercegovina declared themselves to be "Moslems." However, the Serbo-Croatian-speaking Moslems of the Sandžak region of southwestern Serbia for the most part declared themselves to be "Yugoslavs." It is likely in the 1971 census that the same pattern was followed as in 1961, but the nationality data by region were not available to determine this for certain at the time of writing.

Notes

Introduction

1. The classic study of the impact of communism on Russian nationalism is Frederick C. Barghoorn, *Soviet Russian Nationalism* (New York: Oxford University Press, 1956).

2. See, for example, Zbigniew K. Brzezinski, *The Soviet Bloc: Unity and Conflict,* rev. ed. (Cambridge, Mass.: Harvard University Press, 1967); Ferenc A. Váli, *Rift and Revolt in Hungary* (Cambridge, Mass.: Harvard University Press, 1961); Stephen Fischer-Galati, *The New Rumania* (Cambridge, Mass.: MIT Press, 1967); David Floyd, *Rumania: Russia's Dissident Ally* (New York: Praeger, 1965); Paul Lendvai, *Eagles in Cobwebs: Nationalism and Communism in the Balkans* (Garden City, N.Y.: Doubleday, 1969); Adam B. Ulam, *Titoism and the Cominform* (Cambridge, Mass.: Harvard University Press, 1952); Hansjakob Stehle, *The Independent Satellite: Society and Politics in Poland since 1945* (New York: Praeger, 1965).

3. See, for example, Erich Goldhagen, ed., *Ethnic Minorities in the Soviet Union* (New York: Praeger, 1968); Richard Pipes, *The Formation of the Soviet Union: Communism and Nationalism, 1917–1923,* rev. ed. (Cambridge, Mass.: Harvard University Press, 1964); Yaroslav Bilinsky, *The Second Soviet Republic: The Ukraine after World War II* (New Brunswick, N.J.: Rutgers University Press, 1964); Michael Rywkin, *Russia in Central*

Asia (New York: Collier, 1963); Lowell R. Tillett, *The Great Friendship: Soviet Historians on the Non-Russian Nationalities* (Chapel Hill, N.C.: University of North Carolina Press, 1969); Robert S. Sullivant, *Soviet Politics and the Ukraine, 1917–1957* (New York: Columbia University Press, 1962); V. Stanley Vardys, ed., *Lithuania under the Soviets* (New York: Praeger, 1965); Mary Matossian, *The Impact of Soviet Policies in Armenia* (Leiden: E. J. Brill, 1962); Geoffrey Wheeler, *The Peoples of Soviet Central Asia* (London: Bodley, 1966); Robert Conquest, *Soviet Nationalities Policy in Practice* (New York: Praeger, 1967); John A. Armstrong, *Ukrainian Nationalism,* 2nd ed. (New York: Columbia University Press, 1963).

4. See Paul Shoup, *Communism and the Yugoslav National Question* (New York: Columbia University Press, 1968); and George Moseley, *The Party and the National Question in China* (Cambridge, Mass.: MIT Press, 1966).

Chapter 1

1. Cited in Karl W. Deutsch, *Nationalism and Its Alternatives* (New York: Knopf, 1969), p. 3.

2. For a review of the literature on nationalism, see Karl W. Deutsch, *Nationalism and Social Communication,* 2nd ed. (Cambridge, Mass.: MIT Press, 1966), pp. 1–28. See also Karl W. Deutsch and Richard L. Merritt, *Nationalism: An Inter-disciplinary Bibliography, 1936–1965* (Cambridge, Mass.: MIT Press, 1966).

3. Hans Kohn, *The Idea of Nationalism* (New York: Macmillan, 1951), pp. 10–11. See also pp. 3–24.

4. Norman Angell, *The Unseen Assassins* (New York: Harper, 1932), p. 45.

5. Walter Sulzbach, *National Consciousness* (Washington, D.C.: American Council on Public Affairs, 1943), p. 66.

6. See Arnold J. Toynbee, *A Study of History,* Vol. VIII (London: Oxford University Press, 1954), pp. 150–198; also George G. Arnakis, "The Role of Religion in the Development of Balkan Nationalism," in Charles and Barbara Jelavich, eds., *The Balkans in Transition* (Berkeley: University of California Press, 1963), pp. 115–144; and Radu R. Florescu, "The Uniate Church: Catalyst of Rumanian National Consciousness," *The Slavonic and East European Review,* 45:105 (July 1967), pp. 324–342.

7. Rupert Emerson, *From Empire to Nation* (Boston: Beacon Press, 1962).

8. E. H. Carr, *Nationalism and After* (London: Macmillan, 1945), pp. 34–37; and Barbara Ward, *Nationalism and Ideology* (New York: Norton, 1966), pp. 12–15.

9. A series of articles on a number of these national minorities which

have recently become more assertive is found in the special issue *Nationalism and Separatism* of the *Journal of Contemporary History,* 6:1 (1971).

10. For a discussion of the foundation, functioning, and failure of the League provisions on the protection of minorities, see Inis L. Claude, *National Minorities: An International Problem* (Cambridge, Mass.: Harvard University Press, 1955); C. A. Macartney, *National States and National Minorities* (London: Royal Institute of International Affairs and Oxford University Press, 1934); L. P. Mair, *The Protection of Minorities: The Working and Scope of the Minorities Treaties under the League of Nations* (London: Christophers, 1928); Julius Stone, *International Guarantees of Minority Rights* (London: Oxford University Press, 1932); Erwin Viefhaus, *Die Minderheitenfrage und die Entstehung der Minderheitenschutzverträge auf der Pariser Friedenskonferenz, 1919* (Würzburg: Holzner-Verlag, 1960); and Hugo Wintgens, *Der völkerrechtliche Schutz der nationalen, sprachlichen und religiösen Minderheiten* (Stuttgart: W. Kohlhammer, 1930).

11. For a discussion of these interwar nationality problems, see Hugh Seton-Watson, *Eastern Europe between the Wars, 1918–1941* (New York: Harper, 1967), esp. pp. 268–412; Robert Lee Wolf, *The Balkans in Our Time* (Cambridge, Mass.: Harvard University Press, 1956), pp. 143–159; John O. Crane, *The Little Entente* (New York: Macmillan, 1931); Robert J. Kerner and Harry Nicholas Howard, *The Balkan Conferences and the Balkan Entente, 1930–1935* (Berkeley: University of California Press, 1936); Walter Kolarz, *Myths and Realities in Eastern Europe* (London: Lindsay Drummond, 1946); and Norman J. Padelford, *Peace in the Balkans* (New York: Oxford University Press, 1935).

12. See Solomon F. Bloom, *The World of Nations: A Study of the National Implications in the Work of Karl Marx* (New York: Columbia University Press, 1941), pp. 15–23.

13. Friedrich Engels, *Germany: Revolution and Counter-Revolution* in *German Revolutions,* ed. by Leonard Krieger (Chicago: University of Chicago Press, 1967), pp. 174–180, 192, 209–211.

14. Karl Marx and Friedrich Engels, *Manifesto of the Communist Party,* authorized English translation, ed. and annot. by Friedrich Engels (New York: International Publishers, 1932), p. 22.

15. *Ibid.,* p. 28. Emphasis in original.

16. Bloom, *The World of Nations,* pp. 25–32.

17. Marx and Engels, *Manifesto,* p. 28.

18. See R. V. Burks, *The Dynamics of Communism in Eastern Europe* (Princeton, N.J.: Princeton University Press, 1961).

19. See Franz Borkenau, *Socialism: National or International?* (London: George Routledge and Sons, 1942), esp. pp. 114–122; and Andrew Gladding Whiteside, *Austrian National Socialism before 1918* (The Hague: Martinus Nijhoff, 1962), esp. pp. 51–86.

20. On the *Brünner Programm,* see K. Schwechler, *Die österreichische Sozialdemokratie* (Graz and Vienna: Verlagsbuchhandlung "Styria," 1908),

pp. 207–212; and Robert A. Kann, *Das Nationalitätenproblem der Habsburgermonarchie* (Graz and Cologne: Herman Böhlaus, 1964), II, 160–162.

21. Karl Renner published a number of works explaining his views on the national question. The best known are *Staat und Nation* (Vienna, 1899) under the pseudonym "Synopticus," and *Der Kampf der österreichischen Nationen um den Staat* (Vienna, 1902) under the pseudonym "Rudolf Springer." The most complete exposition of his views is found in *Das Selbstbestimmungsrecht der Nationen* (Leipzig and Vienna: Franz Deuticke, 1918) which was published under his own name. Otto Bauer's comprehensive discussion of his theories on the national question is *Die Nationalitätenfrage und die Sozialdemokratie* (Vienna: Wiener Volksbuchhandlung Ignaz Brant, 1907). Analyses of their views are found in Kann, *Nationalitätenproblem*, II, 162–182; and Horace B. Davis, *Nationalism and Socialism* (New York: Monthly Review Press, 1967), pp. 149–163.

22. Oscar Jaszi, *The Dissolution of the Habsburg Monarchy* (Chicago: University of Chicago Press, 1929), pp. 177–184.

23. V. I. Lenin, "Critical Remarks on the National Question," in *Questions of National Policy and Proletarian Internationalism* (Moscow: Progress Publishers, n.d.), pp. 23, 30.

24. Alfred D. Low, *Lenin on the Question of Nationality* (New York: Bookman Associates, 1958), p. 29.

25. There is little doubt that Stalin's views on the national question were derived from Lenin. Stalin himself admitted to Milovan Djilas that *Marxism and the National Question* "was Ilyich's—Lenin's—view. Ilyich also edited the book." Milovan Djilas, *Conversations with Stalin* (New York: Harcourt, Brace and World, 1962), p. 157. See also Bertram D. Wolfe, *Three Who Made a Revolution* (New York: Delta Books, 1964), pp. 579–590.

26. Lenin, "Critical Remarks on the National Question," in *Questions of National Policy*, p. 30.

27. Lenin, "The Right of Nations to Self-Determination," *ibid.*, pp. 66, 69.

28. *Ibid.*, p. 52.

29. For a discussion of Lenin's views on the national question see Low, *Lenin on the Question of Nationality*, and Davis, *Nationalism and Socialism*, pp. 185–211.

30. Iosof Vissarionovich Stalin, *Works*, Vol. III (Moscow: Foreign Languages Publishing House, 1953), p. 55.

31. *Ibid.*, pp. 76–85.

32. See the discussion of the creation of the Soviet Union in Richard Pipes, *The Formation of the Soviet Union: Communism and Nationalism, 1917–1923*, rev. ed. (Cambridge, Mass.: Harvard University Press, 1964).

33. See references cited in note 3 of the Introduction.

Chapter 2

1. "Resolution on the National Question in Central Europe and the Balkans," *International Press Correspondence,* 4:24 (September 5, 1924), p. 684.

2. Wilhelm Winkler, *Statistisches Handbuch der europäischen Nationalitäten* (Vienna and Leipzig: Wilhelm Braumüller, 1931), pp. 94–95.

3. *Itogi vsesoyuzhoi perepisi naseleniya 1959 goda: Ukrainskaya SSR* (Moscow: Gosstatisdat, 1963), p. 176.

4. Ivo Duchacek, *The Strategy of Communist Infiltration: The Case of Czechoslovakia* (New Haven, Conn.: Institute of International Studies, 1949), p. 10.

5. František Němec and Vladimír Moudrý, *The Soviet Seizure of Subcarpathian Ruthenia* (Toronto: William B. Anderson, 1955), pp. 356–357.

6. *Ibid.,* pp. 128–129.

7. Vojta Beneš, "Dr. Edvard Beneš as He Was," *New Yorske Listy,* October 28, 1949, as quoted by Philip Mosely, *The Kremlin and World Politics* (New York: Vintage, 1960), p. 225.

8. Eduard Taborsky, "Beneš and Stalin—Moscow, 1943 and 1945," *Journal of Central European Affairs,* 13:2 (July 1953), p. 173n.

9. Edvard Beneš, "Post War Czechoslovakia," *Foreign Affairs,* 24:3 (April 1946), pp. 397–398.

10. Taborsky, "Beneš and Stalin . . . ," pp. 164–167; J. W. Brügel, "Der Fall Karpathorussland," *Europa Archiv,* 8:20 (October 20, 1953), pp. 6022–6023.

11. Edvard Beneš, *Czechoslovak Policy for Victory and Peace: The Fourth Message of the President of the Republic to the State Council on February 3, 1944* (London: Czechoslovak Ministry of Foreign Affairs Information Service, 1944), pp. 24, 26, 47.

12. *Ibid.,* p. 47.

13. *Ibid.,* p. 26.

14. This argument was advanced by Beneš in a telegram to František Němec in Moscow, January 5, 1945. See Němec and Moudrý, *Soviet Seizure,* pp. 333–336. Beneš also said essentially the same thing in an interview with a British journalist in 1944: Compton MacKenzie, *Dr. Beneš* (London: George G. Harrap, 1946), p. 290.

15. Němec and Moudrý, *Soviet Seizure,* pp. 92, 275.

16. *Ibid.,* pp. 113–114, 140.

17. President Beneš thought this was the case. *Ibid.,* pp. 291–293.

18. See Němec and Moudrý, *Soviet Seizure, passim;* Duchacek, *Strategy of Communist Infiltration,* pp. 10–14; Statement of Dr. Jan Papemec, United Nations Security Council, *Official Records, Third Year,* 272nd Meeting, March 22, 1948, No. 47, pp. 176–179; Brügel, "Der Fall Karpathorussland," pp. 6021–6028; for a pro-Ukrainian but anticommunist treatment, see Vasyl

Markus, *l'Incorporation de l'Ukraine Subcarpathique à l'Ukraine Soviétique, 1944–1945* (Louvain: Centre Ukrainien d'Etudes en Belgique, 1956).

19. Němec and Moudrý, *Soviet Seizure*, p. 357.

20. *Nazi-Soviet Relations 1939–1941: Documents from the Archives of the German Foreign Office*, ed. by Raymond J. Sontag and James S. Beddie (Washington, D.C.: Department of State, 1948), p. 159.

21. *Ibid.*, pp. 161–163.

22. *Anarul Statistic al României 1939* (Bucharest: Institutul Centrală de Statistică, 1939), pp. 60–61, 66–67.

23. *Nazi-Soviet Relations*, p. 78.

24. *Anarul Statistic al României 1939*, pp. 60–61, 66–67.

25. Alexander Dallin, *Odessa, 1941–1944: A Case Study of Soviet Territory under Foreign Rule* (Santa Monica, Calif.: Rand Corporation, 1957), pp. 45–55.

26. *Information Bulletin, Embassy of the Union of Soviet Socialist Republics* (Washington, D.C., April 6, 1944), p. 1. Molotov added that his statement was made "with the knowledge and approval of Great Britain and the United States." Cordell Hull and Winston Churchill both confirmed this.

27. Alexandre Cretzianu, *The Lost Opportunity* (London: Jonathan Cape, 1957), pp. 123–155.

28. *Armistice Agreement between the United States of America, the Union of Soviet Socialist Republics, and the United Kingdom and Rumania*, Department of State Executive Agreements Series, No. 490 (Washington, D.C., 1946), p. 2.

29. Cretzianu, *Lost Opportunity*, p. 142.

30. *Anuarul Statistic al României, 1937 și 1938*, pp. 60–61, 63.

31. *New York Times*, August 24, 1944.

32. *Information Bulletin, Embassy of the USSR*, August 29, 1944, p. 1.

33. *Armistice Agreement . . . [with] Rumania*, p. 4.

34. Letter from Stalin to Rumanian Premier Petru Groza, quoted in Vasile Luca, "The Vienna Verdict and the Solution of the Problem of Nationalities," *Rumanian Review*, 1:2 (June 1946), p. 28.

35. Ferenc Nagy, *The Struggle behind the Iron Curtain*, trans. by Stephen K. Swift (New York: Macmillan, 1948), p. 204.

36. *Ibid.*, pp. 208–211.

37. *New York Times*, May 8, 1946.

38. Luca, "The Vienna Verdict . . . ," p. 26.

39. *Paris Peace Conference, 1946: Selected Documents* (Washington, D.C.: Department of State, 1947), p. 818. For the Hungarian proposals, see pp. 1063–1066, 1097–1102, 1104–1105.

40. *New York Times*, March 11, 1945.

41. *Pravda* (Moscow), March 14, 1945.

42. Luca, "The Vienna Verdict . . . ," p. 28.

43. Stephen D. Kertesz, *Diplomacy in a Whirlpool: Hungary between Nazi Germany and Soviet Russia* (Notre Dame, Ind.: University of Notre Dame Press, 1953), pp. 139–143.

44. *Memorandum of the Government of the Democratic Federative Yugoslavia Concerning the Question of the Julian March and Other Yugoslav Territories under Italy* (Belgrade, [1945]).

45. The threat to the party's popularity was so immediate that it quickly adopted the slogan "Trieste is Italian." See Mosely, *The Kremlin and World Politics*, p. 229.

46. For background on the Trieste problem, see Bogdan C. Novak, *Trieste, 1941–1954: The Ethnic, Political, and Ideological Struggle* (Chicago: University of Chicago Press, 1970); and the chapters on history in Jean-Baptiste Duroselle, *Le Conflit de Trieste, 1943–1954* (Bruxelles: Editions de l'Institut de Sociologie de l'Université Libre de Bruxelles, [1966]).

47. *Memorandum of the Government of the Federative People's Republic of Yugoslavia on Slovene Carinthia, the Slovene Frontier Areas of Styria and the Croats of Burgenland* (Belgrade, 1946).

48. For the relation between Yugoslav claims and the Austrian treaty, see Cary Travers Grayson, Jr., *Austria's International Position, 1938–1953* (Geneva: Librairie E. Droz, 1953); Robert Langer, *The Austro-Yugoslav Problem* ([New York ?], 1951); Sven Allard, *Russia and the Austrian State Treaty* (University Park, Pa.: Pennsylvania State University Press, 1970); and Robert L. Ferring, "The Austrian State Treaty of 1955 and the Cold War," *Western Political Quarterly*, 21:4 (December 1968), pp. 651–667.

49. *The Austrian State Treaty*, European and Commonwealth Series, No. 49 (Washington, D.C.: Department of State, 1957), Article 7.

50. *Anuarul Statistic al României, 1937 şi 1938*, pp. 58–59.

51. *Paris Peace Conference, Documents*, p. 899.

Chapter 3

1. Joseph B. Schechtman, *European Population Transfers, 1939–1945* (New York: Oxford University Press, 1946); and Robert Conquest, *The Nation Killers: Soviet Deportation of Nationalities* (London: Macmillian, 1971).

2. Elizabeth Wiskemann, *Germany's Eastern Neighbors: Problems Relating to the Oder-Neisse Line and the Czech Frontier Regions* (London: Oxford University Press, 1956), p. 62. In the spring of 1939 Beneš definitely favored eliminating the national minorities from postwar Czechoslovakia. Edvard Beneš, *Demokratie heute und morgen* (Zürich: Europa Verlag, 1944), pp. 247–249.

3. Edvard Beneš, *Memoirs of Dr. Edvard Beneš: From Munich to New War and New Victory*, tr. by Godfrey Lias (London: Allen and Unwin,

1954), pp. 186–187, 193, 195, 206–207. The Soviet government was, in fact, the last of the big three to approve Czechoslovakia's expulsion of its German and Hungarian minorities. Soviet approval was not granted until a few weeks after British and American approval had been obtained.

4. "Potsdam Communiqué," *Foreign Relations of the United States: The Conference of Berlin (The Potsdam Conference), 1945* (Washington, D.C.: Department of State, 1960), p. 1511.

5. Stephen Kertesz, "The Expulsion of the Germans from Hungary: A Study of Postwar Diplomacy," *Review of Politics,* 15:2 (April 1953), pp. 179–208.

6. I. Levin, "The Nationality Question in Post-War Europe," *New Times,* 10:20 (October 15, 1945), pp. 3–8.

7. For decrees, laws, and provisions relating to the German minorities, see *Dokumentation der Vertreibung der Deutschen aus Ost-mitteleuropa,* 5 vols., ed. by Werner Conze and others (Berlin: Bundesministerium für Vertriebene Flüchtlinge und Kriegsgeschädigte, 1957–1961). Each volume deals with a single Central European country.

8. Kertesz, "Expulsion of the Germans . . . ," p. 204.

9. See Wiskemann, *Germany's Eastern Neighbors;* G. C. Paikert, *The Danube Swabians* (The Hague: Martinus Nijhoff, 1967); and Joseph B. Schechtman, *Post War Population Transfers in Europe* (Philadelphia: University of Pennsylvania Press, 1962), pp. 50–98, 263–286.

10. Edvard Beneš, "Postwar Czechoslovakia," *Foreign Affairs,* 24:3 (April 1946), pp. 400–401.

11. *Dokumentation der Vertreibung,* Vol. IV. There were numerous demands for rehabilitation and compensation for the Hungarian minority after press censorship was removed in Czechoslovakia in 1968. See *Új Szó,* April 12, 1968, and *Hét,* April 21, 1968.

12. Text of agreement in *Hungary and the Conference of Paris* (Budapest: Ministry of Foreign Affairs, 1947), II, 69–76. This document collection was to have been a five-volume series, but only Volumes I, II, and IV were completed before the communist seizure of power brought publication to an end. Volume I is available in French, Volume II in French and English, and Volume IV in English. References to Volume II cite the English edition.

13. *Ibid.,* II, 80–90; IV, 63.

14. Material in this section is based upon information supplied by György Heltai, who was the communist political director of the Hungarian Ministry of Foreign Affairs from 1945 to 1949. He was arrested in 1949 and later tried as a Rajkist.

On September 10, 1946, Yugoslav and Hungarian representatives in Paris signed an agreement to allow for up to 40,000 Hungarians living in Yugoslavia to move to Hungary if an equal number of Yugoslav peoples living in Hungary wished to go to Yugoslavia. *Keesing's Contemporary Archives,* Vol. 6 (*1946–1947*), pp. 8175–8176.

15. Ferenc Nagy, *The Struggle Behind the Iron Curtain*, trans. by Stephen K. Swift (New York: Macmillan, 1948), p. 208.

16. *Hungary and the Conference of Paris,* IV, 15.

17. Clementis' speeches, in *ibid.,* IV, 25–34, 60–71, 112–115.

18. *Ibid.,* II, 47; IV, 3, 90–91, 95–96, 98–99.

19. *Paris Peace Conference, 1946: Selected Documents* (Washington, D.C.: Department of State, 1947), p. 1114. See also the *Peace Treaty with Hungary,* Article 5.

20. The original Czechoslovak proposal called for five villages. The final article of the treaty required Hungary to cede only three villages with their cadastral lands. *Peace Treaty with Hungary,* Article 1.

21. "Resolution on the National Question in Central Europe and the Balkans," *International Press Correspondence,* 4:24 (September 5, 1924), p. 683.

22. For the history of the Balkan federation idea, see Joseph Rothschild, *The Communist Party of Bulgaria: Origins and Development, 1883–1936* (New York: Columbia University Press, 1959), pp. 205–258; L. S. Stavrianos, *Balkan Federation: A History of the Movement toward Balkan Unity in Modern Times* (Northampton, Mass.: Smith College, 1941); Rudolf Wierer, *Der Föderalismus im Donauraum* (Graz and Cologne: Verlag Hermann Böhlaus, 1960).

23. For detailed discussion of the history of the Macedonian question and the dispute between the Yugoslav and Bulgarian communists, see Stephen E. Palmer, Jr. and Robert R. King, *Yugoslav Communism and the Macedonian Question* (Hamden, Conn.: Archon Books, 1971); Elizabeth Barker, *Macedonia: Its Place in Balkan Power Politics* (London: Royal Institute for International Affairs, 1950); H. R. Wilkinson, *Maps and Politics: A Review of the Ethnographic Cartography of Macedonia* (Liverpool: University Press, 1951); Christ Anastasoff, *The Tragic Peninsula: A History of the Macedonian Movement for Independence since 1878* (St. Louis: Blackwell Wielandy, 1938); Evangelos Kofos, *Nationalism and Communism in Macedonia* (Salonika: Institute for Balkan Studies, 1964); and Paul Shoup, *Communism and the Yugoslav National Question* (New York: Columbia University Press 1968).

24. Letter of Vukmanović-Tempo and Koliševski, in Istorijsko odeljenje Centralnog komiteta KPJ, *Istorijski archiv Komunističke partije Jugoslavija.* Vol. VII, *Makedonija u narodnooslobodilačkom ratu i narodnoj revoluciji, 1941–1944* (Belgrade: Kultura), pp. 359–361.

25. Speech of Georgi Madolev to the Fifth Bulgarian Party Congress, *Rabotnichesko Delo,* December 23, 1948.

26. Letter of Ljupčo Arsov and Vera Aceva, *Istorijski archiv,* VII, 369–375.

27. *Istorijski archiv,* VII, 415. Actually the Bulgarian forces were, in some cases, better armed and organized than the Yugoslav Macedonian partisans and some of them were quite successful against the Germans.

28. *Ibid.,* pp. 366–367.

29. *Ibid.,* pp. 367–369.

30. Aleksandar Ranković, *II kongres Komunističke partije Srbije* (Belgrade: Prosveta 1949), p. 226; Vladimir Dedijer, *Tito* (New York: Simon and Schuster, 1953), p. 304.

31. For the text of this treaty, see Boris Meissner, ed., *Das Ostpakt System: Dokumentenzusammenstellung* (Cologne: Verlag Wissenschaft und Politik, 1951), pp. 125–128.

32. Dimitar Mitrev, *Pirinska Makedonija vo borba na nacionalno osloboduvanje* (Skopje: Glavinot odbor na Narodniot front na Makedonija, 1950), p. 281.

33. The results of the 1946 Bulgarian census were not published by Bulgaria. However, both Yugoslav and Bulgarian sources have consistently stated since 1946 that the census showed 70 percent of the population to be Macedonian but without giving specific figures. See Krste Crvenkovski's speech reported in *Borba,* February 3, 1968. The figures published in *Borba,* August 19, 1971, indicate that there were 169,544 Macedonians in Bulgaria in 1946.

34. Mitrev, *Pirinska Makedonija,* pp. 288–290.

35. Lazar Mojsov, *Bulgarska Radnička Partija (Komunista) i makedonsko nacionalno pitanje* (Belgrade: Borba, 1948), pp. 223–224.

36. Mitrev, *Pirinska Makedonija,* pp. 302–308. See Shoup's discussion of this resolution in *Communism and the Yugoslav National Question,* pp. 151–152.

37. *Documents on International Affairs, 1947–1948* (London: Royal Institute for International Affairs, 1952), pp. 290–292.

38. *Ibid.,* p. 292.

39. *Ibid.,* pp. 293–294; Georgi Dimitrov, *Political Report: V Congress of the Bulgarian Communist Party* (Sofia: Press Department of the Ministry of Foreign Affairs, 1949), p. 65.

40. Dimitrov, *Political Report,* p. 64.

41. See R. V. Burks, *The Dynamics of Communism in Eastern Europe* (Princeton, N.J.: Princeton University Press, 1961), pp. 99–101; and Philip Mosely, *The Kremlin and World Politics* (New York: Vintage, 1960), pp. 230–232.

42. Kofos, *Nationalism and Communism in Macedonia,* pp. 164–166.

43. Mitrev, *Pirinska Makedonija,* pp. 326–335; Dimitrov, *Political Report,* p. 67.

44. Meissner, *Ostpakt System,* pp. 47–50.

45. Mojsov, *Bulgarska Radnička Partija,* p. 274.

46. *Pravda* (Moscow), January 29, 1948.

47. Dedijer, *Tito,* p. 321; see also Milovan Djilas, *Conversations with Stalin* (New York: Harcourt, Brace and World, 1962), pp. 175–178.

48. Dedijer, *Tito,* p. 328.

49. For the main documents exchanged during this period, see Robert

Bass and Elizabeth Marbury, eds., *The Soviet-Yugoslav Controversy, 1948–1958: A Documentary Record* (New York: Prospect Books, 1959).

50. Antun Vratuša, "Multinationality in the Light of Yugoslav Socialist Development," *Socialist Thought and Practice,* No. 5 (January 1962), p. 37.

51. Dedijer, *Tito,* p. 388.

52. Andor Berei, "Tito Clique Foments Nationalist Hatred," *For a Lasting Peace, for a People's Democracy,* May 2, 1951.

53. Vasile Luca, "Fascist Essence of Tito Clique Policy on the National Question," *ibid.,* March 9, 1951.

54. Mátyás Rákosi, "Yugoslav Trotskyists, Shock Troops of Imperialism," *ibid.,* June 1, 1949.

55. *White Book on Aggressive Activities by the Governments of the USSR, Poland, Czechoslovakia, Hungary, Rumania, Bulgaria, and Albania towards Yugoslavia* (Belgrade: Ministry of Foreign Affairs of the FPRY, 1951), pp. 86–87, 98, 99–100.

56. *Bashkimi,* September 4, 1948.

57. *Ibid.,* September 16, 1949.

58. *Zëri i Popullit,* September 25, 1949.

59. *For a Lasting Peace, for a People's Democracy,* November 23, 1951. Yugoslav authorities have revealed that atrocities were committed against the Albanians in Kosovo and Macedonia. However, this occurred not after the Cominform resolution but in 1944–1945, when the partisan armies were seeking to re-establish Yugoslav control of the Albanian minority areas. Shoup, *Communism and the Yugoslav National Question,* pp. 104–105.

60. Dimitrov, *Political Report,* p. 70.

61. See *The Trial of Traicho Kostov and His Group* (Sofia: Press Department, 1949).

62. *White Book on Aggressive Activities . . . ,* especially pp. 151–161. See also Shoup, *Communism and the Yugoslav National Question,* pp. 160–162, 170 ff.

63. Shoup, *Communism and the Yugoslav National Question,* pp. 135–139.

64. Stephen D. Kertesz, *Diplomacy in a Whirlpool: Hungary between Nazi Germany and Soviet Russia* (Notre Dame, Ind.: University of Notre Dame Press, 1953), pp. 180–183.

65. For nationality provisions of the Rumanian constitutions of 1948 and 1952, see Jan F. Triska, ed., *Constitutions of the Communist Party-States* (Stanford, Calif.: Hoover Institution, 1968), pp. 351–352, 362, 374.

66. *Dokumentation der Vertreibung,* IV:1, 308; Triska, *Constitutions,* pp. 435–436.

67. For the provisions of the Yugoslav constitution of 1946, see Triska, *Constitutions,* pp. 456–458.

68. For texts of these treaties, see Meissner, *Ostpakt System.*

69. P. Serebryannikov, "The National Question—How It Is Solved in the People's Democracies," *New Times,* No. 13 (March 23, 1949), pp. 5, 6.

70. I. Nistor, in *Izvestia*, December 27, 1952.
71. N. Matyushkin, in *Literaturnaya gazeta*, April 21, 1953.
72. Serebryannikov, "The National Question . . . ," p. 9.
73. Milovan Djilas, *Članci, 1941–1946* ([Belgrade]: Kultura, 1947), pp. 231–240.

Chapter 4

1. "Report of the Special Committee on the Problem of Hungary," United Nations, General Assembly, *Official Records. Eleventh Session,* Supplement 18 (A/3592), (New York, 1957), pp. 67–70.
2. Charles Andras, *Neighbors on the Danube: New Variations on the Old Theme of Regional Cooperation* (Munich: Radio Free Europe Research, December 1967), pp. 41–47.
3. Imre Nagy, *On Communism* (New York: Praeger, 1957), pp. 238–240.
4. Quoted in Melvin J. Lasky, ed., *The Hungarian Revolution: A White Book* (New York: Praeger, 1957), p. 91.
5. *Veszprém Megyei Népujság,* October 30, 1956.
6. *Magyar Szabadság,* November 1, 1956.
7. Radio Miskolc, October 30 and November 1, 1956.
8. Agence France Press (AFP), November 10, 1956; *Annual Register of World Events, 1956* (London: Longman, 1957), p. 248; Radio Prague, November 10, 1956; Victor Meier, "Slovakia under the Prague Regime," *Swiss Review of World Affairs,* 7:6 (September 1957), p. 12.
9. *Rudé Právo,* October 31, 1956.
10. Československa Tiskova Kancelar (Ceteka), October 31, 1956.
11. Radio Prague, November 3, 1956.
12. *Ibid.,* December 16, 1956.
13. Meier, "Slovakia . . . ," p. 12.
14. Rudolf Olsinski, in *Kulturný Život,* No. 15 (April 12, 1968).
15. Lajos Turczel, in *Új Szó,* April 28, 1968.
16. Radio Prague, November 4, 1956.
17. *Pravda* (Moscow), December 7, 1956.
18. *Ibid.,* November 7, 1956.
19. *Ibid.,* November 18, 1956.
20. *New York Times,* October 29 and 30, November 1 and 3, 1956. (These four reports were written by Wells Hangen, who was expelled from Rumania for writing them.) *New York Times,* November 15, 1956, September 6, 1958; George Urban, *Nineteen Days* (London: Heinemann, 1957), pp. 133–134; Petru Dumitru, "Hungarian Revolution of 1956 and the Roumanians," *Review: A Quarterly of Pluralist Socialism,* 3:4 (October, 1961), p. 19; Elek Telegdi, "Position of the Hungarian Minority in Rumania," *ibid.,* 5:2 (1963), pp. 90–91; Ghită Ionescu, *Communism in Ru-*

mania, 1944–1962 (London: Oxford University Press, 1964), pp. 267–287; *Der Spiegel,* No. 45 (October 31, 1966), pp. 158–162.

21. Agentia Româna de Presa (Agerpres), November 2, 1956.

22. *Scînteia,* October 28, 1956; Radio Bucharest, October 28, 1956.

23. Agerpres, November 2, 1956; Radio Bucharest, November 3 and 4, 1956; *Scînteia,* November 3, 1956.

24. Radio Bucharest, November 5, 1956.

25. *Ibid.,* November 7, 1956.

26. Gheorghe Gheorghiu-Dej, *Artikel und Reden, Dezember 1955–Juli 1959* (Bucharest: Politischer Verlag, 1959), pp. 245–246.

27. *Pravda* (Moscow), November 8, 1956.

28. *Ibid.,* November 26, 1956.

29. *Scînteia,* October 16, 1957.

30. Radio Belgrade, November 4, 1956; *New York Times,* December 10, 1956.

31. *Borba,* November 5, 1956.

32. *Ibid.,* November 16, 1956.

33. *New York Times,* November 20, 1956.

34. *Izvestia,* November 25 and 27, 1956.

35. Radio Bucharest, February 28, 1958.

36. Speech of Gyula Kállai in Tîrgu Mureş capital of the Hungarian Autonomous Region. Radio Budapest, February 25, 1958.

37. Radio Bucharest, February 27, 1958.

38. *Népszabadság,* February 21, 1958.

39. *Rudé Právo,* December 10, 1958.

40. Radio Budapest, December 17, 1958.

Chapter 5

1. *Statistique des Nationalités en Tchécoslovaquie* (Prague: "Politika," 1924), pp. 18–19.

2. *Nova Makedonija* (December 24, 1970, January 31 and February 11, 1971) said Moslems in the Yugoslav Republic of Macedonia who speak Macedonian should be enumerated as Macedonians. The political leaders of the Republic of Bosnia-Hercegovina, which has a sizable Serbo-Croatian-speaking Moslem population that has generally chosen to declare itself to be "Moslem" in postwar Yugoslav censuses, insisted upon the right of citizens to declare themselves to be "Moslem" as a nationality. (*Borba,* December 22, 1970.) The differences of view between these two positions was the subject of a number of exchanges in the Yugoslav press. There were other reports that Turks in Macedonia were being pressured to declare themselves to be Albanians and that Gypsies in Kosovo were being pressured to do the same. (*Politika,* March 23 and April 1, 1971.)

3. For some of the major articles in the controversy, see *Borba,* January

29, February 2, 3, 6, 9, 13, 19, and 20, 1971; *Ekonomska Politika,* February 8, 1971; and *Politika,* February 3, 1971.

4. The changes were announced in *Borba,* February 26, 1971.

5. Károly Patho, in *Új Szó,* March 20, 1968.

6. Kálmán Jánics, in *ibid.,* April 12, 1968.

7. Z. Dávid, in *Magyar Hirek,* April 5, 1969.

8. *Borba,* August 19, 1971.

9. *Ibid.,* February 9, 1967.

10. Krste Crvenkovski speech reported in *Borba,* February 3, 1968.

11. *Makedonskiat vpros: istoriko-politicheska spravka* (Sofia: Institut za istoria pri BAN, November 1968), p. 66.

12. *Borba,* February 3, 1968.

13. In reality the Soviet Union has given very restricted rights to the non-Russian nationalities. See Robert Conquest, *Soviet Nationalities Policy in Practice* (New York: Praeger, 1967); Erich Goldhagen, ed., *Ethnic Minorities in the Soviet Union* (New York: Praeger, 1968); and *Problems of Communism,* 16:5 (September-October 1967).

14. Iosif Vissarionovich Stalin, *Works,* Vol. IV (Moscow: Foreign Languages Publishing House, 1953), pp. 364–365.

15. Khrushchev speech to the Ninth All-German Worker's Conference in Leipzig, March 7, 1959, *Pravda* (Moscow), March 27, 1959.

16. Stalin, *Works,* II, 307.

17. Bolshaya Sovetskaya Entsiklopedia, 2nd ed. (1954), XXVIII, 105–106.

18. *Ibid.*

19. See, for example, the volumes put out by the Moldavian Academy of Science, *Moldavsko-russko-ukrainskie literaturnie svyazi* (Kishinev: Izdatelstvo "Shtintsa" Akademi nauk Moldavskoi SSR, 1962); and *Moldavsko-russko-ukrainskie literaturnie i folklornie svyazi* (Kishinev: Izdatelstvo "Kartya Moldovenyaske," 1967).

20. For example, C. Berezhan, and others, eds., *Kurs de gramatike istorike a limbi Moldovenesht* (Kishinev: Editura "Lumina," 1966); N. Korletyanu, *Studiu asupra sistemei leksikale moldovenesht din anii 1870–1890* (Kishinev: Akademia de Stiintse a RSS Moldovenesht: Institutul de Limba shi Literature, 1964); and *Studii de Limbe Moldovenyaske* (Kishinev: Editura de stat "Kartya Moldovenyaske," 1963). The Moldavian Academy of Science's Institute of Language and Literature also sponsored research and publication of a large Moldavian linguistic atlas. For a summary of some of the more recent works on the Moldavian language, see N. Korletyanu, "Lingvistika moldovenyaske in etapa aktuale," *Komunistul Moldovei,* No. 10 (October 1966), pp. 20–23.

21. For a more complete discussion of the development and acceptance of the Macedonian literary language, see Stephen E. Palmer, Jr., and Robert R. King, *Yugoslav Communism and the Macedonian Question* (Hamden, Conn.: Archon Books, 1971), pp. 153–159.

22. See, for example, the comments on the definition of a nation in Ye. M. Zhukov's article in *Voprosy istorii,* No. 12 (December 1961), pp. 8–9.

23. *Rabotnichesko Delo,* September 22, 1958.

24. *Nova Makedonija,* October 10, 1958.

25. *Ibid.,* October 18, 1958; Ljupčo Arsov's speech reported in *Borba,* September 29, 1958; and Lazar Koliševski's speech of November 2, 1958, reprinted in his *Aspekti na makedonskoto prašanje* (Skopje: "Kultura," 1962), pp. 343–388.

26. *Borba,* September 29, 1963.

27. *Ibid.,* November 20, 1966; *Politika,* November 27, 1966.

28. See H. R. Wilkinson, *Maps and Politics: A Review of the Ethnographic Cartography of Macedonia* (Liverpool: University Press, 1951), p. 310.

29. *Borba,* August 26 and 27, 1946.

30. For Moldavia, see L. V. Cherepnin and others, eds., *Istoriia Moldavskoi SSR* (Kishinev: Izdatelstvo "Kartya Moldovenyaske," 1965 and 1968), I and II. The Macedonians have generally been more concerned with histories showing the distinctiveness of the Macedonian nationality. However, the general histories have considerable material on economic life. See, for example, the Macedonian Institute of National History's three-volume work, *Istorija na makedonskiot narod* (Skopje: Nova Makedonija, 1969). There have also been a few specialized works on this aspect of Macedonian economic history. For example, Dančo Zografski, *Razvitokot na kapitalističkite elementi vo Makedonija za vreme na turskoto vladeenje* (Skopje: Kultura, 1967).

31. On Moldavian culture, see K. V. Korolev, P. A. Kruchenyuk, and B. Z. Tanasevskii, *Doina Radosti: Dekada moldavskovo iskusstva i literaturi provodilas v Moskve s 27 Maya po 5 Iyunya 1960 goda* (Kishinev: "Kartya Moldovenyaske," 1962); R. V. Danielenko, *Razvitie Kulturnovo sotrudnichestva narodov SSSR* (Kishinev: Akademii nauk Moldavskoi SSR, 1968).

32. For a consideration of some of these aspects of Macedonian culture, see Palmer and King, *Yugoslav Communism and the Macedonian Question,* pp. 159–173.

Chapter 6

1. Joseph Stalin, *Marxism and the National Question: Selected Writings and Speeches* (New York: International Publishers, 1942), pp. 220–221.

2. I am particularly indebted to Mr. Charles Andras for his assistance with this chapter. He very kindly made available his unpublished paper entitled "Slovaks and Hungarians in Slovakia," which deals with the Hungarian minority during 1968.

3. For more detailed information on the laws and history relating to Czechoslovak territorial reorganizations, see Rudolf Urban, "Neue Ver-

waltungsgliederung in der Tschechoslowakei," *Zeitschrift für Ostforschung,* 10:1 (March 1961), pp. 119–126; and Helmut Slapnicka, "Die neue Verwaltungsgliederung der Tschechoslowakei und ihre Vorläufer," *Der Donauraum,* 5:3 (1960), pp. 139–158.

4. István Révay, "Die Magyaren in der Tschechoslowakei," in Manfred Straka, ed., *Handbuch der europäischen Volksgruppen* (Vienna and Stuttgart: Wilhelm Braumüller, 1970), p. 609.

5. *Ibid.,* pp. 611–612.

6. The position of the Csemadok CC on the January Resolution of the Czechoslovak CP CC and the Slovak CP CC was published in *Új Szó,* March 15, 1968.

7. See, for example, Rezso Szabo, in *Új Szó,* March 10, 1968; Károly Patho, in *ibid.,* March 20, 1968; the statement of the party organization of *Új Szó,* in *ibid.,* April 2, 1968; Tibor Sabi, in *ibid.,* April 2, 1968; and Mihály Tóth, in *ibid.,* July 14, 1968.

8. The statement of the leadership of the Hungarian section of the Union of Slovak Writers, in *Új Szó,* March 24, 1968, and *Irodalmi Szemle,* April 1968; Rezsö Szabó, in March 10, 1968; József Gyonyor, in *ibid.,* March 19, 1968; Károly Patho, in *Pravda* (Bratislava), April 5, 1968; József Macs, in *Hét,* April 21, 1968, and *Új Szó,* April 26, 1968.

9. *Lud,* April 5, 1968.

10. Ivan Hargas, in *Predvoj,* April 4, 1968.

11. *Rolnické Noviny,* March 2, 1968.

12. *Hét,* April 21, 1968.

13. T. Goldbergerova, in *Práca,* May 21–23, 1968.

14. Géza Vilcsek, in *Új Szó,* April 18, 1968.

15. *Ibid.*

16. Lajos Turczel, in *ibid.,* April 28, 1968, and *Smena,* April 22, 1968.

17. Michal Chorvath, in *Predvoj,* May 2, 1968.

18. Quoted by Samo Sklabinsky, in *Magyar Szó,* May 7, 1968.

19. Rudolf Olinski, in *Kulturný Život,* April 12, 1968.

20. *Hét,* April 21, 1968.

21. *Pravda* (Bratislava), May 24, 1968.

22. *Magyar Nemzet,* April 28, 1968.

23. *Ibid.,* September 5, 1967; *Szolnok Megyei Néplap,* September 24, 1967; *Népszabadság,* May 12, 1968; *Élet és Irodalom,* May 15 and June 15, 1968.

24. Pál Fehér, in *Élet és Irodalom,* May 11, 1968.

25. For example, see the interview with Oldrich Cernik, Hungarian Radio and Television, April 20, 1968; *Népszabadság,* June 1, 1968; *Kisalföld,* June 2, 1968; *Magyar Nemzet,* June 29, 1968; *Magyar Hirlap,* July 16, 1968.

26. *Népszabadság,* June 15, 1968.

27. *Ibid.*

28. *Ibid.,* September 25, 1968.

29. *Ibid.,* October 6, 1968.

30. *Pravda* (Bratislava), May 30, 1968.

31. Robert J. Mikots, in *Hét,* July 21, 1968.

32. *Pravda* (Bratislava), September 12, 1968.

33. Figures calculated on the basis of data in *Új Szó,* May 31, 1970.

34. *Ibid.,* May 3, 1970.

35. The leadership changes in May 1970 were not reported in the Czechoslovak press, but were announced over Radio Budapest on May 12, 1970. Radio Bratislava, March 30, 1971, only announced the election of a new chairman of Csemadok and the removal of the former chairman. It was Radio Budapest, March 30, 1971, which announced that 27 members of the Central Committee had lost their positions.

Chapter 7

1. *Borba,* July 7, 1971.

2. *Statistički godišnjak Jugoslavije* (Belgrade: Savezni Zavod za Statistiku, 1960 and 1970).

3. Data on the number and frequency of these minority-language publications may be found in the annual editions of *Statistički godišnjak Jugoslavije.*

4. See Paul Shoup, "Yugoslavia's National Minorities Under Communism," *Slavic Review* 22:1 (March 1963), pp. 64–81.

5. See reports of the Central Committee plenum of the Serbian League of Communists, September 14–15, 1966, in *Politika,* September 15, 1966, and *Borba,* September 16, 1966.

6. H. R. Wilkinson, *Maps and Politics: A Review of the Ethnographic Cartography of Macedonia* (Liverpool: University Press, 1951), p. 310.

7. See Radoye L. Knejevitch, "The Ethnical Structure of Voyvodina," *Yugoslav Observer,* 2:2 (March 1956), pp. 14–17. The author stresses the Serbian claims, but does give some idea of the complex ethnic situation in the area.

8. Paul Shoup, *Communism and the Yugoslav National Question* (New York: Columbia University Press, 1968), pp. 60–100; and Dinko Tomasic, "Nationality Problems and Partisan Yugoslavia," *Journal of Central European Affairs,* 6:2 (July 1946), pp. 111–125.

9. *Constitution of the Federal Peoples Republic of Yugoslavia* [1946], Article 103.

10. In a speech in Zagreb just after the war, Tito explained that the federal republics were not considered "a group of small nations, rather they have a more administrative character." (*Borba,* May 22, 1945.)

11. Jovan Djordjević, *Novi Ustavni Sistem* (Belgrade: Savremena Administracija, 1964), p. 599.

12. *Ibid.*

13. *Ustav Socijalističke Federativne Republike Jugoslavije* (Belgrade: Novinske ustavone službeni list SFRJ, 1963), Articles 111–112.

14. Djordjević, *Novi Ustavni Sistem*, pp. 602–603.

15. Interview with Iliaz Kurteši, in *Rilindja*, September 30, 1971.

16. Census figures for 1971 are from *Politika*, April 30–May 1 and 2, 1971.

17. Interview with Mahmut Bakali, president of the Provincial Committee of the League of Communists of Kosovo, *Politika*, July 25, 1971.

18. See reports of the plenum of the League of Communists of Kosovo in Priština, June 21–22, 1971, in *Politika*, June 21, 22, 23, and 25, 1971.

19. *Perparimi*, June 1967.

20. *Borba*, December 7, 1968.

21. *Autonomne Pokrajine u Jugoslaviji: Društveno-politički i pravni aspekti* (Belgrade: Institut za uporedne pravo, 1967).

22. *Perparimi*, June 1967.

23. *Borba*, December 7, 1968.

24. Summaries of these proposals are contained in *Politika*, April 24 and July 13, 1968.

25. *Rilindja*, November 4, 1968.

26. *Borba*, May 30, 1968.

27. *Ibid.*, December 1, 1968.

28. *Politika*, December 30, 1968.

29. *Ibid.*, December 5, 1968; and *Borba*, December 14 and 28, 1968.

30. *Borba*, February 6, 1969.

31. Ilija Rajacia, president of the Assembly of Vojvodina, *Borba*, January 8, 1971.

32. Dragoslav Marković, President of the Constitutional Commission of Serbia and President of the National Assembly of Serbia. Telegrafska agenciija Nova Jugoslavija (Tanjug) J,anuary 8, 1971.

33. Arslan Fazlija, president of the Socialist Alliance of the Province of Kosovo, *Politika*, January 8, 1971.

34. For the text of the amendments, see *Službeni List*, July 8, 1971.

35. *Rilindja*, September 30, 1971.

36. *Zëri i Popullit*, October 20, 1958.

37. *Politika*, October 5, 1967; *Perparimi*, June 1967.

38. *Zëri i Popullit*, November 16, 1967.

39. *Ibid.*, November 24, 1968.

Chapter 8

1. Resolution of the Central Committee plenum of June 10–11, 1948, in *Resolutii si hotărîri ale Comitetului Central al PMR*, 2nd ed. (Bucharest: Editura de Stat pentru Literatură Politică, 1952).

2. Peter Meyer, Bernard D. Weinryb, Eugene Duschinsky, and Nicolas Sylvain, *The Jews in the Soviet Satellites* (Syracuse: Syracuse University Press, 1953), pp. 493–556.

3. For a discussion of this and other territorial divisions of Rumania before 1965, see Ronald A. Henlin, "The Volatile Administrative Map of Rumania," *Annals of the American Association of Geographers,* 57:3 (September 1967), pp. 481–502.

4. *Constitution of the People's Republic of Rumania* [September 24, 1952], Article 19.

5. See "Gebietsumfang und Ortsverzeichnis der Autonomen Madjarischen Region in Rumänien," *Wissenschaftlicher Dienst Südosteuropa,* 1:3 (1952), pp. 23–29.

6. *Constitution of the People's Republic of Rumania* [September 24, 1952], Articles 20 and 21.

7. *New York Times,* June 10, 1959.

8. *Scînteia,* July 24, 1958.

9. Wilhelm Reiter, "Die Nationalitäten Politik der Rumänischen Volksrepublik im Spiegel ihrer Statistik," *Osteuropa* 11:3 (March 1961), pp. 189–197; and George Bailey, "Trouble over Transylvania," *The Reporter,* 31:9 (November 19, 1964), pp. 25–30.

10. *Scînteia,* February 20, 1959.

11. *Ibid.,* February 22, 1959.

12. *Ibid.,* July 3, 1959.

13. *Der Spiegel,* No. 45 (October 31, 1966), pp. 158–162. There were a number of Western press reports of the suicides which appeared shortly after the merger of the universities.

14. Figures from *Scînteia,* July 3, 1959; and Michel Tatu in *Le Monde,* November 11, 1967.

15. See "Das Ende der 'Autonomen Madjarischen Region,'" *Wissenschaftler Dienst Südosteuropa,* 9:12 (December 1960), pp. 150–151.

16. See Bailey, "Trouble over Transylvania," and James F. Brown, "The Age-Old Question of Transylvania," *World Today,* 19 (1953), pp. 502–505.

17. Ceauşescu visited the Mureş-Hungarian Autonomous Region on September 24–26, 1965; the Cluj region on November 4–6; the Maramureş region on November 7–8; the Crişana (Oradea) region on February 18–19, 1966; the Banat (Timişoara) region on February 20–22; and he returned to the autonomous region again on August 12–15, 1966. For reports on these visits, see issues of *Scînteia* for the time periods involved.

18. Nicolae Ceauşescu, *România pe drumul desăvîrşirii construcetiei socialiste* (Bucharest: Politică, 1968–1970), II, 581–588.

19. *Scînteia,* December 8, 1967.

20. Ceauşescu, *România pe drumul . . . ,* III, 9.

21. *Ibid.,* p. 11.

22. *Ibid.,* pp. 17–19.

23. See, for example, the article by Zoltán Komócsin, in *Pravda* (Moscow), September 16, 1966, and the speech by János Kádár, reported in *Magyar Nemzet,* July 30, 1968, as well as articles in *Népszabadság,* October 8 and 29, 1966; and *Élet és Irodalom,* May 21, 1966.

24. For a discussion of some aspects of this debate, see Chapter 9.

25. The entire interview was published in *Népszabadság*, July 2, 1966.

26. See Giuseppe Boffa dispatch, in *l'Unita*, December 3, 1966; *Christ und Welt*, December 16, 1966; David Binder, in *New York Times*, May 14, 1966.

27. Ianos Szasz, in *Gazeta literara*, July 25, 1968. The Hungarian articles criticized are found in *Élet és Irodalom*, May 15 and June 15, 1968. See also note 23 in Chapter 7.

28. See the discussion of Rumania's historic debate with the Soviet Union over Bessarabia in Chapter 11.

29. For reports on these developments, see *Scînteia*, August 27 and 31, September 1 and 3, October 25, and November 16, 1968.

30. *Scînteia*, February 21, 1971. See also reports in the German-language newspaper *Neuer Weg*, February 16, 27, and 28, and March 2, 3, and 5, 1971.

31. The best example of this is found in *Korunk*, No. 5 (May 1971), a Hungarian-language cultural journal published in Cluj, which contained a number of articles devoted to the theme that Hungarian culture in Rumania is separate and distinct from Hungarian culture elsewhere.

32. *Népszabadság*, June 25, 1971.

33. *Scînteia*, July 9, 1971.

34. *Ibid.*, July 12, 1971.

35. *Magyar Hirlap*, August 4, 1971.

36. Radio Moscow in Rumanian, July 6, 1971.

37. *Sovietskaya Rossiya*, August 8, 1971; and Radio Moscow in Rumanian, August 8, 1971.

38. For a discussion of the Rumanian government's concessions to the minorities during this period, see Robert R. King, *Rumanian Concern for the National Minorities* (Munich: Radio Free Europe, July 23, 1971).

Chapter 9

1. See Donald S. Zagoria, *The Sino-Soviet Conflict, 1956–1961* (Princeton, N.J.: Princeton University Press, 1962), pp. 28–29; and the statement by J. Kisieliwski, in *Tygodnik Powszechny*, July 6, 1958, as quoted in Robert Conquest, *Power and Policy in the USSR* (New York: Harper Torchbooks, 1961), p. 51.

2. Alexander Solzhenitsyn, *Cancer Ward* (New York: Farrar, Straus and Giroux, 1969), p. 210.

3. A number of works have relied extensively on this kind of analysis, including Myron Rush, *The Rise of Khrushchev* (Washington, D.C.: Public Affairs Press, 1958); William E. Griffith, *Albania and the Sino-Soviet Rift* (Cambridge, Mass.: MIT Press, 1963), *The Sino-Soviet Rift* (Cambridge, Mass.: MIT Press, 1964), and *Sino-Soviet Relations, 1964–1965* (Cambridge, Mass.: MIT Press, 1967); Robert Conquest, *Power and Policy in the*

USSR; Zbigniew K. Brzezinski, *The Soviet Bloc Unity and Conflict,* rev. ed. (Cambridge, Mass.: Harvard University Press, 1967); Michel Tatu, *Power in the Kremlin: From Khrushchev to Kosygin* (New York: Viking, 1969); Uri Ra'anan, *The USSR Arms the Third World: Case Studies in Soviet Foreign Policy* (Cambridge, Mass.: MIT Press, 1969); and Zagoria, *The Sino-Soviet Conflict.* For a discussion of the problems of methodology and a defense of content analysis, see especially Conquest, *Power and Policy in the USSR,* pp. 3–75; Zagoria, *Sino-Soviet Conflict,* pp. 24–35; Wolfgang Leonhard, *The Kremlin Since Stalin* (London: Oxford University Press, 1962), pp. 17–30; Rush, *Rise of Khrushchev,* pp. 88–94, and "Esoteric Communication in Soviet Politics," *World Politics,* 11:4 (July 1959), pp. 614–620; Alexander Dallin and Zbigniew Brzezinski in Dallin, ed., *Diversity in International Communism* (New York: Columbia University Press, 1963), xxxvii–xliv; William E. Griffith, *Communist Esoteric Communications: Explication de Texte* (Cambridge, Mass.: MIT Center for International Studies, 1967; Franz Borkenau, "Getting at the Facts behind the Soviet Façade," *Commentary* 17:4 (April 1954), pp. 393–400; and Roderick MacFarquhar, "On Photographs," *China Quarterly,* No. 46 (April–June 1971), pp. 289–307.

4. *Fundamentals of Marxism-Leninism: Manual,* 2nd rev. ed. (Moscow: Foreign Languages Publishing House, 1963), pp. 146, 145.

5. M. N. Pokrovsky, "Marx as a Historian," *Vestnik sotsialisticheskoi akademii* 4 (1923), p. 372, as quoted in Marin Pundeff, ed., *History in the USSR: Selected Readings* (San Francisco: Hoover Institution, 1967), p. 64.

6. *Voprosy istorii,* No. 2 (February 1949), p. 10.

7. *Ibid.,* No. 3 (March 1957); also in Pundeff, *History in the USSR,* p. 236. For the background of this editorial, see Merle Fainsod, "Historiography and Change," in John Keep, ed., *Contemporary History in the Soviet Mirror* (New York: Praeger, 1964), pp. 20–27.

8. *Fundamentals of Marxism-Leninism,* p. 145.

9. *Ibid.,* p. 147.

10. Griffith, in *Communist Esoteric Communications,* pp. 6–7, lists sources of communications in a suggested order of significance.

11. László Katus, "Über die wirtschaftlichen und gesellschaftlichen Grundlagen der Nationalitätenfrage in Ungarn vor dem ersten Weltkrieg," in *Die nationale Frage in der Österreichisch-Ungarischen Monarchie, 1900–1918* (Budapest: Ungarische Akademie der Wissenschaftler, 1966), pp. 149–216. This volume contains the papers and discussions on the national question at the 1964 Budapest conference of historians. Katus was a candidate of historical science and an assistant at the Historical Science Institute of the Hungarian Academy of Science.

12. Erik Molnar, "Zur Rolle der Arbeiterpartei in Russland und in Österreich-Ungarn," in *Die nationale Frage,* pp. 315–317. At the time Molnar was a member of the Hungarian Academy of Sciences and Director of its Historical Science Institute.

13. M. Constantinescu, L. Bányai, V. Cutricapeanu, C. Gollner, and C. Nutu, "Zur nationalen Frage in Österreich-Ungarn (1900–1918)," in *Die nationale Frage,* pp. 39–147. Constantinescu was the Deputy Minister of Education and a section leader at the Institute for History of the Rumanian Academy; Ladislaus Bányai was Deputy Director of the Institute.

14. See, for example, László Kővágó's review of Czechoslovak, Rumanian, and Yugoslav historical works on the events of 1918, in *Valóság,* No. 10 (October 1966).

15. See Victor Chereştesiu, *Adunarea naţională de la Blaj* (Bucharest: Editura politică, 1966), and the reviews of this volume in *Lupta de clasă,* No. 10 (October 1966), and *Scînteia,* May 19, 1966. See also Miron Constantinescu, "Mesajul lui V.I. Lenin către muncitorii şi popoarele din Austro-Ungaria—2/3 Noiembrie 1918," *Studii revistă de istorie,* 19:1 (1966), pp. 115–127.

16. For a consideration of some of the problems faced by communist historians in evaluating the revolution of 1848 and for some of the early postwar developments in the communist historiography of that period, see John Erickson, "Recent Soviet and Marxist Writings in Central and Eastern Europe," *Journal of Central European Affairs* 17:2 (July 1957), pp. 119–126.

17. Vladimir Minac, "Tu žije národ," *Kulturný Život,* No. 42 (October 15, 1965), p. 1. The second and third portions of Minac's article were published in *Kulturný Život,* No. 43 (October 22, 1965), and No. 44 (October 29, 1965).

18. Erzsébet Andics, "Revízió alá kell-e vennünk Marx és Engels nézeteit az 1848–1849-es forradalomról?" *Valóság* 9:4 (April 1966), pp. 40–53.

19. Minac, "Tu žije národ."

20. *Fundamentals of Marxism-Leninism,* p. 149.

21. Minac, "Tu žije národ." Emphasis added.

22. Daniel Rapant, "Štúr a štúrovci v službe národa a pokroku," *Slovenská Literatura,* 12:5 (1966), pp. 437–457.

23. Minac, "Tu žije národ."

24. Andics, "Revízió . . . ."

25. *Ibid.*

26. Julius Mesaros, "Treba revidovat názory Marxa a Engelsa o revolúcii rokov 1848–1849?" *Predvoj,* No. 30 (July 27, 1966), pp. 10–11. The second half of Mesaros's article appeared in *ibid.,* No. 31 (August 4, 1966), p. 10.

27. Rapant, "Štúr a štúrovci . . . ."

28. Andics, "Revízió . . . ."

29. Mesaros, "Treba revidovat . . . ."

30. Minac, "Tu žije národ."

31. Rapant, "Štúr a štúrovci . . . ."

32. *Ibid.*

33. Mesaros, "Treba revidovat . . . ."

34. Andics, "Revízió . . . ."

35. *Ibid.*
36. Rapant is referring to "Der magyarische Kampf," in *Neue Rheinische Zeitung,* No. 194 (January 13, 1849). This article, as well as most articles on the Hungarian and German revolutions, was written by Engels. See *Marx-Engels Werke* (Berlin: Dietz Verlag, 1959), VI, 165–176, 270–286, 303–307, 507–515; and Friedrich Engels, *The German Revolutions: The Peasant War in Germany and Germany: Revolution and Counter Revolution,* ed. by Leonard Krieger (Chicago: University of Chicago Press, 1967), p. xxxvii.
37. Rapant, "Štúr a štúrovci. . . ."
38. Pál E. Fehér, "Egymás ellen vagy közösen?" *Eilet és Irodalom,* No. 21 (May 21, 1966), p. 1.
39. Andics, "Revízió. . . ."
40. Mesaros, "Treba revidovat. . . ."
41. See Kövágó's review, in *Valóság,* No. 10 (October 1966).
42. Fehér, "Egymás ellen vagy közösen?"

Chapter 10

1. For material on the Macedonian question prior to 1953, see Chapter 3, above.
2. *Nova Makedonija,* August 28, 1968.
3. *Makedonskiat vpros: istoriko-politicheska spravka* (Sofia: Institut za istoria pri BAN, November 1968), p. 63; *Borba,* February 3, 1968; *Nova Makedonija,* August 28, 1968.
4. For more detail on this decline in Soviet-Yugoslav relations, see Vaclav L. Benes and others, eds., *The Second Soviet-Yugoslav Dispute: Full Text of Main Documents—April–June, 1958,* Slavic and East European Series, Vol. 14 (Bloomington: Indiana University Publications, 1959); Robert Bass and Elizabeth Marbury, eds., *The Soviet-Yugoslav Controversy 1948–1958: A Documentary Record* (New York: Prospect Books, 1959); and Donald S. Zagoria, *The Sino-Soviet Conflict, 1956–1961* (Princeton, N.J.: Princeton University Press, 1961), pp. 176–187.
5. *Rabotnichesko Delo,* March 4, 1958.
6. *Novo Vreme,* No. 4 (April 1958), p. 48.
7. *Rabotnichesko Delo,* May 4, 1958.
8. Speech of Boris Vaptsarov, first secretary of the Blagoevgrad district party committee, *ibid.,* June 4, 1958.
9. Speech of Khristo Klaidzhiev, chairman of the Union of Macedonian Societies in Bulgaria and member of the party Central Committee, *ibid.,* August 2, 1958.
10. See, for example, *Nova Makedonija,* May 16, 1958, reprinted in *Borba,* May 21, 1958; *Nova Makedonija,* May 25, 1958, published by Tanjug, May 25, 1958; *Borba,* September 23, 1958.

11. *Rabotnichesko Delo,* September 18, 1958; and *Zemedelsko Zname,* September 18, 1958.

12. Text in *Rabotnichesko Delo,* November 20, 1958.

13. *Ibid.,* September 18, 1958.

14. *Borba,* September 19, 1958.

15. *Ibid.*

16. *Rabotnichesko Delo,* September 20, 1958. An abridged version of this article was broadcast over Radio Sofia in Serbo-Croatian on September 21, 1958.

17. *Politika,* September 21, 1958.

18. *Rabotnichesko Delo,* September 22, 1958. Emphasis supplied.

19. *Ibid.*

20. See the statement of Angel Todorov, secretary of the Bulgarian Writer's Union, *Zemedelsko Zname,* September 25, 1958; and the speech of Anton Yugov on September 27, 1958, at Radomir on the 40th anniversary of the Vladaya soldier's rebellion, as published in *Rabotnichesko Delo,* September 28, 1958.

21. *Politika,* September 24, 1958.

22. *Borba,* September 24, 1958.

23. Radio Belgrade, September 27, 1958. The text of the note was published in *Rabotnichesko Delo* on November 20, 1958, and in *Borba* on October 5, 1958.

24. *Nova Makedonija,* September 29, 1958; there were also reports of the speech in *Borba* and *Politika,* both on September 29, 1958. The speech was given at the "historical" observance of the 30th anniversary of the Zletovo zinc and lead mine in Yugoslav Macedonia.

25. See Stephen E. Palmer, Jr., and Robert R. King, *Yugoslav Communism and the Macedonian Question* (Hamden, Conn.: Archon Books, 1971), pp. 165–173.

26. *Komunist,* October 9, 1958.

27. *Borba,* October 11, 1958. For more information on the dispute between the Yugoslav and Bulgarian communists over Macedonia during World War II, see Paul Shoup, *Communism and the Yugoslav National Question* (New York: Columbia University Press, 1968), pp. 82–91; Evangelos Kofos, *Nationalism and Communism in Macedonia* (Salonika: Institute for Balkan Studies, 1964), pp. 113–119; Elizabeth Barker, *Macedonia: Its Place in Balkan Power Politics* (London: Royal Institute for International Affairs, 1950), pp. 83–98; and Palmer and King, *Yugoslav Communism and the Macedonian Question,* pp. 61–116.

28. *Borba,* October 11, 1958; Nova Makedonija, October 11, 1958.

29. *Borba,* October 13, 1958.

30. *Izvestia na instituta po istoria na BKP* No. 3–4 (1958), p. 509.

31. Lazar Koliševski, *Aspekti na makedonskoto prašanje* (Skopje: Kultura, 1962), pp. 343–388.

32. *Rabotnichesko Delo,* November 20, 1958.

33. *Nova Makedonija,* April 21, 1959, summarized in *Borba,* April 21, 1959; *Nova Makedonija,* May 22, 1959.

34. *Pravda* (Moscow), May 17, 1962. For the reasons behind this *rapprochement* and other indications of it, see William E. Griffith, *The Sino-Soviet Rift* (Cambridge, Mass.: MIT Press, 1964), pp. 43–52.

35. See *Nova Makedonija,* January 7 and April 15, 1962, *Istoricheski pregled,* 17:6 (November–December 1961), pp. 106–114.

36. Speech of Krste Crvenkovski, member of the presidium of the League of Communists of Macedonia, to the Macedonian party Central Committee, February 2, 1968, *Borba,* February 3, 1968. See also *Nova Makedonija,* August 28, 1968.

37. See, for example, *Borba,* April 2, 1964.

38. Speech at Pirot, *Borba,* September 29, 1965.

39. *Delo,* February 12, 1968.

40. *Borba,* February 3, 1968.

41. *Istoricheski pregled,* 21:5 (September–October 1965), pp. 110–115; 21:6 (November–December 1965), pp. 9–22; 22:2 (March–April 1966), pp. 123–125, 126–130; and 22:6 (November–December 1966), pp. 3–13.

42. *Rabotnichesko Delo,* November 5 and December 27, 1965; *Slaviyani* 22:7 (July 1966), pp. 2–11.

43. *Borba,* January 28, 1966; see also *Vjesnik,* September 14, 1961.

44. *Politika,* January 29, 1967.

45. *Rabotnichesko Delo,* January 23, 1967; *Otechestven Front,* January 22, 1967; and *Trud,* January 22, 1967.

46. *Nova Makedonija,* February 6, 1967; *Borba,* February 9, 1967.

47. *Rabotnichesko Delo,* December 1, 1967.

48. Zhivkov speech to the ninth party congress, *ibid.,* November 15, 1966.

49. *Ibid.,* December 21, 1967.

50. *Politika,* January 14, 1968. The article apparently refers to a series by Yono Mitev, in *Narodna Armiya,* January 12, 13, and 14, 1968 (the Yugoslavs would have seen at least the first two of these articles) and to an article by Professor Hadzhinikolov, in *Rabotnichesko Delo,* January 12, 1968.

51. *Rabotnichesko Delo,* January 14, 1968.

52. *Borba,* January 25, 1968.

53. See, for example, *Delo,* February 12, 1968; *Vjesnik,* February 11, 1968; *Borba,* January 31, February 3 and 4, 1968; *Politika,* January 31 and February 7, 1968; *Economska Politika,* January 29 and February 4, 1968; *NIN,* February 3, 1968; *Rad,* February 9, 1968. Even the newspaper of the Bulgarian minority in Yugoslavia (*Bratstvo,* January 31, 1968) denounced Bulgaria's San Stefano aspirations.

54. The text of the Yugoslav note was released by Tanjug, October 5, 1968.

55. *Delo,* February 12, 1968.

56. *Otechestven Front,* February 17, 1968.

57. *Rabotnichesko Delo,* March 3, 1968.

58. *Nova Makedonija,* March 4, 1968.

59. *Trud,* May 4, 1968; other articles appeared at the same time in *Narodna Armiya, Kooperativno Selo,* and *Narodna Mladezh.*

60. *Komunist,* May 30, 1968.

61. Khristo Khristov in *Istoricheski pregled,* 24:2 (March–April 1968), pp. 12–13. The journal is a bimonthly, and this issue should have appeared in March or April. It apparently came out late, however, since the first Yugoslav commentary was not broadcast over Radio Belgrade until June 11. This issue of the journal reflected the interest of the Institute of History in Macedonia. Other articles were on the diplomatic background to the Congress of Berlin (1878) and Vasil Glavinor, "a pioneer of the socialist movement in Macedonia and Adrianople."

62. Tanjug, June 13, 1968.

63. *Pogled,* July 1, 1968.

64. *Borba,* July 5, 1968.

65. *Rabotnichesko Delo,* August 1, 1968.

66. *Trud,* August 6, 1968; *Narodna Mladezh,* August 6, 1968; *Kooperativno Selo,* August 9, 1968; *Otechestven Front,* August 10, 1968; *Zmedelsko Zname,* August 10, 1968.

67. *Otechestven Front,* August 17, 1968.

68. *Rabotnichesko Delo,* August 21, 1968. The same article also appeared in *Otechestven Front,* August 21, 1968.

69. *Vjesnik,* August 26, 1968.

70. *Nova Makedonija,* August 28, 1968. This article was also printed in *Politika,* August 28, 1968, and broadcast by Radio Belgrade in Bulgarian, August 28, 1968.

71. See, for example, the exchange in *Vjesnik,* September 10, 1968; *Zemedelsko Znam,* September 24, 1968; and *Vjesnik,* September 27, 1968.

72. *New York Times,* September 23, 1968.

73. Bulgarska Telegrafna Agentsia (BTA), September 28, 1968.

74. *Nova Makedonija,* October 2, 1968.

75. *Tanjug,* October 5, 1968.

76. *Narodna Armiya,* October 1, 1968; *Borba,* October 2 and 21, 1968.

77. For the Yugoslav celebrations, see *Nova Makedonija,* October 11, 1968, and *Politika,* October 11, 1968. The Bulgarian celebrations were reviewed in *Pirinsko Delo,* October 5, 1968, and *Rabotnichesko Delo,* October 7, 1968.

78. *Rabotnichesko Delo,* November 3, 1968.

79. *Makedonskiat vpros: istoriko-politicheska spravka.* The pamphlet was the basis of a 12-program series broadcast over Radio Sofia during January 1969, and the full text was published in *Pirinsko Delo,* February 4, 1969.

80. *Politika,* January 18, 1969; *Borba,* January 25, 1969.

81. Note from Bulgaria to Yugoslavia of March 4, 1969; note from Yugoslavia to Bulgaria of April 23, 1969; and note from Bulgaria to Yugoslavia of May 27, 1969. The contents of these notes were not made public.

82. *Narodna Armiya,* August 2, 1969; *Trud,* August 2, 1969; *Borba,* August 4, 1969.

83. *Borba,* November 1, 1969; *Oslobodjenje,* November 1, 1969; *Nova Makedonija,* November 14, 1969; *Politika,* November 12, 1969.

84. Institut za Nacionalna istorija-Skopje, *Istoria na Makedonskiot Narod,* 3 vols. (Skopje: Nova Makedonija, 1969).

85. See, for example, *NIN,* November 22, 1970; *Borba,* November 23, 24, 25, and 27, 1970, and January 24, 1971; *Politika,* November 27, 1970; *Vjesnik,* November 28, 29, and 30, 1970; *Nova Makedonija,* December 5, 1970.

86. See, for example, *Borba,* June 16, 1971; *Nova Makedonija,* August 22 and September 14, 1971; *Pirinsko Delo,* August 12 and 14, 1971.

87. *Literaturen Front,* No. 40 (September 30, 1971); *Anteni,* October 15, 1971; *Nova Makedonija,* October 2, 8, and 9, 1971; *Borba,* October 2, 1971; *Vjesnik,* October 7, 1971.

88. *Delo,* September 29, 1971; *Nova Makedonija,* October 1 and 31, 1971; *Vecernje Novosti,* October 11, 1971.

Chapter 11

1. For a discussion of the disposition of these two territories, see Chapter 2.

2. For the view that the Rumanian leaders did seriously entertain thoughts of regaining Bessarabia, see Stephen Fischer-Galati, *The New Rumania* (Cambridge, Mass.: MIT Press, 1967), pp. 101, 107–110, 114–115.

3. A more complete and detailed analysis of Rumania's independent policy can be found in Fischer-Galati, *The New Rumania,* and his *The Socialist Republic of Rumania* (Baltimore: Johns Hopkins Press, 1969), and in John Michael Montias, *Economic Development in Communist Rumania* (Cambridge, Mass.: MIT Press, 1969).

4. V. Liveanu, *1918: din istoria luptelor revoluționare din Romînia* (Bucharest: Editura Politica, 1960).

5. Michael J. Rura, *Reinterpretation of History as a Method of Furthering Communism in Rumania* (Washington, D.C.: Georgetown University Press, 1961), pp. 55–56.

6. Mihail Roller, ed., *Istoria R.P.R.* (Bucharest: Editura de stat Didactică și Pedagogică, 1956), p. 311.

7. *Ibid.,* p. 545–547.

8. *Ibid.,* p. 673.

9. *Istoria Romîniei* (Bucharest: Editura Academiei Republicii Populare Romîne, 1964), III, 611.

10. *Presa muncitorească și socialistă din România, Vol. I (1865–1900), Part 1 (1865–1889)* (Bucharest: Editura Politică, 1964), p. 188.

11. Elias Regnault, *Histoire politique et sociale des Principautés Danubiennes* (Paris: Paulin et le Chevalier, 1855).

12. A. Oṭetea and S. Schwann, eds., *K. Marx—Însemnări despre Români* (*Manuscrise Inedite*) (Bucharest: Editura Academiei Republicii Populare Române, 1964), p. 106; cf. p. 30. Emphasis in original.

13. *Ibid.*, pp. 167, 170, 174; cf. pp. 89, 92.

14. For example, *Tribuna*, February 18, 1965.

15. See the article implying that northern Bukovina is part of "our country" because it was part of ancient Roman Dacia, in *Gazeta literară*, 12:30 (July 22, 1965).

16. Nicolae Ceauşescu, *România pe drumul desăvîrşirii construcţiei socialiste* (Bucharest: Editura Politică, 1968), I, 68.

17. *Pravda* (Moscow), September 2, 1964. The version published in Moscow does not vary from the original version that was published in *Sekai Shoho* (Tokyo), August 11, 1964. See Dennis J. Doolin, *Territorial Claims in the Sino-Soviet Conflict* (Stanford, Calif.: The Hoover Institution, 1965), pp. 42–44.

18. Abdurakhman Avtorkhanov, *The Communist Party Apparatus* (Cleveland and New York: World Publishing Company, 1968), pp. 170-175.

19. *Istoria Moldavskoi S.S.R.* (Kishinev: Izdatelstvo "Kartya Moldovenyaske," 1965), I, 352. The first volume was published in Russian. A "Moldavian"-language version of this volume, which parallels the Russian edition, came out in 1967. The editorial collegium for both the "Moldavian" and the Russian versions is identical; and it is significant that of the eight editors, seven have Slavic names—only one has a Moldavian name. The chief editor is a Slavic professor of Russian history at Moscow University. Volume II, in Russian, appeared in 1968.

20. For an analysis of Soviet historians' treatment of the history of the non-Russian nationalities, see Lowell Tillett, *The Great Friendship: Soviet Historians on the Non-Russian Nationalities* (Chapel Hill: University of North Carolina Press, 1969).

21. *Slavnii yubilei sovetsloi Moldavii* (Kishinev: Izdatelstvo "Kartya Moldovenyaske," 1966), p. 38.

22. *Kommunist Moldavii*, No. 4 (April 1965), p. 77.

23. *Ibid.*, No. 6 (June 1965), pp. 33–39.

24. *Istoria MSSR*, I, 346.

25. *Ibid.*, p. 353.

26. *Pravda* (Moscow), September 12, 1965.

27. *Sovetskaya Moldaviya*, March 5, 1966.

28. *Ibid.*, March 2, 1966.

29. Ceauşescu, *România pe drumul* . . . , I, 360.

30. *Documente din Istoria Partidului Comunist din România, 1923–1928* (Bucharest: Editura pentru literatură politica, 1953), II, 257.

31. *Ibid.*, pp. 593–594.

32. Ceauşescu, *România pe drumul* . . . , I, 361.

33. See the account of one such appeal to Moscow by factions of the

Rumanian party given by Sandor Korsi-Krizsan (a former Rumanian party member of Hungarian origin), "Rumania and the Comintern," *East Europe*, 15:12 (December 1966), pp. 13–15.

34. *International Press Correspondence*, 4:27 (May 1, 1924), p. 262.

35. *Ibid.*, 4:64 (September 4, 1924), p. 684.

36. *Ibid.*, 9:22 (May 10, 1929), pp. 492–493.

37. *Pravda* (Moscow), May 14, 1966.

38. *Ibid.*, May 8 and 11, 1966.

39. *Kommunist*, 43:7 (May, 1966), p. 75.

40. *Pravda* (Moscow), June 29, 1966, mentioned the anniversary in a short notice on page 6.

41. *Sovetskaya Moldaviya*, June 22, 1966; *Kommunist Moldavii*, No. 6 (June, 1966); *Moldova Socialista*, June 14, 1966.

42. *Kommunist Moldavii*, No. 6 (June 1966), pp. 19–24. Emphasizing past Rumanian party statements on Bessarabia is a continuing feature of Soviet commentary on the question. See *Sovetskaya Moldaviya*, February 6 and May 23, 1971; *Kommunist Moldavii* No. 5 (May 1971), pp. 66–74.

43. I. Bobeiko and Ya. Kopanskii, *Dvadtsat dva goda geroicheskoi borbi* (Kishinev: Partiinoe izdatelstvo Ts. K.K.P. Moldavii, 1966). The manuscript was sent to the typesetter on May 23, 1966, and it was approved for printing on June 8.

44. *Meeting of the Political Consultative Committee of Warsaw Treaty Member States, Bucharest, July 4–6, 1966* (Bucharest: Agerpres, 1966), p. 7.

45. Two of the major speeches delivered to this conference are printed in *Kommunist Moldavii*, No. 1 (January 1967), pp. 48–58.

46. *Sovetskaya Moldaviya*, February 16, 1967.

47. *Ibid.*, February 25, 1967.

48. See, for example, *Kommunist Moldavii*, No. 6 (June 1967), pp. 28–33. This has continued to be a recurring theme of the polemic. See *Sovetskaya Moldaviya*, April 15, 1971.

49. Radio Moscow, July 28, 1967. Emphasis supplied.

50. *Sovetskaya Moldaviya*, October 9, 1966.

51. *Ibid.*, January 16, 1968.

52. One of the better examples of this is the collection of documents on the period immediately before and after the Rumanian annexation, *Borba trudyashchiikhsya moldavii protiv interventov i unutrennei konterrevolyutsii v 1917–1920 g.g.: Sbornik dokumentov i materialov* (Kishinev: Izdatelstvo "Kartya Moldovenyaske," 1967).

53. S. K. Brysyakin and M. K. Sytnik, *Torzhestvo istoricheskoi spravedlivosti: 1918 i 1940 gody v sudbakh moldavskogo naroda* (Kishinev: Izdatelstvo "Kartya Moldovenyaske," 1969), pp. 7–12, 130–131, 145–150, 222.

54. *Kommunist Moldavii*, No. 5 (May 1970), p. 75; and *Sovetskaya Moldaviya*, December 18, 1970.

55. *Sovetskaya Moldaviya*, January 14, 1971.

56. See *Kommunist Moldavii,* No. 9 (September 1970), pp. 38–45.
57. *Sovetskaya Moldaviya,* January 13, 1970; *Kommunist Moldavii,* No. 7 (July 1970), p. 30.
58. *Sovetskaya Moldaviya,* February 26, 1971.
59. *Pravda* (Moscow), April 4, 1971.
60. The text of Ceauşescu's speech is in *Scînteia,* May 8, 1971. During an interview with Austrian newsmen prior to a state visit to Austria, Ceauşescu refused to answer a question about Bessarabia. See *Volksstimme* (Vienna), September 11, 1970.

Chapter 12

1. Josif Vissarionovich Stalin, *Works,* Vol. II (Moscow: Foreign Languages Publishing House, 1953), p. 307.
2. V. I. Lenin, "Critical Remarks on the National Question," in *Questions of National Policy and Proletarian Internationalism* (Moscow: Progress Publishers, n.d.), pp. 30, 32.
3. *Filosofskie nauk,* No. 5 (1964), p. 28.
4. *Voprosy istorii KPSS,* No. 2 (February 1971), pp. 100–101. For Western analyses of the Soviet discussion, see Grey Hodnett, "What's in a Nation?" *Problems of Communism,* 16:5 (September–October, 1967), pp. 2–15; Erwin Oberländer, "Der sowjetische Nationsbegriff heute," *Osteuropa,* 21:4 (April 1971), pp. 273–279. A recent review of the debate by a Soviet historian, with extensive footnote references to previous Soviet contributions, is to be found in M. P. Chernov, "O nekotorikh aspektakh marksistsko-leninskoi teorii natsionalnogo voprosa v sovetskoi literature," *Voprosy istorii KPSS,* No. 2 (February 1971), pp. 98–108.
5. *Pravda* (Moscow), June 20, 1950.
6. See, for example, *Bolshevik,* No. 6 (June 1951), pp. 57–62.
7. "The 1961 Party Program," in *Soviet Communism: Programs and Rules,* ed. by Jan Triska (San Francisco: Chandler, 1961), p. 107.
8. See, for example, *Elet es Irodalom,* August 26 and September 2, 1967.
9. Edward Kardelj, *Razvoj slovenačkog nacionalnog pitanja* (Belgrade: Kultura, 1958).
10. For a consideration of some of the aspects of Kardelj's views, see Paul Shoup, *Communism and the Yugoslav National Question* (New York: Columbia University Press, 1968), pp. 201–207.
11. Dobrica Cosić, *Delo,* No. 2 (February 1962).
12. Dušan Pirjević in *Borba,* December 4, 1961.
13. *Osmi kongres SKJ* (Belgrade: Kultura, 1964), p. 32.
14. *Borba,* July 24, 1966.
15. Lazar Koliševski, speech to the third congress of the League of Communists of Macedonia, in *Aspekti na makedonskoto prašanje* (Skopje: Kultura, 1962), pp. 406–407.

16. *Socijalizam,* No. 3 (March 1971), pp. 295–306.

17. Interview given by Tito to the Hungarian-language newspaper *Magyar Szó,* also published in *Borba,* May 23, 1971.

18. For an account of these recent debates in Yugoslavia, see Slobodan Stankovic, "Jugoslawiens Nationalitätenkonflikt," *Osteuropäische Rundschau,* No. 5: 1 and 2 (January and February 1972), pp. 16–21, 6–10.

19. Nicolae Ceauşescu, *România pe drumul desăvîrsirii construcţiei socialiste* (Bucharest: Editura Politică, 1968), I, 58–63.

20. *Ibid.,* pp. 395–398.

21. Constantin Vlad in *Contemporanul,* No. 31 (August 5, 1966).

22. *Ibid.*

23. Petre Constantin, in *Lupta de clasă,* No. 11 (November 1967), pp. 57–60. For other Rumanian commentary on the nation, see *ibid.,* pp. 51–62.

24. *Népszabadság,* March 24, 1966.

25. *Ibid.,* July 2, 1966.

26. *Magyar Nemzet,* February 25, 1966.

27. *Kortárs,* February 1967, p. 289.

28. *Népszabadság,* March 12, 1967.

29. For a consideration of some aspects of the Hungarian debate over nationalism and a comparison with the Rumanian debate, see William F. Robinson, *Nationalism: Hungarian Problem Child* (Munich: Radio Free Europe Research, July 5, 1967). Other articles appeared in *Vilagossag,* July–August 1967; *Látóhatár,* July–August 1967; *Új Irás,* September 1967; and *Kortárs,* December 1967.

Bibliography

I. Documents, Statistics, and Speeches

Bass, Robert, and Elizabeth Marbury, eds. *The Soviet-Yugoslav Controversy, 1948–1958: A Documentary Record.* New York: Prospect Books, 1959.

Beneš, Edvard. *Czechoslovak Policy for Victory and Peace: The Fourth Message of the President of the Republic to the State Council on February 3, 1944.* London: Czechoslovak Ministry of Foreign Affairs Information Service, 1944.

——— *Demokratie Heute und Morgen.* Zürich: Europa Verlag, 1944.

——— *Memoirs of Dr. Edvard Beneš: From Munich to New War and New Victory.* Translated by Godfrey Lias. London: Allen and Unwin, 1954.

——— "Postwar Czechoslovakia," *Foreign Affairs,* 24:3 (April 1946), pp. 397–410.

Benes, Vaclav L., and others, eds. *The Second Soviet-Yugoslav Dispute: Full Text of Main Documents.* Slavic and East European Series, Vol. 14. Bloomington: Indiana University Publications, 1959.

Borba trudyashchikhsia moldavii protiv interventov i vnutrennei konterrevoliutsii v 1917–1920 g.g.: Sbornik dokumentov i materialov. Kishinev: Izdatelstvo "Kartya Moldovenyaske," 1967.

Bulgaria. Tsentralno statistichesko upravlenie pri ministerskiya svet. *Prebroiavane na naselenieto b Narodna Republika Blgariya na 1.XII. 1956 godina,* 2 vols. Sofia, 1959–1960.

Bibliography

———— *Rezultati ot prebroiavane na naselenieto na 1. XII.1965 g.*, 31 vols. Sofia, 1967–1968.

———— *Statisticheski godishnik na Narodna Republika Blgariya.* Sofia, various years.

Ceauşescu, Nicolae. *România pe drumul desăvîrsirii constructiei socialiste: Rapoarte, cuvîntări, articole,* 4 vols. Bucharest: Politică, 1968–1970.

Conze, Werner, and others, eds. *Dokumentation der Vertreibung der Deutschen aus Ost-Mitteleuropa,* 5 vols. Berlin: Bundesministerium für Vertreibene Flüchtlinge und Kriegsgeschädigte, 1957–1961.

Czechoslovakia. Ústřední komise lidové kontroly a statistiky. *Sčítání lidu, domů a Bytů v Československé Socialistické Republice k 1 Březnu 1961,* 3 vols. Prague, 1965.

———— *Statistická Ročenka ČSSR.* Prague, various years.

Dimitrov, Georgi. *Political Report: V Congress of the Bulgarian Communist Party.* Sofia: Press Department of the Ministry of Foreign Affairs, 1949.

Djilas, Milovan. *Članci, 1941–1946.* [Belgrade]: Kultura, 1947.

———— *Conversations with Stalin.* New York: Harcourt, Brace and World, 1962.

Ello, Paul, ed. *Czechoslovakia's Blueprint for "Freedom": Statements—the Original and Official Documents Leading to the Conflict of August, 1968.* Washington, D.C.: Acropolis Books, 1968.

Engels, Friedrich. *The German Revolutions: Germany—Revolution and Counter Revolution and the Peasant War in Germany.* Edited by Leonard Krieger. Chicago: University of Chicago Press, 1967.

Fundamentals of Marxism-Leninism: Manual, 2nd Revised Edition. Moscow: Foreign Languages Publishing House, 1963.

Gheorghiu-Dej, Gheorghe. Artikel und Reden, Dezember 1955–Juli 1959. Bucharest: Politischer Verlag, 1959.

Hungary. Központi Statisztikai Hivatal. *Statisztikai Évkönyv.* Budapest, various years.

———— Külügyminisztérium [Ministry for Foreign Affairs]. *Hungary and the Conference of Paris,* Vols. I, II, and IV. Budapest, 1947.

Institutul de Istorie a Partidului de pa Lăngă C.C. al P.M.R. *Documente din Istoria Partidului Comunist din România, 1923–1928,* 2 vols. [Bucharest]: Editura pentru literatură politică, 1953.

Istorijsko odeljenje Centralnog komiteta K.P.J. *Istorijski archiv Komunističke partije Jugoslavije.* Vol. VII, *Makedonija u narodnooslobodilačkom ratu i narodnoj revoluciji, 1941–1944.* Belgrade: Kultura, 1951.

Kardelj, Edvard. *Razvoj slovenačkog nacionalnog pitanja,* 2nd Edition. Belgrade: Kultura, 1958.

Lenin, V. I. *Questions of National Policy and Proletarian Internationalism.* Moscow: Progress Publishers, n.d.

Marx, Karl, and Friedrich Engels. *Manifesto of the Communist Party.* Authorized English Translation, edited and annotated by Friedrich Engels. New York: International Publishers, 1932.

—— *Sochineniia,* 30 vols. Moscow: Gosudarstvennoe izdatelstvo politicheskoi literaturi, 1957.

—— *Karl Marx-Friedrick Engels: Werke,* 30 vols. Berlin: Dietz Verlag, 1959.

Meissner, Boris, ed. *Das Ostpakt System: Dokumentenzusammenstellung.* Hamburg: Forschungsstelle für Völkerrecht und Ausländisches öffentliches Recht der Universität Hamburg, 1951.

Nazi-Soviet Relations, 1939–1941: Documents from the Archives of the German Foreign Office. Edited by Raymond J. Sontag and James S. Beddie. Washington, D.C.: Department of State, 1948.

Rumania. Directia Centrală de Statistica. *Anuarul Statistic al României.* Bucharest, various years.

—— *Recensămîntul Populatiei si Locuintelor din 15 Martie 1966,* Vol. I, *Rezultate General,* Part 1, *Populație.* Bucharest, 1969.

—— *Recensămîntul Populatiei din 21 Februarie 1956: Structura Demografică a Populatiei.* Bucharest, n.d.

Saveza komunista Jugoslavija. *Osmi kongres S.K.J.* Belgrade: Kultura, 1964.

Slavnii yubilei sovetskoi Moldavii. Kishinev: Izdatelstvo "Kartya Moldovenyaske," 1966.

Stalin, Iosif Vissarionovich. *Works,* 6 vols. Moscow: Foreign Languages Publishing House, 1953.

Statistique des Nationalités en Tchécoslovaquie. Prague: Politika, 1924.

Triska, Jan F., ed. *Constitutions of the Communist Party-States.* Stanford, Calif.: The Hoover Institution, 1968.

Union of Soviet Socialist Republics. Tsentralnoe statisticheskoe upravlenie pri Sovete Ministrov SSSR. *Itogi vsesoiuznoi perepisi naseleniia 1959 goda: Moldavskaya SSR.* Moscow: Gosstatizdat, 1962.

—— *Itogi vsesoiuznoi perepisi naseleniia 1959 goda: SSSR.* Moscow: Gosstatizdat, 1962.

—— *Itogi vsesoiuznoi perepisi naseleniia 1959 goda: Ukrainskaya SSR.* Moscow: Gosstatizdat, 1963.

United Nations. General Assembly. *Official Records. Eleventh Session.* Supplement, no. 18, "Report of the Special Committee on the Problem of Hungary." New York, 1957.

United States. Department of State. *Foreign Relations of the United States: The Conference of Berlin (The Potsdam Conference), 1945.* Washington, D.C., 1960.

—— *Paris Peace Conference, 1946: Selected Documents.* Washington, D.C., [1947].

Ustav Socijalističke Federativne Republike Jugoslavije sa Ustavima socijalističkih republika i statutima autonomnih pokrajina. Belgrade: Novinski ustanove službeni list SFRJ, 1963.

Winkler, Wilhelm. *Statistisches Handbuch der europäischen Nationalitäten.* Vienna and Leipzig: Wilhelm Braumüller, 1931.

Yugoslavia. Ministry of Foreign Affairs. *Memorandum of the Government of the Democratic Federative Yugoslavia concerning the Question of the Julian March and other Yugoslav Territories under Italy.* Belgrade, [1945?].

———— *Memorandum of the Government of the Federative People's Republic of Yugoslavia on Slovene Carinthia, the Slovene Frontier Areas of Styria and the Croats of Burgenland.* Belgrade, [1946].

———— *White Book on Aggressive Activities by the Governments of the USSR, Poland, Czechoslovakia, Hungary, Rumania, Bulgaria and Albania towards Yugoslavia.* Belgrade, 1951.

Yugoslavia. Savezni zavod za statistiku. *Jugoslavija, 1945–1964: Statistički pregled.* Belgrade, November 1965.

———— *Konačni rezultati popisa stanovništva od 15 marta 1948 godine,* 9 vols. Belgrade, 1954.

———— *Popis stanovništva 1953,* 12 vols. Belgrade, 1959.

———— *Popis stanovništva 1961,* 16 vols. Belgrade, 1967.

———— *Statistički godišnjak Jugoslavije.* Belgrade, various years.

Zinner, Paul, ed. *National Communism and Popular Revolt in Eastern Europe: A Selection of Documents on Events in Poland and Hungary, February–November, 1956.* New York: Columbia University Press, 1956.

II. East European Periodicals Cited

Bashkimi. Daily of the Central Democratic Front, Tirana.

Bolshevik. See *Kommunist.*

Borba. Daily of the Socialist Alliance of Working People of Yugoslavia, Belgrade.

Contemporanul. Social-cultural weekly, Bucharest.

Delo. Daily of the Socialist Alliance of Working People of Slovenia, Ljubljana.

Economska Politika. Economic and business weekly published by the Borba Publishing Institute, Belgrade.

Élet és Irodalom. Literary and political weekly, Budapest.

For a Lasting Peace, for a People's Democracy. Organ of the Cominform, discontinued after 1956. Originally published in Belgrade; after 1948 published in Bucharest.

Gazeta literară. Weekly of the Rumanian Writer's Union, Bucharest.

Hét. Weekly of the Association of Hungarian Working People in Czechoslovakia (Csemadok), Bratislava.

International Press Correspondence. Publication of the Communist International, Berlin, Vienna, and other cities.

Irodalmi Szemle. Literary review of the Union of Slovak Writers, published in Hungarian, Bratislava.

Istoricheski Pregled. Bimonthly of the Bulgarian Academy of Science, Institute of Bulgarian History, Sofia.

Izvestia. Daily of the Union of Workers' Deputies of the USSR published by the Presidium of the Supreme Soviet of the USSR, Moscow.

Izvestia na instituta po istoria na BKP. Publication of the Institute of History of the Bulgarian Communist Party, Sofia.

Kisalföld. Daily of the Gyor-Sopron county party committee and county council, Gyor.

Kommunist. Theoretical and political monthly of the Central Committee of the Communist Party of the Soviet Union, previously published under the title *Bolshevik,* Moscow.

Kommunist Moldavii. Theoretical monthly of the Central Committee of the Communist Party of Moldavia, Kishinev.

Komunist. Weekly of the Central Committee of the League of Communists of Yugoslavia, Belgrade.

Kooperativno Selo. Daily of the Ministry of Agriculture and of the Central Committee of the Academy of Rural Sciences, Sofia.

Kortárs. Monthly literary and critical review of the Hungarian Writer's Union, Budapest.

Kulturný Život. Weekly of the Slovak Writer's Union, Bratislava.

Literaturen Front. Weekly of the Bulgarian Writer's Union, Sofia.

Literaturnaya gazeta. Weekly of the Board of the Soviet Writer's Union, Moscow.

Lud. Daily of the Slovak Revival Party, Bratislava.

Lupta de clasă. Theoretical monthly of the Central Committee of the Rumanian Communist Party, Bucharest.

Magyar Hirek. Biweekly of the World Association of Hungarains, Budapest.

Magyar Hirlap. Political daily, Budapest.

Magyar Nemzet. Daily of the Patriotic People's Front, Budapest.

Magyar Szó. Daily of the Hungarian minority in Yugoslavia, Novi Sad.

Moldova Sochialista. Organ of the Central Committee of the Communist Party of Moldavia and of the Supreme Soviet of the Moldavian SSR, published in the Moldavian language, Kishinev.

Narodna Armiya. Daily of the Ministry of National Defense, Sofia.

Narodna Mladezh. Daily of the Central Committee of the Dimitrov Communist Youth League, Sofia.

NIN (Nedeljne Informativne Novine). Weekly published by the Politika Publishing House, Belgrade.

Népszabadság. Daily of the Hungarian Socialist Workers' Party, replaced *Szabad Nép,* Budapest.

Neuer Weg. German language daily published in Rumania, Bucharest.

New Times. Weekly published by the newspaper *Trud,* Moscow.

Nova Makedonija. Daily of the Socialist Alliance of Working People of Macedonia, Skopje.

Novo Vreme. Theoretical monthly of the Bulgarian Communist Party, Sofia.

Oslobojdenje. Daily of the Socialist Alliance of the Working People of Bosnia-Hercegovina, Sarajevo.

Otechestven Front. Daily of the presidium of the National Assembly and of the National Council of the Fatherland Front, Sofia.

Perparimi. Monthly published in the autonomous region of Kosovo, Priština.

Bibliography

Pirinsko Delo. Daily of the district committee of the Bulgarian Communist Party, of the district People's Council, and of the district committee of the Fatherland Front, Blagoevgrad.

Pogled. Weekly of the Bulgarian Journalists' Union, Sofia.

Politika. Daily published by the Politika Publishing Enterprise, Belgrade.

Práca. Publication of the Slovak Council of Trade Unions, Bratislava.

Pravda. Daily of the Communist Party of Slovakia, Bratislava.

Pravda. Daily of the Central Committee of the Communist Party of the Soviet Union, Moscow.

Predvoj. Political, cultural, and economic weekly of the Central Committee of the Communist Party of Slovakia, Bratislava.

Rabotnichesko Delo. Daily of the Central Committee of the Communist Party of Bulgaria, Sofia.

Rilindja. Daily of the Socialist Alliance of the Working People of Kosovo, published in Albanian, Priština.

Rolnické Noviny. Daily of the Slovak National Council on Agriculture, Bratislava.

Rudé Právo. Daily of the Central Committee of the Communist Party of Czechoslovakia, Prague.

Rumanian Review. Literary review, also published in German, French, and Russian editions, Bucharest.

Scînteia. Daily of the Central Committee of the Communist Party of Rumania, Bucharest.

Slaviyani. Monthly of the Bulgarian Slavic Committee, Sofia.

Slovenská Literatura. Literary quarterly of the Slovak Academy of Sciences, Bratislava.

Službeni list. Official gazette of the Socialist Federal Republic of Yugoslavia, Belgrade.

Smena. Organ of the Slovak Central Committee of the Czechoslovak Youth League, Bratislava.

Socijalizam. Theoretical monthly of the League of Communists of Yugoslavia, Belgrade.

Sovetskaya Moldaviya. Daily of the Central Committee of the Communist Party of Moldavia and of the Supreme Soviet of the Moldavian SSR, Kishinev.

Sovetskaya Rossia. Daily of the Central Committee of the Communist Party of the Soviet Union, Moscow.

Studii revistă de istorie. Publication of the Institute of History of the Academy of the Socialist Republic of Rumania, Bucharest.

Szolok Megyei Néplap. Daily of the Szolnok county committee of the Hungarian Socialist Workers' Party and of the county council, Szolnok.

Tribuna. Political, social, and cultural weekly, Cluj.

Trud. Daily of the Central Council of Trade Unions, Sofia.

Új Irás. Literary monthly, Budapest.

Új Szó. Hungarian-language daily published by the Central Committee of the Communist Party of Slovakia, Bratislava.

Valóság. Sociological monthly of the Society for the Dissemination of Knowledge, Budapest.

Večernje novosti. Daily published by the Borba Publishing Enterprise, Belgrade.

Világosság. Ideological monthly of the Society for Scientific Education, Budapest.

Vjesnik. Daily of the Socialist Alliance of the Working People of Croatia, Zagreb.

Voprosi istorii. Monthly of the Historical Institute of the USSR Academy of Sciences, Moscow.

Zemedelsko Zname. Organ of the Bulgarian National Agricultural Union, Sofia.

Zëri i Popullit. Daily of the Central Committee of the Albanian Workers' Party, Tirana.

III. Books and Articles

Akademiia Nauk Soyuza SSR: Institut Geografii akademii nauk SSSR i Moldavskii nauchno-issedoratelskii institut. *Moldavskaya SSR*. Moscow and Leningrad: Izdatelstvo akademii nauk SSSR, 1947.

Anastassoff, Christ. *The Tragic Peninsula: A History of the Macedonian Movement for Independence since 1878*. St. Louis, Mo.: Blackwell Wielandy, 1938.

Andras, Charles. *Neighbors on the Danube: New Variations on the Old Theme of Regional Cooperation*. Munich: Radio Free Europe Research, December 1967.

Angell, Norman. *The Unseen Assassins*. New York: Harper, 1932.

Armstrong, John A. *Ukrainian Nationalism*, 2nd Edition. New York: Columbia University Press, 1963.

Autonomne Pokrajine u Jugoslaviji: Društveno-politički i pravni aspekti: Referati i diskusija sa simpozijuma održanog u Novom Sadu 8, 9, i 10 juna 1967. Belgrade: Institut za uporedno pravo, 1967.

Avtorkhanov, Abdurakhman. *The Communist Party Apparatus*. New York and Cleveland: World Publishing Company, 1968.

Bailey, George. "Trouble over Transylvania," *The Reporter*, 31:9 (November 19, 1964), pp. 25–30.

Barclay, Glen St. J. *20th Century Nationalism*. London: Weidenfeld and Nicolson, 1971.

Barghoorn, Frederick C. *Soviet Russian Nationalism*. New York: Oxford University Press, 1956.

Barker, Elizabeth. *Macedonia: Its Place in Balkan Power Politics*. London: Royal Institute of International Affairs, 1950.

Bauer, Otto. *Die Nationalitätenfrage und die Sozialdemokratie*. Vienna: Wiener Volksbuchhandlung Ignaz Brand, 1907.

Beloff, Max. *The Foreign Policy of Soviet Russia*, 2 vols. London: Oxford University Press, 1949.

Bibliography

Berezhan, C., and others, eds. *Kurs de gramatike istorike a limbii Moldo-venesht.* Kishinev: Kartya Moldovenyaske, 1964.

Berki, R. N. "On Marxian Thought and the Problem of International Relations," *World Politics,* 24:1 (October 1971), pp. 80–105.

Betts, R. R., ed. *Central and Southeast Europe, 1945–1948.* London and New York: Royal Institute of International Affairs, 1950.

Bilinsky, Yaroslav. *The Second Soviet Republic: The Ukraine after World War II.* New Brunswick, N.J.: Rutgers University Press, 1964.

Bloom, Solomon F. *The World of Nations: A Study of the National Implications in the Work of Karl Marx.* New York: Columbia University Press, 1941.

Bobeiko, I., and Ya. Kopanskii. *Dvadtsat dva goda geroicheskoi borbi.* Kishinev: Partinoe izdatelstvo Ts.K.K.P. Moldavii, 1966.

Bolsheviki moldavii i Ruminskogo fronta v borbe za vlast Sovetov. Kishinev: Kartya Moldovenyaske, 1967.

Borkenau, Franz. *Socialism: National or International?* London: George Rutledge and Sons, 1942.

Brailsford, H. N. *Macedonia: Its Races and Their Future.* London: Methuen, 1906.

Braun, Robert. *The Dismemberment of Hungary and the Nationalities.* Budapest: Victor Hornyanszky, [1919].

deBray, R. G. A. *Guide to the Slavonic Languages.* London: J. M. Dent and Sons, 1951.

Brown, James F. "The Age-Old Question of Transylvania," *World Today,* 19 (November 1963), pp. 498–506.

——— *Bulgaria Under Communist Rule.* New York: Praeger, 1970.

——— *The New Eastern Europe: The Khrushchev Era and After.* New York: Praeger, 1966.

Brügel, J. W. "Der Fall Karpathorussland," *Europa Archiv,* 8:20 (October 20, 1953), pp. 6021–6028.

Brysyakin, S. K., and M. K. Sytnik. *Torzhestvo istoricheskoi spravedlivosti: 1918 i 1940 gody v sudbakh moldavskogo naroda.* Kishinev: Kartya Moldovenyaske, 1969.

Brzezinski, Zbegniew K. *The Soviet Bloc: Unity and Conflict,* Revised Edition. Cambridge, Mass.: Harvard University Press, 1967.

Burks, R. V. *The Dynamics of Communism in Eastern Europe.* Princeton, N.J.: Princeton University Press, 1961.

Cabot, John Moors. *The Racial Conflict in Transylvania.* Boston: Beacon Press, 1926.

Carr, E. H. *Nationalism and After.* London: Macmillan, 1945.

Cherepnin, L.V., and others, eds. *Istoriia Moldavskoi SSR,* 2 vols. Kishinev: Izdatelstvo "Kartya Moldovenyaske," 1965–1968.

——— *Istoriia RSS Moldovenesht.* Kishinev: Editura "Kartya Moldoven-yaske," 1967.

Christowe, Stoyan. *Heroes and Assassins.* New York: Robert M. McBride, 1935.

Claude, Inis L. *National Minorities: An International Problem*. Cambridge, Mass.: Harvard University Press, 1955.

Connor, Walker F. "Minorities in Marxist Theory and Practice," paper prepared for delivery at the 65th Annual Meeting of the American Political Science Association, New York, September 2–6, 1969.

Conquest, Robert. *The Nation Killers: The Soviet Deportation of Nationalities*. London: Macmillan, 1971.

——— *Power and Policy in the USSR: The Struggle for Stalin's Succession, 1945–1960*. New York: Harper Torchbooks, 1961.

——— *Soviet Nationalities Policy in Practice*. New York: Praeger, 1967.

Constantinescu-iaşi, P., and others, eds. *Istoria Romîniei*, 4 vols. Bucharest: Editura Academiei Republicii populare Romîne, 1964.

Crane, John O. *The Little Entente*. New York: Macmillan, 1931.

Cretzianu, Alexandre. *The Lost Opportunity*. London: Jonathan Cape, 1957.

——— "The Soviet Ultimatum to Rumania (26 June 1940)," *Journal of Central European Affairs*, 9:4 (January 1953), pp. 396–403.

Daicoviciu, C., and M. Constantinescu, eds. *Destrămarea Monarhiei Austro-Ungare, 1900–1918; Comunicări prezentate la Conferenta istoricilor din 4–9 mai 1964 de la Budapesta*. Bucharest: Editura Academiei Republic populare Romîne, 1964.

Dakin, Douglas. *The Greek Struggle in Macedonia, 1897–1913*. Thessaloniki: Institute for Balkan Studies, 1966.

Dallin, Alexander. *Odessa, 1941–1944: A Case Study of Soviet Territory under Foreign Control*. Santa Monica, Calif.: Rand Corporation, 1957.

Danilenko, R. B. *Razvitie Kulturnogo sotrudnichestva narodov SSSR (1959–1967 g.g.)*. Kishinev: Akademii nauk Moldavskoi SSR, 1968.

Davis, Horace B. *Nationalism and Socialism: Marxist and Labor Theories of Nationalism to 1917*. New York: Monthly Review Press, 1967.

Dedijer, Vladimir. *Tito*. New York: Simon and Schuster, 1953.

Deutsch, Karl W. *Nationalism and Its Alternatives*. New York: Knopf, 1969.

——— *Nationalism and Social Communication*. 2nd Edition. Cambridge, Mass.: MIT Press, 1966.

——— and Richard L. Merritt. *Nationalism: An Interdisciplinary Bibliography, 1935–1965*. Cambridge, Mass.: MIT Press, 1966.

Djordjević, Jovan. *Novi Ustavni Sistem*. Belgrade: "Savremena Administracija," 1964.

Doditse, G., and B. Marin. *Istoriia limbii shi a literaturii vek moldovenesht*. Kishinev: Editura "Lumina," 1966.

Dominian, Leon. *The Frontiers of Language and Nationality in Europe*. New York: American Geographical Society of New York, 1917.

Duchacek, Ivo. *The Strategy of Communist Infiltration: The Case of Czechoslovakia*. New Haven, Conn.: Institute of International Studies, 1949.

Durcansky, Ferdinand. "Czech-Slovak Relations—CSSR's Unsettled Issue," *Central European Journal*, 16 (March 1968), pp. 89–95.

Duroselle, Jean-Baptiste. *Le Conflit de Trieste, 1943–1954*. [Brussels]: Editions de l'Institut de Sociologie de l'Université Libre de Bruxelles, [1966].

Dzyuba, Ivan. *Internationalism or Russification?* London: Weidenfeld, 1968.

Emerson, Rupert. *From Empire to Nation.* Boston: Beacon Press, 1962.

d'Entreves, Alexander Passerin. *The Notion of the State.* Oxford, Eng.: Clarendon Press, 1967.

Erickson, John. "Recent Soviet and Maxist Writings: 1848 in Central and Eastern Europe," *Journal of Central European Affairs,* 17:2 (July 1957), pp. 119–126.

Fadner, Frank. *Seventy Years of Pan-Slavism in Russia.* Washington, D.C.: Georgetown University Press, 1962.

Fainsod, Merle. *International Socialism and the World War.* Cambridge, Mass.: Harvard University Press, 1935.

Fischer-Galati, Stephen. *The New Rumania.* Cambridge, Mass.: MIT Press, 1967.

———— *The Socialist Republic of Rumania.* Baltimore: Johns Hopkins Press, 1969.

Fisher, Jack C. *Yugoslavia—a Multi-national State: Regional Difference and Administrative Response.* San Francisco: Chandler, 1966.

Florescu, Radu R. "The Uniate Church: Catalyst of Rumanian National Consciousness," *Slavonic and East European Review,* 45:105 (July 1967), pp. 324–342.

Floyd, David. *Rumania: Russia's Dissident Ally.* New York: Praeger, 1965.

Frankel, J. "Communism and the National Question in Yugoslavia," *Journal of Central European Affairs,* 15:1 (April 1955), pp. 49–65.

George, Alexander L. *Propaganda Analysis: A Study of Inferences Made from Nazi Propaganda in World War II.* Evanston, Ill.: Row, Peterson and Company, 1959.

Goldhagen, Erich, ed. *Ethnic Minorities in the Soviet Union.* New York: Praeger, 1968.

Gomułka, Władysław. "Lenin's Approach to National Question," *World Marxist Review,* April 1970, pp. 77–85.

Grayson, Cary Travers, Jr. *Austria's International Position, 1938–1953: The Re-establishment of an Independent Austria.* Geneva: Librairie E. Droz, 1953.

Griffith, William E. *Albania in the Sino-Soviet Rift.* Cambridge, Mass.: MIT Press, 1963.

———— *Communist Esoteric Communications: Explication de Texte.* Cambridge, Mass.: MIT Center for International Studies, 1967.

———— *Sino-Soviet Relations, 1964–1965.* Cambridge, Mass.: MIT Press, 1967.

———— *The Sino-Soviet Rift.* Cambridge, Mass.: MIT Press, 1964.

————, ed. *Communism in Europe: Continuity, Change and the Sino-Soviet Dispute,* 2 vols. Cambridge, Mass.: MIT Press, 1964–1965.

Groshev, I. *A Fraternal Family of Nations.* Moscow: Progress Publishers, 1967.

Grosul, Vladislav Yakimovich. *Reformi v Dunaiskikh Khiazhestvakh i Rossiia (20–30 godi xix veka)*. Moscow: Izdatelstvo "Nauka," 1966.

Gyorgy, Andrew. "Ideological Diversity and Political Nationalism in Eastern Europe," paper prepared for delivery at the 65th Annual Meeting of the American Political Science Association, New York, September 2–6, 1969.

Hammond, Thomas T. "Nationalism and National Minorities in Eastern Europe," *Journal of International Affairs*, 20:1 (1966), pp. 9–31.

Haustein, Ulrich. *Sozialismus und nationale Frage in Polen: Die Entwicklung der sozialistischen Bewegung in Kongresspolen von 1875 bis 1900 unter besonderer Berücksichtigung der Polnischen Sozialistischen (PPS)*. Cologne: Böhlau Verlag, 1969.

Hayes, Carlton J. H. *Essays on Nationalism*. New York: Macmillan, 1928.

Helmreich, E. C. *The Diplomacy of the Balkan Wars, 1912–1913*. Cambridge, Mass.: Harvard University Press, 1938.

Henlin, Ronald A. "The Volatile Administrative Map of Rumania," *Annals of the Association of American Geographers*, 57:3 (September 1967), pp. 481–502.

Hoffman, George W., and Fred Warner Neal. *Yugoslavia and the New Communism*. New York: Twentieth Century Fund, 1962.

Hondius, Frederik Willem. *The Yugoslav Community of Nations*. The Hague and Paris: Mouton, 1968.

Hoptner, J. B. *Yugoslavia in Crisis, 1934–1941*. New York: Columbia University Press, 1962.

Inglehart, Ronald F., and Margaret Woodward. "Language Conflicts and Political Community," *Comparative Studies in Social History*, 10:1 (October 1967), pp. 27–45.

Institut istorii partii pri Ts.K.K.P. Moldavii. *Ocherki istorii Komunisticheskoi partii Moldavii*. Kishinev: Partiinoe izdatelstvo Ts.K.K.P. Moldavii, 1964.

Institut za nacionalna istorija—Skopje. *Istorija na Makedonskiot Narod*, 3 vols. Skopje: Nova Makedonija, 1969.

Ionescu, Ghiță. *Communism in Rumania, 1944–1962*. London: Oxford University Press and Royal Institute of International Affairs, 1964.

———— *The Politics of the European Communist States*. New York: Praeger, 1967.

Istoriia literaturii moldovenesht, Vol. I. Kishinev: Editura de Stat a Moldovei, 1958.

Janos, Andrew C. "Ethnicity, Communism, and Political Change in Eastern Europe," *World Politics*, 23:3 (April 1971), pp. 493–521.

Jaszi, Oscar. *Dissolution of the Habsburg Monarchy*. Chicago: University of Chicago Press, 1929.

Jelavich, Charles and Barbara, eds. *The Balkans in Transition: Essays on the Development of Balkan Life and Politics since the Eighteenth Century*. Berkeley and Los Angeles: University of California Press, 1963.

Kann, Robert A. *Das Nationalitätenproblem der Habsburgermonarchie*, 2 vols. Graz and Cologne: Hermann Böhlaus, 1964.

Keep, John, ed. *Contemporary History in the Soviet Mirror*. New York: Praeger, 1964.

Kepeski, Krume. *Makedonska gramatika*. Skopje: Državno knigoizdatelstvo na Makedonija, 1946.

Kerner, Robert Joseph, and Harry Nicholas Howard. *The Balkan Conferences and the Balkan Entente, 1930–1935*. Berkeley: University of California Press, 1936.

Kertesz, Stephen D. *Diplomacy in a Whirlpool: Hungary between Nazi Germany and Soviet Russia*. Notre Dame, Ind.: University of Notre Dame Press, 1953.

———— "The Expulsion of the Germans from Hungary: A Study of Postwar Diplomacy," *Review of Politics*, 15:2 (April 1953), pp. 179–208.

Kirschbaum, J. M. "Ludovít Štur and His Place in the Slavic World," *Slavistica*, No. 32 (1958), pp. 1–34.

Knejevitch, Radoye L. "The Ethnical Structure of Voyvodina," *Yugoslav Observer*, 2:2 (March 1956), pp. 14–17.

Kofos, Evangelos. *Nationalism and Communism in Macedonia*. Thessaloniki: Institute for Balkan Studies, 1964.

Kohn, Hans. *The Idea of Nationalism*. New York: Macmillan, 1951.

———— *Pan-Slavism: Its History and Ideology*. 2nd Edition. New York: Vintage, 1960.

Kolarz, Walter. *Myths and Realities in Eastern Europe*. London: Lindsay Drummond, 1946.

Koliševski, Lazar. *Aspekti na makedonskoto prašanje*. Skopje: Kultura, 1962.

Korletianu, N. *Studiu asupra sistemei leksikale moldovenesht din anii 1870–1890*. Kishinev: Akademiia de Stiintse a RSS Moldovenesht: Institul de Limba shi Literature, 1964.

Korolev, K. V., P. A. Kruchenyuk, and B. Z. Tanasevskii. *Doina Radosti: Dekada moldavskovo iskusstva i literaturi provodilas v Moskve s 27 Maya po 5 Iyunya 1960 goda*. Kishinev: Kartya Moldovenyaske, 1962.

Kosinski, Laszek Antoni. "Population Censuses in East-Central Europe in the Twentieth Century," *East European Quarterly*, 5:3 (September 1971), pp. 279–301.

Kousoulas, Dimitrios. *Revolution and Defeat: The Story of the Greek Communist Party*. London: Oxford University Press, 1965.

Langer, Robert. *The Austro-Yugoslav Problem*. [New York?], 1951.

Lasky, Melvin J. *The Hungarian Revolution: A White Book*. New York: Praeger, 1957.

Lederer, Ivo J. *Yugoslavia at the Paris Peace Conference: A Study in Frontier-making*. New Haven, Conn.: Yale University Press, 1963.

Lendvai, Paul. *Eagles in Cobwebs: Nationalism and Communism in the Balkans*. Garden City, N.Y.: Doubleday, 1969.

Liveanu, V. *1918—din Istoria luptelor revolutionare din Romînia*. Bucharest: Editura politică, 1960.

Low, Alfred D. *Lenin on the Question of Nationality.* New York: Bookman Associates, 1958.

Lunt, Horace G. *Grammar of the Macedonian Literary Language.* Skopje, 1952.

———— "A Survey of Macedonian Literature," *Harvard Slavic Studies,* 1 (1953), pp. 363–396.

Macartney, C. A. *National States and National Minorities.* London: Royal Institute of International Affairs and Oxford University Press, 1934.

MacKenzie, Compton. *Dr. Beneš.* London: George G. Harrap, 1946.

Mahaijlov, Vancho [Macedonicus]. *Stalin and the Macedonian Question.* Translated from the Bulgarian by Christ Anastasoff. St. Louis: Pearlstone Publishing Company, 1948.

Mair, L. P. *The Protection of Minorities: The Working and Scope of the Minorities Treaties under the League of Nations.* London: Christophers, 1928.

Markert, Werner, ed. *Osteuropa-Handbuch: Jugoslawien.* Cologne and Graz: Böhlau Verlag, 1954.

Markus, Vasyl. *L'incorporation de l'Ukraine Subcarpathique à l'Ukraine Soviétique: 1944–1945.* Louvain: Centre Ukrainien d'Etudes en Belgique, 1956.

Matossian, Mary. *The Impact of Soviet Policies in Armenia.* Leiden: E. J. Brill, 1962.

Meissner, Boris. *Das Selbstbestimmungsrecht der Völker in Osteuropa und China.* Cologne: Verlag Wissenschaft und Politik, 1968.

Meray, Tibor. *That Day in Budapest: October 23, 1956.* Translated by Charles Lam Markmann. New York: Funk and Wagnalls, 1969.

———— *Thirteen Days that Shook the Kremlin.* Translated by Howard L. Katzander. New York: Praeger, 1959.

Mitrev, Dimitar. *Pirinska Makedonija vo borba na nacionalno oslobodu-vanje.* Skopje: Glavinot odbor na Naridniot front na Makedonija, 1950.

Mojsov, Lazar. *Bulgarska Radnicka Partija (Komunista) i makedonsko nacionalno pitanje.* Belgrade: Borba, 1948.

Moldavsko-russko-ukrainskie literaturnie i folklornie svyazi. Kishinev: Izdatelstvo "Kartya Moldovenyaske," 1967.

Moldavsko-russko-ukrainskie literaturnie svyazi. Kishinev: Izdatelstvo "Shtiintsa" Akademii nauk moldavskoi SSR, 1962.

Moodie, A. E. *The Italo-Yugoslav Boundary: A Study in Political Geography.* London: George Philip and Son, 1945.

Mosely, Philip. *The Kremlin and World Politics.* New York: Vintage, 1960.

Nagy, Ferenc. *The Struggle Behind the Iron Curtain.* Translated by Stephen K. Swift. New York: Macmillan, 1948.

Nagy, Imre. *On Communism.* New York: Praeger, 1957.

Die nationale Frage in der Österreichisch-Ungarischen Monarchie, 1900–1918. Budapest: Akadémiai Kiadó Verlag der Ungarischen Akademie der Wissenschaften, 1966.

Nationalism and Separatism. Special issue of *Journal of Contemporary History,* 6:1 (1971).

Němec, František, and Vladimír Moudrý. *The Soviet Seizure of Subcarpathian Ruthenia.* Toronto: William B. Anderson, 1955.

Nikolić, Miodrag. *Autonomous Province of Kosovo and Metohija.* Belgrade: Medjunarodna Politika, 1965.

Novak, Bogdan C. *Trieste, 1941–1954: The Ethnic, Political, and Ideological Struggle.* Chicago: University of Chicago Press, 1970.

Otetea, Andrei, ed. *Istoria poporului român.* Bucharest: Editura ştiintifică, 1970.

———— and S. Schwann, eds. *K. Marx—Însemnări despre Români (Manuscrise Inedite).* Bucharest: Editura Academiei Republicii Populare Române, 1964.

Padelford, Norman J. *Peace in the Balkans.* New York: Oxford University Press, 1935.

Paikert, G. C. *The Danube Swabians.* The Hague: Martinus Nijhoff, 1967.

Palmer, Stephen E., Jr., and Robert R. King. *Yugoslav Communism and the Macedonian Question.* Hamden, Conn.: Archon Books, 1971.

Pesaković, Milentije. *Autonomous Provinces in Yugoslavia.* Studies Series, 1964, No. 5. Belgrade: Medjunarodna Politika, 1964.

Petrovich, Michael B. "Ludovít Štur and Russian Pan-Slavism," *Journal of Central European Affairs,* 12:1 (April 1952), pp. 1-19.

Pipes, Richard. *The Formation of the Soviet Union: Communism and Nationalism, 1917–1923,* Revised Edition. Cambridge, Mass.: Harvard University Press, 1964.

Pundeff, Marin, ed. *History in the USSR: Selected Readings.* San Francisco: Hoover Institution, 1967.

Rakowska-Harmstone, Teresa. *Russia and Nationalism in Central Asia.* Baltimore: Johns Hopkins Press, 1969.

Regnault, Elias. *Histoire Politique et Sociale des Principautés Danubiennes.* Paris: Paulin et le Chevalier, 1855.

Reiter, Wilhelm. "Die Nationalitätenpolitik der Rumänischen volksrepublik im Spiegel ihrer Statistik," *Osteuropa,* 11:3 (March 1961), pp. 189-197.

Renner, Karl. *Das Selbstbestimmungsrecht der Nationen in besonderer Anwendung auf Österreich.* Part I, *Nation und Staat.* Leipzig and Vienna: Franz Deuticke, 1918.

Research Institute for Minority Studies on Hungarians Attached to Czechoslovakia and Carpatho-Ruthenia. *Hungarians in Czechoslovakia.* New York: the Institute, 1959.

Riveles, Stanley. "Slovakia: Catalyst of Crisis," *Problems of Communism,* 17:3 (May–June 1968), pp. 1–9.

Robinson, William F. *Nationalism: Hungarian Problem Child.* Munich: Radio Free Europe Research, July 5, 1967.

Roller, Mihail, ed. *Istoria R.P.R.: Manual pentru învătămîntul mediu.* Bucharest: Editura de stat Didactică şi Pedagogică, 1956.

Rothschild, Joseph. *The Communist Party of Bulgaria, Origins and Development, 1883–1936.* New York: Columbia University Press, 1959.

Roucek, Joseph S. *Balkan Politics: International Relations in No Man's Land.* Stanford, Calif.: Stanford University Press, 1948.

Rura, Michael J. *Reinterpretation of History as a Method of Furthering Communism in Rumania.* Washington, D.C.: Georgetown University Press, 1961.

Rywkin, Michael. *Russia in Central Asia.* New York: Collier, 1963.

Schechtman, Joseph B. *European Population Transfers, 1939–1945.* New York: Oxford University Press, 1946.

———— *Post War Population Transfers in Europe, 1945–1955.* Philadelphia: University of Pennsylvania Press, 1962.

Schwechler, K. *Die österreichische Sozialdemokratie: Eine Darstellung ihrer geschichtlichen Entwicklung, ihres Programmes und ihrer Tätigkeit.* Graz and Vienna: Verlagsbuchhandlung "Styria," 1908.

Seton-Watson, Hugh. *The East European Revolution,* 3rd Edition. New York: Praeger, 1956.

———— *Eastern Europe between the Wars, 1918–1941.* New York: Harper and Row, 1967.

———— *Nationalism and Communism: Essays, 1946–1963.* New York: Praeger, 1964.

Seton-Watson, R. W. *The Rise of Nationality in the Balkans.* London: Constable and Company, 1917.

Shafer, Boyd C. *Nationalism: Myth and Reality.* New York: Harcourt, Brace and World, 1955.

Shoup, Paul. *Communism and the Yugoslav National Question.* New York: Columbia University Press, 1968.

Skilling, Gordon H. "Ferment among Czechs and Slovaks," *International Journal,* 19 (Autumn 1964), pp. 496–512.

Slapnicka, Helmut. "Die neue Verwaltungsgliederung der Tschechoslowakei und ihre Vorläufer," *Der Donauraum,* 5:3 (1960), pp. 139-158.

Spector, Sherman D. *Rumania at the Paris Peace Conference.* New York: Bookman Associates, 1962.

Stavrianos, L. S. *Balkan Federation: A History of the Movement toward Balkan Unity in Modern Times.* Smith College Studies in History, Vol. 27. Northampton, Mass.: Department of History of Smith College, 1941-1942.

———— *The Balkans since 1453.* New York: Rinehart, 1958.

Stone, Julius. *International Guarantees of Minority Rights: Procedures of the Council of the League of Nations in Theory and Practice.* London: Oxford University Press, 1932.

Straka, Manfred, ed. *Handbuch der europäischen Volksgruppen.* Vienna and Stuttgart: Wilhelm Braumüller, 1970.

Stranitsi istorii komsomola moldavii. Kishinev: Izdatelstvo "Kartya Moldovenyaske," 1966.

Bibliography

Studii de Limbe Moldovenyaske. Kishinev: Editura de Stat "Kartya Moldovenyaske," 1963.

Sugar, Peter F., and Ivo J. Lederer. *Nationalism in Eastern Europe.* Seattle and London: University of Washington Press, 1969.

Sullivant, Robert S. *Soviet Politics in the Ukraine, 1917-1957.* New York: Columbia University Press, 1962.

Sulzbach, Walter. *National Consciousness.* Washington, D.C.: American Council on Public Affairs, 1943.

Swire, J. *Bulgarian Conspiracy.* London: Robert Hale, 1939.

Symmons-Symonolewicz, Konstantin. *Nationalist Movements: A Comparative View.* Meadville, Pa.: Maplewood Press, 1970.

Taborsky, Eduard. "Beneš and Stalin—Moscow, 1943 and 1945," *Journal of Central European Affairs,* 13:2 (July 1953), pp. 154-181.

Tillett, Lowell R. *The Great Friendship: Soviet Historians on the Non-Russian Nationalities.* Chapel Hill, N.C.: University of North Carolina Press, 1969.

Tomasic, D. A. "Nationality Problems and Partisan Yugoslavia," *Journal of Central European Affairs,* 6:2 (July 1946), pp. 111–125.

Ulam, Adam B. *The Bolsheviks.* New York: Macmillan, 1965.

———— *Expansion and Coexistence: The History of Soviet Foreign Policy, 1917–1967.* New York: Praeger, 1968.

———— *Titoism and the Cominform.* Cambridge, Mass.: Harvard University Press, 1952.

Urban, George. *Nineteen Days.* London: Heinemann, 1957.

Urban, Rudolf. "Neue Verwaltungsgliederung in der Tschechoslowakei," *Zeitschrift für Ostforschung,* 10:1 (March 1961), pp. 119-126.

Váli, Ferenc A. *Rift and Revolt in Hungary.* Cambridge, Mass.: Harvard University Press, 1961.

Vardys, V. Stanley, ed. *Lithuania under the Soviets: Portrait of a Nation, 1940–1965.* New York: Praeger, 1965.

Viefhaus, Erwin. *Die Minderheitenfrage und die Entstehung der Minderheitenschutzverträge auf der Pariser Friedenskonferenz 1919.* Würzburg: Holzner Verlag, 1960.

Vinogradov, V. N., and others. *Istoriia Ruminii: novogo i noveishego vremeni.* Moscow: Nauka, 1964.

Ward, Barbara. *Nationalism and Ideology.* New York: Norton, 1966.

Wheeler, Geoffrey. *The Peoples of Soviet Central Asia.* London: Bodley, 1966.

Whiteside, Andrew G. *Austrian National Socialism before 1918.* The Hague: Martinus Nijhoff, 1962.

Wierer, Rudolf. *Der Föderalismus im Donauraum.* Graz and Cologne: Verlag Hermann Böhlaus, 1960.

Wilkinson, H. R. *Maps and Politics: A Review of the Ethnographic Cartography of Macedonia.* Liverpool: University Press, 1951.

Wintgens, Hugo. *Der völkerrechtliche Schutz der nationalen, sprachlichen, und religösen Minderheiten.* Stuttgart: W. Kohlhammer, 1930.

Wiskemann, Elizabeth. *Germany's Eastern Neighbors: Problems relating to the Oder-Neisse Line and the Czech Frontier Regions.* London: Oxford University Press, 1956.

Wolfe, Bertram D. *Three Who Made a Revolution.* New York: Delta, 1964.

Wolff, Robert Lee. *The Balkans in Our Time.* Cambridge, Mass.: Harvard University Press, 1956.

Zagoria, Donald S. *The Sino-Soviet Conflict, 1956–1961.* Princeton, N.J.: Princeton University Press, 1962.

Zaninovich, M. George. *The Development of Socialist Yugoslavia.* Baltimore: Johns Hopkins Press, 1968.

Zeman, Z. A. B. *The Breakup of the Habsburg Empire, 1914–1918.* London: Oxford University Press, 1961.

Index

323

Index